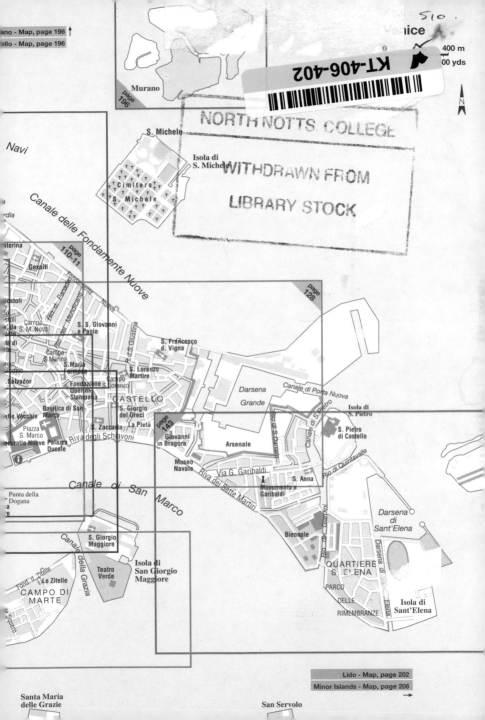

510.

Venice

KT-406-402

400 m
00 yds

N

Murano

page 196

Navi

S. Michele

Isola di
S. Michele

Cimitero
S. Michele

Canale delle Fondamente Nuove

page 110-11

Gesuiti

postoli
S. M. Nova
te di
no
fudge

Campo
S. M. Nova

Campo
S. Marina

S. S. Giovanni
e Paolo

S. Maria
Formosa

Fondazione s.
Querini-
Stampalia

Basilica di San
Marco

atte Vecchie

Piazza
S. Marco

ecuratie Nuove

Palazzo
Ducale

CASTELLO

S. Salvador

Campo
S. Lorenzo

S. Lorenzo
Martire

S. Giorgio
dei Greci

S. Zaccaria

La Pietà

Riva degli Schiavoni

S. Francesco
d. Vigna

page 128

Darsena
Grande

Canale di Porta Nuova

Isola di
S. Pietro

S. Pietro
di Castello

page 143

Giovanni
in Bragora

Arsenale

Museo
Navale

Via G. Garibaldi

Riva dei Sette Martiri

S. Anna

Rio di Quintavalle

Punta della
Dogana
a

Canale di San Marco

Monumento a
Garibaldi

S. Giorgio
Maggiore

Canale della Grazia

Teatro
Verde

Isola di
San Giorgio
Maggiore

Biennale

Darsena
di
Sant'Elena

QUARTIERE
S. ELENA

Le Zitelle

Fond. d. Zitelle

CAMPO DI
MARTE

Squero

PARCO
DELLE
RIMEMBRANZE

Isola di
Sant'Elena

Santa Maria
delle Grazie

San Servolo

INSIGHT CITY GUIDE

Venice

APA PUBLICATIONS
Part of the Langenscheidt Publishing Group

✼ INSIGHT GUIDE
Venice

Written by
Lisa Gerard-Sharp
Edited by
Cathy Muscat
Art Director
Klaus Geisler
Picture Editor
Hilary Genin
Cartography Editor
Zoë Goodwin
Editorial Director
Brian Bell

Distribution

UK & Ireland
GeoCenter International Ltd
The Viables Centre, Harrow Way
Basingstoke, Hants RG22 4BJ
Fax: (44) 1256-817988

United States
Langenscheidt Publishers, Inc.
36-36 33rd Street 4th Floor
Long Island City, New York 11106
Fax: (1) 718 784-0640

Canada
Thomas Allen & Son Ltd
390 Steelcase Road East
Markham, Ontario L3R 1G2
Fax: (1) 905 475 6747

Australia
Universal Publishers
1 Waterloo Road
Macquarie Park, NSW 2113
Fax: (61) 2 9888 9074

New Zealand
Hema Maps New Zealand Ltd (HNZ)
Unit D, 24 Ra ORA Drive
East Tamaki, Auckland
Fax: (64) 9 273 6479

Worldwide
**Apa Publications GmbH & Co.
Verlag KG (Singapore branch)**
38 Joo Koon Road, Singapore 628990
Tel: (65) 6865-1600. Fax: (65) 6861-6438

Printing

Insight Print Services (Pte) Ltd
38 Joo Koon Road, Singapore 628990
Tel: (65) 6865-1600. Fax: (65) 6861-6438

©2005 Apa Publications GmbH & Co.
Verlag KG (Singapore branch)
All Rights Reserved

First Edition 1988
Fourth Edition 2005

ABOUT THIS BOOK

This guidebook combines the interests and enthusiasms of two of the world's best-known information providers: Insight Guides, whose titles have set the standard for visual travel guides since 1970, and Discovery Channel, the world's premier source of nonfiction television programming. The editors of Insight Guides provide both practical advice and general understanding about a destination. Discovery Channel and its Web site, www.discovery.com, help millions of viewers explore their world from the comfort of their home.

How to use this book

The book is carefully structured both to convey an understanding of the city and its culture and to guide readers through its sights and activities:

◆ The Best of Venice section at the front helps you prioritise what you want to see. Top churches and museums, festivals and bars, the best islands to visit and a rundown of unmissable Venetian experiences.
◆ To understand Venice, you need to know something of its past. The first section covers the city's history and culture in lively, authoritative essays.
◆ The main Places section provides a full run-down of all the attractions worth seeing. The main places of interest are coordinated by number with full-colour maps.
◆ Photographic features show readers around major attractions such as

St Mark's Basilica and the Accademia, and identify the highlights.

◆ Photographs throughout the book are chosen not only to illustrate geography and buildings but also to convey the moods of the city and the life of its people.

◆ The Travel Tips listings section provides a point of reference for information on travel, hotels, shops and festivals. Information may be located quickly by using the index printed on the back cover flap – and the flaps are designed to serve as bookmarks.

The author

Insight Guides have a reputation for calling on a variety of authoritative experts to provide essays and information. This new edition of *Insight Guide: Venice,* however, is an exception. **Lisa Gerard-Sharp**, a gifted writer and major contributor to the series' Italian titles, took on the whole book. Although a writer and broadcaster with a special interest in Italy, she was wary of tackling Venice, a reluctance shared by most Italians. In foreign eyes, Venice may be a dream city we have all visited, if only in our imaginations. However, in Italian eyes, the slithery nature of the lagoon, coupled with the indomitable Venetian spirit, provoke admiration rather than affection. Like many visitors, Gerard-Sharp was first drawn to the glistening surface of Venice, a carnivalesque stage-set for idle posing and romantic shenanigans. "In time, this deepened into an appreciation of the deliciously sinister nature of Venice in winter, with its undertow of decadence," she says. While living in Italy, Gerard-Sharp worked as a film editor, documentary-maker and language specialist. She has also reported on the changing Venetian political scene.

Other contributors

Much of the photography for this new edition was provided by **Anna Mockford** and **Nick Bonetti**, Insight regulars. Among the other photographers whose images bring the city so vividly to life are **Bill Wassman**, **Ross Miller** and **Glyn Genin**. The managing editor was **Cathy Muscat**, proof-reading was by **Neil Titman** and the book was indexed by **Elizabeth Cook**.

CONTACTING THE EDITORS

We would appreciate it if readers would alert us to errors or outdated information by writing to:

Insight Guides, P.O. Box 7910, London SE1 1WE, England. Fax: (44) 20 7403-0290. insight@apaguide.co.uk

NO part of this book may be reproduced, stored in a retrieval system or transmitted in any form or means electronic, mechanical, photocopying, recording or otherwise, without prior written permission of *Apa Publications*. Brief text quotations with use of photographs are exempted for book review purposes only. Information has been obtained from sources believed to be reliable, but its accuracy and completeness, and the opinions based thereon, are not guaranteed.

www.insightguides.com

Contents

Maps

Oroiogio
Piazza
San Marco **6** Basilica di San Marc
Museo **7** Campanile (St Mark's Basilica)
heologico di S. Marco P. dei Sospir
(Bridge of Sigh
Nuove Piazzetta Pri
Palazzo **3** S. Marco
Reale **4**
Bibl. Naz. Palazzo
Marciana Molo Ducale
GIARDINI (Doge's Palace)

Map Legend **241**
Street Atlas **241–8**

Travel Tips

THE BEST OF VENICE

Unique attractions, festivals and events, top palaces and islands, best bars and boat trips, family outings... here, at a glance, are our recommendations

BEST PALACES & ART MUSEUMS

- **Doge's Palace**. A masterpiece of graceful High Gothic style. *See page 94.*
- **Accademia**. The world's finest collection of Venetian art. *See pages 188–9.*
- **Guggenheim collection**. *The museum of modern art. See page 113.*

ABOVE: Tintoretto's *The Fall of Man* in San Rocco.
ABOVE RIGHT: crossing the canal on a gondola ferry.
BELOW RIGHT: Fondaco dei Turchi on the Grand Canal.

- **Ca' Rezzonico**. Sumptuous 18th-century palace with art to match. *See page 115.*
- **Ca' d'Oro**. Landmark Gothic palace with beguiling museum of art. *See page 120.*
- **Ca' Pesaro**. Baroque palace housing museums of modern and oriental art. *See page 122.*
- **Palazzo Mocenigo**. Showcase of 18th-century living and

interior decoration. *See page 156.*
- **Palazzo Vendramin-Calergi**. Both a patrician palace and the city casino. *See page 123.*
- **San Rocco**. Virtuoso mannerist display by Tintoretto. *See page 160.*
- **San Giorgio degli Schiavoni**. Cycle by Carpaccio, the most intimate of Venetian artists. *See page 138.*
- **I Carmini**. Showcase for Tiepolo's artistry. *See page 184.*
- **Fondaco dei Turchi**. Turkish merchants' palace, now a museum of natural history. *See page 124.*

WATER EXPERIENCES

- **The Grand Canal** by *vaporetto* (line 1): leisurely palace-spotting along the city's greatest waterway. *See pages 109–124.*
- **Gondola ride** Clichéd but memorable, particularly along the romantic back canals, rather than the bustling Canal Grande. *See pages 116 and 215.*
- ***Traghetto* crossing** Standing room only on the cheap but authentic

gondola ferry across the Grand Canal. *See page 215.*
- **Water Taxi Trip** A private motor launch around the lagoon is wildly extravagant but worth it to travel in style to lesser-known Venice. *See page 215.*
- **The Brenta Canal** Water-borne day trip from Venice to Padua, by barge, to see a clutch of Palladian villas, ideally in summer. *See page 210.*

ONLY IN VENICE

- **The Ghetto**. The heart of Jewish Venice is home to the world's first ghetto, as the Venetians coined the concept. *See pages 172 and 173.*
- **The Rialto market**. Once a crossroads of the world, this is still a fascinating warren of backstreets, from the fish and vegetable markets to the cluster of inns. *See pages 155–6.*

ABOVE: the bustling Rialto fish market, or Pescheria, is set in an arcaded neo-Gothic hall by the quayside.

- **Concerts in *scuole*.** These sumptuous confraternity houses are the setting for superb classical concerts throughout the year, often performed in period dress. *See page 222.*
- **Palazzo Grassi**. Block-buster art exhibitions staged in this grand palace. *See page 102.*
- **Bacari** (traditional wine bars). Having *cichetti e l'ombra,* a snack and a glass of wine, is a Venetian

tradition similar to Spanish tapas. *See page 154.*
- ***Cichetti*** (Venetian tapas). These rustic tapas are the city's in-expensive signature snacks, and best eaten in a *bacaro. See pages 75 and 154.*
- **The Grand Canal** by night. A line 1 *vaporetto* (ferry) winds down the city's greatest waterway, illuminating secret lives in the city palaces. *See page 122.*
- **Masks and Murano glass**. These are the two top city souvenirs, but only if bought from reputable outlets. *See page 227.*
- **Legendary hotels.** The Gritti, the Danieli and the Cipriani are world-renowned, but most of the luxury hotels have romantic waterside bars and roof terrace restaurants which welcome non-residents. *See pages 217–21.*
- **Gondola serenade**. Be a total tourist, just once in your life. *See pages 116 and 215.*

BEST SQUARES

- **Piazza San Marco**. The city's ceremonial stage-set of a square. *See page 87.*
- **Campo Santo Stefano**. The most stylish square, with a top *gelateria. See page 101.*
- **Campo Santa Margherita**. The liveliest square for local nightlife and bars. *See page 185.*
- **Campo San Giacomo dell'Orio**. Venice's most enchanting neighbourhood square. *See page 157.*
- **Campo Santa Maria Formosa**. The quintes-sential canalside *campo. See page 133.*

ABOVE: one of a cluster of lively bars on the Campo Santa Margherita.
BELOW: Piazza San Marco, the heart of Venice, home of the belltower, the basilica and the Doge's Palace.

8

BEST WALKS & TOURS

- **The Zattere**. Follow the waterfront from La Salute around Punta della Dogana past the Gesuati church all the way to western Dorsoduro. *See page 179.*
- **The Ghetto**. The official walking tour visits the synagogues and Jewish museum in off-the-beaten-track Cannaregio. *See page 172.*
- **Backwaters of Dorsoduro**. From the Accademia, stroll to San Trovaso, San Sebastiano, Sant' Angelo, and Calle Lunga San Barnaba. *See pages 177–86.*

- **The Arsenale**. Follow Riva degli Schiavoni to the island of San Pietro, skirting the Arsenale shipyards and the Giardini. *See Castello and Eastern Castello chapters.*
- **Secret Itinerary**. Dungeons and devilish plots on a tour of the Doge's Palace. *See page 97.*
- **The Tintoretto Trail**. Visiting the mannerist artist's masterpieces. *See page 61.*
- **Nature in the lagoon**. Unusual nature tours with Naturavenezia. *See pages 200 and 228.*

ABOVE RIGHT: the Renaissance church of Santa Maria dei Miracoli. **BELOW:** the washing-festooned backstreets of Castello. **BELOW RIGHT:** the island of San Giorgio Maggiore, with a belltower modelled on St Mark's.

BEST CHURCHES

- **Basilica di San Marco**. The grandest private chapel in the world. *See page 89.*
- **La Salute**. Landmark basilica. *See page 177.*
- **Il Redentore**. Palladian masterpiece on Giudecca. *See page 195.*
- **Santi Giovanni e Paolo** (Zanipolo). Vast Gothic church and square. *See page 135.*
- **Santa Maria dell' Assunta**. Torcello's Veneto-Byzantine

cathedral. *See page 201.*
- **I Frari**. Franciscan church and canvas for Titian's masterpieces. *See page 159.*
- **San Sebastiano**. Magnificent shrine to the art of Veronese. *See page 182.*
- **Santa Maria dei Miracoli**. Renaissance jewel-box of a church. *See page 170.*
- **Madonna dell'Orto**. Tintoretto's church. *See page 167.*

BEST ISLANDS

- **San Giorgio Maggiore**. A great first-day-in-Venice crossing to see the island closest to St Mark's, and enjoy the view from the monastery belltower. *See page 192.*
- **Murano, Burano and Torcello**. Taking the ferry to visit the three most popular yet diverse lagoon

islands – all on a day trip. *See pages 197–202.*
- **Giudecca**. Exploring an island unscathed by tourism. *See page 193.*
- **San Lazzaro degli Armeni**. An exotic Armenian island retreat. *See page 211.*
- **San Clemente**. Drinks and dinner on a luxurious monastic island resort. *See page 211.*

ABOVE: *Regatta on the Grand Canal*, by Luca Carnavelis (1663–1730).
BELOW: the understated entrance to Harry's Bar and the gilded interior of Caffè Florian.

FESTIVALS & EVENTS

- **Carnival**. This pre-Lenten masked extravaganza is a surreal 10-day party. *See pages 66–8 and 224.*
- **So e Zo I Ponti**. This Lenten non-competitive marathon crosses bridges and canals, with both children and adults participating. *See page 224.*
- **La Festa della Sensa and La Vogalonga.** May Ascension Day festival and regatta (the first Sunday after Ascension Day) followed by the Vogalonga, a 33km-race around the city and lagoon. *See pages 70–1 and 224.*
- **La Festa del Redentore.** The July festival celebrates the city's salvation from the 1575 Plague with a water-borne picnic and procession. *See pages 70–1 and 224.*

- **Il Biennale**. The major six-month-long art extravaganza is staged in uneven years. *See page 148.*
- **Regata Storica**. The September Historical Regatta is Venice's best water festival. *See pages 70–1 and 224.*
- **Venice Film Festival**. Hollywood comes to town every September for the Golden Lion awards. *See page 204.*
- **Festival Galuppi**. Autumn concerts held in unusual venues and islands. *See page 224.*
- **La Fenice**. The opera season in the recon-structed opera house is now unmissable. *See pages 65 and 222.*
- **Festa della Madonna della Salute.** 21 November festival celebrating the city's salvation from the Plague of 1630 with a procession to the church. *See page 225.*

BEST BARS

- **Harry's Bar**, over-hyped and over here, is Italy's most legendary bar, and where the Bellini cocktail was invented. *See pages 100 and 104.*
- **Caffè Florian** This "prince of coffee houses" was founded in 1720 and is the oldest surviving café in Italy, home to a pretentious string quartet and a sumptuous interior. *See pages 89 and 105.*
- **Caffè Quadri**. When the uber-Venetian

Florian sets its band to playing Strauss's *Radetsky March*, celebrating the vanquishing of Venice, Quadri's rival band responds with Céline Dion. *See pages 77 and 105.*
- **Bancogiro**. A deceptively rustic water-front Rialto bar popular with Vene-tians and visitors alike. *See page 154.*
- **Centrale**. A slick Manhattan moment – with gondola waiting in the wings. *See page 104.*
- **Cantina Do Mori**. A *bacaro*, or traditional wine bar, for a taste of everyday Venice, including *cichetti* (savoury bar snacks). *See page 154.*
- **Vino Vino**. A homely inn where gondoliers rub shoulders with visitors. *See page 105.*

VENICE'S ALLURE

More like a stage set than a city, Venice has captivated visitors for centuries. It dazzles and mesmerises, although it can also overwhelm and confuse the unprepared

Endlessly portrayed by writers, painters and philosophers, Venice is a canvas for every clichéd fantasy. Almost everyone who is anyone has been there. Even the cafés of St Mark's Square are awash with famous ghosts. As a result, Venice can play cultural one-upmanship better than most cities. The Romantics were rewarded with a feeling of having come too late to a world too old. The Victorians saw Venice as dying, while contemporary doom-mongers now seek to bury the city anew. Although entombment by the sea would show symmetry, this resilient city rejects such neat scenarios.

The only city in the world built entirely on water, Venice is no mere fantasy land, but a superior theme park that can uplift the spirit. The city offers a cradle-to-the-grave experience in the best possible taste. You can sleep in Tchaikovsky's bed or wake up in cavernous apartments that once welcomed princes and doges, Henry James and Hemingway. For romance, you can literally walk in Casanova's footsteps; for baroque passion, succumb to a Vivaldi concerto in Vivaldi's church, or savour the gondoliers' songs that inspired Verdi and Wagner. If you are feeling adventurous, explore the world of Marco Polo in his home city, bargain in the Rialto with latter-day merchants of Venice, or pick up the cobalt-blue cabbages that sent Elizabeth David into culinary raptures.

If you are feeling contemplative, you can ponder the passing of time with Proust's ghost in Caffè Florian. If fortunate, you can capture Canaletto's views with your camera, or see Titian's painting in the church it was designed for. If gregarious, you can savour the gossip and Martinis at Harry's Bar, Hemingway's favourite. The morbid can play roulette in Wagner's death chamber, now the city casino; the melancholic can even die in Thomas Mann's Venice, followed by a costly but atmospheric burial in Stravinsky's cemetery.

For more than a millennium, the Republic of Venice used all its strength to repel unwelcome invaders. Today one of the world's greatest maritime powers has become one of the world's greatest tourist attractions. Its singularity can disorient those who arrive unprepared, but it is this sheer uniqueness that makes it a wonder of the world. ❑

LEFT: the Basilica, centrepiece of St Mark's Square.

CITY IN THE LAGOON

It had an unpromising start, founded by refugees among stagnant marshes on the shores of the Adriatic. Yet Venice became the most powerful city in the West

Venice as a city "was a foundling, floating upon the waters like Moses in a basket among the bulrushes. It was therefore obliged to be inventive, to steal and to improvise." Writer Mary McCarthy sets the scene for the city's mythic status. The legendary foundation of Venice was in AD 421, on 25 March, a date conveniently coinciding with the feast of the city's patron saint, St Mark. Venice readily spun itself a romantic tapestry that has hoodwinked many a historian. Unlike its mainland rivals, Venice had been born free and Christian but without a golden Roman past.

To make amends, the city claimed descent from ancient Troy and cultivated the mystique of Byzantium, its one and only master. Early settlers in Venice brought Roman souvenirs salvaged from their ruined homes on the mainland. This city without antiquity also looked east for its aesthetic identity, with Constantinople (modern Istanbul) the unwitting provider of purloined memorials to a fabricated golden age.

"Who in their senses would build more than a fishing hut on the malarial, malodorous shoals and sandbanks of the Venetian lagoon?" The historian John Julius Norwich answers his own question: "Those who had no choice." The barbarians swept through Italy in the 5th and 6th centuries, leaving a trail of devastation. The refugees, driven from the remnants of a glorious Roman past, found themselves washed up on these inhospitable islands.

LEFT: detail from *The Bucintoro* (the Doge's Barge) by Canaletto. **RIGHT:** early settlements in the lagoon, a 16th-century drawing by Sabbadino.

Early settlements

Conventional wisdom has it that Venice was founded by migrants from the mainland fleeing to safety in the lagoon. However, it is conceivable the lagoon was already home to a fishing community. The first exodus was prompted by the arrival of Attila the Hun bearing down on northern Italy. Mass migrations began in AD 568 after a wave of Goths swept through the Veneto, terrorising the populations of Padua, Altino and Aquileia. The fugitives fled to the marshy coast and lagoon islands, settling in Chioggia, Malamocco, Torcello, Murano and Burano. The island of Torcello was colonised in AD 639 and remained the leading Venetian lagoon city, site of a magnificent cathedral, until the population's definitive move to the Rialto in AD 814.

As a vassal of Byzantium, the Eastern Roman Empire, Torcello acted as an effective trading post with Constantinople. Unlike many mainland cities, Venice was never feudal but born mercantile. A keen commercial spirit was bolstered by protectionism and monopolies. The shortage of land and the exposed position in the lagoon turned the island dwellers into skilful traders.

The medium of exchange was salt and salted fish, called "edible money" by the chronicler Cassiodorus. Yet even in the 8th century Venetian traders visited the Lombard capital of Pavia laden down with velvets and silks, peacock feathers and prized furs.

Trade brings wealth

Venice bordered two worlds: the Byzantine and Muslim East and the Latin-Germanic West. As the gateway to the East, the city traded Levantine incense, silks and spices for northern staples, including salt and wheat. Venice was helped by its command of the river mouths leading into northern Italy. The city conveniently lay at the crossing of rival trading routes: the Byzantine sway over Mediterranean trade was challenged by Muslim commercial routes, a consequence of the Arab conquest of Syria,

HOW THE BUILDING BEGAN

Venice is built on mudflats and sandbanks divided by canals and swept by the ebb and flow of tides. To make marshy pockets suitable as building land, the early city government permitted the dumping of ballast and wood; this caused silting and the formation of mudbanks. However, the instability of the terrain – made up of layers of mud, clay, sand and peat – meant that the foundations needed to be very deep and very solid. Buildings were supported by a forest of timber piles *(pali)* driven deep into the subsoil. The oak piles came from the Lido and were later supplemented by oak, larch and pine from the Alps and Dalmatia (modern-day Croatia), a Venetian territory.

Working from the outside in, concentric circles of piles were driven through the unstable lagoon floor to the bedrock of compacted clay. The number and thickness of the piles depended on the weight of the building: La Salute church, for instance, is supported by over a million piles. The piles provided the base for a platform of horizontal beams, the *zatterone*, a raft-like structure made of larchwood, cemented in place with a mixture of stone and brick. The floor was then reinforced with Istrian stone; this marble-like stone, resistant to salt erosion, helped create damp-proof foundations. Oak beams and boards were placed on top, often finished by a traditional light marble floor.

North Africa and Spain. By the 9th century, slaves were the mainstay of Venetian trade, along with salt, fish and timber. Slaves were mainly Slavs but Greek Orthodox and Anglo-Saxon captives were not unknown.

When the population moved to the relative safety of the Rivo Alto (literally the "high bank", the site of today's Rialto markets), the Venice we know today was born. The election of the first doge in AD 726 paved the way for the oligarchy that founded Venice's fortune. Work on the doge's first fortress-palace commenced in AD 814, laying the foundations for the present palace. The institution of the doge was a marker in Venetian independence, a confident identity crowned by the patronage of St Mark. Venice was only nominally under Byzantine rule, and its independence was tacitly acknowledged in AD 840 when the city signed a treaty with the Holy Roman Emperor without seeking permission from Constantinople.

The theft of St Mark's relics from Alexandria in AD 828 showed the Venetian gift for improvisation and myth-making: the deed granted the city instant status, mystique and the presumed protection of St Mark. The Venetian triumph was marked by the decision to build St Mark's Basilica the following year. Under the protection of St Mark, Venice could equate material gain with spiritual riches. Trade was turned into a means of glorifying the fledgling city; Christian duty later sanctioned the Crusades against the infidels (and entitled the victors to spoils). If Venice enjoyed a reputation as a virtuous state, it was a reflection of its perceived stability rather than its morals. Yet this continuity was the product of a singular government.

Conquests and crusades

By AD 1000, Venice controlled the Adriatic coast, having eliminated piracy, although piracy still existed on the Aegean and Ionian seas. The conquest of Dalmatia (Croatia) was achieved under the leadership of Doge Pietro Orseolo (991–1009). His diplomatic skills were even greater than his military prowess, and he successfully juggled the powers of East and West. Ready supplies of timber, iron and hemp provided a stimulus to the burgeoning Venetian shipbuilding industry. The Venetians were soon the leading ship operators in the Mediterranean. Nonetheless, from the 11th century Venice faced naval challenges from the merchant republics of Pisa and Genoa. The Venetians defeated the Pisans off Rhodes in 1099, signalling the despatch of a former maritime power. From then on, the main threat was posed by the Genoese and the Turks.

The First Crusade was launched by Pope Urban II in 1095 to protect Byzantium and free the Holy Land. Jerusalem was captured in 1099 and a feudal kingdom established

there. Venice participated eagerly, shamelessly exploiting both sides. Not only did the Venetian fleet return from the East laden with booty in 1100, but the episode acted as a spur to their maritime ambitions. Venice extended its foothold in the Aegean, Syria and the Black Sea. In 1122 the Venetians defeated the Egyptian fleet that was besieging Jaffa and then went on to sack Byzantine ports in the Aegean and the Adriatic. Trade in the Levant increased with ships sailing to Haifa, Jaffa and Tyre.

The Fourth Crusade (1201–4) marked a turning point in Venetian history, the spur to its formation of a maritime empire, commanding the Adriatic and eastern Mediterranean. During

LEFT: detail from *The Sack of Byzantium* by Tintoretto, who had a gift for dramatic storytelling.
RIGHT: arrival of the relics of St Mark, a 13th-century mosaic on the west facade of Basilica di San Marco.

Marco Polo

Modern scholars are divided as to whether Marco Polo's epic journeys into Asia are wondrous fact or glorious fabrication. Some critics feel that he strayed no further than Persia, although his uncles, Nicolò and Maffeo, went into Asia. Supporters prefer to see Polo as the first explorer and chronicler of China, a talented merchant and administrator who found favour with Kublai Khan.

Like many Venetian merchant families, the Polo clan maintained trading houses

abroad, at Constantinople and in the Crimea. The family home was in Cannaregio, where the atmospheric courtyard still stands *(see page 170)*. Tradition has it that there were two journeys, the first in 1265 ending in the East, and the second in 1271–95, which centred on an extended stay in China. On the first voyage, Nicolò and Maffeo Polo traded a cargo of Venetian goods in Constantinople before sailing on to the Black Sea. There, merchandise was bartered for Russian and Turkish goods before the final thrust into the East. This journey is accepted by most historians, but the second expedition to China, involving

Marco Polo and his uncles, is more controversial. After a three-year journey through Baghdad, Persia and central Asia, they reached Peking in 1275. There Marco Polo claimed to have met Kublai Khan, the Mongol emperor, and to have been appointed governor of the Yangzhou region.

There have been attempts to debunk the Marco Polo story, but some facts are beyond dispute. He was imprisoned in 1298 by the Genoese, and he recounted his adventures to a fellow-prisoner, with whom he recorded his exploits in *Il Milione*, or *The Travels of Marco Polo*. Yet there are no references to him in Chinese records. Polo did not mention the custom of foot-binding, the Great Wall of China escaped his attention and he failed to notice tea ceremonies despite visiting such tea-growing centres as Hangzhou and Fujian.

The case for Marco Polo rests on the fact that he was a merchant, not a historian, primarily interested in the East for the purposes of trade. His defenders argue that women with bound feet would be closeted at home; that he probably had interpreters; and if Chinese records fail to mention the Venetian, he was mere wallpaper in the splendid court of the Great Mongol Kublai Khan at Shangdu.

Polo chronicled everything from the system of taxation and administration to the abundance of cotton and silk, sugar, spices and pepper. Chinese novelties Polo recorded include the practice of coal mining and the Chinese skill at making porcelain.

Critics claim that Marco Polo based his book on his uncles' genuine forays into the East, interwoven with tales told by other merchants and information plagiarised from Persian guidebooks. Even on Polo's return to Venice in 1295, contemporaries found his tales hard to believe, such as his description of Hangzhou, which, with a population of 2 million, was the biggest city in the world. Most historians admit that Marco Polo was prone to exaggeration but not a fantasist. Whatever the veracity of his accounts of the "lands of spices", he fascinated and influenced generations of seafarers, including Christopher Columbus.   ❏

LEFT: woodcut of Marco Polo from the German edition of his book of travels.

the Crusades, the Venetians traded with both sides as well as profiting from the transport of pilgrims; since the Venetians supplied the fleet, pilgrims who failed to pay were sold as slaves. The Crusades reached a climax in the sack of Constantinople, led by the blind but charismatic 90-year-old Doge Enrico Dandolo. The Venetians were skilled at siege operations and returned in 1204 for a successful assault on a city that, as the seat of the Byzantine Eastern Empire, had never fallen. Venice was rewarded with the lion's share of the new Latin empire.

The Venetian victory is regarded as a shameful episode, with the invaders charged with wanton destruction and the deposing of the Greek emperor. In addition to receiving three-eighths of the empire, vital trading ports, Constantinople's arsenal and docks, the Venetians looted the city. Booty, now in St Mark's, included the rearing Roman horses from the stadium in Constantinople and the Madonna Nicopeia, a sacred icon which acted as the Byzantine battle standard. The orgy of looting enriched Venice but did irreparable harm to East–West relations. Yet although the Venetians were responsible for deposing the Greeks, they saw themselves not as usurpers but as the true heirs of Constantine, the Catholic restorers of the rightful empire.

The Sea State

The emergence of the Sea State *(stato da mar)* showed that dominion of the seas was paramount to Venetian policy. However, mainland conquests in Padua, Treviso and Ferrara were also welcome. The period from 1260 until 1380 reflected the transition from Byzantine rule to the Venetian imperial age. With Genoese help, the deposed Byzantine emperors recovered Constantinople in 1261 and Venice lost a number of privileges. However, underlying the conflict was the Venetians' great rivalry with the Genoese, which continued into the next century.

The 1379–80 War of Chioggia was sparked by the Venetian claim to control the Dardanelles. In response, the Genoese mounted a naval blockade at Chioggia. The Genoese penetrated the lagoon, but they failed to challenge the city of Venice, a waterbound maze without gates, walls or escape routes. The result was a

decisive Venetian victory and the once-great naval power of Genoa no longer posed a threat.

Much more troubling was the devastation caused by the Black Death. The plague of 1348 reached Venice from the east and reduced the populous city by three-fifths. In the 14th century, Venice had 160,000 inhabitants at a time when a city of 20,000 was considered large. It took the city almost 200 years to return to the same size. However, for all the tribulations of this period, it also marked the emergence of the Republic's unique system of government.

Machiavelli, the great political thinker, praised the city's statecraft as "deserving to be celebrated above any principality in Italy". He

was impressed by the Venetians' imperialist ambitions, their skill at diplomacy, and a name which "spread terror over the seas". The State's reputation for ruthlessness was merited. When Doge Vitale Michiel was assassinated in 1172 his murderers sought refuge in San Zaccaria. As a punishment, neighbouring houses were razed to the ground and a ban imposed upon building in stone, one that survived until this century. Treason was always punishable by death. Antonio Foscarini, a 17th-century ambassador to France and England, was falsely condemned as a spy and hanged by his foot in the Piazzetta, a common Venetian end. This successful, if sinister, state was run by a closed circle, with its

RIGHT: Marco Polo leaving Venice on his second trip to China (1271), from a 14th-century manuscript.

workings inscrutable, not merely to outsiders but to many of its participants as well.

Despite the ebb and flow of political events, Venetian grandeur was built on the bedrock of a unique system of government. The State was governed according to an extraordinary combination of monarchical, patrician and democratic principles. Its stability was guaranteed by a sophisticated system of checks and balances, which prevented any one family or individual from seizing power. Not that the system was immune to abuse, however. One aspect suggests that the Italian propensity for political corruption has a Venetian origin. Before each major

vote, members of the *Maggior Consiglio* (Great Council) used to gather in front of the Doge's Palace, where the richer members tried to buy the votes of the impoverished nobles, who were called the *barnabotti*. Named the *broglio,* after the area in front of the palace, this practice has also bequeathed us the term "imbroglio".

As the bedrock of the Republic, the Great Council confirmed political appointments and passed laws. Although it could not propose laws, it had the power of veto. One of its major functions was to elect the doge, the leader of the Republic. The Council sat in the Doge's Palace, with the doge in the centre, on the bench of St Mark, and the nobles ranged

around him. Designed to represent the whole city, in time the Council became an élite corps of the Venetian nobility.

In 1297 a reform known as the "Closure of the Great Council" increased membership to 1,000, with all noblemen over the age of 26 obliged to serve; by 1323 membership was for life, and by the 16th century there were several thousand members, representing various branches of 150 families. In effect, every nobleman was a servant of the State. The onerous nature of this service is clear in the weekly Sunday sittings and numerous unpaid duties. In session, secret notes were circulated with the common plea: "Don't elect me! Don't see me!"

The Senate proposed and debated legislation as well as providing the administrative class. Created *c.*1250, it comprised approximately 60 members chosen from the Grand Council and elected for a year, although this time limit could be extended by re-election. Senators had to be over the age of 40, although the age limit was eventually lowered to 30. They were helped by more than 100 *ex officio* members who had no voting rights. The Council of Ten, which was established in 1310, was designed to safeguard the constitutional institutions of the Republic. Presided over by the doge, the Council was comprised of 10 senators and six "sages". In time, it acquired a sinister reputation, thanks to the pervasiveness and the brutal efficiency of the revered Venetian secret police.

The Council also responded to the anonymous denunciations which were posted in *bocche di leoni* (lions' heads) placed along the walls of public buildings. In addition, the Republic was underpinned by myriad other councils and consultative bodies.

A patrician and patriotic society

Venice was a city-state run along republican lines by an aristocracy. The *Libro d'Oro* (Golden Book), first formalised in 1506, was the register of the Venetian nobility. Only those inscribed therein could seek high office. Exceptional services to the State could make a citizen eligible for membership. Occasionally wealthy commoners could buy their way in, but it took generations for the family to become accepted.

In this seemingly egalitarian society, patricians did not use titles and palaces were known as houses (*case*, abbreviated to *Ca'*). To curb the development of powerful clans, the Republic even forbade patricians from acting as godfathers to other nobles' children. Yet certain elements of egalitarianism prevailed: there was no élite district; the nobility and populace lived cheek by jowl; patrician children played contentedly with retainers' children. However, after the fall of the Republic, egalitarianism didn't prevent the opportunist nobles accepting their new Austrian titles with alacrity. In terms of finances and freedom of movement, the merchant classes often fared better than the patricians. In the charmed but circumscribed circle of the oligarchy, nobility entailed obligations:

class provided civil servants and even the Chancellor of the Republic.

Both the merchant and citizen classes were sustained by countless privileges and powerful confraternities. Devotion to the Republic transcended class, with all citizens fed on a diet of elaborate state ceremonial and sumptuous art, the mirror of the times.

Queen of the Seas

As the supreme naval power of the age, Venice was truly the Queen of the Seas. While Tuscan and Genoese wealth depended on banking and industry, the Venetian Republic

foreign visits required authorisation from the State; gifts to officials had to be declared and relinquished; even an ambassadorship had to be funded by the ambassador himself. As the writer Jan Morris remarked: "Beneath the patrician crust, the merchant classes and working men had carefully defined rights of their own." The merchant classes were allowed to set up trading posts in the empire while the élite of the citizen

LEFT: Bellini's painting of Doge Loredan, the great diplomat, who ruled for 20 years from 1501.
ABOVE: *bocca di leone* letterbox where anonymous denunciations could be posted.
RIGHT: torture chamber in the Doge's Palace.

prospered on foreign trade alone. Although patrician, the governing class were merchants rather than feudal barons or rentiers. From the start, Venice had imperial ambitions only in so far as they secured maritime trade; conquest was secondary.

The emerging empire never lost touch with its mercantile roots. Yet this quest for supremacy would never have been successful without the city's clear sense of identity, a self-confidence verging on vanity. The "soldiers of the seas" cultivated the spirit of a chosen island race, one set apart by its social cohesion and glorious constitution. The writer Jan Morris even compared Venice with England, "another maritime

The Doge

Of the first 25 doges, three were murdered, one was executed for treason, three were judicially blinded, four were deposed, one was exiled, four abdicated, one became a saint and one was killed in a battle with pirates. Yet the time-honoured institution, the monopoly of old men, functioned well. As the mystical standard-bearer of St Mark and the symbol of republican Venice, the doge had no equal in grandeur among the Italian princes. Resplendent in gold and white, the doge stood out from the

red-clad senators and sombrely dressed patricians. Yet behind the pomp and ceremony lay the cornerstone of the Republic, an institution dating back to AD 726. Enlightened for its day, the system effectively prevented the rise of family factions or the emergence of a despot.

Although the doge was an elected office from the 9th century, complicated balloting procedures came into force in the 12th century. For the final ballot, a boy was picked out of the crowd; his job was to distribute and add up the canvas counters used in the vote; his reward was lifetime service with the doge. Despite such care, the names of the

same families had a habit of recurring: the Mocenigo clan alone furnished seven doges and the Contarini eight. "They kill not with blood but with ballots" was an outsider's sharp verdict on Venetian machinations. Even so, the system of State paternalism served its purpose, producing stability and strong government without despotism. The last in a line of 120 doges was elected the year the French Revolution broke out: an oligarchy masquerading as a Republic was challenged by newly republican France.

The doge was elected for life by patrician members of the Great Council. The archetypal Doge was a wealthy, 72-year-old elder statesman from a prominent family. To control family cliques, the doge's immediate relations were banned from high office and any commercial enterprise. The doge himself was watched closely; he was forbidden private contact with ambassadors and always accompanied by councillors on foreign missions. Such was the scrutiny that the doge's correspondence was censored. His income was strictly controlled and he was not allowed to accept any gifts except flowers and fragrant herbs.

The doge presided over the Signoria, an inner Cabinet comprising three heads of the judiciary and six councillors, representing the city districts (sestieri). Their consent was required in all decisions. The Republic's myriad advisory bodies, and the complex rotation of offices, ensured that dictatorship was impossible and conspiracies nipped in the bud. The much-feared Council of Ten policed the patrician order and kept a check on the doge's power.

In a system hallowed by tradition, the doge was addressed as the "most serene prince". Several doges succumbed to princely pomposity, an approach typified by Doge Agostino Barbarigo's addition of a princely staircase to the Doge's Palace. Yet despite the restrictions on his power, the doge should not be portrayed as a figurehead. In truth, he was a leading statesman who could work the checks and balances of the Constitution. ❏

LEFT: the doge, like the pope, was elected for life, but bitter politics could make that life short.

oligarchy", in which Venetians considered themselves "not rich men or poor men, privileged or powerless, but citizens of Venice".

At home, the State had a monopoly on salt and grain, which were stored in imposing warehouses on the Grand Canal. Local trades included tanning, silk-weaving, glassblowing, shipbuilding and textiles. However, real wealth rested on international commerce. The great trade routes out of Turkestan, Persia, Arabia and Afghanistan all converged on the seaports of the Levant. These were the shipping lanes that kept the Republic rich.

Egypt, Beirut and Byzantium were key trading partners, but Venetian outposts were strung along the shores of the Mediterranean and Middle East. Yet in the 15th century the pattern of trade shifted westwards, with the route to the Black Sea becoming less important. This was an import-export economy on a massive scale, including the transport of slaves and pilgrims as well as freight. Consuls, customs officials, administrators and ambassadors were all despatched overseas in the company of merchants and armed convoys.

The empire was highly organised, with bonded warehouses and customs offices imposing levies on all goods that passed through its jurisdiction. The winged lion, the symbol of Venetian ascendancy, flew over countless territories and trading posts throughout the city's expanding empire.

The spice trade

Spices had been a valuable commodity since Roman times, but the Crusades marked the expansion of the trade, one the Venetians monopolised until the 16th century. The outlandish use of spices which soldiers and pilgrims had learnt in the Orient now found its way into European kitchens. Exotic seasonings were prized for their pungency, preservative powers and the flavour of fabled lands. Venetian warehouses were filled with pepper, cinnamon, cloves, ginger, nutmeg and cardamom.

Spices were only a part of the Venetian imports from the East; other luxury goods included silk, furs, velvets, precious stones, perfumes and pearls. The Venetians operated a salt-and-grain cartel in the Adriatic; they traded in wine and wheat from Apulia, jewels from Asia, hides and silver from the Balkan hinterland, furs and slaves from the Black Sea, and wax, honey, wheat, oil and wine from the Greek islands. Such Mediterranean goods were traded for Flemish cloth and English wool. Cotton and sugar were shipped from plantations in Cyprus and Egypt while metalwork and precious cloth came from the Levant. From the late 15th century, Venetian State galleys were routed to the Catalan coast and to North Africa, where spices from either Alexandria or Syria could be bartered for local honey, wax and leather.

Maritime ventures

Oriental goods first reached Venice in Byzantine ships but soon the Venetians developed a large merchant-marine fleet. Ships were built in the Arsenale, medieval Europe's largest industrial complex. Sea voyages were nevertheless a dangerous undertaking, with the risk of pirate attacks, stormy weather and poor navigation. Not until the end of the 13th century did accurate charts and compasses assist navigation, with ships no longer at the mercy of bad weather or forced to seek nightly anchorage.

Improved shipbuilding techniques resulted in greater speed and cargo space. Two types of ship were used in international trade: the

RIGHT: Carpaccio's paintings perfectly capture everyday life in 15th-century Venice. This is a detail from the *Miracle of the True Cross* (1496) in the Accademia.

long galley, complete with sails and oars, and cogs, roomy sailing ships. The galleys, essentially ships of war, benefited from considerable speed and fighting power. They controlled the trade in luxury goods and served on trade routes with regular timetables.

At the beginning of the 15th century, 3,000 trading vessels sailed under the Venetian flag. Most were in the coastal trade, delivering wood, stone or grain, or formed part of the fishing fleet. Overseas trade was carried out by 300 ships which sailed alone or in heavily armed State convoys, a system which survived until the mid-16th century. The costs of safe passage and cargo space acted as an incentive

were mostly obtained from the Black Sea, to where the convoys sailed on from Byzantium. Greek Orthodox Georgians, for instance, who were resold in Egypt and North Africa, could be traded in good faith as "non-Christians" because they were non-Catholics; nor was trade in heathen slaves forbidden. Pilgrimages represented a profitable sideline for the Venetians: pilgrims were offered a package tour, including the return fare, a donkey ride to Jerusalem and the various customs duties imposed upon Christians in the Holy Land.

The Portuguese voyages of exploration posed the greatest threat to the Republic's monopoly of the spice trade. In 1498 Vasco da

for private shipowners to travel at their own risk and reap the rewards. A way of offsetting the business risk of the perilous voyage was to form a partnership, or *colleganza*. This agreement stipulated that one party remained in Venice and provided three-quarters of the capital while the other, who went on the voyage, put up the remaining quarter. The profit was divided between the two.

The Venetians signed a treaty with the Turks and traded in "goods forbidden to Christians" such as arms, shipbuilding materials and even slaves. Although the slave trade had been forbidden since the 9th century, it was nonetheless still a good source of income. The slaves

Gama rounded the Cape of Good Hope to India, opening up the sea route to the East. His success traditionally marks the decline of Venetian trade, but this is not wholly accurate. Of all the spices, the Portuguese were only pre-eminent in pepper; even here, their transport costs were high and the quality inferior. By the mid-1560s, Venice was re-exporting even greater quantities of pepper and cotton.

A colonial power

The empire was divided into overseas dominions *(stato da mar)* and mainland territories *(stato da terrafirma)*, with the former originally more important. As early as the 14th century, the Adriatic was known as the Gulf of Venice, such was their trading monopoly. Venetian sway over the Adriatic led to treaties with Slav-controlled ports and then domination of Dalmatia (Croatia). The Greek islands were an attractive prize, yielding wine and corn from Crete, raisins from Zante, olive oil and wine from Corfu. Dominion over key Greek territories had been established in the 13th century, from Mykonos and Corfu (and, for several years, Athens) to Crete, the most valuable colony.

The Albanian coast also presented conquests, as did the Greek mainland: Morea (the Peloponnese) was prized for its wine and

the Venetians' plans for consolidation. Indeed, these Italian lands later compensated for losses in the East. Under Doge Francesco Foscari, Venice pursued an expansionist policy in mainland Italy: between 1432 and 1454, conquests around Brescia in Lombardy were followed by control of the entire area up to the river Adda, just east of Milan. However, at the same time the Ottomans were battering the doors of Constantinople.

In 1453 Constantinople fell to the Turks, leaving Venice the leading Christian city in the Mediterranean. Ottoman expansion was initially a spur to Venice, since many dominions sought Venetian protection. Moreover, the Turks were

wheat. To secure the Gulf of Corinth, Lepanto was acquired in 1407, and Cyprus in 1489.

The 15th century saw a systematic pursuit of the *stato da terrafirma*, Italian mainland territories. By 1405, Vicenza, Verona and Padua had all come under Venetian sway. A century later, Venetian territory encompassed the modern regions of the Veneto and Friuli-Venezia Giulia, as well as the Istrian peninsula. The mainland territories were not a poor substitute for overseas dominions but part of

LEFT: Carpaccio's *The Lion of St Mark*, showing the Doge's Palace in the background where it is hung.
ABOVE: *The Battle of Lepanto*, from the Doge's Palace.

more interested in slaves and tributes than in disrupting trade. For Venetians, religion was not allowed to interfere with commerce. Pope Pius II berated the Venetians for their lack of belligerence: "Too much intercourse with the Turks has made you the friend of Mohammedans." But Venetian merchants had always traded as readily with Egyptian and Syrian Muslims as with Greek Christians in Byzantium.

The Turkish threat

By the late 15th century the Turks were in a position to challenge the Republic's maritime empire, but relatively few Venetian possessions were lost. Venetian policy in the 16th century was designed to keep its possessions intact in the face of Turkish expansion and the ambitions of the European powers. The League of Cambrai in 1508 was an attempt by the European powers and the Italian city-states to check Venetian expansion. However, by devious diplomacy Venice regained and consolidated its lost possessions. A policy of appeasement with Istanbul (Constantinople) was carried out to protect Venetian trade, helped by the fact that the Turks depended upon Venice for access to European markets. Yet Venice was ready to resist Ottoman expansion: to these ends, great fortresses were erected in Corfu, Crete, Cyprus, on the Greek mainland and in Dalmatia.

In 1570 the Turks brutally captured Cyprus, a Venetian possession, provoking the Christian world to respond to the "infidels". In 1571 the Holy League of Venice, Spain and the papacy engaged the enemy off Lepanto, a Hellenic port. Although outnumbered, the Christians inflicted a crushing defeat on the Turks in one of the greatest Mediterranean naval battles. Around 30,000 Turks were killed or captured, with 9,000 Christian casualties. However, the victory did little to stifle Ottoman expansion, and appears in retrospect to be the high water mark of the Venetian empire. At home, the Serene Republic still flourished, but forces were at work that would lead to its decline.

Sunset on the serene society

Any view of Venice in the 17th century is of an eclipsed empire and a city tainted by terminal decline. Yet only hindsight provides such certainty. To the Venetians themselves, it was a vibrant age which ended in the dazzle and display of 18th-century art. The sunset was pleasurable yet poignant, particularly for the patrician class. In the face of hostility from the great powers, Venice opted for armed neutrality. Thanks to this, and the sure-footedness of its institutions, the Republic became a byword for stability in a troubled Europe.

Objectively, the 17th century brought the Venetians little good fortune. The once flourishing maritime empire was on the wane. The Habsburgs developed the harbour of Trieste and encouraged piratical raids on Venetian ships. Long-running disputes with the papacy also came to a head. Venice had always taken a stand as an independent sovereign state: *Siamo veneziani, poi cristiani* (We are first Venetians, then Christians). While professing faith in the pope as supreme spiritual leader, the Venetians insisted that the doge and his officers were the masters of temporal affairs.

The papacy believed that the Republic treated Protestants too liberally and rejected the assumption that Rome should routinely rubberstamp the Venetian candidate for Patriarch of Venice. After Venice refused to hand over two clerics to Roman ecclesiastical courts, the whole city was excommunicated. The Venetians were unbowed and the interdict was removed a year later, with much loss of face to the papacy.

The plague of 1630 confirmed the waning of Venice's powers, compounded by changing patterns of world trade. The decline was signalled by the circumnavigation of Africa and the subsequent bypassing of the Mediterranean with the development of northern and transatlantic routes. The commercial axis shifted towards the North Sea, favouring Dutch and English ports to the detriment of Venice. However, the eclipse of Venice was also hastened by Turkish naval supremacy in the eastern Mediterranean and by the loss of the colonial empire to the Ottomans. Yet the picture was less bleak than has often been painted. After a protracted struggle, Venice lost Crete in 1669, but this was mitigated by the preservation of Dalmatia and the gain of Morea (1684–8) in a campaign led by Doge Francesco Morosini. The decline was irreversible, but some trade and banking business survived and Venice remained a wealthy and exotic city.

A cosmopolitan city

Venice was termed "the metropolis of all Italy" by delighted visitors. The diarist John Evelyn (1620–1706) was surprised by the Venetian melting pot: "Jews, Turks, Armenians, Persians, Moors, Greeks, Dalmatians all in their native fashions, negotiating in this famous emporium." The far-flung empire in the Levant had turned Venice into the most cosmopolitan of cities, where East and West

lenders. The glittering emporium of Venice also attracted German and Turkish traders, who were granted magnificent warehouses and bases on the Grand Canal.

The end of an era

The 18th century was a time in which Venice withdrew from the world stage. The wars against the Turks had cost the Republic dearly; armed neutrality became the new objective, with a refusal to become involved in the Wars of the French, Spanish and Austrian Succession. The Rialto was no longer a centre of overseas trade; the great clearing houses were now Genoa, Livorno, Trieste and northern Europe.

mingled. The Greeks, the longest-established foreign community, had their own church, school and liturgical centre. The Armenians, ensconced since the 12th century, enjoyed a similarly privileged position, first with their own church and later with a private island granted by the doge. The Albanians and Dalmatians (Croatians) were established enough to have their own confraternity houses. There had been a Jewish community in Venice since the 14th century, acting as traditional money-

However, as commentator Francis Russell says: "Visible wealth, historic ceremonial and a lingering memory of the triumphal defence of Corfu against the Ottoman Turks in 1716 ensured that the city remained far more than a mere magnet for the tourist." But Morea and the Aegean possessions were finally lost in 1718 at the Peace of Passarowitz, a treaty concluded without Venetian participation. The loss signalled the end of the mighty maritime empire and the confirmation of Austrian power.

All that remained of Venice was its republican dignity. According to critic Michael Levey, "Its grandeur and gravity, embodied by red-clad senators, were almost anachronistic, and there

The Dancing Lesson, by Pietro Longhi **(LEFT)** and *The Opera Rehearsal,* by Mario Ricci **(ABOVE)** provide a glimpse of salon life.

was some piquancy in a Europe of monarchs and princes in the tremendous, impersonal dignity of a state that continued to be a republic." Any attempts to democratise the archaic government were stifled by the conservative élite. Yet for the patrician class, this was an inward-looking age of elegance, indulgence and *dolce vita*. The spectacle of Venice's demise held its own fascination, with the 18th century dying in a blaze of artistic glory. The illusionistic effects of Tiepolo *(see page 170)*, Italy's last grand-scale imaginative painter, trumpeted the greatest illusion: that Venice still remained serene and splendid, gloriously in control of its own destiny.

In 1789, the French Revolution broke out. Napoleon, soon embroiled in conflict with Austria, was determined to destroy the Venetian oligarchy. He provoked a quarrel with the Venetians over a frigate and declared: "I want no more inquisitors, no more senate, I shall be an Attila to the Venetian State." In 1796 he marched into the Veneto without encountering any resistance. In 1797 the last in the line of 120 doges abdicated in recognition of the fait accompli of Napoleon's victories in northern Italy. In a tumultuous sitting, the Great Council declared the death of the Republic. Laying down the *cufieta*, the linen cap worn under the doge's crown, Lodovico Manin turned to his

CULTURAL GHOSTS OF THE LAGOON

Tourism is almost as ancient as the city itself. As an essential port of call on the Grand Tour, Venice attracted visitors drawn to the notion of slowly crumbling splendour. Henry James thought that "everyone interesting, appealing, melancholy, memorable or odd" gravitated towards Venice, and the city is awash with the ghosts of poets, novelists, philosophers, artists and musicians.

Charles Dickens was drawn to its seductive decline, Marcel Proust pondered the passing of time in Caffè Florian, while Ernest Hemingway propped up Harry's Bar. Contemporary accounts of Lord Byron have the Romantic poet swimming the length of the Grand Canal, con-

ducting illicit affairs with a string of mistresses, writing or talking to Shelley long into the night. Thomas Mann used the city as a backdrop to his haunting novella *Death in Venice*.

Venice was equally beloved by artists, particularly the French Impressionists. Renoir chose to portray the city bathed in light, while the English Romantic painter, J.M.W. Turner, captured the city's iridescence in his marine studies. Tchaikovsky and Wagner tapped into the romantic emotions that Venice inspired. Even Nietzsche said that, if he searched for a synonym for music, he found "always and only Venice".

valet and declared with great dignity: "Take it away; I shall not be needing it again."

A provisional government was soon installed, but the arrival of French troops spelt disaster for the city. Although Venice was consigned to Austria in 1797, French rule was reinstated between 1805 and 1814, and imposed the style of its empire on the city's architecture.

Even though historians have treated the French rather lightly, their actions were far more destructive than Austrian rule. Carrying off the spoils of war to the Louvre in Paris was unremarkable; after all, the Venetians themselves returned with booty after the sack of Constantinople. It was the destruction of churches, convents, palaces and shipyards that made a lasting impact. The monasteries were also suppressed and their treasures dispersed. The creation of the Giardini Pubblici (public gardens) entailed the demolition of a church, a cluster of historic buildings and medieval granaries next to the Mint. French building schemes were suitably grandiose: in St Mark's Square, a wing was added to enclose the square.

Austrian rule

Delivered into Austrian hands by Napoleon in 1798, Venice became an appendage of the Austrian empire. The new rulers occupied the city three times, finally leaving in 1866 when Venice voted to join the United Kingdom of Italy. William Dean Howells, the American Consul in Venice, spoke of "a nation in mourning", noting the disappearance of "that public gaiety and private hospitality for which the city was once famous". He failed to note any meeting of minds between victors and vanquished. While the Venetians were a mercurial people, "like the tide, six hours up and six hours down", the Austrians were regarded as "slow and dull-witted".

Yet coming under the Austrian yoke was providential in some respects. Although the Austrians were loathed as an occupying power and resented for their burdensome bureaucracy, they governed justly and liberally, at least until the 1848 Revolution, after which a provisional Venetian Republic was set up under the heroic Daniele Manin, but this fell in 1849.

LEFT: the Arsenale under foreign yoke: the French and Austrians alternated rule. **RIGHT:** a young Eleanor Roosevelt visits Venice at the turn of the 20th century.

An island no longer

The Austrians had a practical bent, building bridges, funding questionable restoration projects and filling in insalubrious canals. In 1846 they built the historic causeway linking Venice to the mainland, and the railway system – Venice was an island no more. However, the city was virtually destitute during Austrian rule: there were no more government jobs, Trieste became the favoured Adriatic port, shipbuilding dwindled and tourism was negligible. The legacy of the Austrians' 58-year rule was restricted to bridge-building and the introduction of the apple strudel. During the Austrian era, Howells noted that there was

"inevitably some international lovemaking". Many Austrian administrators married impoverished patricians and settled in Venice. While conquest rankled with the nobility, it was the loss of former glory that saved Venice. The local aristocracy and bourgeoisie were reduced to poverty and could not indulge in the ambitious building programmes that scarred many European cities.

Venetian luck also held out in modern times: during the Second World War, when many other historic cities were being bombed to rubble, Venice was saved because, reputedly, it was the first city to be protected on both the German and the Allied heritage lists. ❏

Decisive Dates

AD 337 First record of a lagoon settlement.
421 Legendary foundation of Venice on 25 March, conveniently the Feast Day of St Mark.
452 Attila the Hun plunders the Veneto.
453 Aquilea sacked by Attila, prompting an exodus of refugees towards Venetian lagoon.
568 Mass migrations take place from the mainland to Venice.
639 The island of Torcello is colonised and the cathedral founded.
697 According to Venetian legend, the election of Paoluccio Anafesta, the first doge.

726 Election of Orso Ipato, the first recorded doge, who rules the lagoon from the now-vanished colony of Heraclea.
800 Charlemagne is crowned Holy Roman Emperor.
814 The population moves to the Rivo Alto (Rialto), a more hospitable and easily defended island. Venetian coins first minted. Work begins on the first Doge's Palace.
828 Theft of St Mark's body, removed from Alexandria to Venice.
832 First St Mark's Basilica completed.
840 Tacit independence from Byzantium.
1000 Venice controls the Adriatic coast. The Marriage to the Sea ceremony is inaugurated

in honour of Doge Pietro Orseolo II's defeat of Dalmatian pirates in the Adriatic.
1096–9 Venice joins the Crusades, providing ships and supplies for the First Crusade to liberate the Holy Land.
1104 The foundation of the Arsenale.
1128 First street lighting in Venice.
1171 The six districts *(sestieri)* founded.
1173 First Rialto Bridge begun.
1202–4 The Fourth Crusade; the sack of Constantinople and the Venetian conquest of Byzantium provides the springboard for the growth of the Venetian empire. The Arsenale shipyards are created.
1200–70 Venice emerges as a world power.
1271–95 Marco Polo's epic journey to China.
1284 Gold ducats are first minted in Venice.
1297 Establishment of a patrician autocracy.
1309 Work begins on the present Doge's Palace.
1310 The Council of Ten is established as a check on individual power and as a monitor of security.
1325 The names of Venetian noble families are first inscribed in the *Libro d'Oro*, the Golden Book, or aristocratic register.
1348–9 An outbreak of plague kills half the population of Venice.
1355 Doge Faliero (Falier) is beheaded for treason against the Venetian Republic.
1373 A Jewish community is established.
1379–80 The War of Chioggia and decisive defeat of the Genoese takes place.
1403–5 The acquisition of Belluno, Padua, Verona.
1453 Constantinople falls to Turks; zenith of Venetian empire: Treviso, Bergamo, Ravenna, Friuli, Udine and Istria are conquered.
1454 Acquisition of Treviso, Friuli, Bergamo and Ravenna.
1457 The powerful Doge Foscari is deposed.
1489 Cyprus is ceded to Venice by Queen Caterina Cornaro (Corner).
1506 Names of ruling families are fixed in the Golden Book: no new entries allowed.
1508 League of Cambrai unites Europe against Venice. Titian's *Assumption* is hung in the Frari church, Venice. Birth of Palladio, architect from the Veneto.
1516 Jews confined to the Venetian Ghetto.
1519 Birth of Tintoretto, the celebrated Venetian mannerist painter.

1528 Birth of the painter Paolo Veronese.
1570 Loss of Cyprus to the Turks.
1571 Battle of Lepanto, decisive naval victory against the Turks.
1577 The architect Palladio designs Il Redentore (The Redeemer) church.
1567 Birth of the composer Monteverdi.
1580 Birth of the baroque architect Baldassare Longhena.
1630 Venice is struck once again by an outbreak of plague.
1669 Loss of Crete – the last major Venetian colony – to the Turks.
1693 Birth of Tiepolo, the rococo artist.
1703 Antonio Vivaldi is appointed musical director of La Pietà.
1708 A severe winter freezes the lagoon, allowing Venetians to walk to the mainland.
1718 Venice surrenders Morea (Peloponnese) to the Turks, signalling the loss of the Venetian maritime empire; Venice left with the Ionian islands and the Dalmatian coast.
1720 The opening of Caffè Florian.
1752 Completion of the sea walls.
1755 Giovanni Giacomo Casanova is imprisoned in the Doge's Palace.
1757 Antonio Canova, the neoclassical sculptor known for his realism, is born.
1790 Opening of La Fenice opera house.
1797 The fall of the 1,000-year-old Venetian Republic. Doge Lodovico Manin abdicates. Napoleon grants Venice and its territories to Austria in return for Lombardy.
1800 Papal conclave in Venice to elect pope.
1805–14 Venice under Napoleonic rule.
1815–66 After Venice is ceded to Austria under the terms of the Congress of Vienna, Austria occupies the city.
1846 Venice is finally joined to the mainland by a railway causeway.
1848 The failed Venetian uprising against the Austrians takes place.
1861 Vittorio Emanuele crowned King of Italy.
1866 Venice annexed to the Kingdom of Italy.
1885 First Biennale art exhibition.
1902 The campanile (belltower) in Piazza San Marco collapses.
1926 The Porto Marghera industrial zone is constructed.

1931 A road causeway is constructed to the mainland.
1932 First Venice Film Festival takes place.
1945 British troops liberate the city from its Nazi occupiers.
1960 Construction of the Marco Polo airport.
1966 The worst flood in Venetian history hits the city, provoking a debate about restoration.
1979 The Venice Carnival is revived.
1985 Centenary of Biennale art exhibition.
1988 The first stage of the flood barrier is completed.
1995 Gianni de Michelis, Venetian politician and former foreign minister, is subject of a corruption scandal.

1996 Burning down of La Fenice. The worst floods and *acqua alta* (high tides) since 1966.
1997 Radical separatists briefly capture the belltower of St Mark's.
2003 MOSE, the mobile dam project, gets the go-ahead and work begins on the controversial new barrier, due for completion in 2011.
2004 La Fenice opera house finally reopens after its reconstruction. The city gains a new bridge over the Grand Canal. The Arsenale celebrates its 900th year and is where much of the mobile dam is being built. Cutting-edge Venice gets broadband via fibre-optic cables, dispensing with the need for incongruous and ugly satellite dishes. ❑

LEFT: the Rialto district in the 17th century.
RIGHT: La Fenice after the fire in 1996.

SAVING THE CITY

The new flood barrier is a key factor in the future of Venice, as is the balance between the needs of the mainland and the "floating world"

Oh Venice! Venice! When thy marble walls
Are level with the waters there shall be
A cry of nations o'er thy sunken halls
A loud lament along the sweeping sea!

In his epic *Childe Harold*, Lord Byron sounded the city's death knell. But in truth Venice has been in peril since the first foolhardy settlers sank the first stakes into the lagoon. Reports of the dowager's death may be exaggerated, but the politicians still need to protect the fragile ecological balance of the lagoon and solve the intractable problems between historic Venice and the modern mainland.

Venice's unique situation means that the city has myriad would-be saviours, from UNESCO, Venice In Peril and Save Venice to the newly resurgent Green lobby and an interventionist Italian government. In 2003, Premier Silvio Berlusconi stepped into the breach to lend his support to the controversial new mobile flood barrier that will either safeguard Venice for centuries or spell its downfall.

Murky waters

Venetian politics are rarely dull: a former Foreign Minister, the disco-loving local boy Gianni di Michelis, left the political scene ignominiously after proposing a misguided plan to drain the lagoon for the site of Expo 2000. His nemesis was Massimo Cacciari, who presented himself as the antithesis of the proverbially corrupt politician. When first invited to enter politics in

LEFT: building of the MOSE dam.
RIGHT: the *murazzi*, the city's colossal sea walls.

the 1980s, this future city mayor roundly snubbed de Michelis with the quip; "No thanks, my family's got plenty of money already." Whether Cacciari or his less charismatic successor, Paolo Costa, have fared much better with the city's problems, is a moot point.

Not that preserving Venice as a viable living community is ever straightforward. In the last decade, the city has faced the burning down of its opera house, a separatist siege, the declaration of an independent toytown state, deadly floods, the depositing of toxic waste in the lagoon, and gas exploration off the coast. The most bizarre event of recent years was the independence bid to mark the 200th anniversary of the fall of the Republic. In 1997, separatist commandos unfurled the Lion of St Mark, declaring: "The Most Serene Venetian government has occupied the belltower of St Mark's. Long live the Serenissima." This protest was foiled by *carabinieri* (armed police), who scaled the tower and caught the commandos by surprise. Separatist sentiment had been inflamed by corruption, and resentment of high taxes and Roman rule. "Our problems will not be solved by this kind of behaviour," shrugged a waiter in St Mark's Square. "We are more worried about subsidence and rising water levels." It was a similar story a year earlier, when the separatist leader of the League, Umberto Bossi, launched

his "march on the river Po" and proclaimed Venice capital of Padania, his make-believe kingdom. The mayor of Venice rejected Bossi's view of his city as a mythical northern Italian state, while Arrigo Cipriani, owner of Harry's Bar, was forthright: "Bossi belongs in an asylum with people who think they are Napoleon."

Divided city

The old city motto used to be: "Drink in the culture of Venice – find inner serenity in the Serenissima." Today's citizens are a little short of serenity. Venice is the capital of the Veneto, one of the richest regions in Italy, yet the city struggles to survive. Venice and its islands form the natural "floating world" of the lagoon, but over the causeway lies Mestre, the missing half of Venice and another world. The two communities share a city council and a certain nostalgia, but that is all. While the mainland is industrial, entrepreneurial and left-wing, the historic centre is elderly, conservative, tourism-led and ecologically minded. In the last referendum, both parts of the city voted to remain together. However, the benefits of this are rather one-sided: the mainland gains from the lustre of historic Venice, while the lagoon city remains shackled to its bullying younger brother.

Yet despite the undoubted tensions, the picture is muddied by economic interdependence and family ties. In the past 25 years there has been a flight from the islands to the mainland, *al di là dall'acqua* (over the water), even if the administration now claims that the tide is slowly turning. When people leave, a precious slice of Venetian life is lost.

The population has halved since 1945: only 64,000 people live in historic Venice, with a further 45,000 on outlying islands and 190,000 on the mainland. Yet over 30,000 people commute into the city daily, mostly to work in a tourist industry that serves 15 million visitors a year. There is a premium to pay for living in Venice, with the cost and upkeep of city housing beyond many families. To stem the tide to the mainland, there are housing grants for the poorest, and plans for business and tax incentives.

In recent years there has been a realisation that Venice should not have to swing between the twin poles of tourism and industrialisation. Citizens "over the water" will not renounce the jobs that industry brings unless Venice can pro-

THE LIVING LAGOON

Sea water enters the lagoon through three inlets in the sandbars at the Porto di Chioggia, Malamocco and the Lido. While the "dead" lagoon is only fully covered at high tide, the "living" lagoon is fully navigable, with the tides coursing through the channels, cleansing it of debris and sediment. The marshes are criss-crossed with canals and sandbanks, with an outlying area of dyked lakes used for fish farms. Despite pollution, lagoon life survives, from kingfishers, cormorants and coots to grey herons and little egrets. Even so, the surest way of safeguarding the lagoon would be through the mooted creation of a marine park, stretching from the Lido to Chioggia.

vide a range of alternatives. Venice will always be a costly place, so added-value economics is a logical path to follow: this entails developing the high-tech sector, supporting the crafts tradition and competing for the conference trade. To this end, a Palladian convent has been converted into a conference centre, and the huge neo-Gothic flour mill, the Mulino Stucky, is being turned into a mixture of affordable housing, hotel and conference centre.

The ancient crafts tradition has rested too long on masks and Murano glass, but there are signs of diversification into restoration, textiles, fine art and interior design. As for major job-creation schemes, the city is using the prestige

The endangered ecosystem

The economic challenges arc dwarfed by even more pressing environmental concerns. If Venice is not to be doomed to a watery grave, the precarious lagoon world must be protected, both from the elements and from polluting human interference. The sight of oil tankers bearing down on the Doge's Palace may be just a bad memory, but cruise ships and hulking naval ships are not. The latest threat is the probing for gas close to Chioggia, with the fear that any long-term exploitation of reserves may threaten the seabed and the delicate lagoon ecosystem.

The lagoon city has always faced the contradictory dangers of death by drowning and death

and funds generated by the mobile-dam project as a means of reviving the Arsenale district. The reconversion of these sprawling historic ship-yards, which remain in naval hands, is the biggest urban challenge. The city is in the process of wresting control of the site, and creating a cultural complex and a cutting-edge civil-engineering centre. So far, new theatres have opened, linked to the art Biennale, while in the naval zone, MOSE, Venice's controversial new mobile barrier, is being partially assembled.

LEFT: Grand Canal rally of the Northern League in 1996 to proclaim the self-styled Republic of Padania.
ABOVE: an ocean liner sweeps into the fragile lagoon.

by suffocation: the encroaching sea had to be tamed and the silting sands held at bay. The Venetians buttressed the mud banks to protect the city and closed the gaps between the sand-bars *(lidi)*, leaving only three entrances. Then as now, these served to strengthen the city defences and channel the cleansing tides. Breakwaters have always played a key role, notably the Mur-azzi sea walls, which were one of the Repub-lic's greatest feats of civil engineering. The legendary Magistracy of the Waters still exists to supervise the lagoon's precarious ebb and flow, the dredging of shipping lanes and the maintenance of sea walls. After decades of neglect, the side canals are also benefiting from an ongoing dredging programme, allowing for repairs to household pipes and repair of the wooden piling that supports the houses.

No matter how welcome these improvements, many of Venice's ecological problems can be traced back to the mainland. The industrial port of Marghera is blamed for many of the city's ills, from pollution to subsidence and flooding. Yet like historic Venice, it too was born from necessity. The Arsenale was closed during World War I, to the despair of the 8,000-strong workforce. To save the citizens from ruin, local benefactors created a modern industrial centre on the mainland. Porto Marghera was born, built over the mudflats, and served

by the dormitory suburb of Mestre. After World War II, a second industrial zone was built over more reclaimed land and the exodus from historic Venice was unstoppable. The attraction of easily heated homes with damp-free ground floors and properly functioning bathrooms played no small part in helping people decide.

With hindsight, many of the ensuing problems were predictable. Over the years, the Mestre-Marghera industrial complex has dumped tons of pollutants into the lagoon. Closing the petrochemical complex is the obvious solution but too daring for politicians to contemplate. Instead, the proposed solution is to lay pipelines to take the waste out to the open

sea: a kind gift from Venice to tourism on the Adriatic. Toxic fumes from the port are also damaging Venice's fragile buildings and statuary. Sulphur-based emissions are produced by industrial fumes as well as by the natural decay of vegetation on the lagoon mud flats. Sulphur dioxide combines with the salty air to form a toxic cocktail that damages the city fabric.

No longer sinking

Venice officially stopped sinking in 1983, after the extraction of underground water was forbidden. The drawing of millions of gallons of water from artesian wells in Marghera had led to a sharp fall in the water table and threatened subsidence. In the 1970s aqueducts were built to pipe water from inland rivers to the industrial zone. However, Venetian subsidence is partly caused by the weight of the city, with many monuments under threat. Buildings are supported by wooden piles driven deep into the mudflats; change in the water levels means that at low tides the piles are exposed to the air, causing decay.

Nor is Venice itself blameless. While domestic sewage is treated, baths and sinks still drain into the canals. Phosphate-enriched household detergents have been banned as plant and marine life in the lagoon were being suffocated by the algae that thrive on these phosphates. As for the canals, the wash from the *vaporetti* (water buses) causes erosion, eating away at the stonework of Grand Canal palaces, and has led to the closure of certain ferry routes.

On a positive note, Venice is finally taking its responsibilities seriously, and has embarked on a programme to consolidate the city foundations, from quaysides to canal banks and palaces, both in historic Venice and on the islands of Giudecca and the Lido. Salt marshes and wetlands are being reinstated on the edge of the lagoon, even if the impact is mitigated by pollution in the upper Adriatic, where effluents are disgorged into the sea from the river Po. Green groups are introducing Venetian families on the mainland to the wonders of the lagoon. Since many know little of their heritage, the hope is that ecological awareness will encourage the émigrés to return. Aquatic extinction is still some way off. ❏

LEFT: pollution on mainland Mestre and Marghera.

Dams and Deadly Floods

Named MOSE (Moses) after the prophet who parted the waves, a new tidal barrier looks set to save Venice from perilous floods. The debate has raged for decades, but a dramatic increase in the frequency and severity of the floods forced the government to act (between 2002 and 2004, flooding occurred several hundred times). This water-defence system based on mobile barriers is scheduled for completion in 2011.

Although the sight of hordes crossing duckboards in St Mark's Square seems picturesque, it is deeply disruptive. *Acqua alta* (high water) is one of the city's biggest problems, and occurs when south-easterly sirocco winds combine with tides to trap the high water in the lagoon. Global warming, human intervention and industrialisation are all culpable. The 20th century saw the delicate balance of the lagoon disturbed by land reclamation, the deepening of shipping channels and the enclosure of sections for fish farming.

Venice has always been threatened by floods, particularly between September and April. However, the massive flood of 1966 mobilised the world. A tidal wave breached the sea walls and the water level rose by 1.9 metres (6 ft) above mean high tide. St Mark's Square, the lowest point in the city, was submerged under 1.2 metres (4 ft) of water, with a filthy tide of debris seeping through the Basilica doors and waves crashing against the Doge's Palace.

The MOSE tidal barrier is being installed across the three lagoon inlets, using steel floodgates lying on the seabed to form a submerged barrage 2 km (1¼ miles) long. If dangerous tides threaten, air is pumped into the gates and the barrier springs into action. Since it will only be used to prevent floods forecast at over the 110-cm mark, the barrier should operate three times a year, based on current sea levels. As further measures, the authorities have

RIGHT: the disruptive *acqua alta* in St Mark's Square occurs with increasing frequency.

strengthened the coastal defences and reinstated sandbanks. The lagoon's 60-km (40-mile) outer coastline has also been reinforced with artificial reefs and new beaches backed by effective breakwaters.

The city has also gone part of the way down the environmental route, allowing some reclaimed land to be flooded and seeking to ban oil tankers. The raising of the canal banks in flood-prone areas also finds favour with citizens. Yet most environmentalists are against MOSE, citing vested interests, and questioning the need for a barrier that only operates in cases of severe flooding; the regular flooding of the

low-lying San Marco area will still occur.

Instead, detractors favour a return to the *status quo ante*, letting the tides regulate themselves, halting land-reclamation, letting shipping lanes revert to their original paths, and creating a cruise terminal outside the lagoon. Since the jury on the mobile barrier is out until 2011, Venetian writer Damiano Rizzo is resigned to the wait: "The city will go on fighting the high tides with traditional weaponry: wailing sirens, wooden duckboards, wellington boots and buckets of patience. Some day visitors might look back nostalgically at the quaint experience of high tide." ❏

THE VENETIANS

They're often characterised as being cold and contradictory, but the lagoon-dwellers do have a surprisingly hedonistic streak

The character of the city "is old, conservative and resistant to change. Here in the historic centre we lack the capacity for renewal, or even the numbers required to effect a change". Massimo Cacciari, the recent mayor of Venice, speaks as ponderously and lugubriously as ever. Certainly, the population is ageing, with the number of visitors greatly exceeding that of the resident population.

Yet the elusive Venetian spirit transcends such truisms, defies the simple arithmetic of the doom-mongers, and refuses to be confined by the straight-jacket of tourism. In a city defined by the sea, there can be no fortress mentality, only ebb and flow. In short, the slippery lagoon-dwellers retain their distinctiveness, or as much of it as they ever had.

Virtual city

Paolo Costa, the current mayor, is positive about the future of Venice, pointing out that depopulation has finally been halted, helped by new housing projects on the Giudecca and elsewhere. As a symbol of hope, he cites the recent rebirth of the Fenice opera house, rebuilt "as it was, where it was" after its seemingly fatal fire in 1996. He is also proud of the city's move to cutting-edge technology, with the installation of fibre-optic cables promoting his dream of Venice as a virtual city, not a theme park. In his ideal city, Venetians will be involved in nebulous high-tech industries and be free from the yoke of tourism. Ambitious though this vision

is, at least it challenges the view that Venice is mired in inertia as deep as lagoon mud.

Although tolerant, Venetians will admit to impatience with mass tourism. Every few years, a new administration flirts with the idea of controlling access to the city by means of computerised entry cards. Tourists have always been deplored, yet remain part of the picture. Not that Byron, Ruskin, Proust or Wagner would have tolerated such a vulgar term for themselves. But as the cliché runs: Venice without visitors would not be Venice. The locals resent day-trippers who spend little and leave quickly, are puzzled by foreigners who drink a cappuccino with a savoury, and are amused by those who remain

---

LEFT: a washing-bedecked backstreet of Cannaregio.
RIGHT: the tide may be high, but it's business as usual.

rooted to the floating pontoons until told that, in order to travel, they have actually to board a boat. Off-duty gondoliers continue to "blank" tourists with their age-old fish-eyed stare, while many Venetians feel their city has already become a theme park, a travesty of its former self. Patrician Francesco da Mosto decries Venetian pageants as "pantomime on water", and worries that the few remaining schools will close before his children have finished their education. His barber's response is more pragmatic, admitting that "if tourism collapsed, we would too". Bartender Claudia Ruzzenenti concurs, while deploring the summer deluge: "Any Venetians who can, go away – we have to stay

and work. Still, *non si sputa dove si mangia* – you don't spit where you eat, as we say, and tourism is all Venice has got."

The survival of the local dialect, Venexian, forms a strong bond with the Venetians who have moved to the mainland *al di lá dall' acqua*. The impenetrable dialect is also a way of keeping in touch with Venetian values and of preserving privacy. Not that the Venetians wish to be unfriendly to visitors: they are naturally sociable, and happy to share their home with like-minded spirits. Nor do they wish to live in a museum, but in a living city.

To this end, they are courteous and tolerant, as befits a cosmopolitan people who have come to terms with the loss of empire. Their philosophical detachment is often mistaken for aloofness, with their calm and sanguine air likened to Anglo-Saxon aplomb.

Eternal outsiders

The outside view of Venetians has not always been so charitable. Indeed, Italians from elsewhere still harbour a vague antipathy to the city, fuelled by historical grievances. The Republic was feared and respected but not much loved. Venetian justice was severe and far-reaching, with cruel deaths reserved for traitors to the Republic. Widespread fear was engendered by the Venetians' skill at spying. Within Venice, postboxes for secret denunciations, known as *bocche di leoni* ("lions' mouths"), were placed along the walls of public buildings. But in marked contrast to modern-day Italian political ethics, the Republic was no respecter of rank – even a doge could be condemned. Moreover,

CASANOVA

Casanova (1725–98) is a name synonymous with seduction, yet this complex character cannot be dismissed as an amorous rogue. As a subversive adventurer, soldier, spy, gambler, musician and man of letters, Giacomo Casanova embodied the spirit of La Serenissima. His adventures took him from literary salons and royal courts to noblewomen's beds, nunneries and prisons. He was a charming opportunist, yet led a dissolute life that was entirely in keeping with the decadence of his age. In 1755, Casanova was arrested on charges of freemasonry and licentiousness, but managed a daring escape from the notorious Doge's Palace prisons. He then led a clandestine existence until returning to Venice in 1774, craftily acting as a spy for the Venetian Inquisition. Casanova's Venice is still largely intact: you can see his birthplace in the romantic San Samuele quarter, or visit Campo Sant'Angelo, where he indulged in childish pranks, untying moored gondolas or summoning sleeping midwives and priests to imaginary emergencies. From his home, the city's finest clubs and salons were within easy walking distance, including gambling dens in the Frezzeria such as the Ridotto, the casino where Casanova learnt his trade. Although dismissed as a libertine, charlatan and dilettante, Casanova was as mercurial as the Venetian lagoon, with more lives than a Venetian cat.

the system was fair: if the charge was false, the accuser was punished as if he had been guilty of the very same crime. Venice was also the first state in Italy to abolish slavery and the death penalty. Even rivals grudgingly admired the Venetians' autonomous approach and the mercantile spirit of a great trading empire, as well as their shrewd mastery of foreign affairs and good governance of the Republic at home.

Today, the lingering image of the Venetians is that of a cool, closed people, cosmopolitan, canny and conservative but concealing a sinister heart. Yet there is a lighter side: a satirical, playful nature sustained by pageantry, carnivals and masked balls. The Venetians were always prone to social ostentation, lavish expenditure and a love of finery. This hedonistic reputation was acquired in the 18th century during a period of decadence, even if strict sumptuary laws and dress codes supposedly restricted the use of luxury fabrics. Yet the greater the decline, the sharper the sense of fun.

City of Casanova and illicit liaisons

From medieval times onwards, Venice was famed for its courtesans and enjoyed a risqué image that persists to the present. Situated midway between seductiveness and salaciousness, Venice still relishes its reputation as a place for mistresses and illicit assignations. In the 15th century, prostitution in the Frezzeria quarter near San Marco was officially sanctioned, supposedly to preserve the honour of Venetian ladies. Brothels also flourished in the banking district of the Rialto, the commercial hub of the Republic, which was soon to become equally famous for its fleshpots.

A 16th-century survey noted that the city had 3,000 noblewomen but more than 11,000 prostitutes. Yet in a city graced by gondolas, dreamy mists and Casanova, the arch-seducer, seduction was raised to a fine art.

A well-deserved reputation for pleasure-seeking should not obscure the Venetians' more refined tastes. Their pronounced aesthetic sense is evident in art and architecture. In painting they show a poetic sensibility and a penchant for colour and sensuality, rather than for more

rational, monumental forms. As for architecture, while the Florentine *palazzo* is austere and unadorned, the Venetian equivalent is opulent and ostentatious, a showy symbol of prestige.

The Venetians are also noted for their curiosity and spirit of intellectual enquiry, a disposition that led to great empire-building. Yet this lofty outlook is tempered by a profound indifference to matters beyond the lagoon. Even Marco Polo, the legendary explorer, remained a home-town boy at heart: "Every time I describe a city, I am saying something about Venice." If this sounds contradictory, bear in mind that consistency is not a virtue held in high esteem by the Venetians.

Labyrinthine Venice

The Venetians are victims of classic Italian *campanilismo*, a firm attachment to their roots. This can partly be explained by the physical uniqueness of Venice: the shimmering light and the slow pace of life of this watery, chimerical city are reasons enough for loving the place.

Venice is a labyrinth, even with a map. Venetians, when asked the way, are famed for always declaring: "*sempre diritto, cinque minuti*" (straight ahead, five minutes), no matter how misleading this may be. Yet as the writer J.G. Links says: "If he does not answer *sempre diritto*, he is not a Venetian and his directions must be treated with caution."

LEFT: gamblers in Il Ridotto. Venice still enjoys a reputation as a city for pleasure-seekers.
RIGHT: gambling gondoliers.

The city is split into six *sestieri*, or districts, each with its main church and *campo* (square). Although the distinctiveness of individual parishes is fading, Cannaregio, in particular, retains its character as the last bastion for working-class Venetians who have not moved to the mainland. As in parts of Castello, washing-bedecked alleys are home to children and cats. Around the Rialto lies a humble slice of Venetian life, with a popular market, one of the few places where both Italian and the sing-song of Venetian dialect predominate. But throughout Venice, the *campo* is at the heart of community life. Away from San Marco, Sunday is still spent streaming from church to a trattoria for lunch.

blici, the main park, most prefer their parish *campo*. San Giacomo dell'Orio, one of the city's most domesticated squares, is typical, home to daredevil children kicking footballs against the Byzantine apses while parents look on fondly. Although teenagers fare less well, there is a vibrant university quarter around Ca' Foscari and San Barnaba in Dorsoduro. To outsiders, the quirkiness of studious Venice, and especially of everyday Venice, holds a rarified, undeniable charm.

The Venetian philosophy

Walking slowly echoes the languid pace of city life; such is the Venetian philosophy. There is

Yet even if the slow exodus from the city has been stemmed, the Venetians are in a deadly vice, exacerbated by the cost of housing and lack of help for new businesses. The middle classes are the most vociferous, complaining that they are too poor to buy property but deemed too rich to be eligible for subsidised housing. Venetian demographics also mean that there are almost three times as many pensioners as children under 14. Churches are under threat of closure, with an average of 30 parishioners who attend Mass, all elderly.

By contrast, Venice's 4,000 children seem to lead a charmed life, despite the lack of facilities. Although they play in the Giardini Pub-

always time to greet friends, gossip, choose between the grand Caffè Florian and a cosy neighbourhood bar in the Rialto market. Venetians love stretching out a social greeting into a leisurely chat. Standing at a bar counter, the locals sip an *ombretta*, a small glass of wine, and choose *cichetti*, savoury snacks of meatballs, baby squid or marinated sardines. A Venetian has no qualms about tucking into *nerveti*, boiled ox tendons served with vinaigrette and onions.

A stranger watching this scene might dismiss Venice as provincial. Far from it: Venice is a cosmopolitan stage where virtues and vices are visible for all to see. Apart from summer strollers, the city is relatively quiet at night. High rents have forced many ordinary Venetians to abandon the city at nightfall, returning to their homes in Mestre, leaving Venice to *foresti* (outsiders), as well as to wealthier Venetians or staunch working-class residents. Nightlife is relatively restrained, restricted to cafés, concerts and gentrified wine bars.

A Venetian élite may still meet to strains of Vivaldi at the fireside of a freshly gilded salon. However, most Venetians prefer a prosaic stroll and a meal out, knowing that a "prosaic" stroll around the canal sides can encompass more magic and drama than is on offer in any of the city's formal theatres. However, Venetian culture-vultures are well catered for. The Gol-

At the first hint of summer, Venetian nobles fled the city for the Palladian villas of the Brenta Canal, a practice that still prevails on a small scale. Today's Venetians are vigorous outdoor folk, on the water in summer and on the ski slopes in winter. Thanks to its unique location, Venice has much to offer nature-lovers: the lagoon provides contemplation for fishermen and bird-watchers. The seaside resort on the city's doorstep is the Lido, that elegant bathing beach which becomes a second home to Venetians in summer. On sweltering Sundays, the Lido's manicured beaches may be packed, but the more knowing choose to cycle along the Lido's Lungomare (Esplanade), from the quay-

doni Theatre stages plays by the eponymous playwright (1707–93), author of delightful comedies in Venetian dialect. Classical concerts are held in St Mark's as well as in La Pietà, Vivaldi's church, while opera has returned to the resurrected La Fenice and Teatro Malibran. Gamblers with a musical bent will choose the Casino, in Palazzo Vendramin-Calergi, on the Grand Canal, formerly Wagner's home. Apart from the opera season, the Film Festival, the Biennale and Carnival are the highlights of the Venetian social calendar.

sides to the Adriatic sea walls. Known as the lagoon run, it is a most poetic ride.

In a city where everything is conditioned by water, cool, independent Venetians are nothing if not survivors. Massimo Cacciari is sanguine about the future of his fellow citizens and beloved city: "If Venice has any vitality left, it will seize the moment. If it is dead in human terms, it will die. After all, Babylon, Alexandria and Rome have all died." While at odds with the Venetians' positive approach to life, this view echoes the citizens' classic philosophical detachment. As such, the former mayor shows himself to be a contradictory character, and that is the mark of a true Venetian. ❏

LEFT: there are almost three times as many pensioners as children under 14. **ABOVE:** Venetian students.

ARCHITECTURAL STYLE

Building here was never easy, but the unique setting inspired generations of architects to produce an eclectic blend of Byzantine, Gothic and Renaissance influences

rchitects call Venice an artificial city, "a city born adult". It was never a blank slate, but built from remnants of ruined cities: Venice salvaged Roman bricks from Adriatic villas and recycled arches and statuary from churches and palaces in the romantic colony of Torcello. As the gateway to the East, Venice raided Byzantium for booty to adorn its noble facades. From marble to mosaics, the eastern colonies provided precious materials to transform the inhospitable lagoon islands into an imperial capital.

Oriental allure

Architecturally, the city succumbed to the spell of the East, with a Byzantine spirit poured into a Gothic mould; only reluctantly was Venice lured into the Renaissance. The palace (*palazzo*) is the classic unit of Venetian architecture, a form influenced by the Roman country villa and by Byzantine buildings in Ravenna and Constantinople. Characterised by colour, decoration and eclecticism, the result is a synthesis of styles simply known as Venetian. Plaques and roundels created chiaroscuro effects and offset the flatness of the facade; the vivid marble also reflected the local love of colour.

Although many of the frescoed facades have not survived the ravages of time and humidity, some have been sympathetically recreated on the Grand Canal. Yet the vernacular Venetian style is a hybrid. A typical cluster of buildings may show influences from East and West,

LEFT: the courtyard of the glorious Ca' d'Oro.
RIGHT: the Palazzo Loredan on the Grand Canal.

sporting Moorish windows, a Gothic structure, Veneto-Byzantine decoration and Renaissance or baroque flourishes.

Materials were shipped to Venice with great difficulty: piling and timber came from the Lido, from alpine forests and from the Balkans; carved stones and friezes were raided from Greek and Roman classical temples; white Istrian stone was used for facings, arcading and windows; small, flat Roman bricks served as building blocks, salvaged from villas destroyed by the barbarian hordes; red Verona marble provided flooring; exotic marble came from Greece, with semi-precious stones from Constantinople; only glass was home-made in Murano, although brick was later made from local clay.

Venice is a city of brick rather than stone: it is at most a stone-clad city, where pink-hued bricks predominate, with cool stone restricted to finishings. According to the writer Mary McCarthy, the city's beauty comes from "the thin marble veneers with which the brick surface is coated". Its sheer weight made stone unsuitable as the prime building material, at least until piling techniques became sophisticated enough to cope with such structures as La Salute church, supported by a million piles.

Since Venice began as a satellite of Byzantium, the oriental legacy is tangible. Craftsmen

from Constantinople worked on the oldest buildings, as did Greek mosaicists. In Venice, Byzantine religious architecture is far more impressive than the civil equivalent. To appreciate the early city settlement, there is no substitute for visiting the remote island of Torcello. The basilica feels deeply Byzantine, founded in AD 639 and modified between the 9th and 11th centuries. Inspired by Ravenna, its centrepiece is the Byzantine mosaic-studded apse.

Next door, the domed church of Santa Fosca is the perfect expression of the Byzantine notion of space. The Greek cross plan is complemented by small oriental apses; outside, an octagonal portico rests on Veneto-Byzantine capitals. This stilted portico is considered to have been the prototype for arcades on traditional Venetian palaces. Here, as elsewhere in the church, Romanesque austerity is shot through with Byzantine decorative motifs.

In central Venice, the majority of Byzantine buildings lie around the Rialto, the oldest section of the city, or close to San Marco. San Giacomo di Rialto is considered to be the oldest church, and displays the Byzantine Greek cross design. Austere San Nicolò dei Mendicoli, built for the poor, also retains its 7th-century basilican plan and small double-mullioned windows. However, San Marco remains the supreme example of Byzantine architecture, an elongated version of the five-domed Greek cross design, based on the Church of the Apostles in Constantinople.

Veneto-Byzantine style

Given the Venetian talent for fusion, the emergence of a unique Veneto-Byzantine style was a matter of course. Popular from the 11th to 13th centuries, this was an oriental, flowery form, with ornate capitals, pediments and niches and Byzantine arches. Slender columns (cushion or basket capitals) and stilted arches gave way to Moorish design, especially the horseshoe arch and the inflected arch, resembling a quivering flame. A taste for crenellations was acquired from the Muslim world, though most crenellated parapets have long gone.

The Byzantine legacy is a love of voluptuous materials, from inlaid marble to porphyry and jasper. Facades were adorned with *paterae*, decorative stone or marble plaques, often bearing symbolic foliage and animal motifs – griffins,

---

WELL-HEADS

Carved well-heads are a familiar feature of Venice, from the drum-shaped Roman well-head outside the basilica in Torcello to a trio of delightful wells situated on Campo Santa Maria Formosa. The well-heads mask a complex and costly system below, acting as an outlet for an underground chain of storage tanks which often run the entire length of the *campo*. The rainwater used to be collected through apertures in the *campo* floor, purified through sand-filters and then channelled into cisterns. Since the late 19th century, however, the city's water has come from artesian wells on the mainland.

eagles, lions and peacocks symbolising eternal life through baptism, or vine leaves representing the "true vine" of St John's Gospel.

The Ca' da Mosto on the Grand Canal is one of the best-preserved Veneto-Byzantine palaces. This 12th-century residence has an elegant loggia on the first floor, with arches adorned by fine *paterae*. The Ca' Loredan, which is also on the Grand Canal, retains ground-floor arcading surmounted by an open gallery. The original marble plaques and 12th-century capitals remain.

In Cannaregio, Veneto-Byzantine friezes and roundels adorn the recently excavated courtyard of the Corte del Milion, where Marco Polo's family reputedly lived.

covered loggia *(liagò)*, a feature of 13th- and 14th-century Venetian houses.

The Fondaco dei Tedeschi on the Grand Canal is a monumental square structure, previously a warehouse and residence for German merchants. The arcade at water level made for easy unloading; above is a bare facade which was frescoed by Giorgione and finished by Titian; poetic fragments remain in the Ca' d'Oro museum. The inner courtyard is framed by a loggia and porticoed facades, which were once frescoed by Titian.

The nearby Fondaco dei Turchi has been radically restored but remains close to its original form if not spirit. As an emporium for

Merchant homes

This eclectic Venetian style has left its mark on palaces and warehouses *(fondaci)*. The model was the *casa-fondaco*, combining the roles of commercial office and family home. The house followed a three-tiered plan that became the pattern for centuries to come. In the Veneto-Byzantine merchant's house an arcade ran along the ground floor with a loggia running across the floor above. Side turrets or parapets *(torreselle)* were a reminder of the days of defensive fortifications. The top floor could have a

Turkish merchants, the crenellated building was practical yet decorative, with waterside loading bays below a Romanesque portico.

The aesthete John Ruskin believed that Venetian post-Gothic architecture was a desecration. While this is blind prejudice, it is the Gothic palaces of the 13th to 15th centuries that are one of the city's chief glories. Gothic is the most common city style and also the loveliest. The great Venetian building boom of this period coincided with the expansion of the Ottoman empire. Although this meant the relinquishing of Venice's eastern colonies and retrenchment abroad, the city architecture benefited from the recall of resources and master-craftsmen.

LEFT: well-head on Campo San Marziale.
ABOVE: basilica of Santi Maria e Donato, Murano.

Noble Gothic palaces

Compared with its Byzantine predecessor, the Gothic palace was a nobler yet more ostentatious creation. The pure curve of a Byzantine arch progressed to a pointed Moorish arch and then to a Gothic ogival arch. The Byzantine continuous loggia evolved into a fully-fledged loggia with cusped arches and quatrefoil (four-leaf) motifs. Glorious windows were framed by filigree stonework, with brick and stucco used in delicate two-tone colour combinations. Yet Venetian Gothic is as idiosyncratic as the city: trade with the Levant in the period ensured palaces bore an Islamic and Byzantine stamp.

The Venetian love of *paterae* to embellish facades was extremely resilient and survived until Renaissance times. By the same token, facades continued to be studded with classical Greek sculpture or Byzantine carvings copied from Constantinople.

The Ca' d'Oro is arguably the finest Gothic palace, with detail as delicate as an that on an oriental carpet. Decorated in a Venetian interpretation of the Flamboyant Gothic style, the palace's stone tracery becomes lighter and more fragile as it reaches the top, creating a giddy sensation of space. This clever inversion of space and solids is a characteristic feature of Venetian vernacular.

THE CAMPO

San Marco is the only square in Venice to be called a *piazza;* every other square is either a *campo* or a tinier *campiello.* Major *campi* contain a monastery or an oratory as well as a *scuola,* a confraternity which acted as the hub of social life for the bourgeoisie. But it's the homely neighbourhood square that encapsulates the distinctiveness of Venice. The quintessential *campo* is probably a lopsided space containing a church, a cluster of decrepit palaces, russet pantiled roofs, a bridge, a gondoliers' station, a carved well-head sprouting weeds, and an alley cat lurking in a smelly *sottoportego.* Beneath a facade with a chipped lion's head, a mangy dog suns himself by a flower stall while his master plays cards or chess with a friend from the news-stand next door.

Each *campo* has its own individual charm, from stately Campo Santo Stefano, the place for a chic aperitif in stylish Dorsoduro, to huge Campo San Polo, once the stage for popular fairs and bullfights but now a lively square overrun by boisterous children. Particularly in summer, certain squares are taken over by students, notably Campo Santa Margarita, Campo San Luca, Campo San Barnaba and Campo San Bartolomeo. The tiny *campi* and *campielli* in the Castello district, representing the cheery underside of working-class Venice, are always worth exploring.

The Doge's Palace began life as a 9th-century castle but it was transformed into a masterpiece of graceful High Gothic style. Seeming to float on air, the loggia and portico form a lacy latticework. As for church architecture, from the 14th century, the intricate floriated Gothic style became common. The Frari is the most glorious of Venetian-Gothic churches, based on a Latin cross plan with three aisles. It has a severe facade with a curved crowning and cross-vaulted roof with sturdy tie-beams. Santi Giovanni e Paolo, known as Zanipolo, is almost as grand, with a similar cross-vaulted roof. Exposed beams are a feature of many Gothic city churches, with the finest taking the form of ship's-keel ceilings, as in Santo Stefano, San Polo and San Giovanni in Bragora.

Renaissance splendour

The end of the 15th century was a golden age for all Venetian art forms. Yet although palaces acquired a classical air, native conservatism prevailed and a hybrid of Venetian Gothic survived well into the 15th century. However, much was built in sandstone rather than brick, and supported by exceptionally strong foundations. Inspired by classical architecture, this was a symmetrical style using such motifs as Corinthian capitals, fluted columns, projecting roof cornices and rustication.

The Arsenale, with its crenellations and ceremonial land gate, is considered to be the first flowering of Renaissance architecture. Built in 1460, the land gate leads to the armaments and shipbuilding complex. Other key structures were Antonio da Ponte's Rialto Bridge and the Giants' Staircase in the Doge's Palace.

The delightful church of Santa Maria dei Miracoli and Ca' Dario were designed by the Lombardi brothers, master-craftsmen. If the Venetian Renaissance was a compromise between classical precision and local convention, then Ca' Dario expresses its essence. The palace conveys an oriental richness with its coloured marble reliefs and interlacing design. The flowing arabesques were inspired by Byzantine mosaics in the Basilica of San Marco. Venice owes much to Mauro Coducci (1440–1504), an architect from Bergamo who

was inspired by the city. He imposed symmetry on the Venetian model but did not dispense with Byzantine decorative reliefs. His Palazzo Vendramin-Calergi, which is now the city casino, is a magnificent work, subtly introducing Tuscan sophistication to Gothic Venice. His designs were used for the Clocktower by San Marco and the grandiose Palazzo Zorzi. In addition, he rebuilt the church of Santa Maria Formosa and created the graceful facade of San Zaccaria, his masterpiece.

High Renaissance and baroque

The High Renaissance was led by Jacopo Sansovino (1486–1570), who quickly adapted

to the Venetian sensibility despite his Tuscan background and Roman training. In his role as Superintendent of the Works, he had great influence over Venetian architecture. Ca' Grande on the Grand Canal is a magnificent classical triumph. Here, as in other Venetian palaces, Sansovino established triple water-entrance arches and spandrels adorned with sculpture. He is also responsible for several buildings at San Marco, from the Zecca (Mint) to the Libreria Sansoviniana, his great library.

If the Renaissance was the apogee of refinement, baroque Venice belonged to a bold yet less inspired age. By turns ponderous and whimsical, this was a relatively sober form of

LEFT: *Campo Santa Maria Formosa*, by Canaletto.
RIGHT: the Renaissance Contarini-Bovolo staircase.

baroque, tempered by Palladianism. The style is characterised by stone rustication and heavy ornamentation. It revels in exuberant stucco-work and flamboyant friezes, with every surface studded with garlands, cherubs, coats of arms or grotesque masks. The inner courtyard became a grand feature of a palace, with gardens often disappearing.

As the prime exponent of Venetian baroque, Baldassare Longhena (1598–1682) created the theatrical church of La Salute, with its grandiose plan indebted to Palladio's Il Redentore. In both churches and palaces, Longhena was noted for his sense of chiaroscuro, with dynamic and dramatic facades, heavily charged with rich carving. He is also responsible for breaking the three-part rhythm of the Venetian palace by introducing a continuous sequence of windows. Ca' Pesaro has a theatrical inner courtyard and a rusticated Grand Canal facade rich in ornamentation and chiaroscuro effects. Ca' Rezzonico, which was also designed by Longhena, is more restrained.

Classical revival

In the 18th century there was a reaction against baroque and a return to Palladian values. Grandiose palaces were designed for wealthy *arrivistes*, with stateliness emphasised by monumental staircases. Palazzo Grassi, for example, was based on baroque plans by Longhena but then completed by Massari (1686–1766), an architect who was drawn to the new spirit of the classical revival. Massari also created the Palladian facade of the Gesuati church and his great masterpiece, the church of La Pietà. The classical revival can also be seen in the design of La Fenice opera house. Completed in 1790, La Fenice was one of the last significant neo-classical structures to be built in Venice.

The end of the Republic signalled an end to building, although there was a slight blip during the Napoleonic era. Modernist plans by architects such as Le Corbusier and Frank Lloyd Wright were rejected as out of place in a conservative city. Yet local fears were probably unjustified. By tradition, non-Venetian architects tend to go native, attuning their designs to the aesthetic sensibility of the city and the uniqueness of the lagoon. ❑

PALLADIO

Andrea Palladio (1508–80) was born in the Veneto and worked as a mason on mannerist monuments, but only fully formulated his classical philosophy after visiting Rome in the 1540s. He dedicated the end of his career to transforming the Venetian skyline with his bold buildings.

Although his sublime churches were consigned to the outskirts, with their creation Venice's waterfront vista was complete. His churches are there, framing the space where the sky meets the sea. This is true of San Francesco della Vigna, the church and hospice of Le Zitelle (now a conference centre) and Palladio's two masterpieces: San Giorgio Maggiore and Il Redentore.

San Giorgio, built in 1565, is a model of stylistic unity and coherent classicism, a monastic stage-set with a cloister more fitting for a sumptuous palace than a place of prayer. Il Redentore, built in 1576, is a model of rigour and restraint, inspired by the Pantheon in Rome. An unwavering sense of proportion and perspective is reflected in the facades, the pedimented porticoes and the bold yet airy interiors. The subtle, spare designs are enhanced by broad domes, graceful columns and Corinthian capitals. Taken as a whole, Palladio's work on Venetian churches and patrician villas of the Veneto make him one of the most outstanding and influential architects of all time.

The Venetian Palace

The Venetian palace, whether decrepit or ruthlessly restored, remains a cornerstone of city life. Closed in, compact and surrounded by water, it seems a hermetically sealed world. Designed for commercial and ceremonial purposes, the palace reflects both the city's mercantile character and an avowedly aesthetic sensibility.

All palaces were built with both a land and a water entrance. The waterside entrance is always the principal facade, decorated with Byzantine *paterae*, roundels or precious marbles. The flatness of the facade is relieved by balconies *(pergoli)* rather than loggias or colonnades. The watergate opens on to the *androne* or great hall. Once lit by torches or heavy lanterns, this gallery runs the depth of the palace. The dark rooms on either side of the hall often housed the kitchens. Nowadays, canalside ground floors are rarely lived in because of the damp.

Some palaces had a mezzanine floor where the offices were situated. As the commercial function of the palace gave way to noble living, these quarters were transformed into libraries and treasure rooms. By the 17th century, the draughtiness of the main reception rooms caused nobles to convert these quarters into cosy sitting rooms. The *piano nobile*, the elegant first floor, which has the most elaborate windows in the palace, contains the *portego*, the main drawing room, and a series of reception rooms and bedrooms leading off it. Suitable for lavish banquets, this central gallery often runs the length of the house, culminating in a balcony. Later forming a loggia, this provided the ventilation necessary to survive both the winter humidity and the stifling summer heat.

Despite ostentatiously frescoed ceilings, this was a spartan interior offset by the use of luxurious fabrics. From Gothic times, gilded leather lined the walls, with the *portego* hung with brocades, damask and silks. These products of trade with the Levant were preferred to tapestries. Although stuccowork and paintings became popular in the 17th century, objets d'art, Murano glass chandeliers, a chaise longue and oriental rugs still encapsulate the austere elegance of the grandest Venetian palaces.

Flooring is typically made of *terrazzo* – layers of powdered marble, clay and lime, strewn with fragments of coloured marble, smoothed down and polished. Elaborate floors included glass, mother-of-pearl or fragments of gold mosaics. This impressive but costly flooring solution is still used today.

The upper floors were reached by secondary staircases, and housed a warren of

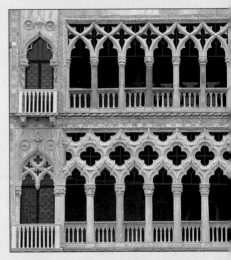

rooms for relatives and children. The attics tended to be used as servants' quarters and for the kitchens, which were often situated here to allow smells to escape. The decorative chimney pots were also highly functional, the tall upended cone acting as a spark-trap.

Perched on the roof was an *altana*, a wooden platform where noblewomen relaxed. Internal courtyards were introduced in the 17th century. These were reached by imposing land gates displaying the owner's coat of arms. Space constraints meant that many courtyards were swallowed up by encroaching buildings. However, delightful courtyards and secret, wisteria-clad gardens remain, often the preserve of cats. ❑

LEFT: Palladio's San Giorgio Maggiore by night.
RIGHT: the lattice-work facade of the Ca d'Oro.

ARTISTS OF COLOUR AND LIGHT

International trade brought the city into contact with
varied artistic schools, but the Venetians adapted
these new influences to suit their own taste

Venetian sensibility reflected a shimmering, watery world. The constantly changing lagoon light created a fluid sense of space and an ambiguity that is absent from landlocked schools of art. Partly in response to the environment, the Venetian school embodied a poetic, painterly sensibility at odds with the rational, monumental and sculptural Florentine style. By the same token, Venice turned its back on the classicism and intellectual rigour of the Romans. To the Venetians, colour, light, texture and space were more important than form.

Venice's status as a great trading empire exposed it to new artistic influences, first from Byzantium and later from Flanders and the Italian schools of Padua, Mantua, Ferrara and Florence. However, Venetian insularity prevailed, with new ideas seeping in slowly and artistic developments transformed into a uniquely Venetian way of seeing things. Paradoxically, thanks to the inclusiveness of the Venetian vision and the varied sources of patronage, Venetian art was less formulaic than other schools, with the greatest painters free to form their own inimitable personal styles.

The Bellini family

Giovanni Bellini (*c.*1430–1516) was the leading exponent of Renaissance art in Venice. Although his brother, Gentile Bellini (1429–1507), rose to be official State painter, Giovanni ("Giambellino") was the unworldly genius. In

later years, he succeeded his brother as State painter. Venice was slow to absorb Renaissance values but, largely thanks to Bellini, evolved its own expressive style.

With Bellini, oil paint displaced tempera (egg-based pigment). Its slow drying-time encouraged experimentation, with oils offering more subtle tonal gradation and a greater simulation of textures. Influenced by Mantegna, his Paduan brother-in-law, Bellini had an understanding of perspective, and was one of the first Venetian artists to include landscapes in the background of his paintings. He revitalised Venetian painting, infusing his art with light, literally seen as a medium of grace.

LEFT: detail from the Bellini altarpiece (1505) in San Zaccaria. **RIGHT:** Bellini's altarpiece, *Madonna and Child* (1488), in the Frari.

Carpaccio

Vittorio Carpaccio (c.1465–1523/6) is the most Venetian of painters, though by no means the greatest. Unlike Giovanni Bellini, Carpaccio was more interested in everyday life than in mood. Compared with Giorgione and Titian, Carpaccio was not innovative, and his paintings have a static quality beneath the surface bustle. Yet the influence of Flemish art is apparent in his miniaturist precision, the details of faces and scenery. While no great master of perspective, he captured the texture of Venetian life and mastered the minutiae without ever losing the unity of the scene. Critics claim that in some respects this is a fantasy Venice in which colours are brighter than in real life and the architecture more extravagant.

This is to neglect the celebratory spirit of an artist who offers an enticing vision of Venetian life: canal-sides crowded with onlookers, pink-hued palaces, ceremonial galleys and gondolas; the noble profiles of confraternity worthies; prelates in damask copes; cocky young blades in red hose and black Venetian caps; cool Venetian ladies at leisure. The sense of a cosmopolitan melting pot is achieved by background figures, from enigmatic Moors to Jewish merchants and turbaned Turks. In the corners lurk a multitude of animals: symbolic lions, doves and dragons compete with whippet-like hunting dogs, Ara-

THE BYZANTINE TRADITION

The Byzantine tradition confirmed Venetian art in its conservatism and love of ornate decoration. One of the city's earliest known artists, Paolo Veneziano (c.1290–c.1360), created static symmetrical works set against a shimmering Byzantine gold background. His great work in the Accademia is the gloriously decorative *Coronation of the Virgin*, in which the central figures are rendered nearly invisible among the large amounts of decorative gold.

Veneziano is credited with introducing the taste for panel paintings to Venice, particularly into the churches. His methods also made sacred art more intimate, with panels placed at eye level to their admirers, by contrast with the inaccessibility of mosaics and murals, which either decorated floors or were tucked away at the top of lofty domes.

Iconic Byzantine influences resurface in Venetian Renaissance art, in Bellini's decorative backgrounds or Veronese's shimmering surfaces. The Byzantine tradition was at one with the Venetians' painterly sensibility and love of surface colour. These are luminous, vibrant, harmonious colours: rich reds, glittering golds and warm sepias. Veronese added to this repertoire with his velvety greens and deep blues, while Tiepolo brought with him a palette of subtle pastels, including mauves and pinks, creams and pale greens.

bian mounts and pampered lapdogs. Carpaccio's *The Lion of St Mark (see page 26)* in the Doge's Palace is both a symbolic depiction of the might of the Republic and an animated portrayal of the winged beast dominating St Mark's and the Doge's Palace.

Giorgione

Giorgione (*c.*1478–1510) has been called "the first modern artist" thanks to the subjectivity of his vision. There are tantalisingly few of his paintings in existence, and those that remain are labelled enigmatic. In Venice, he is noted for two works in the Accademia. *La Vecchia* is both a realistic portrait of an elderly woman and a meditation on old age. Poignantly, Giorgione died young, probably of the plague. *The Tempest* is a poetic and puzzling work that conveys a sense of enchantment disturbed by a mysterious inner tension. In a sense, Giorgione was a Romantic before his time. His understanding of *sfumato*, the soft gradations from light to dark, weaves a spellbinding atmosphere. Some critics impose a modern interpretation of this Renaissance artist's vision, reading in his works vulnerability, loneliness and existential angst.

Titian

Titian (*c.*1487–1576), known as Tiziano Vecellio in Italian, was the polished master of the Venetian High Renaissance style. After Bellini's death, Titian became the undisputed leader of Venetian painting. Indeed, he was the complete Renaissance artist, with ineffable technique, varied subject matter and mastery of different media. His range remains unsurpassed in Western art, encompassing portraits, paintings, mythological poesy, allegories and altarpieces.

His style is characterised by a monumentality akin to Roman painting, by bold design, sweeping forms and sensuous modelling. Allied to this is his expressive style, gorgeous use of colour and the carnal confidence of his nudes. In spite of this enormous scope, he preferred the soft contours of the Venetian school to the sculptural monumentality of the Roman school.

Titian's virtuosity and prolific output made him much in demand throughout Europe. At the height of his career he received commissions

from the pope, the emperor Charles V and Philip II of Spain. If he is not particularly well represented in his home town, it is partly because Napoleon commandeered a clutch of Titian paintings as the spoils of war – Venice's loss was the Louvre's gain.

Titian's greatest paintings in Venice are in the Frari, with the revolutionary nature of *The Assumption* vying with the secular opulence of the Pesaro altarpiece. *The Assumption* echoes the vital confusion of life itself, reinforced by the image of mortals being swept up by the spiritual world. The Accademia possesses several of Titian's works, notably his powerful *Pietà*, which he had intended for his own

tomb. Elsewhere, a luminous depiction of the Annunciation graces the Scuola Grande di San Rocco, while the Doge's Palace has several works by Titian, including a dramatic St Christopher, which is frescoed over a door of the Philosophers' Chamber.

Tintoretto

Tintoretto (1518–94) acquired his nickname ("the little dyer") after his father's trade as a silk-dyer. The artist boldly stated that his aim was to "reconcile the drawing of Michelangelo with the colours of Titian". Michelangelo's influence is clear in Tintoretto's virile compositions and battles with perspective: the bold foreshorten-

---

LEFT: Carpaccio's *St George and the Dragon* .
RIGHT: detail from Titian's Pesaro altarpiece

ing, the striking poses struck by his subjects, the passion for paint. Indeed, it is not fanciful to call the Scuola Grande di San Rocco Tintoretto's Sistine Chapel.

Tintoretto's debt to Titian is clear in his love of colour and mood, but these are from a bold, less subtle palette, dominated by virtuoso chiaroscuro effects. In short, Tintoretto's mannerist sensibility sacrifices luminosity for overwhelming contrasts and theatrical effects. But Tintoretto should not be underrated: he brought a new passion and religious fervour to Venetian painting. Although unworldly, he worked on sumptuous decorative schemes for the State, including mythological battles interpreted as allegories glorifying the Serene Republic.

Veronese

Veronese (1528–88) was nicknamed after his native city, Verona, but his concerns were utterly Venetian. As the art critic John Steer says: "If colour is the most characteristic quality of Venetian art, then the most essentially Venetian artist of his period is Veronese." As a colourist, he was the true successor to Bellini, while in his striving for splendour and decorative detail, his works echoed the Byzantine style. As a society painter, he portrayed the patrician ideal, a civilised life of leisure, a parade of sumptuous fabrics and Palladian decors. It is a fantasy world of formal and spiritual harmony, grace

and Olympian perfection. These heroic, classical paintings are concerned with pictorial effects rather than narrative: on such dazzling stage-sets colour is used to convey mood, often one of eternal spring. Veronese captured the taste of the times, and was chosen to work on the decoration of the Doge's Palace: *The Apotheosis of Venice* is one of his finest mythological scenes.

To great acclaim, he created the sumptuous painting in the church of San Sebastiano, where appropriately the artist is buried. After the death of Veronese, art in Venice declined, and more than a hundred years passed before La Serenissima was able to produce another great painter.

Canaletto

Antonio Canal (1697–1768), known as Canaletto, was greatly admired for his limpid landscapes and photographic observations. In Venice he worked from nature, which was unusual for the period, creating detailed views which influenced generations of landscape painters. Yet his early career as a painter of stage-sets meant that a theatrical approach coloured these scenes. Canaletto's "photographic eye" captured cloud formations and changing light but was not averse to creating exaggerated perspectives. The desired effect was a subtly idealised stage-set, with a sense of order and realism, grandeur and prosperity.

Venice was beloved by Grand Tourists, notably the English, French and Germans. As the forerunners of modern souvenir-hunters, these acquisitive nobles became collectors of Venetian keepsakes, of which the most prized were paintings. Given that Canaletto's work was exported or copied by the grateful, little remains in Venice itself, apart from a few works in Ca' Rezzonico and the Accademia. Although his depiction of San Giacomo di Rialto is better known, Canaletto's architectural whimsy in the Accademia was the work that won him membership of this august body.

Tiepolo

Giambattista Tiepolo (1696–1770) is celebrated for his sublime artifice, heroic style and a virtuosity reminiscent of the Old Masters. Tiepolo was taken under the wing of the Venetian aristocracy: his heroic style, inventiveness and bravura display of skills struck a chord with his patrons, leading to commissions to decorate the finest palaces. Art critic Adriano Mariuz comments on Tiepolo's desire to become another Veronese, "steeped in the flamboyance and airiness of the baroque as well as in the elegance and playfulness of the rococo".

Tiepolo was a fresco painter with a love of grand designs. Created in a Venice on the wane, these pyramids of allegorical figures aspire to Olympian grandeur. The art is decadent in that it is not life-assertive but bound by conventions, albeit forged by an unfettered imagination. Critics claim that Tiepolo lacked real passion, replacing it with bursts of motiveless intensity. Certainly, he was a master of elusive mood, excelling at languorous figures whose moods are not matched to the narrative reality.

era that exalted virtuosity and the glorification of the patron, Tiepolo's triumphal allegories gave expression to the autocratic political ideology that dominated the Europe of his day.

The end of an era

The death of Tiepolo marked the end of an era. However, even after the fall of the Republic, Venetian "minor" painters were still superior to many "major" painters elsewhere in Europe. The final flowering came with perspective and genre painters. Venetian painters followed in Canaletto's footsteps, focusing on picturesque, seemingly photographic views, pastiches custom-made for the collecting mania of the aristocracy. Francesco Guardi (1712–93) was

Tiepolo's palette consisted of pastel tones; delicate, airy colours make the space within his pictures shine with an unearthly radiance. This has earned him the epithet of "poet of light". Yet despite the ethereal settings, his figures have a fleshy, corporeal quality. His was a grandiose vision, but also one throbbing with sensuality. Such mastery of the medium of fresco made him much in demand, and his career took him from Venice to the royal courts of Europe. In an

LEFT: *The Theft of St Mark's Body,* part of Tintoretto's Life of St Mark cycle in the Accademia.
ABOVE: Tiepolo's flights of fantasy in the Carmini.

an impressionistic painter whose views and caprices are, according to the art critic Michael Levey, an "intense response to Venice as a watery setting, its scattered islands, its sense of illimitable distance and silence amid crumbling fragments of ruin". Longhi (1733–1813) was most at home languishing in patrician palaces: as the leading genre painter, he mirrored Venetian high society with charm and intimacy. ❑

● *The best places to see Venetian art are the Accademia (see pages 188–9), the Frari (page 159) and the Scuola Grande di San Rocco (page 160). For a tour of works by Bellini and Tintoretto, see the Artists' Trails (pages 60–1).*

ARTISTS' TRAILS

**Tracking down the works of
Venice's most prolific painters
will take you all over the city,
from Cannaregio to San Polo,
Dorsoduro to the Doge's Palace**

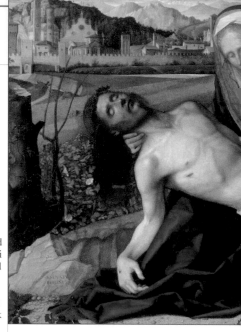

Venice is awash with artists'
trails, but Bellini and Tintoretto are the most represen-
tative, revealing different
facets of Venetian art – the
soft and the harsh, the rapt and
the dramatic. Giovanni Bellini
("Giambellino") is considered
the founder of the Venetian school. His contribution was expressiveness, conveying moods of
grace, tenderness and poignancy. The **Accademia**
is the natural place to appreciate his mystical work
before moving on to the city churches. These are
not all limpid, idealised Madonnas: in his
poignant *Pietà*, the suffering Virgin cradles her
son, her careworn face a testament to the painter's
expressive powers.

Then take ferry line 1 two stops to San Tomà
and head for the **Frari**, a barn-like church housing
The Madonna and Saints, a Bellini masterpiece,
graced by musical cherubs, reinforcing the notion
of music as a symbol of order and harmony.
Ferry line 1 then whisks you to **San
Zaccaria**, where the delightful church
of the same name contains a superb
Bellini altarpiece showing a beguiling interplay of colour and light
in a rich blend of reds, golds and
blues. Next stop is the vast church
of **Santi Giovanni e Paolo** for
Bellini's St Vincent Ferrier altarpiece, showing the saint flanked by
St Christopher and St Sebastian.
Finally, stroll to the remote church
of **San Francesco della Vigna** for
The Madonna and Saints, set in a
luminous landscape.

The dedicated can finish the
day in style with a Bellini cocktail
in Harry's Bar.

ABOVE LEFT: Giovanni Bellini, founder of the Venetian school.
ABOVE: in the Accademia, Bellini's *Pietà* shows the city of Vicenza
looming in the background, indicating the artist's love of landscape
and his skill at opening out a canvas. Other Bellini masterpieces in
the Accademia include the San Giobbe altarpiece, intended for the
church of St Job. Painted at the height of his powers, it is a cunning
illusionistic space with a coffered ceiling heightening the perspective.

LEFT: Bellini's St Vincent Ferrier altarpiece
(1460–5), in the church of Santi Giovanni e Paolo, is a panel painting
charting the passage from Gothic
to Renaissance art. Although the
figures are presented in separate panels, the painting is
given a unity by the new use of
perspective. Bellini admired
Flemish art for its realism and
Florentine art for its purity and
perspective, but was himself
a master of painting without
modelling in line. Bellini's
success in freeing Venetian
painting from Byzantine stiff-
ness can be appreciated in the
masterpieces such as this one
he made for his home city.

THE TINTORETTO TRAIL

The place to begin exploring the works of Venice's most prolific painter is **Madonna dell'Orto** (ferry line 52), where the artist lived and worked, assisted by his children. Despite becoming official painter to the doge in 1574, Tintoretto lived precariously and died penniless. However, his humble background gave him a sympathy for the poor, a theme which, combined with religious fervour, distinguishes him from his contemporaries. The parish church is a shrine to the artist, who is buried in a chapel to the right of the chancel. Here, *The Presentation of the Virgin* shows his characteristic traits of theatricality and grandiosity.

Cross the Rio Madonna dell'Orto canal to reach Rio della Sensa and **Tintoretto's house** (Fondamenta dei Mori 3399), a humble affair, where he lived until his death in 1594. Then take line 52 to Fondamente Nuove and the **Gesuiti**, a baroque church containing Tintoretto's *The Assumption of the Virgin*, influenced by Veronese's luminous colours. Stop for lunch in a rough-and-ready *bacaro* in the Rialto market.

The rumbustious Do Mori on Calle do Mori has operated since 1462, so it's not inconceivable that Tintoretto was a patron. He would have approved of such mixing with the unwashed populace, and eating *crostini* with salt cod or a paste of chicken liver and capers. After lunch, stroll to the church of **San Polo**, which displays Tintoretto's *The Assumption* and *The Last Supper*.

The church is a stepping stone to the real shrine: **Scuola Grande di San Rocco**, Tintoretto's crowning glory. Magnificent mannerist paintings adorn every surface: the works are larger than life, full of chiaroscuro effects and floating, plunging figures in dramatic poses. Before taking line 1 to the Accademia, pause for an ice cream at Millevoglie, in Salizzada San Rocco. From the Accademia stop, either visit the gallery for more by the master or stroll towards pretty **Rio di San Trovaso** and the church of the same name, which boasts several Tintoretto paintings. By the bridge is the engaging wine bar of Cantinone Giá Schiavi. You might find it hard to tear yourself away from the delightful Dorsoduro quarter, even for another work by Tintoretto.

ABOVE: the Doge's Palace is the place to view Tintoretto's splendid works for the Venetian State. The Sala del Senato contains grandiose works (panel pictured above), while the Sala del Maggior Consiglio is decorated by his vast *Paradise*, one of the largest single canvases ever painted. **BELOW:** *The Visitation* in the Scuola Grande di San Rocco, Tintoretto's crowning glory.

THE OPERATIC TRADITION

Venice's liking for masks, romance and drama
combine in opera, which has long been
a high point in the city's cultural life

As one of the world's most operatic cities, Venice has a distinguished tradition in this field. A decisive factor in establishing the genre in the city was the opening of the first public opera house. Taken out of the private chamber, this complex and sophisticated music entered the public domain, and was no longer exclusively the preserve of the nobility. Venice's status as a state with a republican constitution, beyond the control of outside forces, also played an important role in making opera a popular national art form. The leading composers of their day wrote works for Venice, from Rossini and Bellini to Verdi and Wagner. Handel and Scarlatti both conducted their own operas in

Venice. Opera remains close to the Venetian heart despite the tragic fire at La Fenice in 1996 *(see page 65).*

The golden age

Although opera first emerged in 16th-century Florence, the baton was quickly passed on to Venice. The 17th and 18th centuries were the golden age of Venetian music, celebrated by Monteverdi and Vivaldi, and, by the time opera had been defined as a special genre, the city had become the most important centre in Italy.

In the last 20 years of the 17th century, more than 150 operas were performed in the city, including 20 new ones. The operas of the early period perfectly reflected the tastes of Venetian society. Although classical mythology provided the colourful plots, the characterisation reflected the great scandals of the day. This realism was one of the reasons for opera's success in the city, with Venetians only too familiar with the traditional operatic themes of intrigue, conspiracy and betrayal.

In time, it was Venetian composers who developed the sensuous melodies that have come to be considered the hallmark of all Italian opera. Claudio Monteverdi (1567–1643) is regarded as the founder of Venetian opera. Summoned to Venice after an early musical career at the Mantuan court, he was appointed

Teatro San Cassiano, founded in 1637, was the first of many grand public opera houses. By the 18th century, there were 19 such venues in Venice, including La Fenice *(see page 65)*. These theatres were owned by prominent Venetian families who mounted short seasons, hence the constant renewal of the repertoire.

The Venetians were a demanding audience who expected strong librettos and elaborate staging. They got what they craved, and audiences were held spellbound by fantastic stage effects, which could convey dreams and ghostly visitations. Buildings were made to collapse, waves, thunder and lightning could all be simulated, and the clouds on which the gods were

choirmaster of San Marco and Master of Music for the Republic, remaining in his post for 30 years. He was the traditional successor to Andrea Gabrieli (1510–86) and his nephew Giovanni Gabrieli (1557–1612), the early masters of massed choirs and baroque polyphonic music. Monteverdi wrote seven of his operas in Venice, proving his command of musical characterisation, especially in *Poppea*, a late work.

enthroned could divide into three as they sank, then re-form as they rose.

In the 17th century the craze for opera swept the city, but the stage action often played second fiddle to the social aspects: the opera was the place to pick up the latest gossip, play cards, or simply to dine in the privacy of one's box. Yet outstanding vocal performances could provoke storms of applause. Spectators vied with one another in their cries of *"Bravo!"* or threw roses and lace handkerchiefs at the feet of the prima donnas. After the premiere of Rossini's *Semiramis*, an enthusiastic crowd escorted him home in a convoy of gondolas while an orchestra reprised melodies from the opera. Singers who

LEFT: angelic musicians in a Bellini altarpiece in the Frari. **ABOVE:** Giuseppe Verdi (1813–1901), one of the greatest composers of his age, and Claudio Monteverdi (1567–1643), founder of Venetian opera.

did not live up to expectations, however, felt the public's wrath with a fusillade of rotten eggs and tomatoes, radishes or leeks.

Prima donnas and castrati

The 18th century saw the emergence of the concept of the star soloist, the female prima donnas and the castrati, their male counterparts. Their way was paved by the enrichment of operatic forms, the creation of fine arias and *coloratura*, or virtuoso, voice passages. Giving the *primo uomo* (leading man) a treble voice was a popular custom which started in the 16th century and was all the fashion in 18th-century Italy, finally dying out only in the 19th century. The custom

of castrating young boys before puberty to preserve their clear soprano or contralto voices may have been linked to an earlier prohibition against women singing opera in public.

The castrato possessed a unique tone of voice, as well as the lung capacity necessary to sing with great power and the skill to scale the opera's most florid vocal passages. Castrati and prima donnas were so worshipped by their public that they became capricious divas. As overindulged soloists, they decided which arias to sing and which to leave out, as well as laying down the *coloratura* passages which best suited their own vocal virtuosity, regardless of the composer's original intentions.

Verdi in Venice

The appointment of Verdi was a milestone in the history of La Fenice; here was the greatest composer of Italian *bel canto* creating works for Venice. Giuseppe Verdi (1813–1901) was a patriot who found a responsive audience in republican-minded Venice. As one of the greatest composers of his age, Verdi inflamed Venetian passions with five of his finest dramatic works. After diplomatically announcing that Milan's La Scala needed a rest from him (with four of his operas in as many years), Verdi signed a contract with La Fenice. Milan's loss was Venice's gain, and *Hernani* was premiered there in 1844. The public were enchanted by Verdi's music and left humming the melodies.

The heroic composer gave his operas stirring undertones during Italy's struggle for national unity. From 1848, Verdi's name became a rallying cry for his countrymen in the fight for freedom from Austrian domination. The acronym **V**(ittorio) **E**(manuele) **R**(e) **D'I**(talia) was used as a reference to the first king of Italy, eventually crowned in 1861. In 1866, during a performance of *Il Trovatore*, the stage was bombarded by bouquets of red, white and green, the colours of the Italian tricolour flag.

La Fenice

The golden age passed, but La Fenice sustained its reputation, staging the Italian premiere of Wagner's *Rienzi* in 1873, and, after the composer's death in 1883, presenting the entire Ring cycle in German. While most European opera houses could only offer makeshift programmes during World War I, La Fenice presented 68 premieres.

In 1930, the opera house created a festival of contemporary music, proof that Venice was committed to more than the classical canon. Its innovative approach reaped rewards: the world premieres of Stravinsky's *The Rake's Progress* (1951), Britten's *The Turn of the Screw* (1954) and Gershwin's *Porgy and Bess* (1935).

The resurrection of La Fenice has been matched by the reopening of Teatro Malibran, a tiny jewel of an opera house dating back to 1678. The Teatro Malibran, right by the Corte del Milion, an ancient courtyard where Marco Polo once lived, has also reopened its doors after a 10-year closure, again offering a musical venue in the historical heart of Venice. ❑

La Fenice

On 29 January 1996 fire raged through La Fenice opera house. Many Venetians sobbed as their beloved Phoenix burnt down before their eyes, unable to contemplate the loss of this jewel-box of a theatre. The rest of the city awoke to discover that the conflagration had engulfed musical instruments, paintings, costumes and sets; 200 years of history were reduced to four smoke-charred walls. Dame Joan Sutherland, the celebrated diva, was stunned: "It was probably the most beautiful opera house in the world; singing in the Fenice felt like being inside a diamond."

In a sense, this was the third fire in its history. The first Fenice (Phoenix) replaced a 17th-century theatre which had burnt down in 1774. Inaugurated in 1792, the opera house lived to rue its name when, in 1836, fire razed it to the ground. However, just a year later, La Fenice rose from the ashes, rebuilt as before, in all its neoclassical splendour. The jinx appeared to have been broken until 1996, when the Phoenix again seemed doomed. This third fire would resemble the plot of a comic opera if the consequences were not so grave. Ironically for Venice, the draining of the canals left firefighters suffering from a water shortage. An electrical fault was soon ruled out and a more sinister story emerged. Conspiracy theorists made links with the Mafia-led cultural terrorism that struck Italy in the 1990s, but the truth was more banal: two electricians, behind schedule and due to face financial penalties, started a blaze to cover their tracks.

The decision was swiftly taken to rebuild the theatre, com'era, dov'era (as it was, where it was) and in 2004, eight years of scandals, lawsuits and delays ended in the flamboyant reopening of this tiny theatre. The curtain rose on the crowd-pleasing La Traviata, a symbolic opera which received its world premiere in the same theatre in 1853. Marcello Viotti, the musical director, declared his faith in the new Fenice: "We have always

been in the vanguard and in the future I would like to see one new opera presented here every year." The 2004–5 season promised works by Rossini, Strauss and Wagner, supported by a world-class concert and ballet programme, all of which should help dispel La Fenice's reputation for mediocrity.

Yet the city cannot decide whether the Phoenix has taken flight or lost its soul. The theatre has always represented a contrast between a restrained exterior and the richly decorated auditorium. Beyond the gilt and stucco surface, performers appreciate the acoustics and greater intimacy compared with La Scala. Yet while the neoclassical

facade survived the blaze, the auditorium had to be reconstructed, from the glittering chandelier to the gilded balconies and plump putti. In its new guise, the opera house has gained 160 seats yet remains intimate, with its jewel-box ornateness accentuated.

The critical response to the resurrected phoenix has been mixed. Supporters praise the state-of-the-art sets and the improved acoustics, while sentimentalists lament the brightness of the colours and the lack of finesse in the stuccowork. The fiercest art critics decry this kitsch and fake imitation of the past – but to conservative Venetians, the Phoenix has risen again. ❑

LEFT: poster for a performance of Verdi's *Aida* in La Fenice (1881). **RIGHT:** La Fenice resurrected.

CARNIVAL

The colourful pre-Lenten carnival, dating from pagan times, is a 10-day extravaganza of masked balls, pantomime and music

E very year the city indulges in a 10-day masked ball – a Lententide "farewell to the flesh" – when a combination of poseurs and voyeurs come to wallow in the ghostly beauty of Venice as La Serenissima awakes to a whirl of colour, masks and costumes. Carnival has much to answer for: prices soar and the city has more mask shops than butchers; fashion shoots and foreign film crews swamp San Marco; cavorting crowds of motley Europeans dress as gondoliers and bosomy courtesans. Amidst air-kissing and cries of *"bellissimo"*, there are displays of pan-European bad taste. These are all travesties of carnival, but carnival is a time for trav-

esty. Despite the commercialism, this kitsch masquerade retains its magic.

Carnival lore

The Venetian carnival is the inheritor of a rich folk tradition, embracing pagan and Christian motifs. Linked to the winter solstice and fertility rites, such mid-winter folk festivals pre-date Christianity. According to pagan rites, winter was a force to be overcome, with the sun persuaded to return by a show of life at its most vital. Thus in Rome, the fertility rites of Saturnalia were celebrated with a riotous masquerade in which even slaves took part.

Christianity gave the carnival new significance: the words *carne vale*, the Latin for 'farewell to meat', meant a last blow-out, particularly on Mardi Gras (Fat Tuesday), before the start of the long and rigorous Lenten period, marked by abstinence from the pleasures of the flesh and a focus on the spiritual.

In the past, the Venetian carnival was something of a moveable feast, beginning as early as October or Christmas and lasting until Lent. This long carnival season incorporated an element of "bread and circuses", with crowd-pleasing performances intended to curry favour with the populace. In addition to masquerades, there were rope dancers, acrobats and fire-eaters who routinely displayed their skills on Piazza San Marco. The diarist John Evelyn visited Venice in 1645–6 and reported on "the folly and madness of the carnival", from the bull-baiting and flinging of eggs to the superb opera, the singing eunuch and a shooting incident with an enraged nobleman and his courtesan, whose gondola canoodling he had disturbed. During the 1751 carnival, everyone gathered to admire an exotic beast, the rhinoceros, captured in a famous painting by Longhi, which is now displayed in the Ca' Rezzonico.

Carnival was not without barbaric flourishes, including spectacular blood sports with Venetian twists. As well as bear-baiting and Spanish-style bull chases, dogs were shot out of cannons for the crowd's amusement.

Another gory event commemorated the conquest of Aquileia in 1162, when the patriarch of Venice was captured along with 12 of

It is fashionable to mock the carnival as a commercial fabrication, but its roots extend deep into the Venetian psyche. The city has an instinctive love of spectacle and dressing up, dating back to the glory days of the Republic. The carnival reaches back to medieval times and represents a cavalcade of Venetian history, tracing political and military events, factional rivalries and defeats.

Festive calendar

"The finest drawing room in Europe" was Napoleon's overworked description of Piazza San Marco. Here the carnival opens in the presence of thousands of masqueraders, with a

his priests and ransomed for 12 pigs and a bull. After this incident, 12 pigs were flung from the campanile at every carnival, while a bull was beheaded.

When Napoleon conquered Venice in 1797, the carnival went the tragic way of the Venetian Republic. Although revived sporadically in the early part of the 20th century, it was only fully restored in 1979. The event was eagerly reclaimed by Venetians, with playful processions and masquerades.

LEFT: posing in primary colours outside the Procuratie. **ABOVE:** masked revellers in the winter sunshine parading through Piazza San Marco.

different theme each year. No theatre could provide a better setting. During the 10-day spectacle leading up to Shrove Tuesday, revellers come tumbling out of every alley, with the sound of Renaissance and baroque music echoing from every courtyard. Pantomime, operetta, concerts and literary readings are held in theatres and in the open-air spaces of the city *campi*. Campo San Polo, one of the largest squares, is a popular site for outdoor events, thus maintaining a role it has played here since medieval times. Many of the finest masked balls, fireworks and historical happenings are led by the Compagnie della Calza, the local carnival companies.

The high point of the festival is on Shrove Tuesday, when revellers gather for a masked ball on St Mark's Square before moving on to private parties or, in the case of celebrities, to the ball at the Cipriani, across the water. In the past, the midnight fasting bell would ring out from San Francesco della Vigna, signalling an end to licence and the onset of atonement. The end is signalled when the effigy of Carnival is burnt on St Mark's Square.

Devilish disguises

From Epiphany to Ash Wednesday *Sior Maschera*, the masked reveller, reigns supreme. Venetians love to attend the carnival in groups,

all dressed in the same costumes. Revellers are addressed as *Sior Maschera*, since carnival erases distinctions in rank and sex. During the Republic's official ceremonies a strict order of precedence had to be observed, but carnival was a time for the breaking of social taboos: the mask makes everyone equal.

Venetian carnival masks seem timeless. In fact, the most traditional masks form a dramatic monochrome disguise, often harking back to periods of Venetian history or the dramatic tradition of the *commedia dell'arte*. Masks not based on traditional designs are generally known as *fantasie,* or fantasy masks. One of the very finest is the *maschera nobile*,

the white sculpted mask, with a black tricorn and black silk cloak. *Columbina* (Columbine) is the name given to the elegant Venetian domino mask; more catlike and seductive is the mask commonly called *civetta* (flirt). Some masks are quite sinister, notably the menacing Plague Doctor, which features a distinctive beaked nose and black gown and was once worn as a protection against the plague.

If you want to buy a mask, it is worth visiting one of the traditional made-to-measure mask shops, where they can whip you up anything from a brightly coloured festive Harlequin to a Medusa wreathed in snakes or even a sinister death mask.

The most traditional masks are made of leather *(in cuoio)* or papier mâché *(in cartapesta)*, with modern creations worked in ceramics or covered with luxurious fabrics. Leather masks are the hardest to fashion, while hand-held masks make very effective wall decorations. (If you are seeking inspiration for historically authentic carnival costumes, study Pietro Longhi's exquisite carnival paintings, which are in the Ca' Rezzonico.)

Lavish lifestyles

Today's carnival plays homage to the lavish lifestyles of 18th-century Venice. It is ironic that the carnival's heyday coincided with the terminal decline of the Republic. Costumes currently in vogue extol the voluptuous femininity of 18th-century dress for both sexes. The classic costume of the 17th and 18th centuries was the *maschera nobile*, the patrician mask. The head was covered with a *bautá*, a black silk hood and lace cape, topped by a voluminous cloak *(tabarro)*, in black silk for the nobility and in red or grey for ordinary citizens. The *volto*, the white half-mask, covered the face, with the finishing touch provided by a black tricorn hat adorned with feathers.

The elegant *maschera nobile* and *commedia dell'arte* masks are not the only authentic disguises. Masks representing or ridiculing the Republic's enemies, such as an exotic Moor or swarthy Turk, remain popular, as do esoteric costumes associated with the carnival companies. Certainly, the Venetian love of disguise masks a desire to slip into a different skin. As Oscar Wilde said, "A man only reveals himself when wearing a mask." ❏

Commedia dell'Arte

Many of the most distinctive carnival costumes are inspired by the *commedia dell'arte*. The essentially comic genre emerged in 16th-century Italy and featured improvisation, a fast pace and witty regional parodies. Given the physical nature of the comedy, the actors had to be skilled mime artists and acrobatic tumblers. In addition to stagecraft, the genre relied on stock characters who wore costumes and masks to differentiate their roles.

A typical feature of the popular comedy was that characters spoke in regional dialects, leading to comic contrasts and misunderstandings. Thus, the classic pair of manservants, Harlequin *(Arlecchino)* and *Brighella*, come from Bergamo and speak the local dialect. The merchant *Pantalone* speaks Venetian while the Doctor *(Dottore)* favours Bolognese and the lovers Tuscan. The manservants, known as *zanni*, include *Brighella*, the wily servant: always plotting and intriguing, the bilious green colour of his mask shows his bitter nature, as does his broken nose and ugly face. He wears white livery, with green diagonal stripes. The acrobatic *Arlecchino* is often the butt of *Brighella's* jokes. Harlequin's costume of colourful rags is a symbol of his poverty, and later became his red, orange and green suit.

Harlequin's master is the miserly old Venetian merchant, *Pantalone*. Anglicised to "Pantaloons", this was a nickname for Venetians, derived from the name of a popular city saint. The image was reinforced by the character's trousers *(pantaloni)*, worn with a black cloak and red stockings. A brown mask with a bristling moustache and a long crooked nose complete the ensemble.

The foil to *Pantalone* is the pompous and lecherous *Dottore*. As a tedious doctor-at-law, his trademark is pedantry and tirades larded with Latin tags. His black half-mask features a bumpy forehead simulating an injury caused by a disgruntled student. The Captain *(Capitano)* is a braggart of Spanish extraction who has a huge ruff, plumed hat and a mask with a protruding nose.

Many other characters have sprung from these main types, including the maidservant *Columbina*, Harlequin's partner, and *Pulcinella*, the lovable clown, ever popular with children. In England he has turned into Mr Punch, half of the seaside Punch and Judy puppet show. Other characters are seen in France, including the winsome *Pierrot*, a pantomime extension of Harlequin. As well as laying the foundations for pup-

pet shows throughout Europe, the *commedia dell'arte* greatly enriched Continental comic drama, and led to mime in France, and to pantomime in England and Denmark. By the 18th century the *commedia* was in decline, with the characters frozen in time, though Carlo Goldoni (1707–93) raided the repertoire to create his Venetian comedies of manners, plays which are still performed in the city.

Visitors of a consumerist bent can buy the cute velour slippers used by *commedia* characters, including *Pierrot* and *Columbina*, at La Pantofila, Calle della Mandola, San Marco 3718 *(see page 172)*. ❑

LEFT: modern masks for sale all year round.
RIGHT: the miserly merchant *Pantalone* (1550).

REGATTAS AND WATER FESTIVALS

The doges have gone and the great navy is no more, but Venice still celebrates its festivals by staging spectacular water pageants

Water festivals are the glory of Venice, with palaces on the Grand Canal festooned with streamers and silks, redolent of the pomp and pageantry of the Republic. From March to September, the lagoon is awash with regattas. All these events trace their origins back to naval exercises or military training for crossbowmen on the Lido. The most prestigious regatta honours Italy's four ancient maritime republics (Venice, Amalfi, Pisa and Genoa), with a different "republic" staging the event every year.

April's **Festa di San Marco**, honouring the patron saint of Venice, culminates in a gondola race across St Mark's Basin, and the eating of *risi e bisi*, thick rice-and-pea soup. **La Sensa**, the Ascension festival, celebrates Venice's Marriage with the Sea. Until the fall of the Republic, the doge would sail from San Marco to the Lido in the Bucintoro, the ceremonial State barge. With great pomp, a ring was cast into the Adriatic, symbolising Venice's sacred union with the sea.

Today's re-enactment is a pale imitation; the water marathon that follows is more memorable: **La Vogalonga** (Long Row) races from St Mark's Basin to Burano before returning via the Grand Canal. But the most magnificent water festival is September's **Regata Storica**, featuring participants in Renaissance costume. The water-borne parade down the Grand Canal is followed by rowing races best watched from a café by the Rialto Bridge.

ABOVE AND RIGHT: the Festa del Redentore, with barges laden with fireworks and a cavalcade of everyday and ceremonial craft, is the most moving night spectacle. Foghorns are sounded and the festival fireworks explode, turning Venice into a baroque dream. Venetians with views retire to well-positioned terraces, known as *altane*. From these eyries, they eat watermelon while watching the fireworks blaze over the lagoon.

ABOVE: the Regata Storica dates from 1825, the year after the gutting of the last Bucintoro, and was a way of preserving the great memories of the Republic. The cavalcade winds its way from the Giardini quarter to Ca' Foscari on the Grand Canal, where the prizes are presented from dignitaries gathered on a decorated barge.

ABOVE: all classes of Venetian craft appear in regattas, from gondolas to *gondolini*, racing gondolas used in the Regata Storica, and *sandoli*, flat-bottomed boats good for skimming the shallow lagoon. Races also feature the *puparin*, a narrow boat with a platform at the back; the six-man *caorlina*; and the *mascareta*, a light skiff used as a women's racing boat.

BELOW: the greatest Venetian boat of all was the State barge, the Bucintoro. It was lavishly decorated with gilded carvings and used for important state visits. On Ascension Day, it carried the doge to the Lido, where he would perform the ceremony of Venice's Marriage with the Sea, a tradition captured by Canaletto. The Bucintoro was dismantled after the fall of the Republic in 1797.

THANKSGIVING FESTIVALS

Water festivals served to bind the patricians and people together to honour the State, both in times of triumph and disaster. **La Festa del Redentore**, the Feast of the Redeemer, takes place in July and is the most touching and intimate of Venetian festivals. Begun under Doge Alvise Mocenigo, the festival focuses on Il Redentore, the Palladian church built as a token of thanks after salvation from the plague of 1575–7. Then as now, Venetians wend their way to the church, carrying candles and reciting the rosary. A sweeping bridge of boats stretches across the Giudecca canal to the church, enabling people to attend Mass and listen to the chanting monks. The firework display on the eve of the feast day has been a feature since the 16th century. At night, crowds line the Zattere and the Giudecca or take to boats of every description. From stately yachts to refuse barges and gondolas, the watercraft are bedecked in finery and glow like festive gazebos. Boisterous families enjoy on-board picnics of duck, lobster, mulberries, mandarins and sparkling Prosecco. Visitors who are not pulled into picnic boats by high-spirited Venetians must content themselves with the "redemptive" dinners on offer at Harry's Bar. Energetic souls carouse all night before rowing to the Lido for a dawn swim.

La Festa della Madonna della Salute, celebrated on 21 November, also commemorates the city's deliverance from the plague – of 1630. Here, too, there is a votive procession to the church, reached by a pontoon bridge from Santa Maria del Giglio. Venetians make the pilgrimage to La Salute to light candles in gratitude for the continuing good health of the city and its citizens. This baroque church makes a spectacular sight, its main doors finally flung open and crowds ascending the steps.

● *For a full listing of Venice's festivals and cultural events, see page 223.*

LEFT: *The Women's Regatta* by Bella (1730–99) shows costumed girls standing up and rowing down the Grand Canal. First staged in 1493, in honour of Beatrice d'Este, wife of the duke of Milan, the race is still held today as part of the Regata Storica.

EATING OUT

Venice is noted for top-quality seafood and for fine restaurants. But you shouldn't ignore the traditional bars and inns, known as *bacari*

Food critics tend to damn Venetian food as overpriced and underachieving, but you can eat well if you choose wisely. Even so, the difficulty of transporting fresh produce adds 20 percent to restaurant prices. Mass tourism also means that the city can get away with grim tourist menus, indifferent service and inferior breakfasts. Yet for seafood lovers, the cuisine can be memorable, with soft-shelled crabs from the lagoon, plump red mullet, pasta heaped with lobster or black and pungent with cuttlefish ink.

According to Alastair Little, the British gourmet chef and Italophile, "the city's cosmopolitan past and superb produce imported from the Veneto have given rise to Italy's most eclectic and subtle style of cookery." Fine praise indeed. Like the Sicilians, the Venetians absorbed culinary ideas from the Arabs; they also raided Byzantium and, according to the Middle Eastern cookery writer, Claudia Roden, translated it into their own simple style: "If you could see the fish come in live at dawn in barges on the Grand Canal straight onto the market stalls, you would understand why all they want to do is lightly fry, poach or grill it."

As the hub of a cosmopolitan trading empire, Venice was bristling with foreign communities – Arabs, Armenians, Greeks, Jews and Turks – each with its own culinary tradition. Venetian trading posts in the Levant gave the city access to spices, the secret of subtle Venetian cookery. Pimiento, turmeric, ginger, cinnamon, cumin, cloves, nutmeg, saffron and vanilla show the

oriental influences; pine-nuts, raisins, almonds and pistachios also play their part.

Reflecting later conquests of Venice, these exotic ingredients are enriched with a dash of French or Austrian cuisine. From the end of the 18th century, French influence meant that oriental spices were supplanted by Mediterranean herbs. The French brioche was added to the breakfast repertoire, as was the Turkish *crescente* (literally a crescent). The appearance of the croissant dates back to the Turkish defeat at the walls of Vienna in 1683. The Austrian conquest may have left Venice with a bitter taste in its mouth but it also left the city with an appetite for apple strudel and *krapfen* (doughnuts).

LEFT: dining beside the Accademia Bridge.
RIGHT: *cichetti* at Bancogiro, in the Rialto.

Eclectic tastes

A classic Middle-Eastern-inspired dish is *sarde in saor*, tart sardines marinated in standard Venetian sauce. *Melanzane in saor*, made with aubergines, is the vegetarian version. *Saor* means savoury or tasty, and is a spicy sauce made with permutations of onions, raisins, vinegar, pine-nuts and olive oil. *Riso* (rice), rather than pasta, predominates, prized for its versatility ever since its introduction by the Arabs. Creamy Venetian risotto offers endless possibilities, flavoured with spring vegetables, meat, game or fish. *Risi e bisi* (rice and peas) is a thick soup blended with ham, celery and onion. Equally delicious are the seasonal risot-

tos, cooked with asparagus tips, artichoke hearts, fennel, courgettes or pumpkins. An oriental variant involves sultanas and pine-nuts. To achieve the creamy consistency, the rice is fried with onions and ladled over with stock and wine. Venetians look for a rippling wave effect forming on the silky surface of the risotto; called *all'onda*, it is proof that the rice is cooked to perfection.

Fishy dinners

Given the European climate of health scares, some visitors avoid the lagoon fish, fearing mercury contamination. However, the fish on most local menus come from the Adriatic. Inland fish-

DINING TO ORDER

For visitors who spurn the tourist menu, there is often a choice between basking in the beauty of Venice over an exorbitantly priced dinner or hunting down an unpretentious trattoria in a malodorous back canal. Without unlimited means, it is hard to satisfy soul and stomach in one sitting. Yet, with perseverance, you can find that elusive table with a courtyard, a view and genuine home cooking. The *antipasti* (appetisers) will feature fresh seafood, raw, fried or boiled, including *tartuffi di mare* (sea truffles) or *peoci saltati*, pan-fried mussels with parsley and garlic. Those who don't care for seafood should try *crostini* or roast-vegetable dishes. A typical *primo* (first course) is a *minestra* (soup) such

as *pasta e fasioi*, based on pasta and beans. If eating pasta, try *bigoli in salsa* (wholewheat spaghetti in a spicy sauce), *pappardelle alla granseola* (pasta with crab), or *spaghetti con astice* (with lobster). Expect a variety of seafood dishes using tiny sea snails *(garuzoli)*, mussels *(cozze)* and cuttlefish *(seppie)*. As a *secondo* (main dish), there is fish of every description, including *seppie alla veneziana*, cuttlefish cooked in its own ink, served with polenta. As for *dolci* (desserts), a typical one is *crema fritta alla veneziana*, squares of solid custard fried in egg and breadcrumbs. Those with a sweet tooth will like *tiramisu*, which was originally brought from Byzantium by the Venetians.

ing also occurs in *valli*, fenced-off sections of the lagoon, mainly for mullet *(cefalu)* and eel *(anguilla)*. It is hard to better *antipasti di frutti di mare*, a feast of simply cooked shellfish and molluscs, dressed with olive oil and lemon juice; prawns and soft-shelled crabs vie with baby octopus and squid. A trademark dish is cuttlefish risotto, served black and pungent with ink, or *granseola*, spider crab, boiled and then dressed simply in lemon and oil. Another staple is *baccalà*, dried salt cod, prepared with milk and herbs or parmesan and parsley, and served in countless ways, including on toasted bread. In Venice, fish features more often than meat, but offal is favoured, particularly in *fegato alla*

Wine

The Veneto produces a number of superior (DOC) wines, from the fruity, garnet-red Bardolino to the less prestigious Valpolicella. Soave is the Veneto's best-known but bland white, which comes from vineyards dotted along the eastern shores of Lake Garda. Dry whites from the Veneto and Friuli, such as Soave or Pinot Grigio, bring out the best in seafood dishes.

Venetians drink much more white wine, partly through habit, partly because it better accompanies seafood. Regional wines can also be sampled in traditional wine bars: these *bacari* are a Venetian institution dating back to the Middle Ages. To eat *cichetti e l'ombra*, a snack

veneziana, calf's liver sliced into ribbons and cooked with parsley and onion.

Sweet treats

Biscuits, cakes and desserts are a forte, flavoured with exotic spices ever since the discovery of cinnamon and nutmeg. The Venetians introduced cane sugar to Europe, and have retained their sweet tooth. Spicy sweets are popular, including *fritelle di zucca*, sweet pumpkin doughnut served hot, while the best ices can be found in *gelaterie* on the Zattere.

LEFT: fish features on menus more often than meat.
ABOVE: a modern interpretation of the traditional *bacaro*.

and a glass of wine, is a Venetian tradition. These snacks make an engaging choice for a light lunch or supper, and represent the Venetian equivalent of Spanish tapas.

Where to eat

San Marco and Castello are home to some of the city's most prestigious restaurants, but privacy is rare in these goldfish-bowl settings. Further away from the bustle, dining experiences tend to be more varied, and prices lower. Not that visitors should ignore overtly glamorous spots; the Venetians patronise them too. But beyond St Mark's, a number of ethnic restaurants have opened, and late-night dining has become far easier *(see Nightlife, page 223)*, even if in most places you would do well not to arrive for dinner much after 8.30pm.

In style, Venetian restaurants seem to opt for cool, 18th-century elegance, or the exposed beams and copper pots that spell rustic gentility. Yet individualistic inns abound, whether tucked under pergolas or spilling onto terraces and courtyards. Reservations are required for the grander restaurants, which tend to be fairly dressy affairs, reflecting the elegant setting. The opposite is true of the *bacari*, the traditional wine bars, where you can dress as a market trader if you feel like it. More upmarket places are termed *ristoranti*, but may be called *osterie*

(inns) if they focus on homely food in an intimate or rustic setting. To confuse the issue, some inns have bars which act like traditional *bacari*, so that one can opt for a quicker, cheaper snack at the bar or a full sit-down meal at a table.

The distinction between bars and restaurants is tricky in Venice, as most *bacari* also serve food, essentially Venetian tapas, known as *cichetti*, ranging from *polpette* (spicy meatballs) to *carciofini* (artichoke hearts), *tramezzini* (tiny sandwiches), *crostini* with grilled vegetables, *baccalà mantecato* (salted cod on polenta), *seppie roste* (grilled cuttlefish) and anchovy nibbles. For a taste of everyday Venice, especially in the Rialto market, little beats a *bacaro*.

Cocktail hour

Venice is noted for its cocktails, especially the Bellini, the delicious peach-and-prosecco aperitif which was created in Harry's Bar. Prosecco, the sparkling wine from the Veneto, makes a fine *aperitivo* whether drunk dry *(secco)* or medium sweet *(amabile)*. As such, it is Italian champagne, yet drunk at the drop of a hat in Venice.

But to look like a Venetian, risk the lurid orange cocktail known as *spritz* (pronounced "spriss" in Venetian dialect). The bright-orange drink was introduced under Austrian rule (named after the introduction of "selzer", fizzy soda water) and soon became a firm favourite. It consists of roughly equal parts of dry white wine, soda water and an aperitif, usually Campari or Aperol, and garnished with a twist of lemon or an olive. Ask for a *spritz al bitter* for a stronger, less cloying taste. The *spritz* may be an acquired taste, but once acquired, it's the clearest sign that you've fallen for Venice.

The cocktail hour between 7pm and 8pm is a Venetian ritual: the locals can be seen sipping wine or classic cocktails in chic cafés, old-fashioned neighbourhood bars or *bacari*. New wine bars are springing up everywhere, including cool reinterpretations of the *bacaro*, where one can still request *un'ombra* (literally a shadow), a tiny glass of white Veneto wine, downed in one go. At the other end of the scale, once staid hotel cocktail bars have been successfully relaunched as cool lounge bars *(see Nightlife, page 223)*. As a result, Venetian bar culture is far broader than time-warp piano bars in sophisticated hotels.

Not that much changes in the historic cafés close to San Marco, where coffee has been drunk for centuries and post-prandial grappas downed since the days of the doges *(see Café Society, opposite)*. Yet just beyond St Mark's are serious wine bars *(enoteche)*, where tastings rather than tapas are the main draw. Then there are sleek new designer gastro-bars that would be at home in Manhattan, apart from the gondola moored by the back door. In fact, against all the odds, Venice is acquiring a burgeoning nightlife scene, from slick lounge-bar-restaurants to hip late-night eateries. ❑

LEFT: dining in Dorsoduro with a view of Giudecca.

Café Society

After a morning spent enthusing and emoting in churches and museums, it is easy to while away the rest of the day in a chic Venetian café on St Mark's Square. Under the arcades are a cluster of distinguished coffee houses: Florian, Quadri and Lavena. In winter, the cafés turn in on themselves and, during *acqua alta* (high water), when the piazza is often submerged, are only accessible by rickety duckboards. Yet as soon as the first rays of spring sunshine promise warmer weather, the tables and chairs are set out on the square and the spectacle begins.

Like Paris and Vienna, Venice relishes its reputation as a café society, with all the spurious glamour this implies. Yet, historically, Venice is first and foremost a coffee society, ever since the Republic's trade with the Orient brought the Arabian stimulant to Europe. The first *bottega del caffè* (coffee bar) opened on Piazza San Marco in 1638, and caffeine has been the Venetian drug of choice ever since. With their stagy string quartets, pirouetting waiters and pretentious airs, the coffee houses are part of the performance art that is Venice. Each café has its charms: Quadri basks in the morning sun and an 18th-century ambience, while Florian, its celebrated rival, lies in the shade until noon; Lavena simply serves the best coffee without the beau-monde atmosphere. Caffè Florian, considered the prince of coffee houses, was founded in 1720 and is the oldest surviving café in Italy. As an erstwhile literary haunt, it has welcomed Byron and Dickens, Goethe and Thomas Mann – although Wagner kept away from Florian for fear of running into Verdi. Although trading on its past, Florian's air of *fin-de-siècle* Habsburg nostalgia is misplaced. After the Austrian army had quelled the 1848 Venetian uprising, Florian's became the meeting place for republican patriots. The Austrians preferred to survey their uncowed subjects from Caffè Quadri across the square.

RIGHT: Florian's rival, Caffè Quadri, in St Mark's Square.

To ponder on the ghosts of Venice, choose a sophisticated stage set at the glitsiest hotel bars: the Gritti Palace, overlooking the Grand Canal, was one of Hemingway's drinking haunts; the lagoon-side Londra Palace was where Tchaikovsky composed his Fourth Symphony. But for romantic watering holes, look beyond the Grand Canal: the monastic island of San Clemente is the place to sip chilled Prosecco on a summer's day, as is the stylish Linea d'Ombra pontoon bar on the Zattere. Yet even in touristy San Marco, traditional, rustic bars flourish, such as Vino Vino, by the Fenice opera house, where gondoliers rub shoulders with visitors.

Just a stone's-throw away is Centrale, the Venetian take on Manhattan, a slick lounge bar with the requisite cool sounds, beautiful people, great cocktails – and passing gondolas.

A serious wine crawl, or *giro di ombre*, as they say in dialect, is the best way to appreciate the range of bars, from designer temples to *bacari* (traditional wine bars), with each tasting accompanied by *cichetti*, local tapas, eaten at the bar. "Venetians do not know how to eat or drink," declared Pietro Aretino, a visitor to Venice in the 16th century. He clearly had not been invited on a wine crawl. ❑

PLACES

A detailed guide to the city, with the principal sites clearly cross-referenced by number to the maps

The first fleeting glimpse of Venice from the air is a foretaste of the watery puzzle that awaits below. At low tide, the lagoon reveals an expanse of mudflats, shifting sandbanks and brackish marsh; the sunlight momentarily withdraws from the glassy greyish-brown waters, showing the same desolation that failed to daunt the early settlers. Yet, as the plane circles the lagoon, the sinuous red-brick city floats into view, changing foreboding into fantasy.

Venice is traditionally divided into six *sestieri* (districts), a practice followed in this book. In addition, each main island is treated separately, as is the Grand Canal, which winds through all the districts. Despite the watery insubstantiality of Venice, most time is spent walking rather than travelling by boat. However, a mastery of key ferry routes can save unnecessary circling of the lagoon: an error can cost an hour on a short journey. *(See the transport map inside the back cover and the Travel Tips section, page 215, for advice.)*

To find an address, ask the name of the closest parish church; this is more helpful than the postal address. Venetians will usually point you in the right direction. Despite the kindness of strangers, all visitors eventually lose themselves in this labyrinthine city.

The uniqueness of the city geography is captured in Venetian dialect, with the names of streets providing clues to the nature of the city. Familiarity with these terms will help in identifying places on your trails through the confusing backwaters. Venetian spelling is variable, so expect alternative versions.

A Venetian lexicon

Ca' (from *casa*): house/palace
calle: alley
campo: square
campiello: small square
corte: external courtyard
cortile: internal courtyard
fontego or fondaco: historic warehouse
fondamenta: wide quayside
punta: a point
ramo: side street or dead end
rio (plural *rii*): curving canal lined by buildings

rio terrà: infilled canal
riva: promenade, quayside
ruga: broad shopping street
rughetta: small shopping street
sacca: inlet
salizzada: main street; means "paved" and dates from the days when few streets were
sottoportico (or *sottoportego*): tiny alleyway running under a building
squero: boatyard
stazio: gondoliers' station

PRECEDING PAGES: panoramic view of the Doge's Palace; Fondamenta Madonna dell' Orto, Cannaregio. **LEFT:** 15th-century relief of Adam and the Bridge of Sighs, Palazzo Ducale.

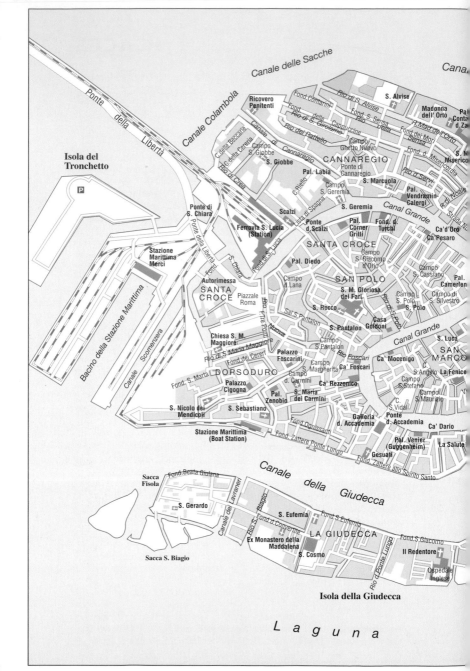

Canale delle Sacche

Cana

Ponte della Liberta

Isola del Tronchetto

Canale Colambola

Ricovero Penitenti

Fond. Contarini

Rio di S. Alvise

S. Alvise

Fond. S. Sensa

Madonna dell' Orto

Pal. Conta d. Za

Fond. delle Cappuccine

R. Mad. de l'Orto

Rio di S. Girolamo

Rio dei Battello

Campo Ghetto Nuovo

Fond. dei Mori

S. M Miseric

Canale d. Cannaregio

CANNAREGIO

Sensa

Fond. d. Misericordia

C. della Beccaria

C. della Cereta

Campo S. Giobbe

S. Giobbe

Pal. Labia

Ponte di Cannaregio

Rio di Servi

Rio di Noale

Rio di Crea

C. Riello

Campo S. Geremia

S. Marcuola

Pal. Vendramin-Calergi

Strada N.

Scalzi

Lista di Spagna

S. Geremia

Canal Grande

Stazione Marittima Merci

Ponte di S. Chiara

Ferrovia S. Lucia (Station)

Ponte d. Scalzi

Pal. Corner Gritti

Fond. d. Turchi

Ca d'Oro

Ca'Pesaro

Ponte della Liberta

Fond. S. Chiara

Fond. S. Lucia

Rio di S. Lucia

SANTA CROCE

Pal. Diedo

Campo S. Giacomo d'Orio

Campo S. Cassiano

Pal. Camerlen

Autorimessa

SANTA CROCE

Piazzale Roma

Campo d. Lana

SAN POLO

S. M. Gloriosa dei Fari.

Campo S. Polo

Campo di S. Silvestro

Bacino della Stazione Marittima

Canale Scomenzera

S. Rocco

Sat S. Pantalon

Casa Goldoni

S. Polo

Rio di S. Polo

Chiesa S. M. Maggiore

Marzene

Fond. dei Cereri

S. Pantalon

Campo S. Pantalon

Canal Grande

S. Luca

Rio di S. Maria Maggiore

Palazzo Foscarini

Foscari

Ca' Mocenigo

SAN MARCO

DORSODURO

Campo S. Margherita

Ca' Foscari

S. Angelo

La Fenice

Fond. S. Marta

Palazzo Cigogna

Campo d. Carmini

Ca' Rezzonico

Campo S. Stefano

Pal. Zenobio

S. Maria dei Carmini

C. S. Maurizio

S. Nicolo dei Mendicoli

S. Sebastiano

Fond. Ognissanti

Galleria d. Accademia

Ponte d. Accademia

C. Vidal

Ca' Dario

Stazione Marittima (Boat Station)

Fond. Zattere Ponte Lungo

Pal. Venier (Guggenheim)

La Salute

Gesuati

Fond. Zattere allo Spirito Santo

Sacca Fisola

Fond. Beata Giulana

Canale della Giudecca

S. Gerardo

Canale dei Lavraneri

Rio Biagio

S. Eufemia

Fond. S. Eufemia

LA GIUDECCA

Fond. S. Giacomo

Fond. a Convertite

Ex Monastero della Maddalena

S. Cosmo

Il Redentore

Sacca S. Biagio

Rio di Ponte Lungo

Ospedale Inglese

Isola della Giudecca

L a g u n a

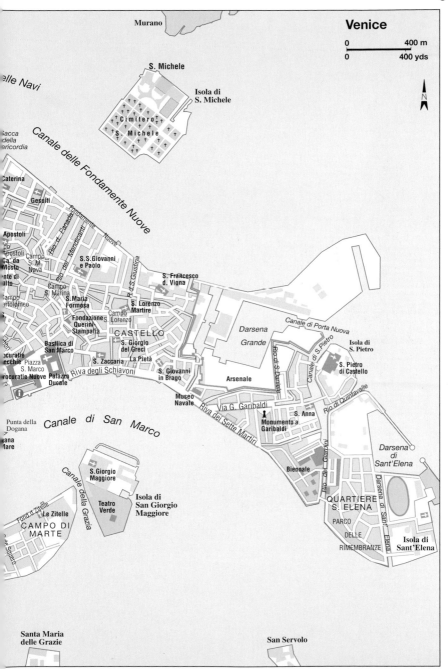

Murano

S. Michele

Isola di
S. Michele

Venice

0 — 400 m
0 — 400 yds

N

elle Navi

Canale delle Fondamente Nuove

Cimitero
S. Michele

Sacca
della
ericordia

Caterina

Gesuiti

Apostoli

po
Apostoli
Ca' da
Mosto
Campo
S.M.
Nova

S.S.Giovanni
e Paolo

Rio dei Mendicanti

Fondamente Nuove

Rio d.S.Giustina

S. Francesco
d. Vigna

ite di
alto

Campo
S.Marina

S.Maria
Formosa

Campo
rtolomeo

S. Lorenzo
Martire

S.

Fondazione
Querini
Stampalia

Campo
S.Lorenzo

S. Giorgio
del Greci

CASTELLO

Basilica di
San Marco

ri

cu rati e
ecchie

Piazza
S. Marco

ocuratie Nuove

S. Zaccaria

Palazzo
Ducale

La Pietà

Riva degli Schiavoni

S. Giovanni
in Brago

Darsena
Grande

Canale di Porta Nuova

Rio di S.Daniele

Canale di S. Pietro

Isola di
S. Pietro

S. Pietro
di Castello

Arsenale

Museo
Navale

Via G. Garibaldi

Rio di Quintavalle

Riva dei Sette Martiri

Monumento a
Garibaldi

S. Anna

Punta della
Dogana

Canale di San Marco

ana
are

Canale della Grazia

S.Giorgio
Maggiore

Biennale

Rio dei Giardini

Darsena
di
Sant'Elena

Teatro
Verde

Isola di
San Giorgio
Maggiore

QUARTIERE
S. ELENA

Darsena di Sant' Elena

Fond. d'Zitelle

Le Zitelle

CAMPO DI
MARTE

Squero

PARCO

DELLE
RIMEMBRANZE

Isola di
Sant'Elena

Santa Maria
delle Grazie

San Servolo

AROUND SAN MARCO

St Mark's Square is the heart of Venice: here are the famous Basilica and belltower, the doge's fabulous palace, the Correr Museum, Harry's Bar and the best cafés in town

Piazza San Marco was famously dubbed "the finest drawing room in Europe" by Napoleon. Like many visitors to Venice, he then proceeded to repaint it in his own image, even rearranging the furniture and literally moving the walls.

However, given the city's talent for fusing influences into an enchanting Venetian whole, the square has retained its essential character. Gentile Bellini's *Procession in Piazza San Marco* (1496) is the most reproduced view of Venice, a grand hierarchical affair of prelates and senators outside the Basilica. Yet unlike many official city squares, St Mark's belongs to the citizens as well as visitors. Venetians themselves will drink at the grand cafés, even if they often save money by standing up. Some may attend Sunday Mass at the Basilica or even dance at the open-air carnival.

For most of the day, though, St Mark's belongs to the pigeons, the crowds and the souvenir-sellers; only in early evening does it revert to a semblance of solitude.

Piazza San Marco acted as the heart of the Republic from the time the earliest settlement shifted from Torcello to central Venice. The piazza's essential design was determined by the building of the Byzantine St Mark's Basilica and the Doge's Palace. However, in the 16th century the square was remodelled to reflect Venetian notions of glory. The Basilica and Palace were embellished, with a new library, mint and administrative buildings clustered around the square. The design remained intact until the bombastic Napoleonic era, when churches and waterside monuments were demolished to create a neoclassical wing, a ballroom and public gardens.

Before braving the hordes in the Basilica, retreat to one of the grand cafés for a prosecco or Bellini in

Map on page 88

LEFT: aerial view of "the finest drawing room in Europe".
BELOW: tourist crowds on St Mark's Square.

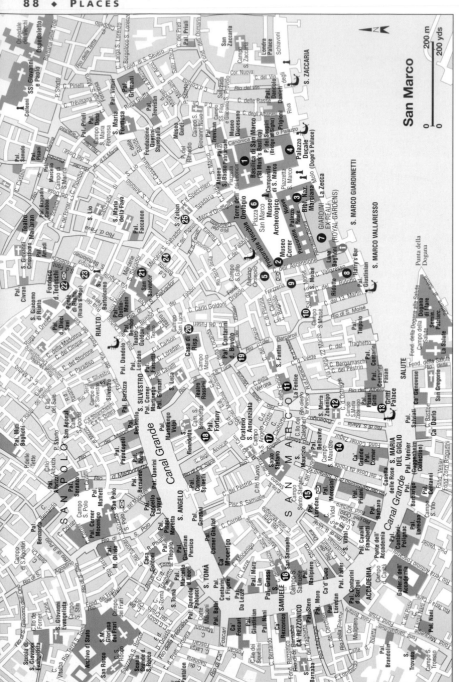

San Marco

style. The most Venetian is **Caffè Florian**, spilling under the arcades of the Procuratie Nuove. **Caffè Quadri** glowers at its rival from the arcades of the Procuratie Vecchie and is only slightly less prestigious *(see page 105)*.

The Basilica

The Basilica di San Marco (St Mark's Basilica) ❶ (9.30am–5pm, Sun 2–4pm; daily from 7am for worshippers; leave all bags in the Ateneo San Basso) is the centrepiece of the square, a place the aesthete John Ruskin called "a treasure heap, a confusion of delight". Best visited in the early morning, the Basilica remains a glorious confusion. Given the crowds, the mysterious design and the varied museums within, several visits are desirable.

San Marco, modelled on Byzantine churches in Constantinople, transposes the essence of an eastern basilica to the West. According to the critic Mary McCarthy, it was "an oriental pavilion, half pleasure house, half war tent, belonging to some great satrap". The French poet Théophile Gautier (1811–72) declared San Marco "a pirate cathedral enriched with the spoils of the universe", while Charles Dickens (1812–70) was spellbound: "opium couldn't build such a place… dim with the smoke of incense; costly in treasure of precious stones and metals; glittering through iron bars; holy with the bodies of deceased saints".

The Basilica was consecrated in AD 832, intended as a mausoleum for St Mark's relics and as the doge's ceremonial chapel. In AD 976 the church burnt down after a riot but was rebuilt between 1063 and 1094, probably supervised by a Greek architect. Since Venice still recognised the cultural supremacy of Byzantium, the Basilica echoed eastern models. At the same time, Doge Selvo (1071–84) asked merchants to return with rare marble and semi-precious stones to adorn the Basilica, from jasper to alabaster and porphyry. John Ruskin admired this "confused incrustation", which incorporated Roman fragments and looted Byzantine booty in an oriental basilica which professed to be a Christian church. Yet for political reasons, this majestic building was technically designated the doge's private chapel for most of the duration of the Republic. San Marco only succeeded San Pietro as the cathedral of Venice in 1807.

The Treasury and Museo Marciano

The Greek-cross plan is inscribed in a square, and crowned by a cluster of five domes, set over each arm of the cross. These are linked to one another by loggias and arcades. The bewildering contrast is between the oriental domes and rounded Byzantine arches, and the Gothic ornamentation of the central roofline. Gothic arches and pinnacles were grafted onto 12th-century facades and completed by a gallery overlooking the square.

Map
on page
88

TIP

Stringent security measures in the Basilica mean that all bags have to be left in the Ateneo San Basso on Piazzetta dei Leoncini, a free left-luggage service.

BELOW: the domes of San Marco.

TIP

The Venice Card is a discounted combined ticket allowing access to all the museums on San Marco, including the Museo Correr.

BELOW: the Basilica's glittering facade.

Most of the garish mosaics on the facade are 17th-century copies, with the only intact 13th-century mosaic depicting the arrival of St Mark's relics in the Basilica (set above the doorway on the far left). A 17th-century mosaic also shows the smuggling of St Mark's remains from Alexandria, supposedly concealed under "a basket covered with herbs and swine flesh which the Muslims hold in horror".

The Basilica was controversially restored in the 1860s and '70s, which led to the removal of the mosaics on the north and south facades. In a letter to his father, Ruskin, who helped mobilise international opinion, literally wept: "They appear to be destroying the mosaics. I cannot draw here for tears in my eyes." Although these mosaics were lost, the international furore stirred up by Ruskin led to the reversal of other restoration blunders in St Mark's.

The exterior brickwork of the central apse is reminiscent of Santa Fosca in Torcello *(see page 200)*. The southern side abuts the Doge's Palace. The baptistery doors are framed by the **Pilasters of Acre**, two ancient Syrian pillars plundered from Acre, in the Holy Land (modern Israel), after a victory over the Genoese in 1258. These sculpted, 6th-century marble columns stand beside a porphyry stump known as the *pietra del bando*, where the laws of the Republic were proclaimed.

In the corner are the **Tetrarchs**, often known as Moors because of their dress, a 4th-century Egyptian sculpture representing Diocletian and his fellow rulers who governed the Roman Empire.

The Basilica is remarkable for its spatial complexity and stylistic synthesis, creating an eclectic yet harmonious design. From the inside, the 13th-century oriental domes seem much lower and smaller than they really are. The **Pavimento**, the Basilica pavement, is an oriental carpet interweaving floral, animal and geometric motifs. The undulating mosaics of marble, porphyry and glass depict allegorical and naturalistic scenes. After the conquest of Constantinople in 1204, Venice celebrated its triumph with lavish cycles

of mosaics and the display of Byzantine booty. Some of the greatest treasures in San Marco were plundered from Constantinople, including the **Madonna Nicopeia**, a sacred 10th-century icon, adorning the Altar of the Virgin.

The **Treasury** incorporates a 9th-century corner tower from the first Doge's Palace and displays Byzantine gold, silver and glassware. Since this collection began with the Venetian looting of Constantinople, it seems only poetic justice that French plundering should have depleted the treasury. But much remains, despite a forced sale of jewels and the Napoleonic melting down of objets d'art.

The **Classical Horses** were also Byzantine booty. The rearing animals stood on top of a triumphal arch in Rome before gracing the hippodrome in Constantinople and finally adorning the facade of San Marco. Given that the horses symbolised the Venetian Republic's untrammelled independence, Napoleon had them harnessed to a chariot in Paris for 18 years. The humiliation ended with

their return to Venice in 1815. Jan Morris mourned the fate of "the supreme talismans of Venetian power, the Golden Horses of St Mark, chafing their gilded hooves in the humiliation of decline." Yet despite the demise of the Republic, the prancing horses are still proud, and remain the only team pulling a chariot to survive from classical times. They are now displayed in the **Museo Marciano**, the gallery above the entrance portal, allowing one to pause for a fine view of the interior before taking in views of the piazza and exterior mosaics from the loggia itself.

The mosaics and altarpiece

Officially, St Mark's remains are encased in a sarcophagus under the altar, but sceptics believe that these were destroyed in the fire of AD 976. Behind the altar, often swamped by crowds, is the **Pala d'Oro**, a superb medieval altarpiece studded with gems and covered in sacred scenes. The panels are enclosed in a gilded frame and encrusted with emeralds, rubies, sapphires and gleaming, translucent enamels bound by a

Map on page 88

Mosaics in the atrium. The mosaics of St Mark's are symbolic rather than realistic, representing a fusion of the decorative and the descriptive.

BELOW: the porticoed buildings surrounding the square are known as the Procuratie.

Carpaccio's Two Venetian Ladies *is the star of the Museo Correr. Though often seen as courtesans, they are probably noblewomen.*

BELOW: love them or loathe them, pigeons are very much part of the St Mark's Square experience.

filigree of gold; each tessera is a separate segment of colour. This 10th-century masterpiece was created by Byzantine goldsmiths but embellished in 1209 and 1345 by the Venetians and Sienese; panels from a sacked church in Constantinople also added to the lustre.

The interior is studded with mosaics, one of the chief glories of San Marco, but visitors are channelled along set routes, making lingering difficult. The mosaics date from 1071, first created by craftsmen from Constantinople; although the majority are from the 11th to 14th centuries, mosaics continued to be added until the 18th century. The result is a bewildering tapestry, an illustrated Bible using 4,000 sq. metres (4,780 sq. yds) of mosaics. Even the windows of this oriental extravaganza were walled up to make more space for mosaics.

The mosaics are rich in geometric forms and symbolic meaning, part decorative, part naturalistic. Relatively naturalistic Old Testament scenes in the **narthex** (atrium) contrast with the more stylised figures

of the central domes. As a rule of thumb, the lower walls depict saints, with the middle section featuring the Apostles, and the domes dedicated to Christ Pantocrator, the Creator of All. The atrium mosaics in the **Genesis Dome** show the Creation, unravelled in concentric circles. The **Pentecost Dome**, rising above the nave, depicts the descent of the Holy Ghost as a dove, and was perhaps the first to be adorned with mosaics. The paired figures between the windows represent the nations in whose languages the Apostles evangelised after Pentecost.

The central **Ascension Dome** shows Christ in Majesty, a 13th-century scene embracing the Apostles and the Virgin Mary. Although newly restored, the 14th-century mosaic-encrusted **Baptistery** and adjoining Zen Chapel remain closed.

The Museo Correr

Facing the Basilica on the far side of the Piazza is the **Museo Correr ②** (9am–7pm, visited on a combined ticket with all the other St Mark's museums). This often overlooked

Map on page 88

museum of Venetian civilisation is housed in the Procuratie Nuove, with the entrance in the Ala Napoleonica, the Napoleonic Wing. The neoclassical rooms make a fitting setting for Canova's sculptures. The first section is a romp through Venetian history, featuring representations of the Lion of St Mark, and paintings of festivities and ceremonies. The final historical section covers the troubled times from the fall of the Republic to French and Austrian domination.

Those without a taste for coins and battle memorabilia can proceed to the more accessible picture gallery, which showcases Venetian art from the 13th to the 16th centuries. While no match for the Accademia, the collection features fine Byzantine-influenced works by Paolo Veneziano and Bartolomeo Vivarini, and paintings by Giovanni Bellini, especially the poignant *Pietà*. However, the symbol of the museum is Carpaccio's *Two Venetian Ladies* (1507), depicted in a pleasure garden, surrounded by birds and dogs.

The Biblioteca Nazionale Marciana ❸ (daily 9am–7pm; combined ticket and access via Museo Correr) is a cool classical building set in an extended loggia around the corner. Designed by Sansovino in 1537, the library is also known as the Libreria Sansoviniana. This long, low building is lined with arches and expressive statues, and graced with a sumptuous stairway. Indeed, Palladio praised it as the richest building since classical times. The library was designed to house the precious collection of manuscripts bequeathed by Petrarch in the 14th century, and by Cardinal Bessarion, the Greek humanist, in 1468. The superb salon of the original library is covered with paintings by Veronese and Tintoretto, and is reward enough for trudging round the duller sections of the Museo Correr and the interconnected archaeology museum *(see below)*.

The piazza is bounded by the Procuratie, the offices and residences of the procurators of the Republic, the highest government officials. The **Procuratie Vecchie** is an elegant porticoed building stretching along the north side of the square. Dating from 1500, this functional affair was

TIP

Visitors to the Basilica are channelled along set routes, so Catholics might consider visiting from 7–9.45am, when only worshippers are welcome.

LEFT: *acqua alta* – high water – on low-lying St Mark's Square occurs around 250 times a year.

Restoration

St Mark's Square is often covered in scaffolding. Pollution, triggered by the combination of sulphur dioxide and the salty lagoon air, acts as a corrosive cocktail on the precious sculpted-marble reliefs on the facades. The British subsidised the cleaning of the capitals on the Doge's Palace, the restoration of the belltower's Loggetta and the Porta della Carta, the ceremonial gateway to the Doge's Palace. The Piazzetta facades of the Basilica are currently being restored, as is the lovely clocktower at the landward end of the piazza. The grand gateway, Cappella Zen and the Basilica crypt have been well restored, but Sansovino's Loggetta is posing a problem. The resins used to protect the restored marble have discoloured the facade, so work is under way to flush the resins out. Equally controversial was the Olivetti-funded restoration of the bronze horses of St Mark, with the originals placed within the Basilica and copies left on the facade.

But much restoration work is aimed at combating the deadly flooding known as *acqua alta*, which invades the piazza, the lowest-lying area of the lagoon, 250 times a year. All around is evidence of one long-term solution, the consolidation of the quaysides, with the final verdict left to future generations (see page 39).

St Mark's Square was transformed into an 18th-century film-set, complete with court-room and gallows, during the making of Disney's Casanova *in 2004, starring Heath Ledger.*

BELOW: Gran Caffè Chioggia, Piazzetta San Marco: pricey, touristy but with a great view of the Doge's Palace.

modelled on Coducci's designs but finished by Scarpagnino. The Marciana was a model for the Procuratie Nuove, the adjoining offices on the south side of the square. The long building was begun in 1586 but finished by Longhena in 1640. Although echoing the Marciana, it is more sober and less graceful than the earlier buildings. Napoleon converted it into a royal palace, creating a ballroom by demolishing a neighbouring church. The **Ala Napoleonica**, the Napoleonic Wing, closes the piazza, sandwiched between the Procuratie Nuove and Vecchie.

The **Museo Archeologico** (9am–7pm, access through Museo Correr, combined ticket) is housed in part of the Procuratie Nuove and the Biblioteca Marciana. The uninspiring core collection consists of Greek and Roman sculpture bequeathed by Cardinal Grimani in 1523, which influenced generations of Venetian artists who came to draw and study here. Among the Roman busts, medals, coins and cameos are Greek originals and Roman copies, including a 5th-century Hellenistic Persephone.

The Doge's Palace

The **Palazzo Ducale** (Doge's Palace) ❹ (April–Oct 9am–7pm; Nov–March 9am–5pm) vies with San Marco for most attention and most plaudits. The facade has been restored and the interior revamped to include a museum of sculpture and sections hitherto off-limits, as well as a bookshop and café. The best way of seeing the palace without the crowds is to pre-book the Secret Itinerary *(see page 97)*, a special visit that explores behind the scenes; the same ticket allows access to the rest of the palace. (The intriguing 90-minute tour is available in English, French and Italian; tel: 041-271 5911 or 041-520 9070).

The Doge's Palace was the seat of the Venetian government from the 9th century until the fall of the Republic in 1797. Yet while rival mainland cities were building grim fortresses, the Venetians indulged in a light and airy structure, confident of the natural protection afforded by the lagoon. Apart from being the doge's official residence, it acted as the nerve centre of the Republic, containing administrative offices and armouries, council chambers and chancellery, courtrooms and dungeons, most of which are now visible.

The palace was a symbol of political stability and independence, as well as a testament to Venetian supremacy and a glorious showcase of Venetian art, sculpture and craftsmanship. Yet there was also a shadowy side to the palace, a secretive machine staffed by State inquisitors, spies and torturers-in-residence.

First built as a fortress in the 9th century, there is now no trace at all of the original Byzantine building, although the massive walls echo its previous role. The palace was enlarged over the course of several centuries, from the 12th century onwards, and was essentially complete by 1438. However, sections

were further embellished between the 14th and 16th centuries. Architecturally, the palace is a Venetian hybrid, a harmonious fusion of Moorish, Gothic and Renaissance.

Although often considered the symbol of Gothic Venice, the palace's distinctive facades were inspired by the Veneto-Byzantine succession of porticoes and loggias. However, the Gothic inversion of spaces and solids reached perfection in the floriated style of the southern corner, with a mass of masonry seemingly floating on air. The palace has two of the finest Gothic facades in existence, a vision of rosy Verona marble supported by Istrian stone arcades. With its noble loggia and arcading, the facade overlooking the piazzetta embodies the majesty of State.

Gothic tracery on the loggia became the model for other palaces throughout the city. The harmonious waterfront facade is a Venetian Gothic masterpiece, including the porticoes and ceremonial balcony overlooking the quays. The **Sala del Maggior Consiglio** was rebuilt in 1340, transforming this waterfront wing. The intricately sculpted capitals and statuary on the facade are a tribute to Venetian Gothic craftsmanship (but some capitals are copies, with the originals on display inside).

The **Porta della Carta**, the main ceremonial gateway, a triumph of Flamboyant Gothic style, is named after resident archivists or clerks who copied petitions nearby. Above the portal is the sculpted figure of Doge Francesco Foscari, who commissioned the gateway, kneeling before the winged lion. Sadly, the sculpture is partly reconstructed, since the lions were obliterated during Napoleonic times. In the Renaissance, attention turned to the eastern wing, courtyard and interior. After a fire in 1483, this wing, tucked between the courtyard and the canal, was remodelled to improve the doge's apartments and provide grander magistrates' offices.

This smooth transition is marked by the meeting of the two styles in the **Foscari Arch**, between the Porta della Carta and the Scala dei Giganti. This deep arch is adorned with the figures of Adam and Eve, copies of the 15th-century originals. Beyond

Map on page 88

Strange but true: 50 percent of visitors to Venice fail to stray further than St Mark's Square.

BELOW:
waterfront facade of the Doge's Palace.

Ceiling of the Scala d'Oro, Sansovino's gilded staircase in the Doge's Palace.

RIGHT: golden winged lion above Porta San Clemente.

lies an elegant courtyard with Renaissance well-heads. The **Scala dei Giganti**, the Giants' Stairway, was built in 1486 to provide access to the loggia on the first floor. In 1567, this triumphal staircase was lavishly sculpted with monumental figures of Mars and Neptune, symbolising Venetian supremacy on land and sea. Doges were crowned, with a ceremonial jewel-encrusted cap, at the top of the stairs.

Many of the carved capitals on the portico have been replaced by 19th-century copies, but the restored originals can now be seen in the **Museo dell'Opera** beside the entrance hall.

The palace interior

The interior reveals the inner workings of the Serene Republic, from the voting procedures to the courts of law. The profusion of wood panelling, coffered ceilings and paintings meant that fire was a constant hazard and destroyed many treasures on several occasions. For this reason, there are few paintings that predate the 1570s. Nonetheless, the interior is magnificent.

The **Scala d'Oro**, designed by Sansovino in 1555, is a ceremonial staircase linking the *piano nobile* with the ostentatious upper floors. Yet even in this most public setting is a *bocca della verità*, a secret box previously used for posting denunciations of one's fellow-citizens. The glittering, gilded setting is a prelude to the superb State rooms, intended to overawe visiting dignitaries. The **Sala del Collegio** was where the Signoria met and ambassadors were received.

Other highlights include the **Collegiate Rooms**, lavishly decorated with Tintoretto's mythological scenes. The **Sala del Consiglio dei Dieci** was the chamber of the feared Council of Ten *(see page 22)*, and has a ceiling decorated by Veronese. The **Sala del Maggior Consiglio**, the Grand Council Chamber, is a highlight of the tour, a grandiose affair studded with coffered ceilings, paintings and embossed surfaces. The paintings in the chamber both reassured Venetians of republican glory and reminded them of their boundless duties to serve the State.

An entire wall is covered by

The Lions of Venice

Venice "crawls with lions, winged lions and ordinary lions, great lions and petty lions… lions rampant, lions soporific, amiable lions [and] ferocious lions". The writer Jan Morris conveys a sense of a city under the wing of a triumphalist lion. For over a thousand years, the lion and the city were inseparable. The Venetians took the symbol in honour of St Mark, but were inspired by eastern models, converting chimeras and basilisks into Christian symbols. Yet lions were often domesticated and kept as pets in palace gardens.

Pacific, playful or warlike, lions pose on flags unfurled over Grand Canal palaces, curl up in mosaics, fly as ensigns above ships, or crouch as statues in secret gardens. In the days of the Republic, the leonine standard was carried into battle, fires and plagues; it guarded palaces, prisons and citadels, fluttering over Venetian ships of war and overseas dominions. A golden winged Lion of St Mark still adorns the city standard, and remains the symbol of the Veneto. Whereas the seated lion represents the majesty of State, the walking lion symbolises sovereignty, whether bearing a traditional greeting of peace or, in times of war, carrying a closed book, or even clutching a drawn sword in his paws.

Domenico and Jacopo Tintoretto's *Paradise*. Veronese's *Apotheosis of Venice* is one of his finest mythological scenes: with his glowing colours, carefree and graceful pictures, Veronese captured the taste of the times. A frieze which runs around the upper walls features the first 76 doges, with the notable exception of the traitor, Marin Falier. The portraits continue in the adjoining **Ballot Chamber**, where votes were counted.

The Secret Itinerary

Few could fail to be enthralled by this exploration of the "shadow-palace", with its maze of alleys, secret passageways, and general air of murk and mystery. The civil service worked behind the scenes here to ensure the smooth running of the Republic, and was supported by a police State. The itinerary leads up the Scala d'Oro and then, via a secret door, disappears into a den of passageways, courtrooms and the chancellery, where all acts of state were drafted. En route, one sees the State inquisitors' rooms, torture chamber and prisons, including the stifling,

timber-lined *Piombi* or Leads, under the eaves of the palace; it was from here that Casanova made his daring escape in 1755. (The Pozzi or wells, the harsher basement cells, can be visited alone, after the tour, along with the armouries and the public face of the palace).

The final secret reveals the tricks of the roof space above the Sala del Maggior Consiglio, where a complex system of struts sustains a ceiling which, from below, has no visible means of support. Through portholes are surprising glimpses of the island of San Giorgio and the Venetian lagoon.

Gondola depot

Just west of the square is the **Bacino Orseolo ❺**, the main gondola depot, too busy a spot for a romantic ride but ideal for watching water traffic. For more privacy, choose gondola stations in quieter parts of Dorsoduro or Castello. The Basin backs onto the Procuratie Vecchie, the earliest of the procurators' offices.

At the far end of the severe building stands the **Torre dell'Orologio ❻**,

Map on page 88

"If a doge does anything against the Republic, he won't be tolerated, but in everything else, even in minor matters, he does as he pleases."
GIROLAMO PRIULI, 16TH-CENTURY NOBLEMAN

BELOW: Sala del Maggior Consiglio, Veronese and Palma il Giovane ceilings.

The clock aided merchants and crews about to sail from St Mark's Basin.

BELOW: climb to the top of the campanile for a sweeping view of the city and lagoon.

the Clocktower, currently being restored. Based on designs by Coducci, this Renaissance tower (1496) has a large gilt and blue enamel clockface which displays the signs of the zodiac and the phases of the moon. Naturally, it also tells the time, with two bronze figures of Moors striking the bell on the hour. In 1646, the diarist John Evelyn records the death of the clock-keeper, hit by the hammer as it struck the hour: "and being stunned, he reeled over the battlements and broke his neck". Behind the clocktower, inveterate shoppers can plunge into the dark alleys of the **Mercerie** *(see page 103)*.

Unlike the clocktower, the **Campanile** or Belltower (9.30am–7.45pm) can be climbed, and provides a superb view across the city and lagoon. Curiously, one cannot see the canals, although on a clear day even the Dolomites are visible. In the past, foreigners were only permitted to climb the tower at high tide, to prevent them from espying secret navigational channels. Standing on the site of an earlier watchtower and lighthouse, the belltower was rebuilt

in the 12th century and crowned by a pyramid-shaped spire. During the Republic, each of the bells played a different role, with one summoning senators to the Doge's Palace and another, the execution bell, literally sounding the death knell. As a symbol of the city, the belltower occupies a special place in Venetian memory: in 1902 it suddenly collapsed, but was rebuilt exactly as before.

The only casualties were the custodian's cat and the **Loggetta**, the classical loggia at the base of the tower, which was completely crushed. Originally a meeting place for the nobility, it was redesigned as a guardsroom by Sansovino in the 1540s. The campanile was at the centre of controversy in 1997 when it was briefly captured by a separatist group before being retaken by Venetian commandoes *(see page 36)*.

Clustered around San Marco are numerous official buildings, including **La Zecca** (the Mint), facing the island of San Giorgio. The severe 16th-century building is attributed to Sansovino. Venice minted silver and gold ducats from 1284, with the latter known as a *zecchino*, the accepted currency until the fall of the Republic. The mint and treasury functioned until 1870, but is now part of the Biblioteca Marciana, with the courtyard covered over and used as a reading room.

Bounded by the mint, the Basilica and the Doge's Palace is the **Piazzetta** (the Little Square), overlooking the Molo, or waterfront. This functioned as the former inner harbour, with ships unloading on the quays. Now a square, it is framed by the **Columns of San Marco and San Teodoro**, which marked the sea entrance to Venice. The columns were named after the city's two patron saints, with St Mark replacing St Theodore in AD 828. The granite columns, from the Levant, were reputedly erected in 1172, and the

engineer's reward was the right to set up gambling tables between the two columns – a lucrative spot for business. This was also the site of public executions, and superstition has it that bad luck follows anyone walking between the columns.

While the statue of St Theodore is a modern copy (the original classical statue is in the Doge's Palace), the **Lion of St Mark** is genuine. This ancient winged beast with agate eyes may be a Middle Eastern hybrid or a Chinese chimera. After the lion was rescued from Napoleon's clutches in Paris, the damaged beast was restored and returned to his pedestal with a Bible placed under his paw. Thus was a beast "from the pagan east converted from a savage basilisk to a saint's companion", remarks the writer Jan Morris.

Grand café retreat

Before exploring the frenetic San Marco district, prepare for the assault by collapsing in one of the grand cafés on the piazza or in one of the modest bars situated off **Piazzetta dei Leoncini**, the tiny square beside the Basilica. Named after the marble lions who guard it, the piazzetta is home to a long-suffering pair of lions used as play horses by countless generations of children. Michel Butor, the French novelist, is sanguine about those who despair of finding solitude or sanity in Piazza San Marco, saying: "The Basilica, like the city around it, has nothing to fear from this fauna or from our own frivolity; it was born under the perpetual gaze of the visitor, and so it has continued."

The San Marco district

Although overshadowed by the attractions of St Mark's Square, this *sestiere* (area) is noted for its bustling *campi* and the maze-like Mercerie, a fascinating shopping quarter. Some of the finest palaces also lie along this stretch of the Grand Canal. The loop in the canal occupied by San Marco is known as the "seven *campi* between the bridges", a succession of theatrical spaces, each with inviting bars. The noblest square is undoubtedly Campo Santo Stefano, one of the most prestigious addresses in Venice. This suggested circular route

Map on page 88

TIP

The Bacino Orseolo is the most central place to begin a gondola ride, but don't pay more than the official rate. Bargain beforehand if you want to book a musical serenade or to see anything outside the gondolier's set route *(see pages 116 and 215)*.

BELOW: the Molo and Columns of San Marco and San Teodoro.

The florid baroque facade of San Moisè, the most unpopular church in Venice. The saving grace of the ponderous interior is a work by Tintoretto.

BELOW: set in a small converted storeroom, the resolutely un-glitzy Harry's Bar is all about food and fun, not romantic views.

embraces the heart of the city before sweeping back to St Mark's.

Heading west along the waterfront you will pass the **Giardini Ex Reali** (Royal Gardens) ❼ and the least brusque **tourist office**, housed in a pavilion. These cool public gardens were supposedly created by Napoleon's nephew, in pursuit of his desire for a sweeping view from his palace in the Procuratie Nuove.

On Calle Vallaresso, the next alley, awaits **Harry's Bar** ❽, the famous watering hole *(see below)*. The *calle* is lined with designer boutiques and is the hub of a chic shopping district, embracing the **Ridotto**, once Venice's licentious casino for masked revellers, but now restored and part of the Monaco e Grand Hotel *(see page 217)*. Just north is the **Frezzeria** ❾, a bustling shopping street, awash with masks and glass of dubious provenance. Named after the arrows it sold in medieval times, the street was also notorious for its prostitutes, who would "open their quivers to every arrow". Not that all clients were satisfied. John Evelyn, the diarist (1620–1706), was informed that

Venetian women were *mezzo carne, mezzo legno* – half flesh, half wood.

Campo San Moisè ❿, which lies at the southern end of the Frezzeria, opens onto the most exclusive, but least charming shopping quarter. The square is framed by an ugly modern hotel and the florid baroque facade of **San Moisè** (9.30am–noon), a church which is almost universally disliked. The novelist L.P. Hartley was one of the few to admire its exuberant architecture, with its "swags, cornucopias and swing boat forms whose lateral movement seemed to rock the church from side to side".

Sophisticated shoppers may be drawn to the district around **Campo Largo XXII Marzo**, with its antique shops, fashion boutiques and jewellers. From here, Calle delle Veste leads north to **La Fenice** ⓫, the famous opera house that was razed to the ground by a mysterious fire in 1996, but rose from the ashes recently, if years behind schedule. The "Phoenix" officially reopened as an opera house in 2004, with a celebratory performance of *La Traviata*. The jury is still out on the quality of

Harry's Bar

On the basis that Harry's Bar is the best bar in the best city in the world, the famed Bellini cocktail is cheap at any price. This is a legendary watering hole, resolutely un-glitzy, apart from a clientele of visiting celebrities and celebrity-watchers. The lure of classic cocktails and a good gossip have drawn prominent personalities, from Churchill and Charlie Chaplin to Bogart and Bacall, Fellini and Mastroianni, Frank Sinatra and Madonna. Ernest Hemingway, footloose in Venice, could always find inspiration or oblivion in his favourite bar. As a macho man in a macho bar, he slugged the Montgomery, a martini made with 15 measures of gin to one of vermouth, the same potent ratio of troops to enemy employed by the military strategist.

Founded by Giuseppe Cipriani in 1931 and still run by the family, Harry's is famous for the creation of the Bellini, a cocktail of crushed, puréed peach and sparkling prosecco. Cipriani is also credited with inventing carpaccio, a dish of finely sliced raw beef fillet doused in oil and lemon, named after the 15th-century Venetian painter Carpaccio, whose paintings favoured a beefy red. Clubby, crowded and cosmopolitan, Harry's, uniquely in Venice, has become accepted by the locals *(see page 104)*.

Map on page 88

the restoration, with detractors pointing to a lack of finesse in the carvings and stuccowork, but most Venetians are content that the Phoenix has risen from the ashes. High society is also delighted not to have to traipse to the Tronchetto industrial zone, home to the opera company while works were in progress. The Fenice remains an appealing district, with atmospheric wine bars such as Vino Vino tucked around encircling canals *(see page 105)*.

Just south lies **Santa Maria Zobenigo** ⓬ (Mon–Sat 10am–5pm, Sun 1–5pm), or Santa Maria del Giglio, a church linked to Antonio Barbaro, a patron who rebuilt it in baroque style. The facade glorifies the Barbaro dynasty rather than God, with reliefs depicting the dominions governed by the Barbaros in the name of the Republic – Candia (Heraklion), Split and Corfu – as well as Rome and Padua, places in which the family held ambassadorial posts.

The adjoining square leads back to the waterfront and the **Gritti Palace** ⓭, a famous Venetian hotel *(see page 112)*. Ruskin, the art critic and aesthete, wrote his influential *Stones of Venice* while staying in both the Gritti and the Danieli. The Gritti terrace offers a grandstand view of the Grand Canal, lying diagonally opposite the church of La Salute.

Just west of Santa Maria Zobenigo is the dilapidated **Campo San Maurizio** ⓮, only of note for the view of the curiously truncated Guggenheim Museum and the haunted Ca' Dario, visible by following Calle del Dose to the waterside and then looking across the canal.

Around Santo Stefano

From Campo San Maurizio, the lively Calle del Spezier leads to **Campo Santo Stefano** ⓯, a long, theatrical space lined with palaces and cafés. This spectacular square makes a seamless link with the

Accademia, the great Venetian gallery on the far side of the bridge. Confusingly also known as Campo Morosini, after a famous doge, the wide square was a backdrop for bull-baiting until 1802, but is now more the setting for a chic evening *passeggiata*, with the occasional baiting of music students by mischievous lawyers. A clutch of cafés occupy the space between the monumental palaces and the tilting belltower of Santo Stefano. The clientele changes with the time of day, but at the cocktail hour these saintly bars tend to be full of sleek Venetian professionals or mothers supervising toddlers enjoying the new play centre by the church.

Few can resist **Paolin**, one of the most prized Venetian bars and ice-cream parlours. On the same side of the square is **Punto Laguna** (weekdays 2.30–5.30pm; information in English and Italian), the friendly new public multimedia centre that presents the case in favour of the dam, along with other environmental projects designed to save Venice and the lagoon.

TIP

Al Volto is one of the oldest wine bars in Venice, set on Calle Cavalli, close to Campo San Luca (tel: 041-522 8945, 5–10pm, closed on Sunday). This popular bar is a good place to sample an array of Venetian wines and snacks.

BELOW: a glut of gondolas.

At the far end of the square stands the Gothic church of **Santo Stefano** (Mon–Sat 10am–5pm, Sun 1–5pm). This Augustinian monastic church has a Gothic main portal facing a café-lined alley. Unusually, a canal flows under the church, through which gondolas can pass if the tide is low. The interior boasts an entrancing ship's-keel ceiling, carved tie beams and notable paintings by Vivarini and Tintoretto. The tomb of Doge Francesco Morosini (1694) is also prominently displayed in the nave. The cloisters, now appropriated by public offices, are accessible through a gateway in Campo Sant'Angelo.

If you lack the energy to visit the Accademia *(see pages 188–9)*, then ignore the bridge over the Grand Canal in favour of an engaging quarter on the bend of the canal. **Campo San Samuele**  was Casanova's parish, with Lord Byron's former home nearby, in Ca' Mocenigo, overlooking the canal. San Samuele, Casanova's baptismal church, is graced with a Byzantine belltower. Beside the ferry landing stage looms the formidable **Palazzo Grassi**, a

major exhibition centre. From here, a circuitous route winds back to San Marco, beginning with **Campo Sant' Angelo** ⑰, a noble quarter lined with the very palaces where Casanova played his practical jokes.

From Sant'Angelo, follow Calle Spezier and take the first turning left to **Palazzo Fortuny** ⑱, a fortress-like, late-Gothic palace and a would-be shrine to Fortuny, the Spanish-born painter. The crumbling palace is currently only open for exhibitions.

From here, cross Rio di San Luca into **Campo Manin**, named after a Venetian patriot who led the ill-fated revolt against the Austrians in 1848. Just south, concealed in a maze of alleys between Calle Vida and Calle Contarini, is **Palazzo Contarini del Bovolo** ⑲ (10am–6pm), a late-Gothic palace celebrated for its romantic arcaded staircase. *Bovolo*, meaning snail-shell in Venetian dialect, well describes the delightful spiral staircase which is linked to loggias of brick and smooth white stone. **Campo San Luca** ⑳, the bustling square east of Campo Manin, is a popular student haunt, with several good bars. Its marble plinth supposedly marks the centre of the city.

Not far from the Rialto, on the far side of Rio di San Salvador, stands **San Salvador** ㉑ (Mon–Fri 9am–noon, 4–7pm), a luminous Renaissance church adorned by Titian's impressionistic *Annunciation* and *Transfiguration*. The church has been a place for romantic assignations ever since the 18th century.

Overlooking the square is the Scuola di San Teodoro, one of the historic confraternity houses, now a venue for classical concerts.

Further north, just beyond the Rialto bridge, is the **Fondaco dei Tedeschi** ㉒, once an impressive trading centre for German merchants but now the city post office *(see page 120)*. On warm evenings, **Campo San Bartolomeo** ㉓, the adjoining

Signposts to the Ferrovia (railway station) and Piazzale Roma (bus station).

BELOW: Sunday morning on Campo Santo Stefano.

square, resembles an open-air club: the statue of the playwright Goldoni, the half-hidden church and the basic bars are usually surrounded by chattering youngsters.

The Mercerie

From here, follow Via 2 Aprile to the **Mercerie ㉔**, the shadowy maze of alleys running between the Rialto and San Marco. Named after the haberdashers' shops that once lined the route, these alleys were among the first paved city streets to be found anywhere in the world. In 1624, John Evelyn was entranced by "the most delicious street in the world", displaying "cloth of gold, rich damasks and other silks... perfumers and apothecaries' shops and the innumerable cages of nightingales".

Today, it remains an engaging bazaar, even if the perfumes of former times have been replaced by Calvin Klein's latest unisex body lotion. Some of the goods are tawdry, but you can also buy such traditional souvenirs as marbled paper, Murano glass and carnival masks of every description. Here,

designer leather goods and hand-crafted jewellery also compete for space with kitsch glass gondolas.

For Venetians, the Mercerie has long been displaced by the district around **Calle Larga XXII Marzo** as the smartest shopping address in town *(see page 226)*. The Mercerie comes out under the **Clocktower** on Piazza San Marco, but en route lies the church of **San Zulian ㉕** (9am–noon, 4.30–6pm), a refuge from commercialism. Dedicated to St Julian, the church was rebuilt in the 16th century and restored thanks to the Venice in Peril fund.

The old Armenian quarter is around the corner, based around **Santa Croce degli Armeni**, the well-hidden Armenian church. For the truest understanding of this ancient community, visit their monastery island of San Lazzaro degli Armeni *(see page 211)*. However, this church can safely be missed in favour of a welcoming bar. As the writer Jan Morris says, "There are 107 churches in Venice, and nearly every tourist feels he has seen at least 200 of them." ❑

Map on page 88

BELOW: Salizzada di San Moisè, in the smarter shopping district west of Piazza San Marco.

RESTAURANTS & BARS

Restaurants

Given that San Marco is home to some of the city's most prestigious cafés and restaurants, there is no shortage of sophisticated places. Many of the top hotels are nearby and have bars and restaurants celebrated in their own right. However, privacy should not be expected in goldfish bowl settings, and a superb setting commands a premium. Further away from the bustle, dining experiences tend to be more varied. Not that visitors should ignore the historic cafés and celebrity restaurants close to St Mark's; the Venetians patronise them too.

Acqua Pazza
Campo Sant'Angelo. Tel: 041-277 0688. Closed Mon. €–€€
This lively pizzeria is a pocket of Amalfi in Venice, with authentic Neapolitan pizzas, pasta and seafood. Bruschetta antipasti and a post-coffee *limoncello* are on the house.

Antico Martini
Campo San Fantin. Tel: 041-522 4121. Open late; closed all Tues, and Wed L. €€€
This classic restaurant, complete with piano bar, began as a coffee house in 1720. The seductive setting is offset by punctilious, slightly overbearing service, yet it is a Venetian institution. The menu follows suit, from seafood risotto and

granseola (spider crab) to *fegato alla veneziana* (liver on a bed of onions), or even lamb cutlets with puréed potatoes. Book.

Le Bistrot de Venise
Calle dei Fabbri. Tel: 041-523 6651. Open until 1am. €€ (menu) and €€€–€€€€ (à la carte).
Set behind St Mark's, this romantic wine bar and softly lit bistro is a touch touristy but redeemed by the canalside terrace, fine wines and seafood staples such as lobster, scampi and elaborate Venetian tasting-menus.

Caffè Quadri
Procuratie Vecchie, Piazza San Marco. Tel: 041-522 2105. Closed Mon in winter. €€€€
In addition to the famous bar, this is the only proper restaurant on the piazza, serving Venetian dishes as well as creative twists on classic Italian cuisine (fish served in a Cabernet Sauvignon sauce). The refined atmosphere is matched by the much-improved menu, with seafood grill, risotto or cuttlefish and polenta recommended, along with pear and parmesan salad or chocolate tart. Book.

Canova
Hotel Luna Baglioni, Calle Larga dell'Ascensione. Tel: 041-528 9840. €€€–€€€€

This historic hotel's elegant restaurant has a serene air and gracious service despite its proximity to St Mark's, and offers both smoking and non-smoking rooms. The menu embraces international fare as well as Venetian staples, all prepared with the freshest ingredients and a light touch; memorable desserts.

Centrale
Piscina Frezzeria. Tel: 041-296 0664. Open 6.30pm–2am; closed Tues. €€
Unlike anywhere else in Venice, this futuristic, sleek bar-restaurant-music club feels more Milanese than Venetian. Set in a converted cinema, the 16th-century *palazzo* incorporates cutting-edge design. Sample a full Mediterranean menu or just snack while chilling out to contemporary sounds – before departing in a gondola, if you wish.

Al Graspo De Ua
Calle Bombasseri. Tel: 041-520 0150. Closed Mon. €€€
Tucked away in the warren en route to the Rialto, this well-established fish restaurant has been serving spider crab, scallops and tagliolini with lobster since 1855.

Harry's Bar
Calle Vallaresso. Tel: 041-528 5777. €€€€
The fresh, utterly consis-

tent menu of this legendary bar attracts wealthy Venetians as well as visitors. Inspired comfort food plays with such ingredients as risotto, seafood and lamb, cooked simply yet superbly. The tone is perfect, set by the current Arrigo (Harry) Cipriani. Guests should refrain from smoking cigars, wearing strong perfumes or using mobile phones. Steep service and cover charge. Book.

De Pisis
Hotel Bauer, Campo San Moisè. Tel: 041-520 7022. **€€€€**
A dazzling damask and candlelit setting with service and cuisine to match, and views from the terrace. Currently considered the best hotel restaurant in Venice: classic Italian cuisine with creative touches. Book.

Trattoria Da Fiore
Calle delle Botteghe, off Campo Santo Stefano. Tel: 041-523 5310. Closed Tues. **€–€€**
Not to be confused with the pricey Da Fiore, this rustic but cosy trattoria is good value, considering its chic setting. The inn is divided into a *bacaro* (traditional bar), for wine and a Venetian buffet eaten at the counter, and the dining room, which serves a fuller menu at higher but still modest prices.

Trattoria Do Forni
Calle dei Specchieri. Tel: 041-523 2148. **€€€**
A quintessentially upmarket Venetian spot masquerading as a mere trattoria. With its reliable cuisine and rambling yet intimate dining rooms, Do Forni provides discreet cover for the stars of the Film Festival in the Orient Express carriage. The broad menu embraces caviar, oysters, steak and pasta, as well as seafood risotto, Adriatic fish and Venetian vegetable pie.

Vino Vino
Calle del Cafetier. Tel: 041-241 7688. Closed Tues. **€**
Close to La Fenice, this cramped but cosy wine bar attracts a mixed clientele, everyone from gondoliers to arty types. A good place to sample *cichetti* (Venetian snacks) such as pasta and bean soup, accompanied by an excellent variety of *ombre* (wine drunk with *cichetti*).

Bars & Cafés

On Piazza San Marco, **Caffè Florian** is the place for a prosecco in style, while drowning in dubious musical offerings. Or sip a Venetian *spritz (see page 76)* at **Caffè Quadri** while closing your ears to the rival quartet but drinking in an interior adorned with stuccowork, red damask and Murano chandeliers. **Bacaro**

Lounge (Salizzada San Moisè) is a cool, cutting-edge wine and cocktail bar with bar snacks and light lunches (more elegant upstairs) and an adjoining ultra-trendy multimedia centre and bookshop. **Boutique del Gelato** (Salizzada San Lio) is the best ice-cream outlet around. **Cavatappi** (Campo della Guerra, near San Zulian) is a fashionable, contemporary-style wine bar serving trusty bar snacks and light lunches or smarter dinners. **Centrale** is moody and modern, great for after-dark cocktails *(see Restaurants)*. **Rosa Salva** (Campo San Luca, no seats) is a branch of the best-known Venetian *pasticceria*, where locals gather for a brioche and cappuccino or an afternoon pastry. Finer still is **Marchini** (Calle

Spadaria), the city's most celebrated cake and pastry shop. **Vitae** (Salizzada San Luca, open until late) is a sleek young wine bar with tasty nibbles (*crostini* and *tramezzini*) at basic prices. **Vino Vino**, despite offering two-tier prices for Venetians and visitors, is still a rarity: a genuine, gruff and fusty all-day wine bar in the touristy opera-house area *(see Restaurants)*. **Al Volto** (Calle Cavalli) is an utterly unfashionable, unpretentious wine bar with decent *cichetti* (tapas).

PRICE CATEGORIES

Prices for three-course dinner per person with a half-bottle of house wine:
€ = under €30
€€ = €30–€50
€€€ = €50–€70
€€€€ = more than €70

LEFT: slick lounge bar Centrale.
RIGHT: St Mark's Square, a vast café terrace.

THE WORLD'S GRANDEST PRIVATE CHAPEL

Everyone who comes to Venice visits San Marco – and with good reason. This golden, marbled pleasure pavilion is simply the city's greatest site.

Although intended as the private chapel of the doges, San Marco soon became a symbol of republican splendour, set beside the Doge's Palace, the centre of Venetian power. The Basilica has always been at the heart of city life, the focus for the greatest celebrations, from thanksgiving for foreign conquests and victories at sea to redemption from the plague.

In recent years, San Marco has been a place of remembrance, with the city commemorating major anniversaries of the tragic 1966 floods through a series of spectacular concerts. After the burning down of La Fenice, the beloved opera house, similar fund-raising events followed, attracting famous politicians and foreign stars.

The eastern inspiration of the Basilica is clear from its oriental domes and lustrous mosaics. Charles Eliot Norton, a 19th-century American scholar, marvelled at this eclectic basilica, "fused into a composition neither Byzantine nor Romanesque, only to be called Venetian… No building so costly or so sumptuous had been erected since the fall of [the Roman] Empire". French writer George Sand, visiting in 1844, found it "a grand and dreamy structure, of immense proportions; golden with old mosaics; redolent with perfumes; dim with the smoke of incense; costly in treasure of precious stones and metals; holy with the bodies of deceased saints".

ABOVE: main entrance. Thirteenth-century carvings on the central doorway (part of the sumptuous decoration added between the 11th and 15th centuries) depict the labours of the month and the signs of the zodiac.
LEFT: bejewelled doorway. A glittering lunette of baroque mosaics is set above the richly decorated west doorway.

ABOVE: a Byzantine mosaic in the Zen Chapel depicts St Mark's arrival in Alexandria. In 828, his relics were smuggled out to Venice, cleverly hidden under barrels of pork – which no Muslim would touch.

BELOW: plundered treasure. Spoils of war, such as the two Turkish pilasters and the 4th-century Egyptian sculpted Tetrarchs, contribute to the eclectic facade.

THE FOUR HORSES OF SAN MARCO

"Below St Mark's still glow his steeds of brass, their gilded collars glittering in the sun." Byron was one of many travellers to admire the four bronze horses, 3rd- or 4th-century Hellenistic or Roman sculptures, which stood guard over the Basilica's central doorway. Like the Lion of St Mark, these noble horses were a symbol of independence. Yet the tale of their travels is a story of imperial envy and an allegory of the Republic's rise and fall.

The horses, which had graced a triumphal arch in Rome, were standing guard over the stadium in Constantinople when the city was sacked by the Venetians in 1204. Centuries of peace in the lagoon city ended in 1797, when they were plundered by Napoleon. This final insult to the crushed Republic was compounded by further humiliation: Napoleon had the noble steeds harnessed to a chariot in Paris for 18 years. After returning to Venice in 1815, the horses decorated the Loggia dei Cavalli on the basilica. The Venetians, never ones to look gift horses in the mouth, were delighted.

The originals are now displayed in the Museo Marciano inside the Basilica, with rather paltry replicas placed on the facade. Many Venetians felt that the beasts should be left *in situ*, but conservationists thought the bronzes ought to be protected for posterity from the corrosiveness of the Venetian climate.

RIGHT: Zen Chapel. Cardinal Zen bequeathed his fortune to Venice on condition that he was buried in the Basilica. His chapel (1504) is decorated with naturalistic Byzantine mosaics. The Treasury of St Mark's contains a number of works that reached Venice from Byzantium, especially after the Sack of Constantinople in 1204. The mosaics brought back as booty were incorporated into great buildings or copied by local Greek masters.

THE GRAND CANAL

A trip on the Grand Canal, Venice's fabulous highway, reveals a pageant of opulent palaces, from the Guggenheim to Gothic Ca' d'Oro and baroque Ca' Rezzonico and Ca' Pesaro, all doubling as superb museums

Venice is a place "where even the simplest coming and going assumes the form and charm of a visit to a museum and a trip to the sea". Marcel Proust captures the entertaining yet educational aspect of a trip along the Grand Canal. Known affectionately as the "Canalazzo", this "Little Canal" follows the course of an ancient river bed. It is nearly 4 km (2½ miles) long and up to 70 metres (230 ft) wide. The surprisingly shallow highway is spanned by four bridges and lined by 10 churches and over 200 palaces. This great waterway sweeps through the six city districts *(sestieri)*, with its switchback shape providing changing vistas of palaces and warehouses, markets and merchant clubs, courts, prisons and even the city casino.

Once a waterway for merchant vessels and great galleys, the canal now welcomes simpler craft, from gondolas to garbage barges. However, the palaces remain as a testament to the city's imperial past. The Grand Canal was considered the register of the Venetian nobility, with the palaces symbolising their owner's status and success. Yet the sea is a great leveller, with low tide revealing the slimy underpinnings of the noblest palace. Venetian eclecticism and the habit of recycling elements from various periods makes the

dating of palaces difficult. Indeed, the writer Jan Morris wryly observes that guidebook writers are the only people who seem capable of distinguishing between the different styles.

A peculiarly Venetian phenomenon is the number of palaces with the same or very similar names. Palaces were often the seats of separate branches of one family, so their names bear witness to Venetian fortunes, feuds and intermarriages; a family member sometimes added the name of the parish or new dynasty to

Map on page 111

LEFT: Ca' Pesaro.
BELOW: a golden gondola.

avoid confusion. The city is littered with palaces linked to the patrician or Dogal dynasties of the Mocenigo, Corner, Giustiniani, Grimani, Pesaro and Pisani families.

Palatial homes

Thanks to inheritance laws, financial vicissitudes and the extinction of the old dogal families, few families inhabit their ancestral homes. Yet impoverished aristocrats may languish in part of a palace or live in one which, while not bearing their name, has been in the family for centuries.

Venice captured the hearts of the Anglo-American colony who moved to the city at the turn of the 20th century and bought dilapidated palaces for a song. Henry James (1843–1916) was at his happiest in Palazzo Barbaro (see page 114).

Many palaces have become hotels or prestigious showcases for Venetian glass and textile manufacturers. Others belong to residents who relish the soft opulence of their second homes. Several of the grandest canalside art collections have been bequeathed to the city, notably the Accademia (Venetian art of all periods), the Guggenheim (modern art), the Ca' d'Oro (medieval and Renaissance art), the Ca' Rezzonico (18th-century art) and Ca' Pesaro (oriental and modern art). The charm of these palaces lies in their variety. As Henry James remarks: "The fairest palaces are often cheek-by-jowl with the foulest, and there are few, alas, so fair as to have been completely protected by their beauty."

Grand Canal procession

Purchase a day pass and trail up and down the Canal to your heart's content, stopping at sights as the fancy takes you. (*vaporetto* lines 1 and 82 both cover the route, but check the direction and be sure to get off before the boat sweeps away to the Lido). Ideally choose the slower route No. 1 and take a return trip to appreciate both banks (it takes about 40 minutes each way). As well as providing a cavalcade of Venetian pageantry, the canal offers a slice of local life. Architecturally, the Grand Canal is a feast for the senses (*see pages 47–53*).

Romantic poet Lord Byron (1788–1824) occupied various palaces on the Grand Canal and often swam its length.

The Grand Canal

0   200 m
0   200 yds

S. Labia
S. Geremia
Canal Grande
Pal. Gritti
S. Marcuola
Pal. Ddonà Balbi
Pal. Corner Gritti
Pal. Giovanelli
Casa Correr
Pal. Erizzo
Pal. Vendramin-Calergi
Pal. Soranzo
Pal. Molin
Pal. Zulian
Pal. Emo
Fond. d. Turchi (Museo Storia Nat.)
Pal. Belloni-Battagià
Deposito del Megio
Pal. Tron
Pal. Priuli
Pal. Barbarigo
Pal. Gussoni
Pal. Boldù
Ca' Pesaro
Pal. Foscarini
S. Stae
Pal. Donà
Ca' Corner della Regina
Casa Favretto
Ca' d'Oro
Gall. Franchetti
Pal. Fontana
Pal. Foscari
Pal. Sagredo
Pal. Michiel d. Colonne
Pal. Valmarana
Pal. Brandolin
Pescheria
Ca' da Mosto
Pal. Querini
Fabbriche Nuove
Pal. Civran
Fabbriche Vecchie
Pal. dei Camerlenghi
S. Giacomo di Rialto
Fondaco dei Tedeschi
Pal. d. Dieci Savi
Ponte di Rialto
S. Bartolomeo
S. Silvestro
Pal. Papadopoli
Pal. Bembo
Pal. Dolfin-Manin
Pal. Barzizza
Pal. Dandolo
Pal. Bernardo
Pal. Businello
Pal. Cappello Layard
Pal. Corner Martinengo
Pal. Querini
Pal. Donà
Pal. Loredan
Pal. Giustinian
Pal. Barbarigo
Pal. Persico
d. Terrazza
Pal. Farsetti
Pal. Marcello d. Leoni
Pal. Pisani Moretta
Pal. Tiepolo
Pal. Martinengo Volpi
Pal. Grimani
Pal. Dandolo Paolucci
Pal. Garzoni
Pal. Corner Spinelli
Pal. Balbi
Pal. Contarini d. Figure
Pal. Corner Gheltof
Ca' Mocenigo
Torre dell' Orologio
Pal. Patriarcale
Basilica di San Marco (St Mark's Basilica)
Pal. Foscari
Pal. Da Lezze
Campanile di S. Marco
P. dei Sospiri (Bridge of Sighs)
Pal. Giustinian
Pal. Moro Lin
Pal. Grassi
Procuratie Vecchie
Piazza San Marco
Museo Archeologico
Pal. Nani
San Samuele
Museo Correr
Procuratie Nuove
Palazzo Ducale (Doge's Palace)
Rezzonico
Musee del Settecento Veniziano
Pal. Malipiero
Palazzo Reale
Bibl. Naz. Marciana
Pal. Stern
Pal. Moro
Pal. Loredan
Ca' d' Duca
Pal. Contarini Scrigni
Pal. Falier
Pal. Cavalli Franchetti
Pal. Pisani
Ca' Corner della Ca' Grande
Pal. Giustinian
Luna Baglioni
La Zecca
Canal Grande
Ponte dell' Accademia
Pal. Barbaro
Casetta delle Rose
Pal. Pisani Gritti
Pal. Contarini
Pal. Tiepolo
Ridotto
Galleria dell' Accademia
Pal. Loredan
Pal. Barbarigo
Canal Grande
Ca' Dario
Ca' Genovese
Pal. Contarini Fasan
Pal. Contarini Polignac
Ca' Contanni
Pal. Venier Salviati (Guggenheim Collection)
San Gregorio
La Salute
Seminario Patriarcale
Punta della Dogana
Dogana di Mare

31 29 28 27 26 25 24 23 22 21 20 19 18 17 16 15 14 13 12 11 10 9 8 7 6 5 4 3 2 1 30 i

TIP

The most heartfelt Venetian festival on the Grand Canal is the Festa della Madonna della Salute (21 November), when a pontoon bridge is created across to the Salute church, in celebration of the city's salvation from the plague in 1630.

RIGHT: Ca' Dario, the bewitched palace where many have met their fate.

From San Marco to the Accademia Bridge

From the **Vallaresso** stop, the *vaporetto* sweeps into St Mark's Basin, with romantic views across to **San Giorgio Maggiore** *(see page 192)*. Set on the right bank, facing the **Customs Point** *(see page 179)*, **Palazzo Giustinian ❶** is the first significant palace on the Grand Canal.

The Giustiniani were an illustrious dynasty tracing their origins to the Roman Empire. Legend has it that, in the 12th century, the line was threatened with extinction, and the sole remaining heir was persuaded to leave his monastery for marriage to the doge's daughter. After saving the line by siring 12 offspring, he returned to a life of celibate seclusion. His sacrifice was a success: the Venetian branch only died out in 1962. In the 19th century, the palace was a hotel where Proust, Turner and Verdi stayed. A newly wed George Eliot stayed here with her unstable husband until he jumped from their window into the canal. The palace is now the headquarters of the Biennale exhibition organisation, the interna-

tional art showcase staged every two years *(see page 148)*.

On the left bank, the baroque church of **La Salute ❷** *(see page 178)* guards the entrance to the canal. Slightly further on, **Palazzo Contarini-Fasan ❸** appears on the right bank. This model of late-Gothic design in miniature has subtle carved cable moulding on the facade. It is nicknamed "Desdemona's House", since it supposedly inspired the setting for Desdemona's home in Shakespeare's *Othello*.

As soon as the boat stops at Santa Maria del Giglio, **Palazzo Pisani-Gritti ❹** comes into view on the same bank. Also known as the Gritti Palace, this is one of Venice's most sumptuous hotels *(see page 217)*, linked to writers as diverse as Hemingway and Graham Greene. Ruskin and his wife stayed here rather than being tempted by the decadent notion of "hiring a house or palace – it sounds Byronish or Shelleyish".

Virtually opposite is **Ca' Genovese ❺**, a neo-Gothic palace, and **Palazzo Salviati**, with its vivid mosaics set in an ochre facade;

The Curse of Ca' Dario

Five centuries of scandals, suicides and suspicious deaths have left Venetians wary of this sinister canalside palace. The Gothic palace belonged to Giovanni Dario, who negotiated peace with the Turks in 1479. Dario's daughter died of a broken heart after marrying into the patrician Barbaro family. Although the Dario family retained ownership until the 19th century, tragedy regularly struck its members, including a family massacre. Another purchaser, an Armenian diamond merchant, swiftly went bankrupt, while, in the 1840s, aesthete Rawdon Brown committed suicide in the drawing room. In 1936, French poet Henri de Régnier died shortly after moving in, while Charles Briggs, a colourful American who held homosexual orgies in the palace, was expelled from the city. In the 1970s the then owner, Kit Lambert, manager of The Who, was murdered over a drugs dispute. In 1979 the jinx struck Count delle Lanze, battered to death with a candlestick by his male lover. The most recent victim was industrialist Raul Gardini, who committed suicide in 1993 after being caught up in corruption scandals. Since then, the palace has lain empty. Prospective purchasers such as Woody Allen have wisely decided not to court disaster.

these gaudy showrooms belong to wealthy Murano glassmakers. On the same side, several palaces further down, is the gently listing **Ca' Dario** ❻ *(see below left)*, one of the most delightful spots on the Grand Canal. Henry James adored this haunted palace, then let to motley foreigners, for its "little marble plates and sculptured circles".

On the right bank looms **Ca' Grande** ❼ (or Ca' Corner della Ca' Grande), one of the greatest palaces, both in terms of importance and sheer size. Built by Sansovino for Jacopo Corner, a nephew of the queen of Cyprus, the palace is the first confident High Renaissance building in Venice. The Corner dynasty had deep links with Venice and owned numerous palaces in the city. The last of the line sold it to the Austrian administration in 1812, and the palace is now the seat of the Prefecture, the provincial government.

Palazzo Venier (Peggy Guggenheim Collection)

Facing Ca' Grande is the **Palazzo Venier** ❽, a white, truncated structure also known as "Nonfinito" (Unfinished). Legend has it that the owners of Ca' Grande forbade further building as it would block their view, but it is more likely that the project simply ran out of funds. Although now restricted to two storeys, the original palace was intended to rival the city's grandest. This 18th-century palace was built for one of the oldest Venetian dynasties, who produced three doges. The Veniers' lion nickname *(dei Leoni)* comes from their habit of having kept a pet lion chained in the courtyard. The building now houses the **Peggy Guggenheim Collection** (10am–6pm; closed Tues, open late in summer), named after the American millionairess, art collector and benefactor who lived here from 1949 until her death 30 years later.

It is appropriate that this startlingly modern-looking building should house a superb collection of modern art. This is a deservedly popular showcase for Chagall, Dalí, Klee, Braque, Giacometti, Kandinsky, Bacon and Sutherland. Most major movements are represented, from Picasso's cubist period to Severini's

The Contarini built more than 25 palaces. Among them on the Grand Canal are the Gothic Contarini-Fasan (above) and Contarini-Corfu, as well as the Renaissance Contarini-Polignac.

BELOW: Grand Canal to La Salute.

Marini's provocative Angel of the Citadel.

BELOW: Palazzo Venier dei Leoni, home of the Peggy Guggenheim Collection.

Futurism; from Mondrian's abstract works to Surrealist masterpieces by De Chirico, Delvaux and Magritte. Max Ernst, Guggenheim's second husband, is well represented. Other highlights include De Chirico's *Red Tower*, Magritte's *Empire of Light* and Pollock's *Alchemy*, forming a complement to the new collection in Ca' Pesaro *(see page 122)*.

Although Peggy helped launch Jackson Pollock, there is little expressionist work, since it did not find favour with the otherwise discerning collector. The sculpture-lined gardens feature works by Henry Moore and Marino Marini, and new pieces continue to be acquired. (Curiously, the watergates are often closed, to conceal the provocative erection sported by the rider in Marini's *Angel of the Citadel*.)

Several palaces further along is **Palazzo Barbarigo**, notable for its gaudy mosaics, and **Campo San Vio**, a pleasant spot from which to watch the water traffic.

On the same left bank, two palaces before the bridge, lies **Palazzo Contarini-Polignac ❾**, one of the first Renaissance palaces in Venice. In fact, a new facade, decorated with marble roundels, was added to the Gothic building. The Princesse de Polignac ran a sophisticated 19th-century salon here, and the palace remains in the same family.

On the right bank, virtually opposite, is **Palazzo Barbaro ❿**, a Gothic gem where Monet, Browning and Henry James were guests of the American Curtis family. James wrote *The Aspern Papers* here, and set *The Wings of a Dove* in his rooms: "part of a palace, historic and picturesque but strictly inodorous". The wheel came full circle with the making of the film of the same name in the palace. Next door is **Palazzo Cavalli-Franchetti**, a grandiose Gothic palace with an appealing garden.

Between the Accademia and Ca' Foscari

Beside the palatial bank is the distinctive wooden **Accademia Bridge**, a popular meeting place for Venetians. Beside it is the Accademia boat stop, with the world's greatest collection of Venetian paint-

ings housed in the neighbouring **Accademia ⓫** gallery *(see pages 188–9)*. Also on the right bank is **Palazzo Falier ⓬**, an early-Gothic palace with typical Venetian loggias *(liaghi)* facing the canal. This was supposedly the home of the infamous Doge Marin Falier, beheaded for treason in 1355.

Ca' Rezzonico

Ca' Rezzonico ⓭ lies on the left bank, by the boat stop of the same name. Henry James likened this bold building to "a rearing sea horse" because of its upward-thrusting cornices. This baroque masterpiece, designed according to Longhena's plans *(see page 52)*, is slightly more restrained than Ca' Pesaro. This is probably the most famous palace in the city, and one of the few on the Grand Canal open to the public. The newly ennobled Rezzonico banking family bought the unfinished palace in 1750 and supervised its completion in conservative baroque style. The effect is harmonious, if rather ponderous, with heavy rustication on the ground floor and a grand

courtyard. It was in this palace that the poet Robert Browning (1812–89) died. (His son, Pen, owned the palace in the 1880s and did much to restore it.) After lying in state in the ballroom, the poet was transferred to San Michele *(see page 207)* and then to London's Westminster Abbey. A wall in the palace bears words taken from Browning's epitaph: "Open my heart and you will see/ Graved inside of it Italy".

Ca' Rezzonico is home of the **Museum of 18th-Century Life** (Museo del Settecento Veneziano) (10am–6pm; closed Tues). The rococo interior has been sumptuously restored in recent years, with the re-hung picture gallery of superior genre artists on the second floor, and the eclectic art gallery on the top floor. In terms of Venetian art, Ca' Rezzonico now takes up from where the Accademia leaves off.

In keeping with Venetian style, the rooms are sparsely but lavishly furnished, with the mirrored wall brackets, lacquered furniture and chinoiserie that characterised the period. A grand staircase leads to the

Map on page 111

TIP

Weary gallery-goers can take a culture break in the Guggenheim's arty café, while visitors to the beautifully restored Ca' Rezzonico can relax and recover in its chic café.

BELOW: Tiepolo fresco in the Ca' Rezzonico.

Gondolas and Gondoliers

According to the writer Mary McCarthy, everything in Venice has an "inherent improbability, of which the gondola, floating, insubstantial, at once romantic and haunting, charming and absurd, is the symbol". The gondola may be as old as Venice itself, and although probably of Turkish origin, it is uniquely adapted for the lagoon waters: it is streamlined yet sturdy, able to navigate the shallowest waters and narrowest canals. To Thomas Mann, the gondola conjured up "visions of death itself, the bier and solemn rites and last soundless voyage". Although red was the traditional Venetian colour of mourning, funeral gondolas were eventually painted gold and black.

The gondola took its definitive form by the 17th century; before then, the craft was less streamlined. A gondola is made of eight different sorts of wood, finished off with 10 coats of black paint. The *ferro*, or metal prow, is the most distinctive feature, much admired by Mark Twain: "The bow is ornamented with a steel comb with a battleaxe attachment." The front of this projection supposedly symbolises the *corno*, the doge's cap, with the six forward prongs representing the six *sestieri* (districts) of Venice, and the seventh the Giudecca. In practical terms, the prow serves as a counterweight to the gondolier and aligns the boat around narrow corners.

Until the 16th century, boats were lavishly decorated, bedecked with satins and silks, brocade and brass sea horses. The Sumptuary Laws *(see margin opposite)* consigned gondolas to perpetual mourning. The gilded cherubs and noble crests on the stern and prow were banished in favour of black livery. Luxurious gondolas were equipped with a *felze*, an upholstered wooden cabin that gave protection from prying eyes and winter weather. (These are on show the Naval Museum, *see page 146.*)

In the 16th century, Venice had about 10,000 gondoliers, but now the number has fallen to 400. Nowadays, the Japanese are the keenest customers, always ready to try a gondola ride in all weathers and to pay a premium for a "music boat", rowed by a serenading gondolier.

The *gondolieri* are a breed apart: only native Venetians can apply for a coveted licence, and the trade is often passed down from father to son. Many are noted for their singing, but serenades are often spiced with lewd language, including lascivious appreciation of brides. (Since this is delivered in Venetian dialect, few visitors are likely to be offended.)

Spokesman Mario Ventin also defends fellow gondoliers against criticisms of colourful language: "Foreign visitors love to hear us shout at each other. If a water-taxi narrowly misses us, are we to bow and say politely, 'Sir, your keel was too near?' No! We dispatch the captain to hell!" Yet gondoliers do occasionally live up to their romantic image. Roberto Nardin met his Californian wife when she took a ride on his gondola. When Roberto described her eyes as "more beautiful than those September days when the sky dissolves into the lagoon", one more heart melted into the Venetian sunset. ❏

● *For more information on gondolas and water transport in general, see page 215.*

LEFT: Grand Canal gondolier.

Map on page 111

Piano Nobile, the ceremonial first floor added by Massari. Here, the opulent setting makes a spectacular showcase for Tiepolo's *trompe l'œil* ceilings and Guardi's memorable genre scenes. The **Sala da Ballo**, or ballroom, is boldly restored, daringly frescoed and richly embellished with glittering chandeliers and period pieces, including ebony vase-stands borne by Moors.

Off the ballroom is the **Sala dell'Allegoria Nuziale** (1758), raised to great heights by Tiepolo's nuptial allegory on the ceiling, ostensibly depicting *The Marriage of Ludovico Rezzonico*. Accompanied by angels and cherubs, careering horses tumble through the billowing heavens, forging a link between the elevated residents and the gods. In the same year, a Rezzonico count was elected pope, thus putting the seal on the family's social acceptability. Elsewhere there are lofty Tiepolo frescos depicting *Nobility and Virtue* and *Fortitude and Wisdom*.

After its recent renovation, the second floor rivals the piano nobile in magnificence, with the huge *portego* used as a **Picture Gallery** for genre scenes by Canaletto, Guardi and Longhi. Genre painters seems a disparaging term for these great 18th-century salon artists at the peak of their powers. Guardi's *Ridotto* (1748) captures the revelry of masked gamblers and revellers in the State casino, while his *Nuns' Parlour* (1768) depicts the spirited and worldly nuns whose reputation for lasciviousness made Venetian convents a byword for dissolute living. Longhi's superior salon pictures show patrician Venice at play, including the famous *Rhinoceros Show*, depicting masqueraders entranced by this exotic beast. Also on display is one of the few works by Canaletto in Venice: his view of *Rio dei Mendicanti* (1725). There are also subtle

paintings and miniatures by Rosalba Carriera, the 18th-century portraitist.

Apart from these genre scenes and Tiepolo's frescoed ceilings, the highlights are the suite of rooms dedicated to frescos salvaged from **Villa Zianigo**, the Tiepolo family home. Giandomenico Tiepolo's provocative yet playful frescos reveal the mood of disenchantment in Venice towards the end of the 18th century. The greatest of these strange and unsettling pictures is *Mondo Nuovo* (New World), depicting a crowd staring out to sea, and suggesting the disorientation created by the fall of the Venetian Republic, with Venetians reduced to being mere bystanders.

If the second floor is a fond farewell to the Serenissima, the top floor is a tribute to the taste of one of Venice's most renowned art patrons, Egidio Martini. This well-displayed **Private Collection** spans four centuries of northern Italian art, including works by Tintoretto and Tiepolo. But its appeal lies in the collection's eclectic nature, fashioned by one man's singular tastes. Here, too, is a quaint period **Pharmacy**, complete

The Sumptuary Laws were established in 1562 to avoid profligacy and curb the patricians' overweaning pride. They were designed to limit the conspicuous display of wealth by restricting the ornamentation of palaces, gondolas and even clothing. But the laws were riddled with loopholes and rich Venetians soon found ways to circumvent them.

BELOW: Ca' Rezzonico.

Entrance to Ca' Foscari, home to Venice University and also the finishing line for the celebrated Regata Storica (Historical Regatta).

BELOW:
Palazzo Loredan.

with ceramic jars, glass bottles and wooden cabinets – but no 18th-century headache remedies for those suffering from sensory overload.

Set on the right bank, the Palazzo Grassi and church of San Samuele can be seen from Ca' Rezzonico. **Palazzo Grassi ⑭** (10am–7pm; www.palazzograssi.it; book exhibitions online) is an imposing patrician palace and model of neoclassical restraint. Although designed by Longhena, there is no trace of baroque exuberance; Massari completed the palace with due regard to classical orders. The palace belonged to a patrician family who died out in the 19th century. Now owned by Fiat, it has been converted into a slick international exhibition showcase.

On the same bank lies a cluster of three palaces, commanding a sharp bend known as the Volta del Canal. **Palazzo Giustinian ⑮** is one of 15 palaces owned by the Giustiniani clan. This Gothic showpiece is a double palace adorned with delicate tracery and linked by a watergate. Here, in 1857–9, Wagner composed *Tristan und Isolde*.

Between Ca' Foscari and the Rialto Bridge

Next door, **Ca' Foscari ⑯** presents similar Gothic coherence, with a waterside facade graced by the Foscari arms. Built at the height of Venetian power, this is a monument to the ambition of Doge Foscari, who ruled from 1423 to 1457. Tommaso Mocenigo, a previous doge, distrusted him: "He sweeps and soars more than a hawk or a falcon." Foscari survived to pursue expansionist goals until a conspiracy caused his downfall, and he died a broken man in this palace.

This Gothic stage-set witnessed countless pageants. During a state visit prior to being crowned, Henri III of France stayed here and was fêted by the Venetians. The mosaic floor of his bedroom was remodelled to Veronese's designs; Titian painted his portrait and Palladio was commissioned to build a triumphal arch. Now the grandest part of Venice University, the palace has been tampered with but is being restored.

On the far (canal) side of the Rio, distinguished by twin pinnacles, is **Palazzo Balbi**, grandiose seat of the regional government.

Around the Rialto

Henry James found this middle stretch of the Canal evoked a "melancholy mood", likening it to "a flooded city". But there is an intriguing contrast between the bold palaces and the bustling quayside close to the Rialto market. As the boat stops at the **San Tomà** landing stage, look across to **Ca' Mocenigo ⑰** on the right bank. This cluster of palaces belonged to the influential Mocenigo family, who produced seven doges. Byron stayed here while writing his mock-heroic poem *Don Juan* (1819–24) and had an affair with the baker's wife, a woman "wild as a witch and fierce as a demon". On the left bank a little

further along is **Palazzo Pisani-Moretta** ⓲, with its Gothic tracery reminiscent of the Doge's Palace. Curiously, the palace has two *piani nobili* or patrician floors instead of the more common one. The palace is also exceptional in still belonging to descendants of the Pisani family.

On the right bank, beside the **Sant'Angelo** stop, is **Palazzo Corner-Spinelli** ⓳, the prototype of a Renaissance palace. Designed by Coducci, it has a rusticated ground floor as well as his trademark windows, two bold round-arched lights framed by a single round arch. Like Ca' Grande, the palace was owned by the Corner family, the royal Cypriot dynasty. The ownership passed to the Spinelli, important dealers in gold and silks, and still serves as the showrooms of noted Venetian textile merchants today.

As the boat stops at **San Silvestro** by the church, look across to the right bank to appreciate the **Palazzo Farsetti** and **Palazzo Loredan** ⓴, two of the finest Veneto-Byzantine palaces in Venice. Ca' Loredan, in particular, is graced with the origi-

nal capitals, arches and decorative plaques. The pair are occupied by the city council and the mayor. The banks between here and the **Rialto Bridge** are lined with deceptively appealing restaurants overrun by tourists rather than market traders.

From the Rialto Bridge to Ca' d'Oro

The **Rialto Bridge** was the only one to span the Grand Canal until 1854. Today, the bridge provides the chance to watch the water traffic, from gondolas to garbage barges. The Rialto is also an ideal place for lunch in a *bacaro*, a rough and ready Venetian version of the Spanish tapas bar *(see page 154)*. On the left bank, just upstream, the severe **Palazzo dei Camerlenghi** ㉑ curves round the canal bend. Now a courthouse, it was built in 1525 as the seat of the exchequer, with the ground floor used as a debtors' prison. Like many multifunctional Venetian buildings, it also served as a merchants' emporium and administrative centre.

On the right bank, facing the

Bancogiro aside, most restaurants clustered on the Rialto quaysides are mediocre at best; for a rustic lunch, retreat to a darkly atmospheric market inn with quirky tapas, but without so much as a canal view.

BELOW: sunset gondola ride on the Grand Canal.

TIP

For good views of the Regata Storica *(see page 70)*, watch the start of the procession from the rooftop terrace of the Gabrielli Sandwirth Hotel. Alternatively, watch the races from the Rialto Bridge – reserve a canalside table if you can. The views, if not the food, will be memorable. Or join the street party after the races, when trestle tables are set up in the market for a communal dinner.

BELOW: view of the Grand Canal from the Rialto markets.

palazzo, lies the **Fondaco dei Tedeschi** ㉒, named after the German merchants who leased the emporium. A healthy trade in precious metals from German mines meant that this privileged community created a cross between an emporium, commercial hotel and social club.

Set close to the Rialto commercial quarter, this self-contained haven even had its own chapel and casino. After a fire in 1505, it was rebuilt in traditional fashion, with a courtyard and towers that recall an earlier defensive function. The merchants left in 1812, abandoning the site to its banal fate as the city post office.

On the left bank stands the **Fabbriche Vecchie e Nuove** ㉓, an arcaded frontage concealing a key pair of mercantile institutions. The buildings around the Rialto were destroyed by fire in 1514 but rebuilt in classical style. The ground floors functioned as shops, while the upper floors were administrative offices and courts. The porticoes of the **Fabbriche Vecchie** housed sectors

devoted to fruit and vegetables, fish, banking and cloth. Above were offices and tribunals to settle trading disputes. Sansovino's larger **Fabbriche Nuove**, built some 30 years later, echo the earlier design. Now the Court of Assizes, they formed the Republic's trading centre, with offices on the upper floors devoted to commerce, navigation and food distribution.

Virtually opposite the Fabbriche Nuove and the covered neo-Gothic fish market is **Ca' da Mosto** ㉔, a crumbling example of Veneto-Byzantine architecture. This 13th-century palace was the birthplace of the explorer Alvise da Mosto (1432–88), credited with discovering the Cape Verde Islands and exploring coastal west Africa. His descendant, writer and television personality Francesco da Mosto, always gives the palace a rueful glance as he ponders on the loss of the ancestral pile by his careless forebears.

The Ca' d'Oro (Palace of Gold)

On the same side is the **Ca' d'Oro** ㉕, one of the loveliest Gothic palaces, set beside the landing stage of the same name. Architecturally, this is a landmark building and a sumptuous version of a Venetian palace. On the facade, the friezes of interlaced foliage and mythological beasts were originally picked out in gold, leading to its popular name, the "Palace of Gold". The Veneto-Byzantine influence is clear in the design, from the oriental pinnacles to the ethereal tracery.

The palace has an arcade rather than the pointed watergate favoured by Gothic palaces. This was a single family courtyard, unlike palaces designed for several branches of the same family, which commanded twin watergates and double courtyards. As well as the watergate on

the Grand Canal, the palace retains its original land gate in a brick courtyard. In 1845 Ruskin wept while watching the brutal "restoration" of the palace demanded by the owner, a famous ballerina. Fortunately, Baron Franchetti, a later owner, restored the Ca' d'Oro to its original glory, even tracking down the original staircases. While suffering from an incurable illness, the baron committed suicide in 1922, but not before bequeathing his beloved palace to the city.

The Ca' d'Oro houses the **Franchetti Gallery** (Mon 8.15am–2pm, Tues–Sun 8.15am–7.15pm), rivalling Ca' Rezzonico as the most appealing city art gallery. If the collection is idiosyncratic, it reflects the refined taste of the owner. The courtyard contains the original Gothic well-head that Franchetti finally retrieved from a Parisian dealer. Although the interior is no longer recognisably Gothic, the coffered ceilings and fine marble floors make a splendid showcase for the medieval and Renaissance exhibits.

The gallery is adorned with Flemish tapestries as well as Gothic and Renaissance furniture. The highlights of the collection include a delightful *Annunciation* by Carpaccio, Guardi's views of Venice and Titian's *Venus*. Andrea Mantegna's *St Sebastian* is the most poignant of his paintings, with other versions existing in Paris and Vienna: this was Franchetti's favourite work. Yet the minor Venetian works give the greatest pleasure, ranging from 12th-century sculptures of interlaced peacocks to Vivarini's poetic Byzantine-style paintings.

The *portego,* or gallery, opens onto the Grand Canal. In fine weather, the loggia makes a delightful place to sun oneself and watch the comings and goings on the canal: looking towards the Rialto, there is a splendid view of the **Pescheria**, the fish market. A wooden Gothic staircase leads to the top floor and works by Guardi and Tintoretto. After a surfeit of serious art, succumb to the pleasure of lunch in Alla Vedova, one of the most authentic wine bars, set down the end of the Ca' d'Oro alley *(see page 175).*

"A man's life often resembles these palaces on the Grand Canal, which begin at the base with an array of stones proudly sculpted in diamond points, and end with the upper floors hastily cobbled together from dry mud."

–PAUL MORAND

BELOW: the Rialto's lively fish market.

One of Rodin's Thinkers, exhibited in the Museum of Modern Art in Ca' Pesaro. Today, Rodin's work is considered a bridge between classical 19th-century sculpture influenced by antiquity, and the Renaissance.

From Ca' d'Oro to the railway station

Just upstream on the left bank is **Ca' Corner della Regina** ㉖, the birthplace of Caterina Corner, queen of Cyprus, who was the victim of a cynical Venetian plot to gain control of the island. As a result of French conquests during the crusades, the island was ruled by King James of Lusignan, whom Corner married in 1468. When he died, leaving her queen of Cyprus, Venetian ambassadors persuaded her it was her patriotic duty to abdicate and grant Cyprus to the Republic. In return, she was given dominion over Asolo, a beautiful but minor town in the Veneto. In the 17th century, descendants of her family rebuilt the palace, which is now owned by the Biennale organisation.

Ca' Pesaro ㉗, the next palace but one, is a stately baroque pile which bemused Henry James: "I even have a timid kindness for the huge Pesaro, whose main reproach, more even than the coarseness of its forms, is its swaggering size." In building Ca' Pesaro, Longhena was inspired by Ca' Corner. The well-restored Grand Canal facade offers a play of chiaroscuro effects created by recessed windows and sharply delineated cornices. The rusticated ground-floor facade is interrupted by a triple-arched water entrance leading to a theatrical inner courtyard lined by balconies, loggias and a portico, with a grand well-head in the centre. In 1899, Duchess Bevilacqua La Masa bequeathed the palace to the city. It is now home to the **Museum of Oriental Art** and the **Museum of Modern Art** (both daily 10am–6pm, closed Tues, combined ticket, San Stae stop).

The **Museum of Oriental Art** draws on the eclectic 19th-century collection assembled by the Count di Bardi on his travels to the Far East. Japanese art of the Edo period (1614–1868) is mixed with oriental decorative screens and lacquerwork. There are also precious fabrics, musical instruments, costumes and armour, plus masks and puppets. While the fate of this fusty time capsule is uncertain, it remains an endearing collection.

By contrast, the **Museum of Modern Art** could not be a slicker showcase for modern art, although the coffered or frescoed ceilings also merit admiration. A sculpture-lined courtyard leads upstairs to both museums, past one of Rodin's quizzical Thinkers. The early rooms contain pastoral paintings by the Tuscan Impressionists and works by early winners of the Biennale. The grand *portego*, or ceremonial salon, displays the show-stoppers, from Klimt's decadent *Salome* and Chagall's *Rabbi of Vitebsk* to Bonnard's *Nude in the Mirror* and Lavery's *Woman in Pink*. Later rooms focus on the Italians, from Morandi to De Chirico and Carlo Carra.

On the same bank is the church of **San Stae** ㉘, with its striking

The Canal by Night

At night, after most tourists have returned to the mainland, is the time for a leisurely look at the Grand Canal. Pick up a No. 1 *vaporetto* and slip into one of the coveted seats on the prow. The palaces present a seductive face at night: the illuminated windows are an invitation to dream, revealing gleaming Murano glass chandeliers, red silk-clad walls and the odd summer party spilling onto the balconies. On the water, you may catch a fleeting glimpse of a *sandolo*, a twin-oared rowing boat, scudding by, its prow lit by a rustic lamp. Afterwards, the tiny *campielli* near the shore provide a good vantage point for watching the water traffic: try the bench on Campo San Vio, between the Guggenheim and the Accademia, or just stand on the Rialto Bridge. Writer Jonathan Keates revels in the elemental delight of walking in Venice after dark, with the city's ghostly stage-sets bathed in "muted brilliance, shadow and absolute murk".

Mark Twain, writing in 1878, was equally entranced: "Under the mellow moonlight the Venice of poetry and romance stood revealed… ponderous stone bridges threw their shadows athwart the glittering waves… Music came floating over the waters – Venice was complete." A conversational stroll or a boat ride are classic Venetian pastimes, activities that pass for nightlife in sleepy Venice.

Map on page 111

Palladian facade. A couple of palaces further on is **Palazzo Belloni-Battaglia**, which stands out for its stylish facade and highly distinctive pinnacles. It was designed by Longhena for the parvenu Belloni family, who bought their way into the local aristocracy.

On the right bank is **Palazzo Vendramin-Calergi** ㉙, a testament to the changing fortunes of the Venetian nobility. It was built before 1500 by Coducci for the patrician Loredan dynasty, but later belonged to the Calergi, a Cretan family who bought their way into the Venetian nobility.

The Vendramin, scions of a banking and dogal family, then owned the palace until 1845, when it was sold to the French Bourbon Duchesse de Berry. Here she based her court in exile, a Versailles on the lagoon, with the interior hung with Renaissance paintings. Wagner rented the mezzanine wing from the family and, with his father-in-law Franz Liszt, gave a concert at La Fenice opera house. In 1883, Wagner suffered a stroke in his apartments and died in his wife's arms. Now the city **Casino**, the place

is banned to Venetian residents in an uncanny echo of ancient Republican law. (To admire the palace from afar, leave the boat at San Stae, but to chance your luck in the Casino, get off at San Marcuola.)

Architecturally, the palace is a classical masterpiece, built in familiar three-part design and faced with Istrian stone. It is notable for its horizontal line, Tuscan projecting cornices, sweeping balconies and a frieze studded with shields and heraldic eagles. The palace still possesses a spectacular interior, despite the sale of the original furnishings by the de Berry heirs. The casino has coffered ceilings, chandeliers, marble fireplaces and mannerist paintings, as well as a hall decorated with jasper columns from the fabulous Turkish ruins of Ephesus. A Wagner Society is housed in the composer's former quarters.

On the far bank stands the fortress-like **Deposito del Megio** ㉚, the state granary. Now a school, the austere 15th-century granary is crenellated, in keeping with the Venetian approach to many public

TIP

To gamble in the impressive Casino, dress smartly and bring your passport (tel: 041-529 7111). It is open all year round 3pm–2am (*vaporetto* lines 1 and 82). Wagner's mezzanine apartments here can also be visited.

BELOW:
Santa Maria della Salute and the Grand Canal at night.

Map on page 111

"Streets full of water, please advise" was the famous cable sent home by the American humorist Robert Benchley on his first visit to Venice.

BELOW: gondolas moored opposite the Fondaco dei Turchi, a former Turkish emporium.

buildings. The Lion of St Mark emblem on the facade is a reconstruction, since Napoleonic troops effaced whatever republican symbols they found. Next door is the **Fondaco dei Turchi**, a former trading base for Turkish merchants. It was built in 1227 for the noble Pesaro family but leased to the Ottomans in 1621, partly as a means of supervision. Bedrooms, shops and servants' quarters were created. In keeping with Muslim custom, doors and windows were sealed off, and the building included a mosque and Turkish baths. The Venetian State insisted that all weapons be surrendered on entry, and forbade Christian women and children from crossing the threshold.

The Fondaco only fell into disuse in 1838 and, after an insensitive restoration, became the **Museum of Natural History** (Sat–Sun 10am–4pm; tel: 041-275 0206). Henry James was stunned by "the glare of white marble without and a series of showy majestic halls within". The museum contains the sarcophagi of previous doges, but one bears no

inscription since it belonged to the disgraced Marin Faliero, the doge decapitated for treason in 1355. The museum has been refurbished, but only the aquarium and dinosaur sections are open, as well as an ecological presentation of the lagoon.

The buildings are less impressive on the next stretch of the canal. Opposite is the church of **San Marcuola ③**, and, upstream on the same bank, stands the square-towered **Palazzo Labia ③**. This eclectic palace is home to the RAI state broadcasting network, and boasts superb Tiepolo frescos (by appointment, Wed–Fri 3–4pm; tel: 041-781 111). Next door is the domed church of **San Geremia** and, just beyond, the severe **Palazzo Flangini ③** marks the last of the major palaces.

On the same bank stands the restored rococo **Scalzi ③** church, "all marble and malachite, a cold hard glitter and a costly, curly ugliness". Henry James thought little of the church, but Venetians have a soft spot for it as the sole monument to survive the building of the grim **Railway Station ③**, which serves to remind us what the real world is like.

Leave the boat at the Ferrovia stop, with a glance at **San Simeone Piccolo ③** on the far bank. This church was modelled on the Pantheon in Rome and created as a counterweight to La Salute, framing the Grand Canal with a baroque church at either end.

But the church is now upstaged by a striking addition to the cityscape, a **Fourth Bridge** over the Grand Canal, and the only one to be illuminated at night. Designed by Calatrava, the acclaimed Spanish architect and bridge fetishist, this elegant, understated sliver of a structure connects the station with the road terminal. Although unremarkable in most capitals, this construction makes a splash in a city as conservative as Venice. ❑

RESTAURANTS & BARS

Restaurants

Al Bancogiro
Campo San Giacometto, San Polo. Tel: 041-523 2061. Closed Sun D and Mon. €–€€

Tucked snugly into ancient porticoes by the busy Rialto crossing, this fashionable wine bar and new-wave *bacaro* stands on the site of the city's earliest bank. Eat *cichetti* with locals at the bustling bar or terrace – or select from the short but ever-changing menu upstairs, with dishes based on produce from the fish and vegetable markets.

Club del Doge
Hotel Gritti Palace, Campo Santa Maria del Giglio. Tel: 041-794 611. €€€€
Traditional cuisine in a palatial setting overlooking the Grand Canal, with probably the best terrace in town; equally atmospheric for lunch, drinks or a dinner based on fish. In this doge's palace, service has a lighter touch than in most other grand hotels. *Vaporetto*: Santa Maria del Giglio.

La Cusina
Westin Europa & Regina, Corte Barozzi, Calle Larga XXIII Marzo, San Marco. Tel: 041-240 0001. €€€€
International, Italian and Venetian cuisine (try the risotto) in an elegant setting, typified by the terrace and a Murano-chandelier-hung interior made intimate by views of the chefs at work. One of the better grand hotel restaurants. Book.

Fiaschetteria Toscana
Salizzada San Giovanni Cristostomo, Cannaregio. Tel: 041-528 5281. Closed Mon L and all Tues. €€–€€€
Set just beyond the Rialto Bridge, this is a reliable, good-value choice for sound Venetian fare, plus a smattering of Tuscan steak dishes, fine wines and cheeses. Book.

Grand Canal
Hotel Monaco & Grand Canal, Calle Vallaresso. Tel 041-520 0211. €€€
Set at the start of the Grand Canal, this elegant, newly revamped terrace restaurant (with piano bar) has fine views over the lagoon, taking in La Salute and San Giorgio. International, Italian and Venetian dishes include fish soup, vegetable risotto and scampi. Book.

Alla Madonna
Calle della Madonna, San Polo. Tel: 041-522 3824. Closed Wed. €€
Tucked away down a tiny canal just beyond the Rialto bank, this reliable, ever-popular old inn specialises In Venetian cuisine, from seafood risotto to polenta and spider crab. Service is brisk and animated but expect to queue with chatty locals.

Bars & Cafés

Close to St Mark's, Calle Vallaresso boasts **Harry's Bar** and the waterside bar of **Hotel Monaco e Grand Canal**. Nearby, on Campo San Moisè, Hotel Bauer's celebrated **B Bar** is a trendy cocktail bar popular with Venetians, thanks to its skilled barmen and the waterside terrace. **Alla Botte** (Campo San Bartolomeo), on the San Marco side of the Rialto Bridge, serves sound Venetian tapas in a rustic setting. **Al Bancogiro**, on the far bank, by the market, is an idiosyncratic yet deservedly popular wine bar *(see Restaurants)*. On the same bank is the **Peggy Guggenheim** (café inside the museum), the smartest gallery eatery in town, suitable for snacks or light lunches. **Paolin** (Campo Santo Stefano, open until late) is just off the Grand Canal, handy for the Accademia over the bridge, and is famous for its ice cream. The cocktails and bar snacks are pretty good too.

PRICE CATEGORIES

Prices for three-course dinner per person with a half-bottle of house wine:
€ = under €30
€€ = €30–€50
€€€ = €50–€70
€€€€ = more than €70

RIGHT: good views can be had from the Rialto Bridge cafés, but better *bacari* are found in the backstreets.

CASTELLO

Lying to the north and east of San Marco, Castello is
a mix of sophistication and local charm. It has the
city's best-known waterfront, Vivaldi's church, and
the most mysterious confraternity seat in Venice

H enry James's evocation of the
essence of Venice easily applies
to Castello: "a narrow canal in
the heart of the city – a patch of
green water and a surface of pink
wall... a great shabby facade of
Gothic windows and balconies". Yet
this fails to do justice to the diversity
of the district. As the most varied
Venetian *sestiere*, Castello offers a
spectrum of sights, from the sophisticated bustle along Riva degli Schiavoni to the quaint fishing-village
ambience of San Pietro.

Castello's seafaring heritage may
be strong but so are its cosmopolitan
roots and mercantile spirit. Sailors,
shipwrights and merchants came
from Dalmatia, Eastern Europe,
Greece and Egypt, attracted by the
prospect of work at the Arsenal shipyards and great quaysides. The cosmopolitan legacy lingers on, with the
district still home to sizeable Greek
and Slav communities, as well as a
small Armenian quarter.

Like Cannaregio, Castello offers
a slice of everyday life, with Sundays ringing with church bells, and
dark alleys opening into bright,
bustling squares. Two of the most
homely areas centre on Campo
Santa Maria Formosa and San Giorgio dei Greci, the Greek church. Yet
culturally the *sestiere* can compete
with any in Venice. The district is

home to La Pietà, Vivaldi's church,
and the Gothic majesty of San Giovanni e Paolo (San Zanipolo). The
distinctive Venetian confraternities
(scuole) are well-represented, with
San Giorgio degli Schiavoni the
most intimate and San Marco the
most prestigious. The Arsenale is the
focal point of the eastern district,
with its looming walls and defensive
towers visible from afar.

While western Castello becomes
increasingly gentrified, with boutique
hotels and eclectic craft shops shun-

Map
on page
128

LEFT: the Bridge of
Sighs linking the
Doge's Palace to the
"new" prison.
BELOW:
waiting for customers.

Castello

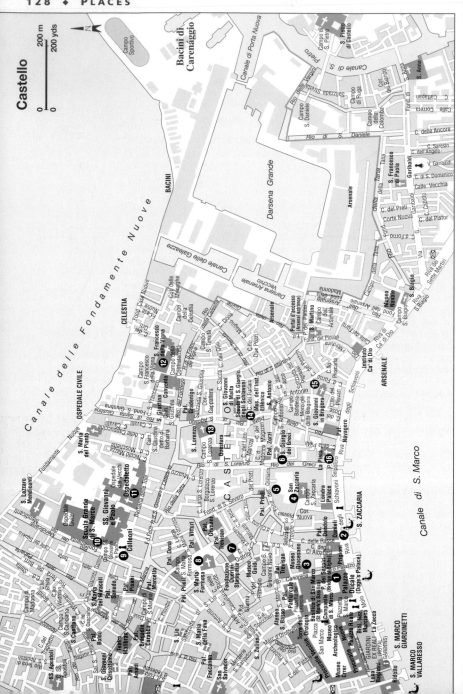

200 m
200 yds

N

Campo Sportivo

Bacini di Carenággio

BACINI

Canale delle Fondamente Nuove

CELESTIA

OSPEDALE CIVILE

Canale delle Galeazze

Darsena Grande

Darsena Arsenale Vecchio

Arsenale

ARSENALE

Canale di S. Marco

S. Pietro di Castello

Canale di S. Pietro

Canale di Porta Nuova

Campo di Porta Nuova

S. Francesco di Paola

V. Garibaldi

S. Biágio

Museo Navale

Istituto Ca' 'di Dio

C A S T E L L O

1 Palazzo Ducale (Doge's Palace)
2 S. Zaccaria
3
4 San Zaccaria
5
6 S. Giorgio dei Greci
7
8
9 Colleoni
10 Scuola Grande di S. Marco
11 Ospedaletto
12 Santa Vigna
13
14 Mus. dell'Inst. Ellénico
15
16 La Pietà

S. Maria del Pianto

S. Lazzaro Mendicanti

SS. Giovanni e Paolo

S. Francesco della Vigna

S. Lorenzo

S. Martino

S. Antonin

S. Giovanni in Brágora

S. MARCO

S. MARCO GIARDINETTI

S. MARCO VALLARESSO

ning carnival masks and Murano glass, the remoter parts of Castello are falling silent as workshops close. However, the eastern area is also the greenest in Venice, with classical gardens, wide waterfronts and the site of the Biennale exhibition. Castello's diversity is encapsulated by its bars: choose a drink in the Danieli, the haunt of the literati, or an *ombretta* of white wine in a secluded neighbourhood bar, under the sole gaze of a Venetian cat.

The Bridge of Sighs

Just beyond the Doge's Palace is the **Ponte dei Sospiri** (Bridge of Sighs) ❶, the most famous bridge in Venice. It crosses the canal to the "new" prisons, providing a link between the Doge's Palace, court-rooms and cells, allowing interrogators to slip back and forth. Built between 1595 and 1600, this covered stone bridge acquired its legendary name after the lamentation of prisoners as they confronted their inquisitors. In reality, by the standards of the day, the prisons were relatively comfortable. The **New Prisons**, designed

to hold the overspill from the "old" prisons in the Doge's Palace, occupy a sober, classical building. The **Old Prisons**, from which Casanova *(see page 42)* made his dramatic escape, were known as *I Piombi* (The Leads), because they were built right under the lead roofs of the palace.

The bridge marks the beginning of **Riva degli Schiavoni** ❷, the best-known stretch of Venetian waterfront. Now bustling with tourists and souvenir sellers, this sweeping quayside once thronged with slave dealers and merchants. Its name refers either to slaves or Slavs, who were often synonymous in Venetian minds. Certainly, the term came to embrace the Dalmatian merchants from Schiavonia, modern-day Croatia, who settled in Venice in great numbers during the 15th century. The quayside was widened and paved in 1782, and has been a popular Venetian promenade ever since.

Nor can visitors avoid the waterfront, since it is the focal point of ferry routes, and of the latter-day merchants of Venice who erect souvenir stalls along its length. As the

Map on page 128

"A Venetian gondola? That singular conveyance came down unchanged from ballad times, black as nothing else on earth except a coffin."

–THOMAS MANN

BELOW: view towards St Mark's along Riva degli Schiavoni.

Poisoned daggers were used by Venetian secret police: when inserted into a victim's body, the glass dagger would snap off and leave virtually no trace of the fatal wound.

RIGHT: the Londra Palace has "a hundred windows on the lagoon."

hub of upmarket tourism, the Riva is lined with distinguished hotels, all vying for the cocktail clientele *(see page 218)*.

The Hotel Danieli

The **Danieli** is the most historic hotel in Venice, with even Proust enchanted by his room: "When I went to Venice I found that my dream had become – incredibly but quite simply – my address." The Danieli was also the scene of an unhappy love affair between George Sand and Alfred de Musset in 1883.

During the Liberation, in 1945, grand hotels were commandeered as officers' clubs, with the Danieli becoming the New Zealand headquarters. The terrace still remains a superb place to toast the ending of a war or the beginning of a romance.

Over the next bridge stands a well-known landmark, the horseback monument to Vittorio Emanuele, the first king of a united Italy. Behind lies the restrained **Londra Palace** hotel, with balconies overlooking the island of San Giorgio and lights reflected in the lagoon waters. The waterfront is

awash with literary and musical links, from Wagner and Tchaikovsky to Dickens. Henry James stayed further along the Riva (at 4145) while finishing *The Portrait of a Lady*. Here, "in the fruitless fidget of composition", he was distracted by "the waterside life, the wondrous lagoon spread before me, and the ceaseless human chatter at my windows".

The **Museo Diocesano di Arte Sacra** ❸ (Mon–Sat 10.30am–12.30pm), the Museum of Sacred Art, is tucked away on Ponte della Canonica, behind the Doge's Palace and Riva degli Schiavoni. The Romanesque cloisters of this canalside museum form an oasis of calm amidst the bustle of San Marco. Ranged around the cloisters are fragments of early medieval sculptures from San Marco, as well as Roman and Byzantine statuary. The museum displays works salvaged from deconsecrated churches along with mannerist and baroque art.

From here follow Salizzada San Provolo east to Campo San Zaccaria. En route are several simple inns, including Alla Rivetta, noted

Rooms with a View

St Mark's Square was described by Napoleon as "the finest drawing room in Europe", which must make the Riva degli Schiavoni its sumptuous bedroom. Here the Danieli was favoured by Wagner, Dickens, Proust, Debussy, Cocteau and Balzac. Here, too, George Sand and Alfred de Musset famously fell in and out of love. Today the Danieli still attracts the rich and famous. Next door is the charming Londra Palace, with "a hundred windows on the lagoon". In splendid rooms overlooking San Giorgio, Tchaikovsky composed his Fourth Symphony. The grand Venetian hotels are still the place to strike a pose, perhaps starting with the Luna Baglioni, which claims to be the oldest hotel in Venice, dating back to Templar times.

On the Grand Canal is the Gritti Palace, once favoured by Ruskin, Hemingway and Graham Greene. Over the water on the Giudecca is the Cipriani, the choice for guests who want luxurious seclusion. Yet even the most illustrious visitors once faced night-time horrors: "The great business before going to bed was the hunt for insects, vicious mosquitoes that particularly torment foreigners, on whom they hurl themselves with the sensual appetite of a gourmet." Fortunately, poet Théophile Gautier's experiences are lost to modern visitors.

for its cuttlefish and polenta (*see page 141*).

San Zaccaria ❹ (Mon–Sat 10am–noon, 4–6pm) is a delightful church graced by Coducci's curvilinear facade. This Renaissance masterpiece conceals a far older basilica, with Byzantine and Gothic churches fused into a harmonious Renaissance whole. Fortunately, elements of earlier incarnations remain. The church was founded in the 9th century, and acted as a Venetian pantheon, with eight early doges buried in the crypt. The original Byzantine basilica forms the crypt below San Tarasio chapel, an atmospheric spot usually lying underwater. The chapel itself is decorated with Gothic frescos and three lovely 15th-century altarpieces.

In the north aisle of the main church, which is essentially Gothic, is Bellini's glowing altarpiece of the *Madonna and Child*. The attractive square is completed by a Gothic belltower.

It is hard to associate this peaceful square with its sinister reputation for skulduggery and licence. Three doges were assassinated in the vicinity, while the adjoining Benedictine convent was a byword for lascivious living. Since noblewomen were frequently dispatched to nunneries to save money on dowries, tales of libertine nuns were rife. Venetian attempts to stem the scandals were half-hearted: although chaplains and confessors had to be in their fifties or older, younger sons were made welcome at the convent's masked balls; the aristocracy encouraged such illicit liaisons as a means of keeping the family estate intact. The nuns' parlour became a celebrated social salon, as portrayed in Guardi's famous painting in Ca' Rezzonico. Men are still made welcome in the former convent: the *carabinieri* barracks sacrilegiously occupy the Renaissance cloisters, linked to the church by a graceful open loggia.

A Gothic portal leads to bustling Campo San Provolo, which opens onto the charming quayside of **Fondamenta dell'Osmarin** ❺, notable for the **Palazzo Priuli**, a superb late-Gothic palace commanding the corner of Rio di San Severo and San

Shop sign of a 'mascheraio'. Mask-makers had their own guild in medieval times.

BELOW: Ca' del Sol mask workshop on the Fondamenta dell'Osmarin.

The baroque campanile of Santa Maria Formosa.

BELOW: *The Geography Lesson*, by Longhi, in the Querini-Stampalia gallery.

Provolo. From the bridge over Rio dei Greci is a view of the radically restored Gothic **Palazzo Zorzi** on the right, now a boutique hotel.

Across the bridge is **San Giorgio dei Greci ❻** (daily 9.30am–1pm, 3.30–5.30pm), the Greek Orthodox church, distinguished by its dome and tilting baroque tower. The Greeks represent one of the oldest ethnic communities in Venice, even if they have only been established within this enclosure since 1526.

After the Turkish conquest of Constantinople in 1453, the Venetian Greek community expanded greatly, working as merchants, scribes and scholars; in fact, only the Jews formed a larger ethnic group. The Greek contribution to Venetian culture can be seen in scholarship and printing, as well as in the production of icons and mosaics.

The 16th-century church has a tall, narrow facade and early-Renaissance purity. In keeping with Orthodox tradition, the interior has a *barco* or *matroneo*, a women's gallery, and an iconostasis, an exotic 16th-century screen separating the sanctuary from

the nave. This intimate church comes alive during the vibrant Easter festivals, when the stylised, golden interior and the scent of incense create a heady exoticism. Wagner visited the church shortly before his death, and was disturbed by the oriental pomp and the mysterious mood created by the dark dome and flickering haloes of saints. An elegantly walled square encloses the church and a cluster of cultural buildings, including the Hellenic Institute, a museum of icons and a tiny Greek cemetery.

The **Museo Dipinti Sacri Bizantini** (daily 9am–5pm), the Icon Museum, is housed in the former Greek *scuola,* or confraternity house, now run by the Hellenic Institute. The confraternity chapter house has kept its baroque decor, while the museum displays an outstanding collection of 16th- and 17th-century Cretan works, which illustrate the synthesis of Greek and Venetian art.

Just around the corner is Da Remigio, a cosy trattoria noted for its gnocchi *(see page 141).* From here, cross Rio dei Greci to Fondamenta dell'Osmarin, before taking the second bridge on the right into **Ruga Giuffa**, a narrow alley with overhanging roofs. This is both an everyday shopping street and Venice at its most insular. Although only a stone's-throw from San Marco, it feels like a private world, deeply Venetian yet historically linked to the Armenian community. The street, now noted for its food shops, was once populated by Armenian cloth merchants, and named after an Armenian enclave in Persia.

Querini-Stampalia gallery

Just before Santa Maria Formosa, turn left into Calle dietro Magazen, which rounds the canal to Calle Querini and comes out at the **Fondazione Querini-Stampalia ❼** (Tues–Sun 10am–6pm, Fri–Sat 10am–10pm). This is one of the best

small galleries in Venice, intimate, eclectic, uncrowded, and a tranquil coffee stop. The Querini belonged to the ancient nobility, the families who elected the first doge. However, a foiled plot led to the dynasty's banishment to the Greek island of Stampalia, a title they later appended. The last count died in 1868 and bequeathed his home to the city.

Count Giovanni left his stamp on this Renaissance palace, from the new library to the gallery hung with family portraits and Venetian paintings, mainly 17th- and 18th-century genre scenes. Highlights include a poetic Bellini painting and the festive and domestic scenes of Gabriele Bella (1730–99). Several famous works by Longhi include *The Geography Lesson* and *The Ridotto*, depicting masqueraders at the Casino. The count's taste in furniture is typical of the refined yet relatively spartan interiors favoured by the nobility.

Given such pared-down chic, it is fitting that the ground floor was remodelled by Carlo Scarpa, the Venetian modernist architect, in the 1960s, creating an airy atrium and a Japanese minimalist garden. Evening classical concerts are held in the frescoed main salon while the chic café is also recommended *(see page 141)*.

Santa Maria Formosa

Campo Santa Maria Formosa ❽, the next square north, is a lovely assymetrical space dotted with flower, fruit and junk stalls. Rivalled only by Campo Santa Margherita and Campo San Giacomo dell'Orio, this is the archetypal Venetian square. Set in the heart of Castello, this *campo* provided a backdrop for traditional festivities, from masked balls to bear-baiting. Today, the square rests on its laurels, sure of each Venetian element: the shadowy alleys running into a sunlit space, a striking Renaissance church, palaces from three different periods, a covered well-head surrounded by pigeons, unpretentious cafés filled with stallholders and visitors alike, a small market, and even a gondola station *(stazio)*.

The **Palazzo Vitturi** (5246) is a 13th-century affair decorated with Gothic and Moorish motifs. The **Palazzo Trevisan** (5250) is a Renais-

"I love the cats of Venice, peering from their pedestals, sunning themselves on the feet of statues."

—JAN MORRIS

BELOW: Campo Santa Maria Formosa.

Antonio Vivaldi

Rarely does *The Four Seasons* fall on fresh ears, but it often falls on deaf ones. As one of the world's best-known pieces of classical music, its fate has been sealed. Its sin was to be too successful. The concerto is a cliché of tasteful background music, signalling anything from seduction to a sophisticated dining experience. The Venetian composer, no slouch at seduction or celebrity, would have been secretly pleased at such popularity.

Although his work acted as a model for future followers, J.S. Bach among them, Vivaldi's music soon suffered a decline, and was only rescued from oblivion in 1926. It seems inconceivable that the works of such a celebrated composer could have been lost for nearly 200 years. To contemporary critics, Vivaldi (1678–1741) is one of the most important composers of late-baroque music. Now a new generation of classical violinists has managed to infuse his work with passion.

Vivaldi's great musical talent was encouraged by his father, Giovan Battista, a barber whose playing was good enough to gain him a place in the orchestra of St Mark's Basil-ica. His son was nurtured in the Venetian musical tradition and, as a budding violin virtuoso, allowed to stand in for his father. The young man entered the priesthood, which gave him time to devote to music, and he was widely known as *il prete rosso*, the red-haired priest.

Vivaldi devoted himself to composition and obtained a post as composer and violin teacher at the Ospedale della Pietà, a famous charitable institution. At once an exclusive girls' conservatoire and an orphanage, it was one of several schools where gifted orphans were elevated from poverty to careers in music. It proved so popular that a plaque had to be erected threatening heaven's wrath on parents who passed off their offspring as foundlings. Vivaldi spent 40 years here, coaxing fine performances from choir and orchestra and introducing his compositions to a wide public.

Vivaldi's relationship with the Ospedale began superbly, with universal acclaim for his concertos, sonatas and sacred music, including oratorios. His gift for melody made him successful in most fields of music, but his favourite instrument remained the violin. However, within 10 years the administration had become aggrieved by the maestro's new star status, his avoidance of Mass and his worldliness.

His reversal of fortune came with allegations of improper conduct with a pupil from Mantua, Anna Girò, a soprano who sang in his operas. The affair damaged his reputation as a teacher, priest and establishment figure. In his disappointment, Vivaldi turned his back on Venice and escaped to concert tours in Paris, Dresden, Prague and finally Vienna, where he died in poverty in 1741.

La Pietà, Vivaldi's musical base in Venice, was remodelled shortly after his death, but his chamber music is still performed in the newly restored church, beneath the splendid Tiepolo ceiling *(see page 140)*. Next door, the composer's home has become the Vivaldi Hotel, an act of blatant commercialism which would probably have found favour with the maestro. ❏

LEFT: *il prete rosso*, the musical red-haired priest whose downfall was caused by a soprano.

sance palace studded with slender columns and ornamentation. On the Rialto end, above Ponte del Paradiso, stands a delicate Gothic archway.

The parish church of **Santa Maria Formosa** (Mon–Sat 10am–5pm, Sun 1–5pm) is an especially endearing sight, with its eccentrically bulging apses. The foundations may date from the 9th century, but the church was redesigned by Coducci, the great Renaissance architect, and acquired a baroque belltower with a grotesque mask at its base. While the canalside facade is by Coducci, the *campo* facade was added in 1604. The cool grey-and-white marble interior contains a Vivarini *Madonna* (1473) and a chapel set aside for students "to pay a little visit on the way to school".

The canalside café beside the church makes a good coffee stop, the place to listen to passing musicians or the backchat of gondoliers waiting for business on their *stazio*.

San Zanipolo (Santi Giovanni e Paolo)

From the square, follow Calle Santa Maria Formosa north across Rio di San Giovanni to **Campo Santi Giovanni e Paolo ⑨**. Familiarly known as Zanipolo, this is one of the most monumental squares in Venice. While less intimate than Santa Maria Formosa, it is far more impressive architecturally. This spectacular square occupies land given to the Dominicans by Doge Orseolo in 1234, and encloses a great Gothic church and Renaissance confraternity, as well as the finest equestrian statue in northern Italy.

This restless horse and rider commemorate **Bartolomeo Colleoni** (1400–76), a celebrated *condottiere* (mercenary soldier) whose bequest to the city came with a stipulation that a monument be erected to him on St Mark's Square. The rider has reason to be restless: the authorities cunningly relegated the idealised

Renaissance statue to this lesser spot, outside St Mark's confraternity.

The *campo* possesses yet another Renaissance treasure, a sculpted well-head attributed to Sansovino, which, like the equine monument and the confraternity seat nearby, is swathed under scaffolding. Any disappointment can be remedied by a visit to Rosa Salva, a historic café set in a Gothic palace *(see page 141)*. Sweet pastries form a prelude to feasting on the city's most authentic Gothic church.

Santi Giovanni e Paolo (Mon–Sat 7.30am–12.30pm, 3–6.30pm, Sun 3–7pm) is also known as **San Zanipolo**, a conflation of Saints John and Paul, to whom the church is dedicated. Sheer size and scale invite comparisons with the Frari, its fellow giant *(see page 159)*. This, too, is an austere church, founded in the late 13th century but only consecrated in 1430. The Gothic pinnacles can be seen from both banks of the Grand Canal, with the roof line displaying statues of the Dominican saints. Close up, the plain brickwork of the church is enlivened by a 14th-century poly-

The Colleoni equestrian statue was sculpted by Verrocchio, but, in his rage at only being asked to sculpt the warhorse, not the rider, he smashed his first attempt.

BELOW: the equestrian statue of Colleoni outside San Zanipolo.

The Cappella San Domenico, in San Zanipolo.

gonal apse. The main portal incorporates Byzantine columns and ornamentation salvaged from Torcello. While characterised by a lofty nave and sparse decoration, the interior is initially more coherent and welcoming that of the Frari. The cross-vaulted ceilings are supported by wooden tie beams and stone pillars.

The church is considered the Pantheon of Venice, honouring illustrious leaders, from admirals and noblemen to the occasional State artist, notably Bellini. Above all, this was the last resting place of the doges, with the pomp of State funerals matched by magnificent monuments to 25 doges. Among the profusion of funerary monuments is the sculpted Renaissance tomb of Doge Giovanni Mocenigo, close to the main portal. Made by the Lombardi family of master-craftsmen in 1500, it is one of many monuments to the powerful Mocenigo dynasty.

In the right aisle, also close to the main portal, is a memorial to Marcantonio Bragadin, the garrison commander flayed alive by the Turks in Cyprus in 1571. In the chancel, by the baroque high altar, lies the finest Renaissance funerary monument in Venice, dedicated to Doge Andrea Vendramin, who died in 1478. Diagonally opposite is the tomb of Doge Michele Morosini, a victim of the 1382 plague. This was the Gothic monument most admired by Ruskin.

The **Chapel of the Rosary**, at the end of the north transept, was built to commemorate the Venetian victory over the Turks in 1571. Over the entrance is the funerary monument to Doge Sebastiano Venier, who commanded the fleet at Lepanto.

The chapel once contained works by Titian and Tintoretto but, after a tragic fire, these were replaced with ceiling panels by Veronese, considered the most pagan and joyous of Venetian painters. The church interior is enriched by other works of art, including Vivarini's *Christ Bearing the Cross* (1474). A controversial Veronese *Last Supper* was painted for this church but is now in the Accademia *(see pages 188–9).* In the right aisle, Bellini's gorgeous *St Vincent Ferrier* altarpiece survives, set in its original gilded frame.

The Scuola Grande di San Marco

The unadorned facade of Zanipolo is flanked by the ornate **Scuola Grande di San Marco ⑩**, once the richest Venetian confraternity, but now mired in long-term restoration. The facade, only partially visible, has become a victim of its beauty: precious marble weathers badly in the damp Venetian climate. This *scuola* is the exception to the rule that Venetian interiors are finer than exteriors.

The confraternity retains its *trompe l'œil* Renaissance facade as well as its assembly rooms and chapter house. Coducci designed the curved crowning of the facade in 1490, conceivably inspired by the domes of St Mark's. The sumptuous marble lower section was decorated by the Lombardi brothers. In keeping with the charitable aims of the confraternity, it is fitting that the city hospital should now be based here.

A grand portal framed by illusionistic lions leads into the hushed hospital, with the foyer occupying the cloisters of the former Dominican foundation. To visit the former *scuola*, slip past reception and walk upstairs to check the current opening times posted on the door of the medical library, housed in the panelled, 16th-century assembly rooms.

From here, **Fondamenta dei Mendicanti** leads past a *squero,* or gondola boatyard, and the hospital chapel of San Lazzaro. Beyond lie the bleak jetties of **Fondamente Nuove**, with fast boat services to the islands. From the canal-side are occasional views of hospital cases arriving by water ambulance.

Alternatively, from San Zanipolo follow Barbaria delle Tole to the cunningly concealed **Ospedaletto ⑪** (Thurs–Sat, 3.30–6.30pm), set in a hospice. This was one of four famous Ospedali, charitable institutions that acted as orphanages and prestigious music conservatoires. The frescoed Sala della Musica formed the main concert hall and can still be visited, ideally for a concert. The ponderous baroque facade of the adjoining Ospedaletto church is attributed to Longhena. Ruskin dismissed these leering masks as "the most monstrous example of the Grotesque Renaissance… the sculptures on its facade representing masses of diseased figures and swollen fruit". The church interior is decorated with 17th- and 18th-century paintings, including an early work by Tiepolo.

Barbaria delle Tole leads east across Rio di Santa Giustina to **San Francesco della Vigna ⑫** (8am–noon, 3.30–7pm), set in an isolated, somewhat shabby area. Goethe even required a compass to reach this remote spot. However, this Franciscan church represents an architectural milestone, both Sansovino's first creation in Venice and the first flowering of the High Renaissance in Venice. The facade and crowning pediment were designed by Palladio, while the tall belltower is a familiar city landmark. San Francesco is a hallowed

Map on page 128

Although the "scuole" (see page 158) were confraternities not guilds, the arts and crafts were well represented, from glassmakers to goldsmiths, stone-cutters to fritter-makers.

BELOW: canalside arcade.

To find a ferry or gondola, return to the Riva degli Schiavoni.

BELOW: dining alfresco on Fondamenta San Lorenzo.

site, built on vineyards associated with a mysterious visit by St Mark. The present building was founded in 1534 by Doge Andrea Gritti, the Renaissance scholar and notorious womaniser. "We cannot make a doge of a man with three bastards in Turkey," declared one envious rival.

The church was built in accordance with NeoPlatonic ideals, using the precision of proportional relationships based on the number three: even the width of the aisles corresponds to a third of their height. The cool but harmonious interior contains a monument to the doge (who died from a surfeit of grilled eels), as well as a clutch of paintings by Venetian masters, from Vivarini to Tiepolo.

Highlights include sculptures from the Lombardi school, Veronese's *Holy Family*, and a *Madonna and Child* by Negroponte (1450). The lovely Gothic cloisters lead to the Cappella Santa where a Bellini *Madonna* can be found.

Behind the church lies a depressing stretch of urban wasteland, with canal-sides abutting one of the oldest walled sections of the Arsenale, out of bounds to visitors. From here, cross Rio del Fontego to the south to **San Lorenzo** ⑬, the presumed burial place of Marco Polo. Since the discovery of ancient foundations in 1987, the deconsecrated church has been undergoing a lengthy restoration. San Lorenzo was also the site of another lax convent, while the canal is flanked by fine palaces, including the police headquarters, which often feature in contemporary thrillers, including best-sellers by a resident writer, Donna Leon.

From here, Fondamenta San Giorgio hugs the canal south to **San Giorgio degli Schiavoni** ⑭ (Tues–Sat 9.30am–12.30pm, 3.30–6.30pm, Sun 9.30am–12.30pm; closed Mon). Tucked into Calle dei Furlani is the loveliest confraternity seat in Venice. The *scuola* was intended to protect the interests of Slavs from Dalmatia (Schiavonia), the first Venetian colony. This community of sailors, skilled artisans and merchants was first accommodated by the Knights of Malta in the building behind San Giorgio before prosperity spurred them to build their own headquarters.

On its completion in 1501, the confraternity commissioned a painting cycle in honour of the Dalmatian patron saints, St George, St Tryphon and St Jerome. As the foremost painter of cycles, Carpaccio was chosen to decorate the upper gallery but, after the *scuola* was rebuilt in 1551, his masterpieces were moved downstairs. Despite remodelling, the *scuola* retains its authentic atmosphere and boasts the only Venetian pictorial cycle to have survived in the building for which it was painted.

Carpaccio's narrative cycle

Carpaccio's vibrant works are displayed in a mysterious, intimate setting, below a coffered ceiling. Unlike his superb cycle in the Accademia *(see pages 188–9)*, a portrayal of pomp, pageantry and everyday life,

this cycle is characterised by dramatic storytelling. In particular, the *St George and the Dragon* paintings are bold chivalric scenes *(see page 56)*, with a captivating depiction of a veritable knight in shining armour, a dying dragon and a place of desolation, with the ground littered with skulls, vipers and vultures. Equally beguiling is the St Jerome trilogy, with *The Miracle of the Lion* showing the saint extracting a thorn from the lion's paw. Despite the scene's presumed eastern setting, Carpaccio has included San Giorgio and the Knights of Malta.

The Vision of St Jerome is both one of the most engaging works and his masterpiece, conveying a mood of contemplative calm and a Tuscan sense of space combined with Flemish realism. St Augustine is depicted in his study writing to St Jerome when a heavenly voice announces his imminent death. Carpaccio shows his customary accuracy in the depiction of a Renaissance humanist's study, from the bookspines to the astrolabes and musical scores. The perky Maltese dog by the saint's feet evokes the Knights of Malta, whose headquarters still lie next door. The upstairs room, hung with minor works and the confraternity pennant, is more memorable for the panelled ceiling and sound of cooing doves.

Behind San Giorgio stands **San Giovanni di Malta**, the secretive seat of the Knights of Malta. The members not only contributed to San Giorgio but continue to have close links with the confraternity.

Fondamenta dei Furlani winds south to Salizzada Sant'Antonin and **San Giovanni in Bragora** ⓰ (Mon–Sat 9–11am, 3.30–5.30pm). This treasured parish church is set on a quiet *campo* beside a handsome Gothic palace. The austere church is essentially late Gothic, despite 9th-century foundations and a Renaissance presbytery. The interior is notable for its ship's-keel ceiling and Renaissance works of art, a style which reached Venice later than elsewhere. While Bartolomeo Vivarini's *Madonna and Saints* (1478) is a stiff, Byzantine-style work, his nephew Alvise shows humanist leanings in his *Resurrection* (1498),

Map on page 128

TIP

All'Aciughetta (Campo Santi Filippo e Giacomo) is an atmospheric inn for a rustic meal or authentic bar snacks, such as tiny, anchovy-encrusted pizzas, stuffed peppers, as well as fine wines and cheeses.

BELOW: Carpaccio's *The Vision of St Jerome.*

Map
on page
128

Pulpit of La Pietà.

BELOW: Riva degli
Schiavoni with the
waterfront church of
La Pietà, once Vivaldi's
musical base.

a dynamic High Renaissance altarpiece. Adorning the high altar is Cima da Conegliano's *Baptism of Christ* (1492), set against a realistic mountain landscape.

Mouldering in a chapel on the right lies the mummified corpse of St John the Almsgiver. However, the church of St John is keener to proclaim birth than death: Vivaldi was baptised in the red marble font, as the proudly displayed copies of the baptismal register prove.

Calle del Dose leads back to bustling Riva degli Schiavoni and **La Pietà** ⓖ (9.30am–noon, 4–6pm), a newly restored church with even stronger Vivaldi connections. The Ospedale della Pietà was the most famous of the Ospedali, institutions that combined the roles of orphanage and musical conservatoire. The church was the backdrop for the concerts given by the choir of orphan girls under Vivaldi's tutelage. After the composer was accused of improper conduct with one of his pupils, the ensuing scandal damaged his reputation as a teacher, priest and establishment figure, leading Vivaldi

to turn his back on Venice for ever.

The church was superbly remodelled by Massari shortly after Vivaldi's death in 1741, and transformed into the city's leading concert hall. The cool, oval interior was designed with acoustics in mind, enhanced by curving lines, low-vaulted ceilings, a vestibule that muffled the street noise, and the filigree-like choir galleries. Since Massari won the commission to rebuild the church in 1735, while Vivaldi was still in residence, it is perhaps not too fanciful to presume that the composer advised the architect on acoustic refinements.

The gleaming gold-and-white interior is crowned by Tiepolo's *The Triumph of Faith* (1775). In the dazzling fresco, the figures appear to come alive and billow into the church itself. Although Vivaldi never lived to see the completion of this church, the young chamber orchestra that plays here now does its best to invoke the master's spirit. The fine acoustics can be appreciated during one of the frequent baroque concerts *(see page 134).* ❏

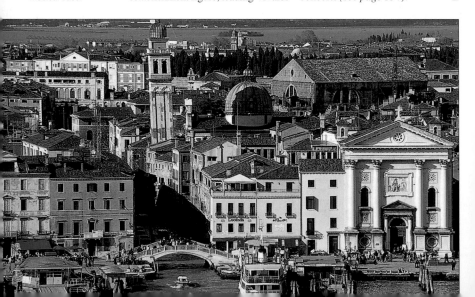

RESTAURANTS & BARS

Restaurants

L'Aciugheta
Campo San Filippo e Giacomo. Tel: 041-522 4292. Closed Mon. €–€€
This unpretentious, value-for-money *bacaro* goes against type by boasting space, a terrace and a proper menu with plenty of choice. It's popular with Venetians, tempted by the fine Friuli wines, Adriatic fish, oysters, truffles and cheeses.

La Corte Sconta
Calle del Pestrin. Tel: 041-522 7024. Closed Sun and Mon. €€€
A renowned yet authentic temple of gastronomy, tucked into a secret courtyard, with a cheerful atmosphere and a menu based on fish fresh from Chioggia market. Tuck into fishy antipasti, from scallops and calamari to sea snails, shrimps and sardines. Book.

Do Leoni
Hotel Londra Palace, Riva degli Schiavoni. Tel: 041-520 0533. Closed Tues in winter. €€€
This revamped restaurant enjoys fine lagoon views and maintains its Venetian character while pleasing international tastes. Fans of Venetian food with a contemporary twist can sample *sarde in saor* and *risi e bisi* as well as seafood grills and gnocchi with shrimps, plus classic Italian fare.

Service is attentive yet discreet, with an informal mood on the terrace. Live music in the evenings.

Enoteca Mascareta
Calle Lunga Santa Maria Formosa. Tel: 041-523 0744. D only (7pm–2am). Closed Thurs. €€
A cosy, rustic wine bar, run by wine buff and wine writer Mauro Lorenzon, with cold cuts or cheeses at the counter, or a select Michelin-inspired menu including bean soup, lasagne and fish at the table. The convivial host, laid-back jazz and the superb wines (all available by the glass) ensure a contented clientele.

Osteria Al Mascaron
Calle Lunga Santa Maria Formosa. Tel: 041-522 5995. No credit cards. Closed Sun. €€
Set in a lively area, this is an ideal introductory Venetian inn. Old-fashioned gentrified-rustic wine bar and inn with friendly but leisurely service, fine wines and reliable cooking. Try the fresh antipasti, bean soup, mixed grill – and the Burano biscuits dipped in dessert wine.

Osteria di Santa Marina
Campo Santa Marina. Tel: 041-528 5239. Closed all Sun and Mon L. €€–€€€
Set in a quiet square, this welcoming new-wave *bacaro* presents reinterpretations of dishes from the Veneto, from seafood ravioli to tuna-and-bean soup

and mixed grills; in summer, sit outside and end with a sorbet or cinnamon apple pie.

Da Remigio
Salizzada dei Greci. Tel: 041-523 0089. Closed Mon D and all Tues. €€
This erstwhile simple trattoria is a local favourite but no longer a secret. Set in a newly revitalised area, the authentic menu includes both meat and Venetian dishes such as grilled fish, with gnocchi a house speciality. Service can be slow but the welcome is genuine. Book.

Alla Rivetta
Ponte San Provolo. Tel: 041-528 7302. Closed Mon. €–€€
Set on the bridge across Rio del Vin, between Campo Santi Filippo e Giacomo and Campo San Provolo, this is an unpretentious place. Despite being close to San Marco, the breezy atmosphere makes it un-touristy. Fish and seafood predominate (grills and cuttlefish), as do polenta and plates of roast vegetables. Trade is brisk and service a touch brusque.

La Terrazza
Hotel Danieli, Riva degli Schiavoni. Tel: 041-522 6480. €€€€
The view alone is worth it: the rooftop terrace of this historic hotel overlooks St Mark's Basin. Highlights of the Mediterranean-inspired cuisine are the

antipasti, chosen from the buffet, the fish soup and the seafood. Book.

Bars & Cafés

Many top hotel bars line Riva degli Schiavoni, but are best in the evening (see *Nightlife*, page 225). **Cichetteria Sara** (Salizzada dei Greci) is a friendly, female-run bar for a sandwich and *spritz* on the run. **Florian Art Caffè**, set in the quirky Querini-Stampalia gallery, is the only branch of Florian, and a peaceful place for coffee or a quick bite. **Zanzibar** (Campo Santa Maria Formosa) remains a lively canalside kiosk-bar for a sandwich, giant *spritz* and eclectic background music. **Inishark Irish Pub** (Calle del Mondo Novo, evenings only) is fake but fun, at least if you're in the mood for Guinness and a live screening of Italian football. **Rosa Salva** (Campo Santi Giovanni e Paolo) is the original Venetian pasticceria, serving coffee, pastries, cakes and ice cream.

PRICE CATEGORIES

Prices for three-course dinner per person with a half-bottle of house wine:
€ = under €30
€€ = €30–€50
€€€ = €50–€70
€€€€ = more than €70

EASTERN CASTELLO

Dominated by the Arsenale shipyards, this elusive district has a scattering of important sites, including the rewarding Naval Museum and the international exhibition pavilions of the Biennale

Map on page 143

BELOW:
a quiet washing-festooned corner.

Venetian romantics call this disparate district "real Venice". Although pockets overlooking the prettier canals near the historic shipyards have been gentrified, much of the neighbourhood beyond is like walking back into a 1950s time warp. Un-designer washing waves in the breeze, and baggy underwear is on sale, along with the sort of checked gingham tablecloths last seen in postwar Mafia movies.

Outlying Eastern Castello is a complex blend of the homely and the international. The district embraces arty geranium-clad cottages on the San Marco side and gritty working-class tenements further east. If the remote island of San Pietro is home to an insular, boat-building community, bustling Via Garibaldi still feels like a forgotten Venice, barely grazed by tourism. Yet plonked beside all this cosy domesticity is the self-conscious internationalism of the Biennale pavilions. And, at its very centre, is the Arsenale, an amalgam of secret military base and shipyards.

Urban regeneration schemes, especially arts complexes, are regularly proposed for the Arsenale, but initiatives are hampered by the secrecy surrounding the site. Still, unless your goal is the Biennale, this is a place for moods not monuments, and daydreams about Venetian naval might.

The district around the naval complex contains a stretch of factory-like modular housing designed for the former Arsenale workers, whose skills were so valued that they were offered jobs for life. One of the newest quarters lies further east, with the ancient island of San Pietro on the outskirts. Napoleonic redevelopment and land-reclamation schemes created the streets and the public gardens that line the eastern waterfront. Following French demolition projects, the Austrians dutifully reclaimed swathes of the watery marsh off Sant'Elena. Intended as a military parade ground, this former island has now succumbed to development, and is home to the city's lacklustre football club.

The Arsenale

Arsenal is a term that the Venetians have bequeathed to the Western world. Although the oldest dockyard of the Venetian **Arsenale** ❶, the Darsena Vecchio, still exists, the Darsena Nuovo and Nuovissimo now form a single basin, swallowed up by the Darsena Grande. Today the site is mainly used as a sheltered anchorage for battleships. In the late 1990s, ships were dispatched from Venice to Albania and former Yugoslavia.

Previously a forbidden zone, public access remains restricted, but two ferries pass through the naval complex. Since the Arsenale remains a working base, naval school and shipyards, officers and crew can be seen strolling around.

The best way to see the Arsenale is to get off at the *vaporetto* stop, Arscnale, on the Riva degli Schiavoni, and wander down to the wooden bridge that stands opposite the entrance to the heart of the complex. Unfortunately, the *vaporetto* no longer runs through this closed military zone, but you can get a good view from the middle of the bridge, and, who knows, you may even meet a friendly naval officer who might let you take a peek inside. The sense of desolation is partly due to the Napoleonic devastation, when buildings and ships were set on fire and cannons and bronzes melted down.

Just east, running along Rio della Tana, stands the hulking **Tana** (or **Corderie**), the former rope-and-cable factory that was founded as a hemp warehouse. Here, hemp plants were carded and spun before being passed to master cordwainers, who made the ropes and hawsers. This functional space was redesigned in the 1540s by

Fifteenth-century engraving of a Venetian cog. As Venetians grew wealthier, it became harder to find native oarsmen. By the 16th century, Dalmatian and Greek crews gave way to convicts who were dragooned into service.

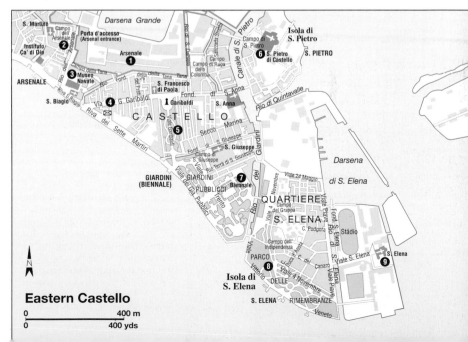

Eastern Castello

0   400 m
0   400 yds

The Arsenale

The Arsenale was the symbol of Venetian maritime might. Founded in 1104, this secretive military and naval complex became Europe's largest medieval shipyard and a powerhouse of industrial planning. The term "arsenal" derives from the Arabic *darsina'a*, or house of industry, a most suitable description of this Venetian production line.

The Arsenale was a city within a city, bounded by 3 km (2 miles) of walls, with wet and dry docks and ordnance depots that were envied abroad. It was also an armaments site. At its height, 16,000 people toiled in the foundries, gunpowder mills, munitions depots, sail factories, rope-works and grain stores. Industrial bakeries produced the dry Venetian biscuits that were suited to preservation for consumption on long sea voyages but less acceptable to modern palates. The Arsenale's industrial caulkers' vats so impressed Dante that he described them in his *Inferno*, making immersion in the bubbling cauldrons of pitch a hellish punishment for corrupt officials.

Before the creation of the Arsenale, shipbuilding and repairs were often carried out in St Mark's Basin. However, even at the height of its production capacity, the Arsenale was supported by numerous private repair yards, including some on neighbouring islands, especially Murano. However, as far as shipbuilding work was concerned, the state exercised a monopoly, with the Arsenale constructing fleets of ships. This was a vast enterprise that stretched over three docks and spawned several hundred successful chartered-shipping companies.

The Arsenale acted as a medieval production line, manufacturing light galleys, ships of war and merchant vessels. Hulls constructed in the "new" Arsenale were towed past a series of openings in the "old" Arsenale, where they were rigged and fitted out with munitions and food supplies. "From one window the cordage, from another the bread, from another the arms, and from another the mortars", as one impressed visitor described the conveyor-belt system in 1436.

Everything from oars and sails to barrels of biscuits was loaded by means of a pulley system; at the end, the galleys would be ready to sail. In its 16th-century heyday, the Arsenale could deliver a fully rigged galley in a day. In 1574, the Venetians clearly impressed Henri III of France by producing a seaworthy vessel complete with a 16,000-pound cannon in the time it took him to devour a state banquet.

Such pioneering methods of prefabricated construction were dependent on a highly skilled workforce. The *arsenalotti* comprised an artisans' élite of master shipbuilders, caulkers and carpenters. They were staunch loyalists, with a privileged section acting as the doge's guards of honour or pallbearers, and another group operating as firemen. So greatly did the State value the experience and skill of these men, that workers were guaranteed jobs for life.

The 900th anniversary of the Arsenale, in 2004, was greeted with some celebration, as plans to restore the complex were finally given new impetus – thanks to the launch of the MOSE dam project, the mobile barrier which will be constructed in part of the Arsenale. ❏

LEFT: the Arsenale, in an old engraving.

da Ponte, the architect of the Rialto Bridge. Nearby is the newly opened Teatro Piccolo dell'Arsenale and ticket office to the Biennale.

From Campo della Tana, Rio dell' Arsenale leads to **Campo dell'Arsenale ❷**, the entrance to the naval complex, with its impressive fortifications bounded by 16th-century walls and towers. Beyond the footbridge lies the water entrance, framed by crenellated brick towers. These picturesque waterside towers were rebuilt in the 17th century.

Beside the watergate stands the ceremonial **Porta Magna**, the majestic land entrance to the Arsenale. Built in 1460, this triumphal arch is celebrated as the first Renaissance monument in Venice. Yet, with typical Venetian eclecticism, the gateway recycles stolen statuary as well as four Greek marble columns and their Byzantine capitals.

Notwithstanding the Venetian victory at Lepanto in 1571 the Republic undertook defensive fortifications in response to fears of Turkish expansion. As a sign of the warlike mood, the winged Lion of St Mark over the gateway holds a closed book, rather than displaying his traditional message of peace. The gateway was embellished with statues at the same time, with the allegorical figures added a century later. These are believed to have been carved from marble looted from the Parthenon during the 1687 Venetian bombardment of Athens. The land gateway is guarded by two lions pillaged from Piraeus during the same attack by Doge Morosini, admiral of the Venetian fleet. The lion sitting upright to the left of the gateway bears a runic inscription on his shoulder and haunches, probably carved by 11th-century Norse mercenaries who were defending the Byzantine emperor against Greek rebels. The smaller pair of lions on the far right may be Greek booty from Delos dating from the

6th century BC. In 1682, a terrace replaced the medieval drawbridge, setting the seal on this ambitious modernisation programme.

Exploring the mysteries of the Arsenale

This is now as far as unauthorised visitors are allowed to go, as even the *vaporetto* that used to slip between the towers of the grand water entrance has been scrapped. Recently, however, neglected warehouses and historic gunpowder-and-munitions depots have been reclaimed from the military by the city. On Campo della Tana, a cavernous warehouse has been converted into the Teatro Piccolo dell'Arsenale, a venue for music, dance or art exhibitions. Virtually next door is the Corderie Cultural Centre and, by the docks, just within the military zone, are the three newly opened arts venues known as Teatro alle Tese, Artiglierie and Gaggiandre.

The best chance to explore this mysterious black hole is during the Biennale, when much of the Arsenale becomes an exhibition space. While viewing the avant-garde art, allow

Map on page 143

A 6th-century BC lion guards the mighty Arsenale.

BELOW:
Italian naval officers outside the Arsenale.

Venetian maritime traditions glorified the doge and the Republic, and no regatta was complete without the presence of the Bucintoro. This State barge resembled a gilded dragon, or some other mythical beast, with the winged Lion of St Mark on the prow. The doge occupied a throne by the figurehead.The last barge was destroyed by Napoleon in 1797, but a scale model made in 1828 is on display at the Naval Museum.

BELOW:
Admiral Morosini's fleet encounters theTurks in 1659 (from the Naval Museum).

yourself to be sidetracked by the monumental 16th-century boathouse, designed by Sanmicheli, the noted civil and military engineer. Until Napoleon stripped it, the ceremonial State barge, the legendary Bucintoro, was housed here. A pale imitation, also housed here, is paraded down the Grand Canal during the Regata Storica (Historical Regatta).

The central waterway of the Arsenale is the **Canale delle Galeazze**, named after the oar-propelled Venetian galleys, lined by 18th-century shipyards where frigates were made, and the **Cantiere delle Gaggiandre** docks, with their dignified 16th-century arches. These were created after the 1571 Venetian victory at Lepanto, and were capable of dispatching a fleet of warships at a single moment's notice. The most significant building here is Sansovino's magnificently roofed boat-house, designed for the armed patrol craft that protected the lagoon ports.

Consider visiting the underrated Naval Museum. A small detour from the Arsenale takes you back to the waterfront via the site of the former

Arsenale bakeries. These stand at the St Mark's Basin end of **Riva Ca' di Dio** (No. 2179–80). Set on the east bank of the canal, the **Forni Pubblici** date from 1473 and are distinguished by a marble frieze.

According to historian Pompeo Molmenti, one batch of long-lived Venetian navy biscuits was left in Crete in 1669 and discovered to be perfectly edible in 1821. Nearby stand workers' houses first designed for the *arsenalotti*, the Arsenale shipwrights and skilled craftsmen.

The Museo Navale (Naval Museum)

Further along the waterfront stands the dignified **Museo Navale** ❸ (Mon–Fri 8.45am–1.30pm; Sat am only; closed Sun). Given the tantalising elusiveness of the Arsenale, the Naval Museum is the only place where you can fully appreciate the greatness of maritime Venice. Before its present incarnation, the 16th-century building was used as a naval granary and biscuit warehouse. The Austrians created the collection from the scant remnants to survive French depredations. (Many Venetian naval treasures are now displayed in the rival Parisian naval museum.)

The Venetian museum is deceptively spacious, so you may wish to restrict your visit to the lower floors; the top floor is devoted to uniforms, pennants and insignia. Apart from naval maps and nautical instruments, the collection includes a range of weaponry, from 17th-century breech-loaders to heavy cannons and World War II torpedoes. The Venetian antiquarian maps depict the development of the Arsenale and the lagoon defences, while Venetian naval supremacy is illustrated by scenes of naval battles such as Lepanto, and by models of Mediterranean fortresses.

Venetian shipyards generally built boats from models rather than draw-

INSEGVISCE L'ARMATA TVRCA, CHE FVGGE SEBENE PIV TA ARRIVA DVE DELLE PIV GROSSE GALERE FLE

Map
on page
143

ings. Models on display range from early Egyptian and Phoenician craft to Greek triremes and a Venetian galley. Gondolas naturally play a prominent role, including ones of boats built with a *felze*, the wooden cabin that protected passengers from prying eyes and winter weather. One highlight is a scale model of the last Bucintoro, the legendary State barge.

From here, a walk through one of the quietest and greenest parts of the city leads to the site of the Biennale exhibition and to the former city fortress, marooned on the island of San Pietro. Strolling east along **Riva San Biagio** takes you past the colonnaded San Biagio, a Greek church now used as the naval chapel.

On the left is **Via Garibaldi ❹**, the widest street in Venice, occupying a filled-in canal. As the commercial hub of Eastern Castello, this working-class street is lined with basic household shops and friendly bars. On the right is the former home of the Venetian navigators, John and Sebastian Cabot, who explored Newfoundland in 1497.

Viale Garibaldi ❺, a tree-lined avenue further down, is a model of French rationality. Napoleon embellished this area, incidentally demolishing churches and monasteries. The avenue runs down to the Napoleonic gardens, a tree-lined promenade dotted with monuments. In 1834 the novelist George Sand found the park as deserted as most Venetian parks, populated only by "grumbling old men, some senseless smokers or some bilious melancholics".

From here, cross the gardens to the Biennale site, or retreat to an authentic canalside *trattoria* – a good choice is the Hostaria da Franz, which was opened in 1842 by an Austrian soldier who fell in love with a Venetian woman (*see page 149*). Once refreshed, return to Via Garibaldi and cross the bridge to San Pietro, set in the far reaches of Castello. At the first

quaint bridge at the end of the street is a distant view across to the Arsenale, with its cranes, walls and defensive towers. This endearingly shabby district is enlivened by the jaunty fishing boats, workshops and boatyards lining the Canale di San Pietro.

San Pietro and the Biennale

A wooden bridge leads to the island of **San Pietro**, the site of the original castle *(castello)* which gave its name to the district. **San Pietro di Castello ❻** (Mon–Sat 10am–5pm, Sun 1–5pm) rests on ancient foundations but is essentially Palladian, topped by a central dome. From the foundation of Venice until 1807, the church was the city cathedral, with the title only passing to St Mark's after the demise of the Republic. Ironically, this remote island church was the official seat of religious power while the splendid St Mark's Basilica was merely the doge's private chapel. This was the Venetian way of keeping the power of the papacy at one remove, with temporal power centred on the St Mark's district.

Garibaldi in his gardens. The revolutionary leader became the first prime minister of the Kingdom of Italy in 1861, but died shortly after – five years before the annexation of Venice in 1866.

BELOW: cafés on Via Garibaldi, the widest street in Venice.

The Biennale

Every two years, the modern-art merchants of Venice bewilder the world with a swirling morass of work, mostly set in the city's historic naval yards and leafy gardens. For those who prefer the past, Ca' Pesaro, the modern-art museum, now displays the best from the Biennale's early back catalogue.

The Biennale has been described as Disneyland for adults: art-lovers want to play with everything at once and end up suffering from sensory overload. This glamorous summer forum for contemporary art is held in odd-numbered years. Sponsorship is precarious and the event is increasingly politicised, but the Biennale remains a highlight in the international art calendar.

It may be garish, sprawling and pretentious, but it is also chic, challenging and commercially successful. There is a place for everything, from postmodernist lampshades and erotic photography to Armenian video installations, a 3-D Japanese tea ceremony and even a Taiwanese cyberworld staged in the ancient prisons of St Mark's. As at Venice carnival, the festival attracts eccentrics, including two bald Germans who always attend dressed as angels.

The Biennale was designed to give Venice a fresh identity as a vital cultural metropolis within the new Italian nation. It aimed to attract leading artists, boost tourism and introduce an international audience to the wonders of Venice. Inaugurated in 1895 by King Umberto I, the show raised a furore because of Giacomo Grosso's symbolist work depicting women draped lasciviously over a corpse. The event has been controversial ever since.

In 1910 a work by Picasso was rejected for being too scandalous; the great artist was only finally deemed acceptable in 1948. Nevertheless, in the early 1920s the Impressionists were well received, as were Degas and Toulouse-Lautrec. The Fascist period marked the lowest point of the Biennale, with Hitler declaring his "disgust" at the degeneracy of the art. Since World War II, however, the festival has paraded its avant-garde credentials. In 1948 the first post-war Biennale displayed works by Picasso, Klee, Schiele and Magritte, as well as by the Metaphysical painters Carrà, De Chirico and Giorgio Morandi. Here, too, the Impressionists vied with Otto Dix and other German expressionists banished by Nazism.

In 1964, an American artistic invasion and the advent of pop art marked another great turning point. Robert Rauschenberg received the major prize, despite protests by staid French Academicians. In recent years, visitors have been scandalised by an Israeli pavilion overrun by a flock of sheep, only outdone by an Italian slaughterhouse. The centennial Biennale in 1995 staged an impressive retrospective, juxtaposing the masters of the 20th century with lesser-known painters. Recent exhibitions have seen the triumphant return of American artists, as well as a successful showing by the British artist, Chris Ofili. At its best, the unofficial fringe still acts as a prestigious springboard for struggling artists.

The Biennale is tied in with parallel events at the major galleries and at such curious exhibition spaces as a former leper colony, the salt warehouses on the Zattere, the Corderie, the old rope factory in the Arsenale, as well as in the Armenian-run Palazzo Zenobio, and even in the republican prisons on the St Mark's waterfront. ❑

LEFT: an interactive artwork.

The disappointing interior contains a late work by Veronese and the Throne of St Peter, a marble seat decorated with Moorish motifs and Koranic inscriptions, cut from an Arab stela. The grassy *campo* beside the church is framed by Coducci's tilting Renaissance belltower and by the hulking might of the Arsenale shipyards across the water channel.

Retracing one's steps through the friendly but faded neighbourhood leads back to the Napoleonic gardens and the site of the **Biennale ❼** (*see left*). The Biennale is based in the **Giardini Pubblici**, gardens lined by paths leading to designer pavilions. About 40 countries are housed in these permanent pavilions, with space set aside for international exhibitions. The pastoral nature of the site makes a pleasing contrast to the slick modernism of the exhibits.

A number of pavilions have been built by famous architects, notably Josef Hoffman's Austrian pavilion (1934), the Venetian architect Carlo Scarpa's Venezuelan pavilion (1954) and Alvar Aalto's Finnish creation (1956). The best spots are taken by the old-world powers. According to art critic Waldemar Januszczak, distortions of national rivalries are alive and well: "The British pavilion stares across at the German"; yet while the British space is vaguely Palladian, and looks as though it would do a nice line in teas, the German building is "one of the few bits of full-blown Nazi architecture to survive outside Germany". The newest star is James Stirling's Book Pavilion (1994), facing the vast Italian pavilion. Inspired by naval design and intended to recall the neighbouring Arsenale, this spacious glass-and-copper structure resembles an overgrown *vaporetto*.

To make full use of the Giardini pavilions, a Biennale for architecture takes place in the intervening years and has already made its mark, attracting renowned international architects. The city is used as a canvas, with provocative architectural puzzles sited in key public squares, and exhibitions staged in underused spaces, such as Palazzo Fortuny, the salt warehouses and the shipbuilding sheds around the dockyard.

On the waterfront, the Giardini-Biennale boat stop returns you to the San Marco area. Energetic walkers can follow the shoreline east through **Parco delle Rimembranze ❽** and the uninspiring island of **Sant'Elena**. The former Austrian parade grounds are now the stamping ground of Venice's football team, while the medieval monastery and seamen's hospital have succumbed to soulless urban sprawl. Dating from the 1920s, these streets bear the names of famous battlefields of World War I.

The goal is the Gothic church of **Sant' Elena ❾**, with its belltower, cloisters and Renaissance portal. Afterwards, the Sant'Elena *vaporetto* whisks the hungry back to San Marco, offering superb views of the Doge's Palace, the Giudecca and San Giorgio Maggiore. ❏

Map on page 143

"There are few more soothing places than a Venetian garden on a blazing summer morning."

–JAN MORRIS

Siesta in the public gardens.

RESTAURANTS & BARS

Dai Tosi
Seco Marina. Tel: 041-523 7102.
Closed Wed. €€
As a rare outpost in Eastern Castello, this dependable pizzeria and trattoria (try the spaghetti with scampi) is convenient for the Biennale gardens. *Vaporetto*: Giardinetto.

Hostaria da Franz
Fondamenta San Giuseppe (San Isepe). Tel: 041-522 0861. Closed Tues. €€€
This quaint canalside trattoria was opened in 1842 by an Austrian soldier who fell in love with a Venetian girl. Sample Venetian seafood dishes with a twist, from risotto to gnocchi with prawns and spinach, marinated prawns, grilled fish, or fish with polenta. Off the beaten track, but convenient for the Biennale gardens. Book.

Trattoria Giorgione
Via Garibaldi. Tel 041-522 8727.
Closed Wed. €€.
Set in the working-class Arsenale area, this inn is popular with Venetians, both for the traditional fish recipes and for the live folk music most evenings.

• • • • • • • • • • • • • •
Prices for a three-course dinner per person with a half bottle of house wine.
€ under €30. €€ under €30–50. €€€ €50–70. €€€€ more than €70

SAN POLO AND SANTA CROCE

These left-bank districts, centred on the Rialto, are a
warren of alleys and markets which hide the great
treasures of Bellini, Titian and Tintoretto in the
Frari and Scuola Grande di San Rocco

San Polo and Santa Croce form
adjoining districts *(sestieri)*
curved into the left bank of the
Grand Canal. Together they encompass the bustling Rialto market and
the picturesque backwaters towards
the station, centred on the quintes-
sential *campo* of San Giacomo dell'
Orio. The hub of the left bank is
the Rialto, "the marketplace of the
morning and evening lands".
Goethe's poetic evocation is fleshed
out by the writer Jan Morris, who
loved the Rialto's "smell of mud,
incense, fish, age, filth and velvet".

The labyrinthine Rialto, with its
dark alleys and tiny squares *(campielli)*, makes a sharp contrast to the
more open spaces around Campo
San Polo. In theory, this is lesser-
known Venice, *Venezia minore*,
implying a humility that does little
justice to a district that contains two
of the city's greatest sights: the Frari
is a huge Franciscan church containing masterpieces by Titian and
Bellini, while San Rocco is a shrine
to Tintoretto. Nor is "minor" a fair
summary of the stretch of Grand
Canal from the Rialto Bridge to the
station, a waterside lined by historic
warehouses and palaces, including
Veneto-Byzantine gems. (Best seen
from the water, this section is covered in the Grand Canal chapter, *see
pages 119–24*.)

The Rialto

"What's new on the Rialto?" was
Antonio's cry in Shakespeare's *The
Merchant of Venice*. Gossip remains
a popular Venetian pastime in this
curiously provincial city, and the
Rialto ❶, with its market and mass
of tiny bars, is still a talking shop. To
Venetians, the Rialto is not restricted
to the graceful bridge but embraces
the district curved around the middle bend of the Grand Canal. The
Rialto (derived from *rivo alto* or
high bank) also refers to the first

Map
on page
152

LEFT: water taxi by
the Rialto Bridge.
BELOW: brightly
painted boats supply
fish and produce to the
Rialto markets.

San Polo and Santa Croce

settlement of central Venice, and became the capital from AD 814.

As the oldest district, the Rialto has the greatest number of Veneto-Byzantine palaces. From its earliest foundation, this was the powerhouse of the Venetian empire, a crossroads between East and West. As "Venice's kitchen, office and back parlour," it also acted as a commercial exchange and meeting place of wholesale and retail merchants.

Even outbreaks of fire failed to crush the city's mercantile spirit. In the past, the Rialto was as prone to fire as it is to flooding today. The fire of 1514 razed the Rialto to the ground in six hours, sparing only the stone church. However, the commercial district quickly recovered and was rebuilt much as before. Thanks to liberal laws and an entrepreneurial culture, the Rialto was a cosmopolitan centre, home to a mixture of races and a babble of tongues.

The Venetians were middlemen, making a profit from the sale of everything in this emporium. Long before Shakespeare's Shylock, the Venetians had a reputation for guile and business acumen. In this exotic marketplace, cargoes of spices and silks from the Levant were sold, along with Slav slaves. Here, northern Italian grain dealers and Flemish wool merchants rubbed shoulders with Jewish moneylenders, Arab spice traders and German silver traders, as well as with Florentine and Lombard cloth merchants.

Trading and banking centre

The district was also home to a cluster of highly functional mercantile buildings that supervised trade and administered justice. From the 13th century onwards, various magistracies governed the Rialto commercial centre, granting leases or supervising fiscal, financial and legal affairs. Foremost among these were the **Fabbriche Nuove** and **Fabbriche Vecchie** ❷ trade offices and tribunals, which stand between the two main Rialto markets *(see page 120)*.

Another key civic building was the **Palazzo dei Camerlenghi** ❸ the former State treasury and debtors' prison, housed in a Renaissance hulk built of Istrian stone.

Also on the Grand Canal are the trading houses for German and Turkish merchants. Craftsmen were equally protected by the authorities, with many guilds located in the Rialto, including those for jewellers, woodcutters and goldsmiths.

The ancient market was also the hub of a foreign-exchange and banking centre, with a cluster of private banks around the bridge. The Venetian ducat was a stable currency, and the Rialto dominated international exchanges. Private banks flourished from the 12th century onwards, with a forerunner to the Banco di Giro, the earliest State deposit bank, opening in 1157. (The engaging Al Bancogiro wine bar now occupies this spot). The *giro* took the form of a written transfer from one account

Map on page 152

At the 2004 Venice Film Festival, Al Pacino won plaudits for his mesmerising portrayal of Shylock in Shakespeare's The Merchant of Venice.

BELOW:
the bustling Rialto market, a refreshing change from monumental Venice.

*San Giacomo di
Rialto is believed to
be the oldest church
in Venice. Its most
distinctive feature is
the Gothic 24-hour
clock dating from
1410, restored in the
16th century along
with the rest of the
building.*

RIGHT: Al Bancogiro,
a popular *bacaro*.

to another; no receipt was given, since the bank register was considered an official record. At night, the money was moved to the mint under an armed escort. With ready access to capital, the Rialto merchants funded fleets and made use of maritime insurance services and a commodity stock market.

The **Rialto Bridge** traditionally divides the city into two, with the right bank, the San Marco side, known as the *Rialto di quà* (this side) and the left bank known as the *Rialto di là* (that side). The Rialto Bridge spans the Grand Canal with a strong, elegantly curved arch of marble, a single-span bridge lined with shops. Henry James appreciated these "booths that abound in Venetian character", but also felt "the communication of insect life", a feeling shared by today's visitors as they run the gauntlet of stalls selling gondoliers' garb and dodgy handbags.

The Rialto Bridge is merely the last in a series of bridges that began with simple pontoons and progressed to wooden bridges with a drawbridge section to allow the passage of tall ships. A new bridge was created in 1588–91 by Antonio da Ponte, who beat the greatest architects of the day, including Michelangelo and Palladio, to secure the commission. The aptly named da Ponte surpassed himself by designing a light, floating structure with shops nestling in the solid, closed arches. From the bridge one can admire the majestic sweep of palaces and warehouses swinging away to La Volta del Canal, the great elbow-like bend in the Grand Canal.

The quayside

Henry James, who stayed in a palace nearby, admired "the old pink warehouses on the hot *fondamenta*". The Grand Canal palaces and warehouses are generally difficult to appreciate from the land, but on this stretch the waterside is lined with *fondamenti* or *rive*, accessible quaysides. Here one can walk along both banks, weaving among the crowded terraces. The **Fondamenta del Vin ❹**, where barrels of wine used to be unloaded, is now a quayside overrun by tempting but touristy trattorias and souvenir stalls. Facing it

Bacari: traditional bars

The Rialto market is the ideal place to indulge in a Venetian bar crawl, a *giro di ombre*, in the traditional wine and tapas bars known as *bacari*. On offer are an array of Venetian snacks *(cichetti)* and glasses of wine *(ombre)* in some of the oldest bars in Venice, dating back to the 15th century. **Da Elio** (Campo delle Beccarie, 7am–7pm, closed Mon) occupies a tiny corner of the fish market to sell delicate *cichetti* and wine, while quaint **Do Mori** (Calle de Do Mori, off Ruga Vecchia, 8am–8pm, closed Sun) offers standing room only for its tiny sandwiches. The strong of stomach can visit **Antico Dolo** (Ruga Vecchia, closed Sun), which specialises in tripe, as well as chicken gizzard and grilled peppers, leaving the squeamish to seek out **Ruga Rialto** (Calle del Sturion, off Ruga Rialto, 11am–3pm, 6–12pm), a bohemian *bacaro* and inn with wooden benches, copper pots and simple but sound dishes. End a Rialto bar crawl in **Al Bancogiro** (Campo San Giacometto), the bar that brings the *bacaro* concept up to date without betraying its rustic roots. Teetotallers, meanwhile, can take refuge in **Bar Rialto** (Ponte del Lovo), an old-fashioned *pasticceria* serving Venetian biscuits, cakes and coffee.

is **Riva del Ferro** ❺, where German barges unloaded iron *(ferro)*. Their trading house, the Fondaco dei Tedeschi, was close by *(see page 120)*. Also on the right bank is Riva del Carbon, where coal merchants moored their barges.

San Giacomo di Rialto ❻, the church nestling comfortably among the fruit and vegetable stalls, is linked to St James, the patron saint of goldsmiths and pilgrims. Both were much in evidence in the Rialto, even if the pilgrims were often in search of gold rather than God. Affectionately known as San Giacometto, this is reputedly the oldest church in Venice, founded in the 5th century but rebuilt in the 11th century.

Its most distinctive features, apart from the market bustle, are the Gothic portico, belltower and bold 24-hour clock. The 16th-century restoration respected the original domed Greek-cross plan, the ancient Greek columns and Veneto-Byzantine capitals. The cramped interior is disappointing but enlivened by the presence of resting market traders and dishevelled customers.

Campo San Giacomo ❼ preserves its mercantile atmosphere, an echo of republican times when money-changers and bankers set up their tables under the church portico. The **Gobbo di Rialto**, the Hunchback of the Rialto, is a curious stooped figure supporting the steps opposite the church: it was on the adjoining pink podium that republican laws were proclaimed, with the burden borne, literally and metaphorically, by this figure, a Venetian everyman. Petty criminals were also chased through the streets to the Rialto and were only given sanctuary from the bloodthirsty crowds when they reached these steps.

Market life

Threading the labyrinthine alleys of the Rialto is an intoxicating experience, especially in the morning. The alleys and quays bear witness to the Rialto's mercantile past, with names such as *olio* (oil), *vino* (wine), *spezie* (spices), *polli* (poultry) and *beccarie* (meat). Ruga degli Orefici, Goldsmiths' Street, begins at the foot of the Rialto Bridge, while Ruga degli Speziali, Spice Traders' Street is nearby. Today, smelly alleys often triumph over spicy perfumes, but the market is rarely squalid and makes a refreshing change from the monumental Venice of St Mark's. Indeed, the market is one of the few places where Italian prevails, along with the guttural sing-song of Venetian dialect.

The Rialto remains a hive of commercial activity, with everything on sale between here and the Mercerie in the San Marco district. Ignore the tourist tat in favour of foodstuffs galore, including cheese and salami around Ruga Vecchia di San Giovanni, and tastings in the remaining *bacari*, traditional wine bars.

The **Erberia** ❽ is the fruit-and-vegetable market overlooking the Grand Canal. Brightly painted boats from the lagoon supply the main

Elizabeth David, the celebrated English cookery writer, was entranced by "the light of a Venetian dawn so limpid and so still that it makes every separate vegetable and fruit and fish luminous with a life of its own".

BELOW: fresh produce from the Erberia.

TIP

Visit the Erberia to see bunches of red peppers, succulent salad leaves and peachy borlotti beans. Apart from spring-artichoke hearts (*castraura*), tasty vegetables are grown on the island of Sant'Erasmo or imported from mainland Veneto, just across the water.

BELOW: the arcaded Pescheria, Venice's main fish market.

markets with fish and fresh vegetables. Close by is the watergate, the "tradesmen's entrance" to the markets. Casanova spoke of the Erberia as a place for "innocent pleasure"; latter-day foodies find sensuous pleasure in the profusion of medicinal herbs, flowers and fruit, not to mention the asparagus, radicchio and baby artichokes.

The markets extend along the bank to the **Pescheria ❾**, the fish market, set in an arcaded neo-Gothic hall by the quayside, a design inspired by Carpaccio's realistic paintings. Under the porticoes, fishermen set their catch on mountains of ice. Elizabeth David waxed lyrical about "ordinary sole and great ugly skate striped with delicate lilac lights, the sardines shining like newly minted silver coins". The sight of so much appetising food is an invitation to a casual lunch in a basic wine bar, probably in the alleys around **Campo delle Beccarie**, the former abattoir but still the beating heart of the market *(see page 154)*.

Just over the canal lies **San Cassiano ❿** (9am–noon), an oppressive church ruined by 17th-century remodelling, and not redeemed by an interior containing Tintoretto's eerie *Crucifixion* and a couple of 9th-century marble pilasters. The district between here and Campo San Polo enjoyed a dubious reputation, with bare-breasted courtesans famed for leaning from their windows to attract clients. In 1608 the visitor Thomas Coryate was impressed by the profusion of prostitutes who "are said to open their quivers to any arrow".

From the former fleshpots, tiny alleys lead across the next canal to **Campo di Santa Maria Mater Domini ⓫**, a harmonious square with a Gothic well-head hemmed in by medieval palaces and a fashionable bar. Set back from the square is the equally beguiling Renaissance church of **Santa Maria Mater Domini** (Tues–Fri 10am–noon, 3–5pm). Often overlooked, the church has a well-restored interior, and a cool but distinctive atmosphere enhanced by clean Roman lines, a Byzantine cube shape and baroque cornices. There are fine 16th-century paintings, including one by Tintoretto.

From here, Calle del Spezier leads across the next canal north to the **Palazzo Mocenigo ⓬** (10am–5pm; closed Mon). This palace-museum is linked to one of the greatest dogal families and to other Mocenigo status symbols on the Grand Canal. This ancestral home was so well-preserved that, after Alvise Mocenigo bequeathed it to the city in 1954, it became a fitting showcase of gracious 18th-century living, from the lavishly decorated ballroom to the frescoed bedchamber. This palatial mansion remains an airless time capsule, defined by its Murano chandeliers, gilded furnishings and rococo frescos. This makes a perfect setting for a display of Venetian period costumes, as well as for a family-portrait gallery worthy of a dynasty which produced seven doges.

A stone's-throw from the palace is the over-restored church of **San Stae** ⓭ (daily 10am–5pm, exhibition centre) overlooking the Grand Canal. The design is closer to Palladian than baroque, with Corinthian columns set on high plinths.

Just east is **Ca' Pesaro** ⓮, a sumptuous palace housing museums of modern and oriental art *(see page 122)*. To the west, also on the Grand Canal, lies the **Fondaco dei Turchi** ⓯, one of the greatest merchant's warehouses, now home to the Museum of Natural History *(see page 124)*.

Behind the Fondaco, Fondamenta del Megio leads to the church of **San Giacomo dell'Orio** ⓰ (Mon–Sat 10am–5pm, Sun 1–5pm), tucked into a corner of a leafy square of the same name. Although slightly off the beaten track, this parish church conveys an inviting Romanesque atmosphere lit by diffuse light. The coherence is particularly remarkable given the eclectic nature of the church, which spans many centuries since its 9th-century foundation. Behind the pulpit and in the right transept are several Byzantine capitals raided from Constantinople, including one made of greenish Greek marble. The poet Gabriele d'Annunzio likened it to "the fossilised compression of an immense verdant forest". Architectural eclecticism is apparent in the Veneto-Byzantine belltower and columns, wooden Gothic arches and Renaissance apses; the pièce de résistance is the Gothic ship's-keel roof.

The finest artworks are a rare 14th-century wooden Tuscan crucifix and, in the **New Sacristy**, a Veronese ceiling. A stroll around the building reveals the characteristic bulbous apses, and is an invitation to linger in a bar on one of the city's most captivating squares.

Labyrinthine quarter

The church is part of a labyrinthine quarter of narrow *calli* and covered passageways *(sottoporteghi)*. A short but confusing stroll south leads to the home of one of the surviving *scuole* or powerful lay confraternities. The **Scuola di San Giovanni Evangelista** ⓱ (concerts or by prior

Map on page 152

Decorative gondola detail. There are gondola stands on Riva del Carbon (the Rialto) and at Santa Maria del Giglio.

BELOW: Campo San Giacomo dell'Orio.

The Scuole

Dating back to the Middle Ages, the *scuole* were charitable lay associations close to the heart of Venetian life. Until the fall of the Republic at the end of the 18th century, they acted as a state within a state, looking after members' spiritual, moral and material welfare. Anything could be provided, from a dowry or loan, to alms, free lodging and medical treatment.

Serving the citizen class, from lawyers and merchants to skilled artisans, the *scuole* were expected to support the State, play a part in processions and contribute to good causes. The richest foundations even recruited and financed military expeditions. For the merchant class, excluded from government, this was an opportunity to show their civic pride and communal spirit. In fact, these associations were the main focus of social life for citizens beneath the patrician class. In a regimented and rather claustrophobic society, the *scuole* also served as a useful safety valve.

While there were great distinctions between the prestigious *scuole grandi* and the humble *scuole minori*, they were essentially democratic, with rich and poor able to

join at different rates of subscription. Four of the *scuole grandi*, the major institutions, originated as flagellant societies in the 13th century. While the *scuole grandi* were more overtly religious, all the *scuole* were devotional associations: they prayed together and performed charitable works in the name of the patron saint.

Such confraternities appealed to the Venetians' puritanical streak as well as to their fondness for self-government. The *scuole* promoted pious living and forbade blasphemy, adultery, gambling, "frequenting taverns and lewd company".

The *scuole grandi* possessed great wealth and prestige, and played a leading role in the ceremonial life of the city. Apart from San Rocco, these include the Scuole di San Giovanni Evangelista, I Carmini, San Marco and Santa Maria della Carità, now home to the Accademia gallery. There were also associations for foreign communities, such as the Scuola di San Giorgio degli Schiavoni, intended for workers from Dalmatia, present-day Croatia.

All *scuole* wished to glorify their patron saint and themselves by employing the great artists who had decorated the Doge's Palace. Corporate funds were lavished on the interiors of meeting houses, of which the grandest is San Rocco. Set on two floors and linked by a magnificent staircase, a typical headquarters had halls decorated by the finest artists of the age, rich in narrative scenes and in dazzling processions.

By the 18th century there were almost 500 confraternities. Although Napoleon sacked their headquarters and disbanded the confraternities themselves in 1806, several have since been revived and still more former meeting houses are now open to the public. The *scuole* remain highly distinctive, whether used as living confraternities, permanent museums or regular concert halls. One has become a school sports hall, and the Scuola Grande di San Marco, one of the greatest, is currently home to the city hospital, thus still serving the community in the broadest sense. ❑

LEFT: detail from Tintoretto's *Slaughter of the Innocents* in San Rocco.

appointment, tel: 041-718 234) still serves its original purpose and, while difficult to gain access to, is worth seeing from outside. The distinctive Renaissance marble portal and courtyard is watched over by an eagle, the symbol of St John, the confraternity's patron saint. The interior is graced by a monumental staircase, a barrel-vaulted, double-ramp affair, but most of the finest paintings are now in the Accademia *(see pages 188–9).* Opposite is the 15th-century church of San Giovanni Evangelista.

From here, Calle del Magazzen leads to the greatest church on the left bank, the **Frari ⓲**, officially known as Santa Maria Gloriosa dei Frari (Mon–Sat 9am–6pm, Sun 1–6pm; the route is signposted from San Tomà *vaporetto* stop, line 1 or 82). Rivalled only by San Giovanni e Paolo, this is the largest and greatest of all the Venetian Gothic churches. The hulking Franciscan complex, founded in the 13th century, was rebuilt in the 14th and 15th centuries.

The adjoining monastic cloisters house the state archives and 1,000 years of Venetian history. Outside and in, the bare brick church is virtually devoid of decoration. The writer Jan Morris likens it to "a stooping high-browed monk, intellectual and meditative". Such simplicity stems from the dictates of Franciscan building rules: poverty was the guiding principle of the great mendicant orders.

Only the three Gothic turrets crowned with pointed gables act as a reminder of the richness of Venetian architecture. Yet inside, even the restricted colour range is used to great effect, with red-brick walls relieved by creamy Istrian stone, colours repeated in the red-and-white marble floor. The interior is a stark framework for the artwork, a pantheon of Venetian glories. The choir chapels are lined with tombs of the doges, including the monument to Doge Francesco Foscari, deposed in 1457.

The nave is dominated by a Gothic choir screen and lovely choir stalls, the only such ensemble to survive in Venice. The high altar beyond is the focal point of the Frari, a space illuminated by Titian's *The Assumption,* his masterpiece, flanked by dogal tombs. His other great work, the Pesaro Altarpiece, lies in the north aisle of the nave. Beside it is the Pesaro Monument to Doge Pesaro (1658), an overblown funerary piece honouring Titian's chief patron. Ruskin disliked the baroque, and this sculpture in particular, decrying it as "a huge accumulation of theatrical scenery in marble… [its] negro caryatids grinning and horrible".

Titian's bombastic tomb, erected three centuries after his death, is set in the right-hand (south) aisle, close to the main portal. Directly opposite is the mausoleum of the neoclassical sculptor Canova, who died in Venice in 1822. Canova designed this as Titian's tomb, but it became a monument to himself. Canova's sinister open-doored pyramid contains the sculptor's heart; the tomb feels cold and even heartless. The querulous

Classical concerts are often held in churches and confraternities, especially San Rocco, the Frari, La Pietà, I Carmini and San Giovanni Evangelista.

BELOW: the Frari, mother church of the Venetian Franciscans.

Ruskin dismissed it as "ridiculous in conception, null and void to the uttermost in invention and feeling".

To the right of the high altar lies the entrance to the Pesaro family chapel, dominated by Bellini's altarpiece, a radiant *Madonna and Child*. Henry James adored the triptych: "It is as solemn as it is gorgeous as it is simple as it is deep." Also delightful is an early-14th-century Byzantine-style *Madonna* by Paolo Veneziano. The writer Ian Littlewood recommends seeing the church in the evening when "the smoking candles and the softness of the light offer the giddy experience of slipping from one world to another".

Venetian cakes and biscuits are on sale in Bar Rialto, an old-fashioned pasticceria on Ponte del Lovo.

The Scuola Grande di San Rocco

The apse of the Frari abuts Campo San Rocco, home to the **Scuola Grande di San Rocco** ⑲ (9am–5.30pm), one of the greatest city sights. San Rocco is the grandest of the *scuole* or charitable lay confraternities, and acts as a backdrop for baroque recitals. The society is dedicated to St Roch, the French saint of plague victims, who so impressed the Venetians that they stole his relics and canonised him. The confraternity's mission was the relief of the sick, a noble aim that soon became conflated with the prestige and social standing of the *scuola*.

The 16th-century building is also a shrine to Tintoretto, the great mannerist painter, whose pictorial cycle adorns the walls *(see page 61)*. Hand-held mirrors are provided to help view the ceiling paintings; even so, most visitors will find they suffer vertigo and sensory overload.

Tintoretto won the competition to decorate the interior, clinched by his cunning submission of a perfectly completed panel rather than the requested cartoon. The painter's overpowering Biblical scenes, executed between 1564 and 1587, provoke strong responses. Henry James found "the air thick with genius" yet palpably human: "It is not immortality that we breathe at San Rocco but conscious, reluctant mortality."

New Testament scenes are displayed in the **Sala Inferiore**, the Ground Floor Hall, including *The Annunciation*, a dramatic chiaroscuro composition. Such works show the painter's profound Biblical knowledge and manipulation of mannerist iconography. Yet, according to art historian Bernard Berenson, "the poetry which quickens most of his works is almost entirely a matter of light and colour".

A gilded staircase leads to the **Sala Grande**, the Great Upper Hall, and the **Sala dell'Albergo**, the smaller assembly room. This upper floor is framed by an inlaid marble floor and by surfaces studded with one of the finest painting cycles imaginable. Tintoretto's genius is revealed in these dynamic orchestrations of colour and light, works marked by drama and strong composition.

Even the artist's faults, from a gaudy palette to the strenuous pos-

Titian

Titian was the supreme artist. The Frari contains two of his masterpieces, including *The Assumption*, a work whose revolutionary nature caused it to be rejected by the friars; when they relented, the work made Titian's international reputation. The altar is dominated by this vibrant piece, completed in 1518. The Virgin floats heavenwards on a wreath of clouds borne aloft by cherubic angels. Unlike his rivals, Titian could make his illusionistic work command attention from afar. Vibrant colours helped: the counterpoint of the golden sky against the glowing red of the Virgin's robes. Titian aligned the whole work exactly with the opening of the rood screen, so that one's eye is drawn through the Gothic choir towards this magnificent altarpiece.

The Pesaro Altarpiece depicts members of the Pesaro family, Titian's patrons, with the steady gaze of the young heir to the family fortune looking out towards us. Titian was a shrewd businessman who flattered his many patrons. This is a Venetian *sacra conversazione* with a difference: worldliness. For the first time, the portraits of a patron and his family were made part of a devotional painting, thus breaking the previous strict division between sacred and secular.

turing of his figures, are a product of his visionary imagination, restless style and volatile changes of mood. The Sala Grande uses telling Biblical scenes to accentuate the confraternity's mission to heal. Stagily set on easels by the altar are Tiepolo's *Abraham and the Angels* and Titian's poetic *Annunciation*, matched by his *Christ Carrying the Cross*, previously attributed to Giorgione.

The Sala dell'Albergo contains allegories linked to the society's patron saint, including *St Roch in Glory*, the ceiling panel that won Tintoretto the entire commission. Facing it is *The Crucifixion*, both a vast masterpiece with a charged atmosphere and a poignant drama. Henry James contrasted the "portentous solemnity" of the paintings with "the bright light of the *campo*, the orange-vendors and gondolas". The orange-vendors have gone, but there are enough bars nearby to restore one's spirits.

San Rocco to San Pantalon

The church of **San Rocco** (7am–noon, 3–5pm), tucked into the tiny *campo* of the same name, is something of an anticlimax. The gloomy interior is lined with works by Tintoretto and Pordenone, another major mannerist artist. From here, follow Calle della Scuola across the next canal south to **Campo San Pantalon**.

Set on this canalside *campo* is the church of **San Pantalon** ⑳ (Mon–Sat 8–10am, 4–6pm). San Pantalon (or Pantaleone) is dedicated to an obscure saint, who was both Emperor Diocletian's doctor and a miraculous healer. The church follows a common Venetian practice, whereby the interiors, with the exception of St Mark's or Palladian gems, are finer than the exteriors. The bare, unfinished 17th-century facade gives no indication of the splendours within. This is one of the most theatrical interiors in Venice, a tour de force of perspective which projects the nave high into the sky.

The baroque ceiling paintings by Fumiani (1650–1710) depict *The Martyrdom and Glory of St Pantalon*. Unlike in San Rocco, there is no need for mirrors, since this majestic work was intended to be viewed from one single perspective,

Map on page 152

San Rocco, temple to Tintoretto. "One of the three most precious buildings in Italy", declared Ruskin.

BELOW: Titian's *The Annunciation.*

Map on page 152

TIP

Linger for a drink in the friendly San Polo neighbourhood. Calle della Madonetta is a pleasant alley that runs over bridges and under buildings towards the Rialto. This is one of several adjoining streets with overhanging roofs, a rarity in Venice.

close to the entrance. This may be the largest painting on canvas ever completed, created on 60 panels and hoisted into place. The illusionistic ascent into heaven is populated by boldly foreshortened figures clambering, floating or ascending. On completion of the ceiling, the artist supposedly stood back to admire his work before slipping off the scaffolding to his death.

Veronese's last work, *The Miracle of St Pantalon,* is in a side chapel on the right, while one on the left houses several Byzantine-style paintings, including a delightful Paolo Veneziano *Madonna and Child* (1333).

Campo San Polo

If feeling claustrophobic and in need of a burst of everyday Venetian life, head towards spacious **Campo San Polo**, via **Campo San Tomà**. (San Tomà *vaporetto* stop is nearby, with lines 1 or 82 returning to the Rialto in one direction and San Marco in the other.) On the far side of Rio San Tomà is the **Casa Goldoni** ㉑ (Mon–Sat 10am–4pm), the birthplace of

Goldoni, the 18th-century Venetian dramatist. Even if you are indifferent to the playwright, glance at the attractive courtyard with its carved well-head and Gothic staircase.

Campo San Polo ㉒, lying just across the canal of the same name, is the heart of a picturesque district. After San Marco, it is the largest Venetian square and lies at the heart of the San Polo quarter. Historically, this amphitheatre of a square was the scene of bull-baiting, tournaments and processions, even a great "bonfire of the vanities" in 1450. Today it is a popular venue for film screenings or carnival balls and, like Campo Santa Margherita, remains a classic Venetian space. At different times of day, the appealing square becomes a crèche, an impromptu football pitch or a place for a picnic lunch. At night, students converge on the square's historic *birreria*.

The lofty, rusticated **Palazzo Corner Mocenigo** is now the headquarters of the Guardia di Finanza, the financial police. However, in the past it was noted for having two doors so that the dead and the living would never pass through the same one. The Gothic **Palazzo Soranzo** (No. 2169–70), at the eastern end of the *campo*, was where Casanova's main patron lived. Here the humble violinist and future libertine was adopted by an ailing senator.

In the south-west corner is the church of **San Polo** (Mon–Sat 10am–5pm), hemmed in by houses. Essentially Gothic, the church features a rose window and ship's-keel ceiling, a frame for Tintoretto's *Assumption and Last Supper* and Tiepolo's *Apparition of the Virgin*.

An early 17th-century plaque outside the church forbids games, shopping and swearing "on pain of prison, the galleys or exile", but Venetians, then as now, paid little heed to such limitations on their pleasures. ❑

Working on Water

Venetians are well-served by *vaporetti*, the work-horses of water-buses, but on quieter canals, look out for the dredgers, refuse barges, and removals boats. Only the emergency services are allowed to break the speed limit of 8 km (5 miles) an hour, rocking passing gondolas in their choppy wake. In practice, few respect the speed limit. The *gondolieri* demonstrate vociferously, but their complaints fall on deaf ears. In Venetian dialect gondoliers are known as *"Pope"* which is what you shout when you want to cross the Grand Canal. The garbage men *(spazzin)* cry *"Pronti!"* as they collect the sacks heaped on the canal-bank, to be carried away by ship and incinerated. Major tidal flooding means the suspension of refuse collection as the boats cannot pass under bridges. When the stormy sirocco winds blow, the high-water siren sounds, provoking a chain reaction. Shop-keepers pile their wares on higher shelves; walkers don gumboots; duckboards are rapidly put down by the *spazzin.* Non-Venetians are distinguished by their inability to divine the different levels of pavements, to comical effect, by turn sinking leadenly into deep water and squelching like a duck on dry land.

RESTAURANTS & BARS

Restaurants

While this district has a few stylish restaurants, it is also an ideal place for sampling the Venetian *bacari (see page 154).*

Antica Bessetta
Salizzada de Ca' Zusto. Tel: 041-721 687. Closed all Tues and Wed L. €€–€€€.
Off the beaten track, just north of San Giacomo dell'Orio, this is a deceptively rustic trattoria where standards (and prices) are suitably high. It is a temple of Venetian home cooking and a foodies' paradise, with risi e bisi (rice and peas), gnocchi, seafood risotto – or the catch of the day, grilled or baked, accompanied by distinctive regional wines.

Da Fiore
Calle del Scaleter, off Campo di San Polo. Tel: 041-721 308. Closed Sun and Mon. €€€€.
Acclaimed as arguably the best restaurant in town, and a celebrity haunt during the Film Festival. The locals find it an accurate reflection of the subtlety of Venetian cuisine, from grilled calamari and granceola (spider crab) to Adriatic tuna, squid, sashimi and risotto al nero di seppia (cuttlefish risotto). Only one (sought-after) table overlooks the canal.

Frary's
Fondamenta dei Frari. Tel: 041-720 050. Closed Tues. €.
Facing the Frari church, this cosy, reliable Arab and Greek restaurant aspires to a "thousand-and-one-nights" atmosphere. Dishes run from Greek salad and moussaka to an array of Lebanese mezze and fish couscous.

Da Pinto
Campo delle Beccarie. Tel: 041-522 4599. Closed Mon. €.
This historic Rialto market inn has been restored, revealing a huge fireplace in the medieval meathouse. Snooty locals say the osteria has sold out by offering pizza, but they still serve cichetti at the bar or a generous menu (pasta, fish grill and dessert for around 20 euros) seated below exposed beams or on the market square.

Al Nonno Risorto
Sottoportego della Siora Bettina, Campo San Cassiano. Tel: 041-524 1169. Closed Wed. €–€€.
A popular pizzeria and trattoria with 30-something Venetians, drawn to this rustic spot, framed by a wisteria-hung courtyard and garden. Changing fish, pasta and pizza menu.

Il Refolo
Campiello del Piovan, Campo San Giacomo dell'Orio. Tel: 041-524 0016. Closed all Mon and Tues L. €–€€.
In a pretty canalside setting, this innovative, upmarket pizzeria is the place for a peaceful meal. Classic as well as creative pizzas.

Alla Zucca
Ponte del Megio. Tel: 041-524 1570. Closed Sun and Aug. €€.
Very popular trattoria set by a crooked bridge over the canal, with a few tables outside. The bohemian atmosphere reflects the eclectic menu, which favours vegetables as well as fish, with pumpkin flan, aubergine pasta and smoked mackerel. Book.

Bars & Cafés

A selection of the best bars and *bacari* in the Rialto district are listed in the box on page 154. Beyond the Rialto: **Bagolo** (Campo San Giacomo dell' Orio) is a striking designer bar offering an array of cold cuts, fine wines and grappas. **Dei Frari**, (Campo dei Frari Bridge) is a boisterous young bar with good tapas and cocktails. Nearby, **Gelateria Millevoglie** (behind the Frari church) has the area's best ice cream. **Easy Bar** (Campo Santa Maria Mater Domini), an arty fusion of high-tech styling and old-fashioned brickwork, is equally popular with locals and visitors.

RIGHT: The Dei Frari *bacaro*, before the midday rush.

CANNAREGIO

This faded, northerly district, once the most fashionable in Venice, is a moody backwater and the site of the world's first Jewish ghetto

Théophile Gautier, the sensitive French poet, wrote: "From alley to alley we had got deep into Cannaregio, into a Venice quite different from the pretty city of water-colours." Far from wanting to escape from this run-down quarter, he lapped up the deserted squares, desolate wharves and green, sluggish canals. Cannaregio is a district for those who have tired of the monumental sights around San Marco. Walks in the melancholic backwaters at the edge of the city trace a landscape of peeling facades and humble workshops, broad canals and wind-buffeted quays; the sense of abandonment creates a poetic atmosphere conducive to wistfulness.

Cannaregio is the most densely populated district and the closest both to the railway station and to the mainland. Before the advent of the causeway, the Canale di Cannaregio was the city's main entry point; it is therefore fitting that the district remains a bridge between Venice and the mainland, between the historic city and modernity. This is an ancient quarter, often scorned by the snobbish in favour of stylish Dorsoduro.

Certainly, the district's working-class credentials are beyond dispute. Ironically, this was once one of the city's most fashionable spots, dotted with foreign embassies and palatial gardens sloping down to the lagoon. The palaces may be faded but Cannaregio remains both a retreat for cognoscenti and the last bastion for working-class Venetians who have not moved to the Mestre mainland. In recent years, it has become more cosmopolitan, with an influx of westernised Hassidic Jews, Middle Eastern immigrants, and a cluster of chic boutique hotels.

This is also the most northerly *sestiere*, bounded by the railway station in the west, by the windswept

Map on page 166

LEFT: washing day in Cannaregio. **BELOW:** 13th-century figure near Campo dei Mori.

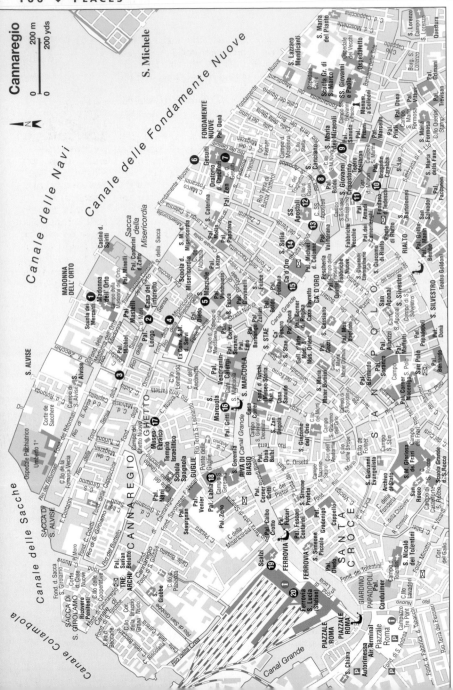

Cannaregio

| 0 | 200 m |
| 0 | 200 yds |

S. Michele

Canale delle Navi

Canale delle Fondamente Nuove

Canale delle Sacche

Canale Colombola

expanses of the northern quays, and by the upper sweep of the Grand Canal. Within this great arc are subtly diverse districts, from the world's oldest ghetto, in eastern Cannaregio, to the quaint, remote quarter around Madonna dell'Orto. The northern quays face the islands and are characterised by wide, melancholy, slightly menacing canals. By contrast, the Grand Canal district contains palaces as fine as any in Venice. Just inland, Strada Nuova is a bustling shopping district linking the station with historic Venice.

Cannaregio has a distinctly neighbourhood feel, with every parish possessing its own church and *campo*. Despite daunting post-war tenements on the fringes of the district, Cannaregio is alive with activity, with the space for chattering children and dozing cats. Glimpses of everyday life on secluded balconies or through half-shuttered blinds reveal elderly Venetians passing the time of day with their neighbours, or leaning out of windows hung with washing.

The tangle of alleys reveals the occasional *bottega* selling wood carvings, as well as earthy, hole-in-the-wall bars, and even *alimentari*, basic food shops which are hard to come by in fashionable parts of Venice, not to mention the odd place selling *vino sfuso* (draught wine). Far removed from San Marco, a Sunday in Cannaregio is still spent streaming from church to a trattoria for lunch.

The northern quays

Cannaregio has a cluster of different neighbourhoods rather than an obvious heart. The northernmost tip, centred on the church of Madonna dell'Orto, is one of the most curious quarters. (Despite its sense of remoteness, the district is easily reached by *vaporetto* 52 from the San Zaccaria stop near San Marco.) Here parallel *fondamente* (quaysides) frame wide *rii* (canals) and

are criss-crossed by smaller canals. The three major canals *(rii)* were created from the Cannaregio marshes in medieval times, with Rio della Sensa arguably the most atmospheric. These faintly mournful waterways are flanked by houses and neglected palaces somewhat reminiscent of Amsterdam, a great contrast to the tall tenements of the Ghetto further west. In the 1890s, the de Goncourt brothers were moved to describe these quays as "a whole district in decay, like an antique sculpture eaten away by rain and sun".

Madonna dell'Orto ❶ (Mon–Sat 10am–5pm, Sun 1–5pm), set on a harmonious square of herringbone design, is named after a miracle-working statue of the Madonna found in a nearby vegetable garden *(orto)*. The three-part composition of the facade, enlivened by a frieze of garlands, is reminiscent of the Frari, albeit on a smaller scale. The quirky campanile is topped by an onion-shaped cupola; this is the first bell-tower to greet visitors as they speed across the lagoon from the airport.

Map
on page
166

TIP

Dip into one of the local wine bars *(bacari)* and sample the classic local aperitif known as *spritz* – a luridly orangey cocktail of dry white wine, soda water and Campari or Aperol, garnished with a twist of lemon or an olive. Ask for a *spritz al bitter* for a stronger, less cloying taste.

BELOW: for glimpses of everyday life, lose yourself in the neighbourhood backstreets.

The Campo dei Mori is named after the turbaned Moors that decorate the facade of the Palazzo Mastelli, near Tintoretto's house.

BELOW: market day on Fondamenta di Cannaregio.

Often bathed in a warm light, the church is a masterpiece of Venetian Gothic. The austere, brick-faced interior, graced by Greek marble columns and a fine wooden ceiling, was well restored by the British Venice in Peril fund after the 1966 floods.

The church also makes a good starting point for exploring Tintoretto's temperamental genius: the painter lived nearby and this, his parish church, is decorated with works he created *in situ*. His tender *Presentation of the Virgin* (1551) graces the Mauro Chapel, as does the over-restored statue of the "miraculous" Madonna. Two other Tintoretto works dominate the chancel.

The aesthete John Ruskin raved about *The Last Judgement*, seeing "the river of the wrath of God, roaring down into the gulf where the world has melted"; his new bride ran out of the church, traumatised by "a death's head crowned with leaves". A memorial bust of the artist watches over his grave in a side chapel. Tintoretto aside, the church is a treasury of Venetian painting from the 15th to 17th centuries.

Before crossing the bridge over **Rio Madonna dell'Orto** to **Campo dei Mori** ❷, stand on the quayside and glance across at the Gothic **Palazzo Mastelli** opposite. To the right of the filigree balcony is an eastern-looking relief of a laden camel, lending the palace an eastern flavour. The owners were Levantine merchants whose origins are alluded to in the worn Romanesque reliefs of turbaned Moors on the **Campo dei Mori** facade. The Moorish name derives from the Fondaco degli Arabi, the Arab trading centre that once stood on the same spot.

Just beyond the *campo* is Tintoretto's house, marked by a plaque and bas-relief of the painter.

Quayside atmosphere

For a fine view, follow **Fondamenta della Sensa** ❸ to **Corte Vecchia** and **Ponte della Sacca**. This bridge looks out over the northern lagoon and San Michele, island of the dead *(see page 207)*. At twilight, especially when the boundary lights of the waterways are lit, this is the place for poignant thoughts. Another atmospheric spot is **Campo de l'Abbazia** at the end of **Rio della Sensa**. Here, the sculpted facade of the former confraternity of the **Scuola della Misericordia** overlooks a quaint well-head and a tiled, herringbone-style square.

The quaysides can feel rather exposed, but, if the weather is bleak, retreat to one of the bars and inns on **Fondamenta della Misericordia** ❹ and **Fondamenta degli Ormesini**, the next quaysides south of Fondamenta della Sensa. This bustling section of quays overlooks **Rio della Misericordia**, with the middle section in particular lined by inns, bars and neighbourhood shops.

Fondamenta della Misericordia is bordered by austere former convents and the baroque church of **San Marziale** ❺ (Mon–Sat 5–7pm), with its boldly ornamented interior.

Map on page 166

From here, head south to bustling **Strada Nuova** if the solitude of the quaysides has seeped into your bones, or stroll to **Fondamente Nuove ❻**, the quays bordering the northern lagoon, to see a baroque church, or set off for the islands. The windswept Fondamente Nuove, or New Quays, were actually created in the 1580s. Before then, this desolate stretch was a desirable residential district, with summer palaces and well-tended gardens lapped by the lagoon waters. These quays offer the fastest ferry times to the islands, as well as services to San Marco.

Vying for your attention are a smattering of basic bars, as well as a plaque marking Titian's home and **Palazzo Donà delle Rose**, a severe 17th-century palace that still belongs to the family that built it. Although the quays can seem inhospitable, especially in winter, the stirring lagoon views, encompassing the cemetery island of San Michele, count for much. On the proverbially clear day, the snowy Dolomite peaks are visible, seemingly suspended over the apparently featureless great plain of the Veneto.

Gesuiti church

The **Gesuiti ❼** (10am–noon, 4–6pm) is often confused with the Gesuati, the other major Jesuit foundation, set in Dorsoduro. The Jesuits were never popular in Venice, a city which put patriotism before the papacy and famously declared: "Venetians first and Christians second". After their banishment was revoked, the Jesuits returned to Venice, and, in 1715, rebuilt this church, which is still run by the Order, and has become the seat of the American Jesuit University. Set into a line of severe houses, the baroque, angel-bedecked facade reveals a stage-set of an interior. The design is typical of a Roman Jesuit church, with a broad nave flanked by deep

chapels and surmounted by a central dome. Gaudy stuccoes and frescos set the tone for an interior decorator's delight, from the vaulted and domed ceiling to the lavish altars, including one encrusted with lapis lazuli.

The impression is of a wedding cake swathed in green-and-white damask, even if it is marble masquerading as drapery. The whimsical Théophile Gautier felt that the decor made "the Chapel of the Holy Virgin look like a chorus girl's boudoir". The highlights are Titian's stormy *Martyrdom of St Lawrence* and Tintoretto's joyous *Assumption of the Virgin*, the painting that most inspired Tiepolo. The flashes of lightning, the darting angels and the sheer creative passion had a lasting effect on the great rococo artist.

Facing the Gesuiti is the **Oratorio dei Crociferi** (Fri–Sat 3.30–6.30pm), which, although dedicated to the crusading mendicant Order of Crutched Friars, later passed into Jesuit control. The interior has a subtle pictorial cycle by Palma il Giovane (1548–1628). Outside, Campo dei Gesuiti is dotted with houses asso-

In Venetian dialect, a fondamenta *is a quayside beside a canal (known as a* rio, *plural* rii)*, while* sottoportego *is a tiny alleyway running under a building.*

BELOW: the ornate facade of the Gesuiti church stands out among the more sober buildings around it.

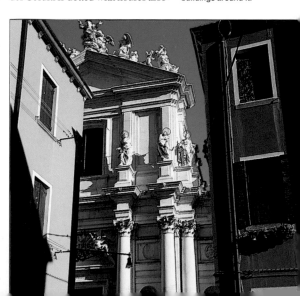

ciated with the guilds; on the walls are symbols or inscriptions referring to coopers, tailors and weavers.

Nearby is Palazzo Zen, a 16th-century palace with an eastern influence. If you do not wish to visit the islands (*see page 191*), leave the bleak quaysides of the Fondamente Nuove for commercial Cannaregio.

From Campo dei Gesuiti, cross Rio di Santa Caterina and head south through a network of alleys, following signs for the Rialto. Well before the Rialto Bridge, take Calle Malvasia across the canal of Rio dei Santi Apostoli to **San Canciano** ❽ (8am–noon, 5.30–7.30pm), an ancient church decorated in bold baroque style.

Just to the south, by the meeting of several canals, the lovely church of **Santa Maria dei Miracoli** ❾ (Mon–Sat 10am–5pm, Sun 1–5pm) rises sheer from the water, marooned like a marble siren awaiting the call of the sea. No wonder the church is a favourite with Venetian brides. Perfect proportions and seductive charm make this a Renaissance miracle in miniature, gleam-

Palaces were not permitted to have projecting eaves which might cast a shadow on the alleys below.

BELOW: bric-a-brac for sale near the church of Santa Maria dei Miracoli.

ing with a soft marble sheen. Its romantic setting invites such clichés as "Renaissance jewel-box", an image for once justified. The church is often compared with Ca' Dario, a palace also created by the Lombardi family of master-builders.

Certainly, this dazzling display of pastel marble is a far cry from the prosaic Venetian brick facade. Even Ruskin, no fan of the Renaissance, was forced to admit the Miracoli to be "the best possible example of a bad style". The interior has a *barco*, a nuns' choir gallery, and a barrel-vaulted and coffered ceiling, with the presbytery surmounted by a starry dome. The surfaces present a vision of pale pinks and silvery greys, and pilasters adorned with interlaced flowers, mythical creatures and cavorting mermaids. After its recent "miraculous" restoration, this bridal church truly bedazzles.

Just south, sandwiched between the canals of **Rio Giovanni Crisostomo** and **Rio dei Tedeschi**, lie Marco Polo's former home and a historic church. **Corte del Milion** ❿ is a quaint courtyard where the great

explorer reputedly lived. While Marco Polo's house burnt down in 1596, the well-head remains, as does a courtyard and arch decorated by Veneto-Byzantine friezes.

On an adjoining square stands the church of **San Giovanni Crisostomo** ⓫ (8.30am–noon, 3.30–7pm). Although founded in the 11th century, this restrained terracotta-coloured church owes more to the Renaissance. As the last work of Coducci, it boasts a tripartite facade reminiscent of San Zaccaria and also contains a delightful Bellini altarpiece (1515). The dome, supported by pillars and arches, is a model of classical coherence. The restrained marble interior contains a delightful Bellini altarpiece (1515), possibly his last work. The surrounding maze of streets was the 17th-century preserve of "hired slaves, bravoes, common stabbers, nose-slitters and alley-lurking villains". Today, however, any aspiring nose-slitter probably finds selling souvenirs to tourists more profitable.

Shopping district

Cannaregio's main shopping district begins at **Campo Santi Apostoli** ⓬, across the canal of the same name. The sombre air of the church of **Santi Apostoli** (8–11.30am, 5–7pm) is offset by the liveliness of the surrounding square. The 16th-century church is built on ancient foundations but is undistinguished, apart from a prominent belltower and Tiepolo's *Communion of St Lucy*, set in the domed Renaissance Corner Chapel, designed for the family of the Caterina Corner (Cornaro), Queen of Cyprus.

Campo Santi Apostoli marks the beginning of the **Strada Nuova** ⓭, which forms the main thoroughfare to the station, undergoing several name changes en route. Created under Austrian rule in the 1860s, the street represents the first piece of

modern town-planning in Venice. Strada Nuova was carved through an ancient quarter, causing Campo Santa Sofia to be severed from its church. Running roughly parallel to the Grand Canal, the broad street offers tempting *bacari* and food shops displaying juicy hams and home-made pasta. Side streets close to the Campo Santi Apostoli end of Strada Nuova conceal inviting inns such as Alla Vedova *(see page 175)*. Despite the demolition of houses to create the Strada Nuova, the church of **Santa Sofia** ⓮ survives, with its ungainly belltower seamlessly merging into the streetscape.

Campo Santa Sofia, with its Veneto-Byzantine palace and two pavement cafés, provides a sunny spot for a rest. The next left turn leads to the **Ca' d'Oro** ⓯, one of the finest palaces on the Grand Canal *(see page 120)*. With several name changes, Strada Nuova continues eastwards towards the station; at Campiello dell'Anconetta, either turn left to visit the Grand Canal or right to explore the Ghetto. Turning left leads to the church of **San Marcuola** ⓰ (8am–

Map on page 166

The residential backstreets are full of delightful architectural details, though some are better-preserved than others.

BELOW: the gleaming marble facade of Santa Maria dei Miracoli.

The Jewish Ghetto

Shakespeare gave Jews a bad press in *The Merchant of Venice*, but they were already stigmatised in the world's oldest ghetto. Jews were first mentioned in Venetian records in the 10th century, as passengers forbidden from travelling on Venetian ships. As an ambitious trading city, Venice feared competition from astute Levantine merchants. Persecution soon drove waves of refugees to Venice, but Venetian policy was ambivalent, wavering between tolerance and persecution, protection and expulsion.

While Jews who practised as doctors, traders or textile merchants were tolerated, pawnbrokers and moneylenders were resented. Jewish "banks for the poor" opened in 1366, but persecution reached its height in the 15th century, when the collapse of private banks forced Venetians to use moneylenders – usury was forbidden to Christians. Jews were forced to wear a distinguishing badge, yellow skullcap or red hat, while attempts to restrict Jews to the mainland resulted in the decree of 1423 forbidding Jewish property ownership.

In 1516, the expanding Jewish community was given its own closed living quarters, both a reward for contributing funds for the defence of the city and as a means of future control. Ringed by canals, like a moated prison, this segregated, unhealthy area was within sight of the former foundry or *ghetto*, which came to mean a closed Jewish quarter. By day, many Jews worked outside the Ghetto, but night curfews prevailed. The locked gates were manned by Christian guards, whom the Jews were forced to pay. Ceilings were made low in order to cram in seven floors, leading to the buildings being dubbed "medieval skyscrapers".

The Venetian ambivalence to Jews was mirrored in the Ghetto itself. Jews often favoured splendid clothes and jewellery, the sole way of displaying status. While the synagogues were outwardly modest, the interiors were sumptuous, but real power was limited. Jews obeyed their contract with the Venetian state, collected taxes, settled legal problems and dealt with new immigrants. Even so, they had free schooling and a printing press in an age when few Christians were literate. Christians often patronised the Ghetto, visiting respected doctors or the three local banks, called the red, yellow and green after the colour of their promissory notes. Yet even in death, the Jews were segregated: they were rowed down the Canale degli Ebrei to the Lido, the cemetery for outcasts.

While Venice's greatness declined during the 16th and 17th centuries, the Jewish community prospered on trade with Levantine Jews. Only in 1796 did the Napoleonic invasion cause the Ghetto gates to be flung open. Jews became full citizens in 1866, but found no peace in the 20th century: a bronze relief in the Ghetto Nuovo recalls the deportations and death of 200 Venetian Jews.

Yet grim though the Ghetto is, Venice was one of the few states to tolerate the Jews. The city was a liberal enclave compared with the brutality of 15th-century Spain or the Ottoman Turks. The Ghetto remains at the heart of Jewish life, with fine synagogues and a cultural centre, a nursery, an old people's home, workshops selling liturgical objects, and a kosher bakery and restaurant. ❑

● *You can explore the Ghetto on a Jewish-led tour; book with the tourist office or at: www.jewishvenice.org*

noon, 4–6.30pm), a Grand Canal landmark. The unfinished brick facade is a feature of many Venetian churches, as is the 18th-century remodelling of a medieval foundation, and even the presence of a fine Tintoretto work, *The Last Supper*.

Nearby is the San Marcuola stop and **Palazzo Vendramin-Calergi**, reborn as the Casino, and best visited in the evening *(see page 123)*.

For now, turn your back on the waterfront and take Calle Farnese to Campo del Ghetto Nuovo, and the Venetian **Ghetto** 🄳. Nothing about the neglected facades of these drab tenements suggests that until the 17th century this was one of the major Jewish communities in Europe. The population density was three times greater than in the most crowded Christian suburbs. After the Ghetto Nuovo (1516), two newer settlements, the Ghetto Vecchio (1541) and Ghetto Nuovissimo (1633), only provided temporary relief from the chronic overcrowding.

Despite its name, **Campo del Ghetto Nuovo** (New Ghetto Square) stands at the heart of the world's old-est ghetto, a fortified island created in 1516. This moated *campo* contains evocative testaments to the deportation of Jews to the death camps, in the form of memorial plaques on several of the buildings around the irregularly shaped square. Three of Venice's five remaining synagogues are set around the square, as unobtrusive as the Ghetto itself. Although hidden behind nondescript facades, the synagogues reveal lavish interiors, often with a Levantine feel. Gilt and stucco are used rather than marble, a material forbidden to Jews by the Venetians.

The synagogues, known as *schole*, were Jewish counterparts to the Venetian *scuole (see page 158)*. The synagogues followed different rites and acted as community centres as well as places of worship.

The **Schola Grande Tedesca**, the German Synagogue, was built in 1528, while its neighbour, the **Schola Canton**, possibly intended for Jews from Provence, dates from 1532. Adjoining it is the **Schola Italiana**, founded for Italians in 1575. Also on the square is a museum of Jewish

Map on page 166

The belltower of Santi Apostoli, a familiar landmark.

BELOW:
Holocaust Memorial, Ghetto Nuovo.

Map on page 166

TIP

Set at the entrance to the Ghetto, Gam Gam (Sottoportego del Ghetto Vecchio; tel: 041-715 284, closed Fri and Sat) is the only kosher restaurant in Venice, and specialises in Italian-Jewish and Ashkenazi dishes. (San Marcuola stop).

BELOW: Ferrovia, the busy *vaporetto* stop for the station and the new bridge.

history, the **Museo Ebraico** (10am-6pm; closed Sat; tours of the synagogues every hour from 10.30am to 4.30pm daily except Sat; tel: 041-715 359). The hinges of the former Ghetto gates can be seen on **Sottoportego Ghetto Nuovo,** evoking a drawbridge leading to a mysterious world. Beyond the spacious square and bridge lies the **Ghetto Vecchio** (Old Ghetto), an overspill ghetto created in 1541, with two more synagogues. The **Schola Spagnola**, designed for Spanish and Portuguese Jews, was built in 1538 but gained a Baroque facade by Longhena. The hall is graced with a *matroneum*, or women's gallery, reminiscent of the grand circles of Venetian theatres.

The nearby **Schola Levantina**, linked to Sephardic Jews from the Middle East, dates from the 1530s and is a variant on the Schola Spagnola since it, too, was remodelled by Longhena. Inside, the highlight is the *tevà* or wooden canopied altar. Outside, a low-key atmosphere prevails, totally unlike the impressions of Théophile Gautier, whose unconscious anti-Semitism was shared by

many 19th-century visitors: "Curious figures, furtive and silent, slipped by close to the high walls with a fearful air… the alleyways got narrower and narrower, the houses rose like towers of Babel, hovels stacked one on top of another to reach for a little air and light above the darkness and filth through which crept misshapen beings." Today's visitors are more likely to be detained by the Jewish bakery or **Gam Gam**, the kosher restaurant by the Ghetto Vecchio.

Palazzo Labia and the railway station

From the Ghetto, head for the station via **Ponte delle Guglie**, the charming bridge over the **Canale di Cannaregio,** an area lined with waterside stalls. Over the bridge awaits **Palazzo Labia** ⓳, a splendidly restored palace, with the ballroom frescoed by Tiepolo *(see page 124)*. The former owners, the noble Labia family, were renowned for their extravagance: once, after a riotous banquet, the gold plates were hurled into the canal as the host cried out: "*Le abbia o non le abbia sarò sempre Labia!*" ("Whether I have them or not, I'll always be a Labia!") The occasion for this extravagant pun had been carefully contrived, with precautionary nets placed in the water to catch the precious heirlooms.

From here, follow the masses along **Lista di Spagna**, the tawdry main thoroughfare redeemed by the occasional inn tucked into a tiny courtyard. Just beside the station looms the restored church of the **Scalzi** ⓳, a lavish baroque edifice ironically built for the barefoot *(scalzi)* order of Carmelites. The street bustle reaches fever pitch by **Ferrovia Santa Lucia** ⓴ and Calatrava's sinuous **New Bridge** *(see page 124)*. In conjunction with the causeway, and now the bridge, this railway station has opened Venice up to the world, for good and ill. ❑

RESTAURANTS & BARS

Restaurants

Da Alberto
Calle Giacinto Gallina. Tel: 041-523 8153. Closed Sun. €–€€
Set close to the lovely Miracoli church, this authentic *osteria* (inn) is a cosy and romantic place to sample pasta, risotto, cuttlefish and a full range of *cichetti* (bar snacks).

Bentigodi-Osteria da Andrea
Calle Selle. Tel: 041-716 269. Closed Sun and Mon. €
A cheery *bacaro*, lined with wooden tables, serving a good selection of *cichetti* from aubergine nibbles to chickpea soup, seafood salad and pasta with swordfish.

Ai Promessi Sposi
Calle dell'Oca. Tel: 041-522 8609. Open 10am–10pm; closed Wed. €
This busy *bacaro* serves a wide selection of *cichetti*, plus clams, pasta and *pasticcio di crespelle al pesce* (fish pancakes) and *castraure* (baby artichokes).

Sahara
Fondamenta della Misericordia. Tel: 041-721 077. D only (6pm–2am). Closed Mon. €
Syrian restaurant with great ambience and cuisine: couscous, falafel, hummus, or rice with aubergine are staples, as is mint tea. Book restaurant, but bar snacks available. (Many other dining options on the same canalside.)

Alla Vedova
Ramo Ca' d'Oro. Tel: 041-528 5324. Closed Thurs, Sun L and Aug. €
Set near the Ca' d'Oro, this friendly and reliable *bacaro* is popular with young Venetians clustered around the bar to sample such tapas as *polpette* (spicy meatballs), *baccalà*, fried artichokes, marinated peppers, or seafood, including cuttlefish gnocchi with salmon. Table service too.

Vini da Gigio
Fondamenta di San Felice. Tel: 041-528 5140. Closed Mon and Aug. €€
Very popular family-run *bacaro* that is both a wine bar and inn but exceptional food but leisurely service. Expect variety, from Venetian risotto to northern Italian game dishes, as well as fine wines. Book.

Bars & Cafés

Cannaregio tends to be a relatively cheap district for restaurants, although many are just bars or basic inns, but fine for lunch on the run.

Algiubagio (Fondamenta Nuove), convenient for the *vaporetto* stop, is a much-needed retreat from the windswept quaysides, and a chance for a coffee, liqueur or snack. On the route to the station, **Vecia Carbonera** (Rio Terra della Maddalena, beside Ponte Sant'Antonio) is a rustic-style wine bar with decent tapas. **Osteria al Bomba** (Strada Nuova, by Santa Sofia) is a traditional inn with a wide range of Venetian treats. Also here is **Gelateria Ca' d'Oro**, the place for an ice cream. **La Cantina** (further down, on Campo San Felice) is an old-style *bacaro* serving fine wines, soups, salami or cheese plates. **Enoteca De Rossi** (Rio Terra San Leonardo) is a gentrified-rustic wine bar with reliable snacks, a mixed crowd and regular jazz concerts. On Fondamenta della Misericordia, virtually next door to one another are a trio of nightspots with decent food: **Cantina Iguana**, a Mexican cantina, the music-minded **Paradiso Perduto** and **Sahara**, a special Syrian eatery *(see left)*.

PRICE CATEGORIES

Prices for three-course dinner per person with a half-bottle of house wine:
€ = under €30
€€ = €30–€50
€€€ = €50–€70
€€€€ = more than €70

RIGHT: traditional inns *(bacari)* are scattered around Cannaregio's quaysides and side streets.

DORSODURO

The smartest area of Venice, and a haven for
expatriates, stretches from La Salute, the
church facing St Mark's, to the Accademia,
the city's most illustrious art gallery

Dorsoduro simply means "hard
back", so called because the
district occupies the largest area
of firm land in Venice. This is upper-
crust Venice, the grandest section
defined by the Punta della Dogana,
the Gesuati and the Accademia. This
most fashionable residential district
has long been favoured by foreigners,
particularly the American and British
communities. Dorsoduro remains a
haven for wealthy expatriates, even if
the southern flank, essentially on the
left bank, contains poorer but picturesque areas towards the west.

Yet, historically, Dorsoduro was a
mixed district, with the nobles and
nouveaux riches ensconced in splendid Grand Canal palaces, the impoverished nobility living close to
Campo San Barnaba, and sailors and
fishermen confined to the scenically
shabby west. Today, socially and geo-
graphically, there is considerable
overlap: Campo Santa Margherita,
the hub of Dorsoduro, is a cheerful
district of shopkeepers, students and
arty types.

The closeness of the university
quarter, centred on Ca' Foscari,
ensures that the bars are full and service is friendly. The parishes of San
Trovaso and San Barnaba offer a similar mixture of youthful high spirits
and discreet privilege. In chic Dorsoduro, foreign bohemianism meets

Venetian conservatism, resulting in
understated good taste spiced with a
touch of the cosmopolitan.

La Salute

Dorsoduro is the most attractive quarter for idle wandering, with wisteria-
clad walls, secret gardens and
distinctive domestic architecture.
Apart from the Accademia gallery
and Salute church, the district is surprisingly free from visitors. The
southern spur of the Zattere makes the
most enchanting Venetian prome-

Map on
pages
178–9

LEFT:
Punta della Dogana.
BELOW: strolling
along the Zattere.

TIP

Particularly for children: La Salute *traghetto* (gondola ferry) makes an enjoyable and inexpensive jaunt across the Grand Canal to Santa Maria del Giglio. It is considered good form to stand up during the crossing.

nade, bracing in winter and refreshing in summer. These quaysides offer panoramic views from the glittering sea-customs post and the stately Salute church.

This landmark basilica is rivalled by several major churches and confraternities. San Sebastiano and I Carmini can compete, with entrancing interiors decorated by Veronese and Tiepolo. Culturally, Dorsoduro is surpassed only by San Marco: the district is home to numerous galleries, of which the Accademia reigns supreme as the treasury of Venetian painting. Many of the finest waterside palaces also lie along Dorsoduro's spine. However, Dorsoduro is essentially understated, with peace and quiet prized more than glittering sights.

One such secluded spot is the fishermen's church of **San Nicolò**, situated on the outer rim of the city. Another quaint corner is the *squero*, the gondola docks, where boats wait to be planed or repainted. Little won-

der, then, that Dorsoduro's more precious residents feel that simply to step outside the *sestiere* produces a lowering of the spirits.

Eastern Dorsoduro is dominated by the baroque basilica of **La Salute** ① (daily 9am–5.30pm), a Venetian landmark guarding the entrance to the Grand Canal. Dedicated to Santa Maria della Salute (Our Lady of Good Health), the church was built as a thanksgiving for delivery from the 1630 plague. Longhena, the great baroque architect, wished it to be "strange, worthy and beautiful". Henry James's celebrated conceit springs to mind: "like some great lady on the threshold of her salon. She is more ample and serene… with her domes and scrolls, her scalloped buttresses and statues forming a pompous crown, and her wide steps disposed on the ground like the train of a robe."

However, Longhena's triumphal and grandiose church is also indebted

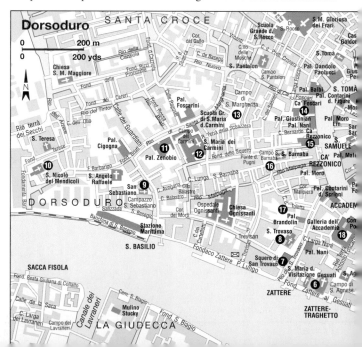

to Palladio's Il Redentore. Although Longhena learnt from his classical forebear's choice of theatrical settings and magnificent use of space, lavish sculptural decoration was his own baroque contribution. Begun in 1631, the church took 50 years to complete, and is the focal point of a lively annual November festival, where even cynical gondoliers bring their oars to be blessed by a priest on the basilica steps *(see page 225)*.

La Salute marks the end of Venetian mannerism and heralds an era of bold baroque statements. Devised before Rome's Bernini and Borromini masterpieces, it became one of the few Italian churches to challenge the supremacy of Roman baroque. The interior boasts a spectacular central plan, with its revolutionary octagonal space surmounted by a huge dome. The octagonal structure alludes to the symbolic eight-pointed Marian star, while the theatrically raised high altar evokes the Virgin's rescue of

Venice. The major works of art include Tintoretto's *Wedding at Cana*, paintings by Titian in the sacristy, and a small Byzantine Madonna, overawed by baroque splendour. While eminently praiseworthy, the interior is rather solemn and cold, clad in Istrian stone. The exterior is more joyous, with the majestic dome dominating the Venetian skyline.

At the bottom of a dramatic flight of steps, a *traghetto* links La Salute with Santa Maria del Giglio on the far bank, while the *vaporetto* sweeps visitors over to San Marco or down the Grand Canal.

The Zattere

Alternatively, stroll around the point, the **Punta della Dogana** (Customs Point), the start of a popular Venetian walk. Occupying the triangular tip of Dorsoduro is the **Dogana di Mare** ❷. This was the sea-customs post, as opposed to the land-based customs post (Dogana della Terrà, on the Riva

One of the most delightful walks in Venice stretches from La Salute to the Zattere quays, rounding the Customs Point. Depending on the number of pauses, the walk lasts from half an hour to half a day, and could easily encompass visits to the Gesuati church and the Guggenheim.

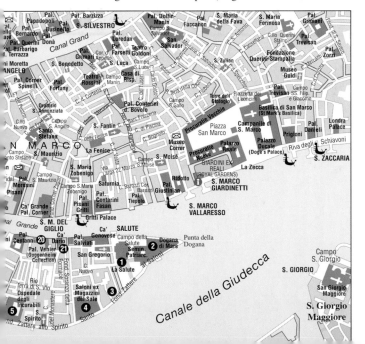

del Vin on the Rialto). Here, ships and cargoes were inspected before being allowed to drop anchor in front of the Doge's Palace. Still used as a customs house, this is the only republican civic building to have maintained its original function. Although the present sea-customs post dates from the 1670s, it occupies the site of an earlier customs house and medieval defensive works.

Facing St Mark's Basin, a porticoed corner tower is crowned by a rich composition: bronze Atlases bear a golden globe, with a weathervane featuring the figure of Fortune glinting in the sun.

The **Zattere** ❸ stretches all the way round Dorsoduro's southern shore, with its quaysides flanked by cafés and churches, boathouses and warehouses. This promenade was created in 1516, and named after the cargoes of wood that were unloaded on these quaysides (*zattere* means "floating rafts"). This is a refreshing *fondamenta*, and the Venetians' favourite walking place; the residents prefer windswept sea views to neat parks, which are usually deserted.

The Zattere is far more appealing than its northern counterpart, the quaysides of the Fondamente Nuove. In all seasons, strolling along the Zattere represents a local ritual. At the first sign of spring sunshine, Venetian sun-worshippers flock to the landing stages and decks that line the shore. Summer *passeggiate* are also de rigueur, partly to combat the heat and city claustrophobia, partly to parade the latest pastel fashions and sip drinks in stylish cafés, such as Linea d'Ombra *(see page 187)*, one of the first of the open-air cafés around the point.

The Gesuati and the Squero di San Trovaso

Facing the island of the Giudecca are the **Magazzini del Sale** ❹, the former salt warehouses, where the city's sole raw material was stored. The low, regular neoclassical frontage conceals a 15th-century structure. The interior, an occasional boathouse, also doubles as an exhibition space during the Biennale art festival. Just before Rio delle Torresele lies **Ospedale degli Incurabili** ❺, an austere former hospice for syphilitics, a medieval building redesigned by Sansovino in the 16th century. Now a children's home, in its time it has been an orphanage, a music conservatoire and a barracks.

Further along the Zattere stands the grandiose church of the **Gesuati** ❻ (Mon–Sat 10am–5pm, Sun 1–5pm), a supreme example of 18th-century Venetian architecture, not to be confused with the Gesuiti in Cannaregio. The facade, with its lofty Corinthian columns and Palladian motifs, was designed by Massari, an early rococo architect. The church is often seen as a counterpoint to Palladio's Il Redentore over the water *(see page 195)*.

The Gesuati, dedicated to Santa Maria del Rosario, dates from 1726, and was commissioned by the Dominicans. The theatrical yet grace-

BELOW: Gesuati church, Zattere.

ful interior (under restoration) holds Tiepolo masterpieces (1739) in their original setting. The master of the rococo adorned the vaulted ceiling with a heavenly vision, the air stirred by the beat of angels' wings. The central panel celebrates the *Institution of the Rosary*, showing the Madonna offering the rosary to St Dominic; the side panels illustrate the *Life of St Dominic*. Easier to see, in the first chapel on the right, is Tiepolo's exuberant altarpiece of the Madonna, accompanied by three venerated Dominican saints. Only a Tintoretto *Crucifixion* disturbs the Dominican orthodoxy and rococo mood.

Next door is **Santa Maria della Visitazione** (8am–noon, 3–7pm), a Renaissance oratory attributed to the Coducci school. On the facade is a lion's-mouth letterbox for secret denunciations. Access to the oratory, with its 16th-century Umbrian coffered ceiling and cloisters, is through the gateway of a charitable institute. The **Zattere Boarding Stage** lies on this stretch of quays, with ferries to the Giudecca and San Marco. Towards the San Trovaso end of the

Zattere are open-air cafés and pizzerias, perched on waterfront rafts. Even if the views are finer than the food, few can complain.

From here, turn down **Rio di San Trovaso** to explore a privileged domestic district dotted with university buildings. Set on the corner of Rio Trovaso and Rio Ognissanti is the **Squero di San Trovaso** ❼, a picturesque gondola repair-yard best viewed from Fondamenta Nani on Rio di San Trovaso. Gondolas are overhauled at one of three *squeri*, the traditional boatyards of which this is the oldest in existence, dating from the 17th century. Naturally, the *squeri* are always set on the waterfront, with the yard sloping down to the canal. Beside the boatyard is a wooden galleried construction, a geranium-clad outhouse with living quarters above. The resemblance to an alpine chalet is not accidental: many of the early boat-builders came from the Dolomites.

Nowadays, the main concern is the maintenance of the 400 or gondolas still in use. In summer, the upturned boats are scraped of weeds

Map on pages 178–9

Globe and weather-vane figure on the customs house.

BELOW:
La Salute with Il Redentore beyond.

For a taste of domestic, down-tempo Venice, wander aimlessly beside the side canals of Rio de Santa Margherita, Rio dei Carmini, Rio di Sant'Angelo, Rio Briati and Rio del Tintor – ideally in the late afternoon.

RIGHT: pulpit detail, Angelo Raffaele.

and retarred, but weeds are less of a problem since the council banned phosphate-rich detergents.

A shortage of skilled craftsmen and the labour-intensive nature of the work means that there is a waiting list for new gondolas: only a handful are made each year, mostly destined for millionaires' pleasure lakes. Today, this asymmetric half-ton craft costs up to $80,000 to make. Yet Nedis Tramontin, the master-craftsman at San Trovaso, recalls the 1920s, "and seeing my father's team make seven gondolas in 21 days for 700 lire each".

Further along **Fondamenta Nani** lies a cluster of university buildings, including the sculpted Palazzo Nani Mocenigo. The scenic Rio di San Trovaso links the Grand Canal and the Giudecca Canal, with the Cantinone Giá Schiavi, an old-fashioned wine bar, beside Ponte di San Trovaso. Towards the Grand Canal end of the *rio* are several wisteria-clad palaces and a small bridge leading across the canal to the church of **San Trovaso 8** (Mon–Sat 3–6pm). Originally medieval, the church was remodelled in Palladian style. Curiously, there are two matching facades, one facing the canal, the other facing a raised stone *campo*. Tradition has it that two entrances were required to keep the warring clans of the Castellani and Nicoletti apart. The square and well-head conceal a rainwater cistern.

Despite its setting, the church is disappointing, with a gloomy interior only partly redeemed by paintings by Tintoretto and his son.

San Sebastiano and San Nicolò dei Mendicoli

The pleasing Calle della Toletta now leads to Campo San Barnaba and the Grand Canal palaces beyond. Alternatively, follow the Zattere westwards to Rio di San Sebastiano and the start of a scruffy but appealing district. **San Sebastiano 9** (Mon–Sat 10am–5pm; Sun 1–5pm) is an early 16th-century church, a classical canvas for Veronese's opulent masterpieces, painted between 1555 and 1565. The church is often praised as a perfect marriage of the arts, with architecture, painting and sculpture in

The Tiepolo Trail

Dorsoduro is dotted with Tiepolo sites, shrines to the greatest rococo artist. His credo was that "the mind of the painter should always aspire to the sublime, the heroic and perfection". This master of scenic illusion produced a riot of picturesque detail to seduce the most casual observer. Ca' Rezzonico is his chief canvas *(see pages 115 and 185)*. On the Zattere nearby, the Gesuati church has illusionistic frescos and a joyous altarpiece *(see page 181)*. From here, a pleasant stroll leads to the Scuola Grande dei Carmini and Tiepolo's sensuous *Madonna of the Scapular (see page 184)*.

Beyond Dorsoduro are other Tiepolo sites. San Rocco in the San Polo district shows Tiepolo in a softer light, as a painter of subtle portraits and altarpieces, notably *Abraham and the Angels (see page 161)*. By contrast, La Pietà in Castello is a feast for the senses, with Tiepolo's celebrated frescos best seen during a Vivaldi concert *(see page 140)*. Art critic Philip Rylands praises the vibrant effects of the ceiling fresco in Vivaldi's church: "The acoustics cause the sacred music to reverberate so that Tiepolo's celestial angels seem to have burst into a trumpeting cantata."

complete accord. Veronese's works are enhanced by lavishly carved ceilings and a galleried choir which adds to the sense of spaciousness. This resplendent cycle of paintings shows Veronese in all his glory, exalting grace, harmony and serenity while indulging in occasional whimsy. Veronese's *trompe l'œil* interior is an architectural flight of fancy created by frescoed loggias, columns and statues. Blocks of pure colour adorn every surface, from the nave ceiling to the organ panels. The individual subjects are secondary to the overall effect, a broad spectrum of religious, historical and mythological motifs.

Although the paintings in the choir illustrating the martyrdom of St Sebastian are looking distinctly dark, the **Sacristy** has recently been restored, revealing a vivid ceiling dedicated to the Virgin and the Evangelists. For 18th-century connoisseurs, Veronese's paintings were the noblest, the most sought after and most pleasing; today they strike a particular chord with the French.

Behind the painter's parish church lies a traditional working-class district once populated by fishermen, now home to port officials. On the next square west is the creamy-coloured **Angelo Raffaele** (tel: 041-529 8711), a restored 17th-century church which stands on ancient foundations.

The adjoining canal leads to the most remote waterside church in western Dorsoduro, **San Nicolò dei Mendicoli ⑩** (10am–noon, 4–6pm). Set in a dilapidated district, this former fishermen's and artisans' church is surprisingly sumptuous. San Nicolò presents a squat Romanesque belltower and a bare brick facade lit by mullioned windows; a rare Gothic portico graces the west facade.

The church, which was founded in the 7th century and then remodelled between the 12th and 14th centuries, is one of the oldest in Venice. It was sensitively restored by Venice in Peril in the 1970s. The endearing interior is one of the best-loved in the city, with a single nave ending in a Romanesque apse. Distinctive aspects include the Byzantine cornices and a nave graced by Romanesque columns, Gothic capitals and beamed ceilings. The interior is

Map on pages 178–9

TIP

In the local inns try *fegato alla Veneziana*, tender calf's liver flavoured with parsley, onion and olive oil, or *bigoli*, dark skeins of wholewheat spaghetti, often served with an anchovy and onion sauce.

BELOW: Gondola yard on Rio San Trovaso.

embellished with Renaissance panelling, gilded statues and school of Veronese paintings.

Palazzo Zenobio and Santa Maria dei Carmini

From here, Rio di San Nicolò winds back to civilisation. Following the eastern bank of the canal, which changes its name to Rio Santa Margherita, brings you to the quayside of Fondamenta Briati. Overlooking the *rio* on the other side is **Palazzo Zenobio** ⓫ (tel: 041-522 8770), a rare example of Roman baroque in Venice. Although originally Gothic, the palace was remodelled in the 17th century and given a long, monotonous facade, softened by Italianate gardens at the back.

The grand interior leads from a *portego* (ceremonial hall) to the sumptuous, frescoed ballroom upstairs, adorned by a minstrels' gallery, gold-and-white stuccowork and *trompe l'œil* effects. The mirrors, chandeliers and door handles are all 17th-century. The palace has been an Armenian college since 1850, but the ballroom can be visited on request.

On the same western bank is **Santa Maria dei Carmini** ⓬ (Mon–Sat 2.30–5pm). The baroque belltower is surmounted by a statue of the Virgin bearing the scapular (these two small white strips of cloth form the distinguishing badge of the Carmelites). The church is often described as a display of Renaissance works in a Gothic setting, but the truth is more complex. The solemn nave has 17th-century arcades and a number of ponderous baroque paintings in honour of the Carmelite Order. Renaissance panelling covers a number of Gothic features, with the choir lofts decorated with 16th-century works. The finest Renaissance painting is a Cima da Conegliano *Nativity* in the second altar on the right. The Gothic cloisters now form part of an art institute.

On the same square is **I Carmini** (Mon–Sat 9am–4pm; Sun 9am–1pm; classical concerts). As the home of the Scuola Grande dei Carmini and headquarters of the Carmelite confraternity, this is one of the city's grandest confraternities, at least in artistic terms. The uninspired facade, built by Longhena, conceals a lavish 18th-century interior. The ground floor comprises a frescoed great hall and sacristy. A monumental twin staircase, its barrel-vaulted ceilings encrusted with stuccowork, leads to a splendid showcase to Tiepolo.

On the left is the **Sala dell'Albergo**, which housed pilgrims, and the Sala dell'Archivio, where the confraternity archives were stored. The decoration of the **Salone** or assembly room on the right was entrusted to Tiepolo. Since the wealthy Order prospered during the Counter-Reformation, with the cult of Mary acting as a counterweight to Protestantism, the Carmelites could afford to summon the services of the greatest rococo painter. Tiepolo repaid their confidence with a series of sensuous masterpieces, a floating world of pale skies and illusionistic effects. In the centre of the ceiling is a visionary work showing the Virgin with the Blessed Simon Stock. Tradition has it that Stock had a vision of the Virgin bestowing the Carmelites with their sacred badge, the scapular. As the order was re-established during the 13th century, Stock became one of the first Englishmen to join, leading the Carmelites during the time of their realignment to the Mendicant Friars. The corners of the ceiling are graced by four voluptuous Virtues, a radiant allegorical work.

Campo Santa Margherita

Just beyond lies **Campo Santa Margherita** ⓭, the liveliest square in the district, and the archetypal Venetian meeting place for bored youth. At one end of the sprawling square is the free-standing Scuola dei Varotari, formerly the tanners' guild. Just above several fish stalls stands an ancient stone sign prescribing the minimum size of fish permitted (eel must be over 25 cm/10 ins long and sardines at least 7 cm/3 ins).

One side of the square is bordered by dignified palaces with overhanging roofs, a style rare in Venice because of the fear of fire and a desire to let light into dark alleys. At the end of the square is the truncated bell-tower of Santa Margherita, with the deconsecrated church now a lecture hall. Students mingle around the market stalls, designer bars, English pubs and alternative herbalists, all set amidst homely palaces. Given the contagiously upbeat mood, blue-rinse matrons from Milwaukee often join peace-protesting students in sipping a lurid orange *spritz* in one of the arty cafés *(see page 225)*.

From here, the splendours of the Grand Canal beckon. Milling students may lead one to **Ca' Foscari** ⓮, the magnificent university palace *(see page 118)*. Just south is **Ca' Rezzonico** ⓯ *(see page 115)*, the museum of 18th-century art and one of the loveliest city galleries, with a major work by Tiepolo featuring large compositions in which mirages of light and air barely contain the orchestrated, dancing figures.

Alternatively, follow Rio Terrà across the canal to **Campo San Barnaba** ⓰. Bordering the scenic

Map on pages 178–9

Sgropin, *lemon sorbet, is made with vodka and prosecco, and traditionally served at the end of a fish course.*

BELOW: Campo Santa Margherita.

Map
on pages
178-9

TIP

To visit the work of the
Venetian great masters
in situ, see the Bellini
Trail *(page 60)*, the Tintoretto Trail *(page 61)*
and the Tiepolo Trail
(page 182).

BELOW:
gondolas beside
Accademia bridge.

square is Rio San Barnaba, signalled
by a colourful barge laden with fruit
and vegetables. The square is reached
by **Ponte dei Pugni**, the main bridge
between San Barnaba and Santa
Margherita. This was the scene of factional fisticuffs between rival clans
until such brawls were banned in
1705. When not at church in San
Trovaso, the Castellani and Nicolotti,
from Castello and San Nicolò respectively, staged their ritual battles here.
Their footprints, embedded in the
stonework, are reminders of the
bloodshed that left many dead.

Yet the square also has decidedly
aristocratic associations, since this
was the parish of the *barnabotti*, the
impoverished nobility, who gambled
or begged in order to survive. An austere 18th-century church does little to
dampen the spirits of this bustling
square, with its boisterous cafés and
picturesque market barge. The fun
spills over onto **Calle Lunga San
Barnaba** and **Rio Terra Canal**, the
liveliest places for designer bars and
reliable trattorias *(see opposite)*.

From here, Sottoportego Casin dei
Nobili, once a refuge for ruined

nobles, crosses Rio Malpaga to the
quaysides of **Calle della Toletta** ⓱.
This pretty, winding alley passes
several bars and a good bookshop
before returning to the delightful Rio
di San Trovaso.

On the far side of the canal,
Campiello Gambara leads to the
Accademia Bridge, a prime spot for
watching water traffic. The distinctive wooden bridge replaced a cast-
iron one rebuilt under the Austrian
occupation. Plans to replace the
bridge with a transparent model were
defeated by conservatives, but modernism has prevailed at the other end
of the Grand Canal, in the form of a
compelling sliver of a new bridge *(see
page 124)*. Visitors flock across the
wooden bridge to the **Accademia** ⓲,
the greatest collection of Venetian art
(see pages 188–9).

Between the Accademia and La
Salute, the Grand Canal is lined with
the finest palaces and museums.
Charming **Campo San Vio** is home
to St George's Anglican Church,
which serves the English-speaking
community in Venice. Here, too, is
Palazzo Cini ⓳ (tel: 041-521 0755;
reopens in 2005), the former residence of Count Vittorio Cini (1884–
1977), a noted industrialist. The count
created the fine Cini Foundation at
San Giorgio *(see page 193)*, but lived
here, filling his palace with period
furniture, silver, ceramics and Tuscan
Renaissance masterpieces.

From here, Calle della Chiesa
leads to the **Guggenheim** ⓴, the
superb collection of modern art *(see
page 113)*. Virtually next door is the
intriguing **Ca' Dario** ㉑ *(see pages
112–13)*. Calle del Bastion slips back
to La Salute, allowing you a last lingering look at the baroque church
before taking the *traghetto* across to
the right bank or a *vaporetto* along the
Grand Canal. Like Henry James, you
may find it hard to leave the Salute
steps, "with all the sweet bribery of
association and recollection". ❏

RESTAURANTS & BARS

Restaurants

Cantinone Gia Schiavi
Fondamenta Nani, Rio di San
Trovaso. Tel: 041-523 0034.
Closed 9.30pm and Sun D. €
Set near the church of
San Trovaso, this old-
fashioned canalside wine
bar is popular with locals
and expats from all walks
of life. A good place for
cichetti. Savour the mood
by popping in for a light
lunch or lingering at the
cocktail hour (7–8pm).

Ai Gondolieri
Ponte del Formager, San Vio.
Tel: 041-528 6396. Closed
Tues. €€€
Set close to the Guggen-
heim and popular with
Americans, the restaurant
thrives on a meaty menu,
supported by exceptional
risotto. Book.

Linea d'Ombra
Ponte dell'Umiltà, Zattere. Tel:
041-241 1881. €€
Close to La Salute and
facing Il Redentore church
on the Giudecca, this
romantic restaurant and
wine bar is perfect on a
summer's evening. Rein-
terpreted Venetian clas-
sics, with fresh fish and a
good wine list. The floating pontoon is preferable
to the chic but minimalist
modern interior. Book.
Vaporetto: La Salute.

Da Montin
Fondamenta delle Eremite.
Tel: 041-522 7151. Closed
Tues D and Wed. €€€

This enchanting but over-
priced arty garden restaurant was once favoured by
such luminaries as Hem-
ingway and Peggy Guggen-
heim. Although most
popular in summer, the
cosy, faintly bohemian
dining room comes into
its own in winter. Book.

Quatro Feri
Calle Lunga San Barnaba.
Tel: 041-520 6978. Closed
Sun. €
This bustling new-wave
bacaro has a youthful
owner, Barbara, and her
reasonable prices attract
a faithful young crowd to
sample Venetian dishes.
As befits a former
sommelier, Barbara
serves superior wines.

Bars & Cafés

Al Chioschetto (Fondamenta Zattere, by Capi-
taneria di Porto) is a
waterfront kiosk-bar serving tasty snack lunches
and sunset aperitifs. **Arco**
(Calle Lunga San Pan-
talon) has an excellent
ciccetteria (traditional
tapas bar) in front of the
main trattoria and pizze-
ria. **Enoteca San Barnaba**
(Calle Lunga San Barn-
aba) is a rustic-style inn
for regional wines and
meaty bar fare from Friuli.
Imagina (Rio Terra Canal)
is a buzzing New York-
style designer bar and
gallery that runs the

gamut from cappuccino
and brioche to prosecco
and late-night bar snacks.
Further down, **Pasticceria
Giobetti** is a pastry shop
noted for *la bomba*, a rich
chocolatey tart. **Linea
d'Ombra** (Ponte dell'U-
miltà, Zattere) is both a
chic restaurant and an
atmospheric waterfront
bar, ideal for drinks, lunch
or ice cream on the floating terrace. **La Piscina**
(Zattere 782) is a smart
waterside café serving
teas, coffees and light
Mediterranean fare. Fur-
ther along (Zattere 922)
is **Gelateria Nico**, a top
place for ice-cream. **La
Rivista** (Calle Larga
Pisani) is a stylish bar-
restaurant, Japanese-
managed but Italian
Futurist in conception and

cuisine. **Suzie Café**
(Campo San Basilio;
closed weekends) is a
studenty place for drinks,
light lunches and live
music in summer. **Campo
Santa Margherita** is
awash with buzzing bars
(and **Causin**, a fine *gelateria*) – places suitable for
all by day but which are
youth-magnets by night,
apart from the sophisti-
cated **Margaret Duchamp**
(see Nightlife, page 225).

RIGHT: Linea d'Ombra's scenic terrace.

THE ACCADEMIA

The world's finest collection of Venetian art is a showcase of ceremonial paintings and sumptuous religious art

This treasury of Venetian art ranges from Renaissance masterpieces and Byzantine panel paintings to vibrant ceremonial paintings, Grand Tour caprices and even portraiture. Yet it remains intimate rather than overwhelming, as memorable for its revealing snapshots of everyday life as for its masterpieces.

The collection is housed in La Carità, a complex of church, convent, cloisters and charitable confraternity. The church was deconsecrated in Napoleonic times and became a repository of work created during the Venetian Republic, particularly paintings saved from suppressed monasteries. However, the core collection was assembled by Venetian artists themselves in the 18th century. Since the gallery is lit by natural light, choose a bright day to explore this vaguely chronological collection, dating from the 14th to 18th centuries. Highlights include intimate works by Carpaccio and Bellini, High Renaissance art by Giorgione, Titian, Tintoretto and Veronese, and genre scenes by Tiepolo, Guardi and Canaletto.

The Republic set great store by the State painter, with artists of the calibre of Bellini, Titian and Tintoretto expected to capture Venetian glory through official festivities. Much effort is dedicated to charting the ceremonial, with the protocol of receiving prelates, ambassadors and dignitaries, all on display here. Yet vibrant colour, luminosity and a supreme decorative sense, tinged with a poetic sensibility, also distinguish Titian, Giorgione and Veronese. The American art critic Bernard Berenson judged Venetian painting the most appealing Italian school: Their colouring not only gives direct pleasure to the eye but acts like music upon the moods.

● *Open: Mon 8.30am–2pm; Tues–Sun 8.30am–7pm.*

ABOVE: Veronese's *Feast in the House of Levi* (1573) invoked the Inquisition's wrath, with its sacrilegious portrayal of buffoons, drunkards, Germans, dwarfs and similar indecencies. Veronese side-stepped the issue by renaming his work in more secular vein.

RIGHT: *The Tempest* by Giorgione (born c.1475–1510) stakes the artist's claim to being the first Romantic painter in the modern sense. This is one of his few surviving works, characterising the ages of man in enigmatic yet artful pastorals.

RIGHT: Carpaccio's *Arrival of the English Ambassadors.* Carpaccio is noted for a love of detail, narrative talent and sensitive use of colour. Carpaccio and Bellini were prime exponents of the narrative cycles known as *istorie*, a Venetian Renaissance phenomenon.

THE COLLECTION

Room I occupies the Gothic chapter house, and is dedicated to Byzantine and Gothic artists, such as Paolo Veneziano and Antonio Vivarini (*c.*1419–76), noted for static yet rapt decorative works on gold backgrounds. **Rooms II to IV** display expressive early Renaissance altarpieces by Giovanni Bellini, brimming with poetic atmosphere.

Room V contains the most celebrated works: Giorgione's *The Tempest* (*c.*1507), a moody and enigmatic canvas, and his *Portrait of an Old Woman*, a meditation on time. **Rooms VI to X** feature Renaissance and mannerist masters, from Titian to Veronese and Tintoretto. Titian's poignant *Pietà*, intended for his own tomb, is lit by a diffuse light and infused with an anguished questioning about the meaning of life; the troubled *Nicodemus* is Titian's last self-portrait. Veronese's *Feast in the House of Levi* (1573) covers an entire wall in **Room X** but was painted for the church of Santi Giovanni e Paolo. Intended as a *Last Supper*, the subject was a pretext for depicting a profane

feast. Also here is Tintoretto's *Miracle of the Slave*, the work that made his reputation.

Works by Veronese and Tintoretto are in **Room XI**, as are rococo frescos from ruined churches, culminating in Tiepolo's *Rape of Europa*, a triumph of pulsating light and shade. **Rooms XII to XVII** display 18th-century landscapes and genre paintings beloved by Grand Tour visitors. Guardi's caprices hang alongside Longhi's patrician homes and a rare Canaletto perspective painting, which uses a pastiche Venetian background.

The final section, from **Room XIX to the end**, returns to the Renaissance, with a showcase for the pomp and pageantry of the Venetian Republic, seen in vibrant ceremonial paintings by Carpaccio and Bellini. The last room retains its Gothic ceiling and displays Titian's *Presentation of the Virgin*. This work was painted for this very room, and so makes a fitting finale to any tour.

LEFT: Paolo Veneziano is credited with introducing the taste for panel painting to Venice. His *Coronation of the Virgin* (1325) is symbolic rather than realistic, and is bathed in radiant colours.

ISLANDS OF THE LAGOON

Visit San Giorgio and Giudecca for the views and churches, Torcello for mosaics, Murano for glass, Burano for lace, and the Lido for its seaside air

The lagoon is a floating world between the smoking oil refineries on the mainland and the fish slithering in the reeds. At times, fumes intermingle with the cedar-perfumed air of the islands and the sound of cicadas. The desolation of the lagoon waters is relieved by sightings of wild ducks, mute swans or the fragile-looking black-winged stilt. Despite their proximity, the lagoon islands are startlingly different, embracing marshland, orchards, vineyards and even beaches.

These low-lying islands have a chequered past as monasteries or munitions dumps, mental asylums or market gardens, leper colonies or crumbling fortifications. However, the strangest places tend to be the "minor" or outlying islands. By comparison with these diverse but dying communities, the main islands survive on their location and separate identities. Certain islands are the preserve of fishermen, lacemakers and glass-makers, while others are home to silk-workers, boat-builders or urban sophisticates.

Visitors with little time available would do well to make the islands of San Giorgio, Burano and Torcello their priorities. San Giorgio, facing San Marco, is the closest to the city, and the only major island untouched by commerce. The belltower offers the most romantic view of Venice. Torcello, the remotest of the islands, offers a stirring impression of the earliest Venetian settlement. The mood is set by the surreal isolation of the site, the air of stagnation, the sluggish canal, the scattered buildings and the solitary red-brick belltower.

Out of season, Torcello is the place for bathing in what the writer Jan Morris calls "an ecstasy of melancholia". By contrast, Burano is a splash of colour in a bleak lagoon, dispelling any mournfulness with its

Map on pages 194–5

BELOW:
Burano: brightly painted houses.

BELOW: view across to
San Marco from San
Giorgio Maggiore

parade of colourful fishermen's cottages. However, visitors tempted by gaudy Venetian glass or soft-shelled crabs will choose its neighbour, Murano. Giudecca, just off Dorsoduro, is celebrated for its Palladian church, but is a raffish yet newly revitalised island in its own right. The Lido cannot compete historically, but its beaches and graceful art-nouveau architecture offer a semblance of escape from the summer heat.

San Giorgio Maggiore

The island of **San Giorgio Maggiore** was once known as *isola dei cipressi* because of the cypress-framed vistas. Seen from afar, the majestic monastery appears suspended in the inner lagoon, with its cool Palladian church matched by a belltower modelled on St Mark's. Together with the baroque beacon of La Salute, these two great symbols guard the inner harbour of Venice. San Giorgio is a hallowed spot, with its famous Benedictine monastery.

Despite the island's proximity to San Marco, the absence of distractions means that San Giorgio still has a secluded air. The monastery boldly looks out over St Mark's Basin, defying the conventional model of an inward-looking institution enclosed by cloisters. The medieval building was remodelled in the late-15th and early-16th centuries, but owes its classical grace to Palladio. Although the Napoleonic suppression of the monasteries in 1806 was accompanied by French plundering of San Giorgio, the monks refused to leave. The harbour was developed at the same time, with part of the monastery used to store munitions during World War II. Today, the Benedictines remain the sole residents, enhancing the mood of spirituality.

San Giorgio Maggiore ❶ (9.30am–12.30pm, 2.30–6.30pm) is undoubtedly the finest monastic church in the lagoon. Only the churlish aesthete Ruskin found it "barbarous" and "childish in conception". Endowed by doges and favoured by humanist scholars, the monastery became a famous centre for learning.

Although most visitors restrict their visit to the church and belltower, to appreciate the size and diversity of the monastic site, you need to tour the Cini Foundation (*see opposite*). In 1565 Palladio was commissioned to rebuild the church, his finest Venetian legacy, rivalled only by Il Redentore. Here Palladio shows his mastery of the classical idiom, using the basic geometric volumes of cube, pyramid and sphere. Based on Alberti's precepts, this is a Christian church founded on classical principles and mathematical proportions.

The facade is composed of two overlapping temple fronts, with a central portico. The cool church is a model of perspective, with a domed interior which is bathed in white light. The overall sense of order is more impressive than the component parts: the vaulted ceiling, elegant choir and choir stalls, the

striking marble floor and two minor works by Tintoretto.

A lift whisks visitors to the top of the **Belltower** for fabulous views over the city, whatever the weather. The angel on top of the tower fell off during a violent storm in 1993 but has been restored, with the original now displayed inside the church and a bronze copy on the roof. If the lift attendant is not too busy, he may be persuaded to unlock the **Sala del Conclave**, where the conclave met to elect Pope Pius VII in 1800, while Rome was occupied by French troops. Although it is now used as a private music room by the monks, members of the public can occasionally attend classical concerts here, as well as performances of Gregorian chant in the church.

The **Fondazione Cini ❷** occupies much of the great Benedictine complex. (Some sections can be viewed during exhibitions, but for a full tour, call the foundation or try to charm the custodian; tel: 041-271 0228.) Count Vittorio Cini (1884–1977) bequeathed his home to the city and created the foundation as a memorial to his son, who died in a flying accident. The centre funds restoration projects and stages major exhibitions. The baroque architect Longhena designed the monastery's ceremonial double staircase and library, built on the site of Michelozzi's Renaissance library.

Other highlights are the huge Renaissance dormitory and the cross-vaulted Palladian refectory. More impressive still are the Renaissance **Cloister of the Laurels** (Chiostro degli Allori) and the Palladian **Cloister of the Cypresses** (Chiostro dei Cipressi). Palladio also designed the ceremonial guest quarters overlooking the lagoon. The sumptuous setting is more reminiscent of a palace courtyard than of a cloistered retreat. The Palladian cloisters lead to the monastic gardens and the **Teatro Verde ❸**, the open-air theatre; this pastoral setting provides an atmospheric stage set for occasional summer concerts.

Giudecca

Giudecca is the most contradictory of Venetian islands, home to the city's most luxurious hotel and to its most raffish district. Until recently, this was a depressed island of decaying tenements and blind alleys, with a polarisation between the gentrified east and the industrialised west. It was easy to forget that the island was once celebrated for palatial villas, exotic gardens and risqué clubs. Giudecca probably began as a place of exile for punished nobles, but became a veritable pleasure garden.

From Renaissance times onwards, the island spelt indulgence for a nobility in search of the decadent *dolce far niente* (sweet idleness) typical of a Venetian summer. Giudecca was also noted for its convents, including one notorious for Casanova's amorous exploits. Industrialisation put an end to the patrician idyll: from the 19th century until the

Giudecca's busy waterfront.

BELOW:
Mulino Stucky housing redevelopment.

1950s, the island became Venice's industrial inner suburb. The horizon was dotted with flour mills, fabric and clock factories, a brewery and boatyards. Decline set in with the growth of the industrial zone on the mainland, which left Giudecca an urban wasteland.

And then a rock star moved in, with his camp collection of Warhol, Damien Hurst and Murano glass, and resurgence followed. Simplistic though it sounds, the locals credit Elton John with turning the tide in this resolutely un-glitzy island. What is beyond dispute is that this *popolare* or working-class district, is undergoing a rebirth, with the restoration of landmark buildings.

While parts of Giudecca remain shabby, abandoned lofts are being bought by artists, giving the district a bohemian air. Given that property prices are far lower than in historic Venice, old flour mills and furniture factories are being converted into fashionable apartments. On the waterfront facing the city, the foundations are being restored, and functional buildings have been put to creative new uses, including a granary converted into a youth hostel and a brewery turned into flats.

However, apart from the great Palladian church and the quayside facing the city, Giudecca feels immune to tourism. The churches may have been restored, but the women's prison is still in service, the boatyards remain active, and the waterfront bars are favoured by matronly locals sipping lurid orange *spritzes*. They may enjoy one of the finest views of St Mark's, but now have to contend with fans in search of Elton John's Gothic home, conveniently close to the Cipriani.

Although it is tricky to walk across the island, tiny pastoral pockets survive. Dirk Bogarde, while filming *Death in Venice* (1970), luxuriated in solitude on Giudecca, with the lagoon lapping beside him, "the wheeling swifts, swooping like commas high above the dome of the Redentore, and the distant bells of the city drifting across the lagoon, all mixed with the bumble of pollen-heavy bees nudging into the white and pink discs of hollyhocks".

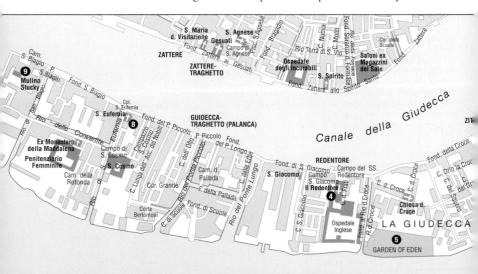

Il Redentore ❹ (Mon–Sat 10am–
5pm, Sun 1–5pm) is a Venetian landmark, visible from every side of St
Mark's Basin, and a key reason for
visiting the island. The church of the
Redeemer was built in thanksgiving
for the end of the 1576 plague.
Designed as a votive temple, this
graceful church is still the scene of
Venice's most beguiling summer festival. Architectural purists feel that
this Palladian masterpiece, inspired
by the Pantheon in Rome, surpasses
even San Giorgio *(see page 192)*.

The newly restored facade is
undoubtedly more subtle, resting on
a rusticated pediment, with a sweeping flight of steps echoing the style
of a gracious Palladian country villa.
From here, the eye is inevitably led
to the lantern surmounted by the figure of Christ the Redeemer.

However, compared with the
lovely view of the floodlit facade,
visible from the quaysides across
the water, the interior can feel disappointing, despite its rigorous
respect for classical principles, mastery of geometrical forms and effort-
less grandeur. Palladio was also

influenced by contemporary Roman
architecture, with the choir of Il
Redentore echoing Bramante's central plan for St Peter's.

From the church, Ramo della
Croce leads to the exotic **Garden of
Eden ❺**, named after the English-
man who created it. Facing the garden is the former English Hospital,
which cared for impecunious British
expatriates during Edwardian times.
Retracing one's steps leads back to
the waterfront and another Palladian
gem. **Le Zitelle ❻** bears the Palladian hallmarks of stylistic unity,
coherent classicism and an inspired
sense of proportion. In keeping with
Venetian tradition, the complex was
originally designed as a convent but
became a noted musical conservatoire. Recently restored, the complex
has now taken on the role of a convention centre, making access difficult. Although Le Zitelle has a
landing stage, with frequent services
back to central Venice, many visitors
end up in Cip's Club, the elegant
waterfront bar which lies just beyond
the convent.

The **Hotel Cipriani ❼**, set on the
eastern spit of the island, enjoys
sweeping views over the lagoon,
especially from the summer terrace.
Now one of the world's most exclusive hotels, the Cipriani originally
belonged to the founders of Harry's
Bar *(see page 100)*. Cipriani's liver-
ied motor boats regularly ferry guests
across from San Marco to this oasis
of peace. The hotel incorporates a
Gothic palace and has gardens full of
azaleas, rhododendrons and olean-
ders framing the wide expanse of the
swimming pool. For Harry's without
the hype, retreat to Harry's Dolci, a
slightly less pricey offshoot, located
on Fondamenta San Biagio.

The section from Campo di San
Cosmo to Rio Ponte Lungo runs
through the area's old manufacturing district. Fans of industrial architecture can walk back along the

Map
below

*"Of all the colours,
none is more proper
for churches than
white, since the
purity of the colour,
as of life itself, is
particularly satisfy-
ing to God."*

PALLADIO

*The facade of Palla-
dio's Il Redentore.*

*Cool, Palladian
interior of Il
Redentore.*

Giudecca and
San Giorgio

Fondazione
Cini
Campanile di
San Giorgio
Maggiore
S. GIORGIO
San Giorgio
Maggiore ❶
San Giorgio
Maggiore
Canale di S. Giovanni
Canale di S. Giorgio
Bacino di
S. Giorgio
Hotel
Cipriani
Teatro Verde ❸
Zitelle ❼
MPO
ARTE
N

0   200 m
0   200 yds

Elton John's Gothic Palazzo on Giudecca.

waterfront past distinctive factories to the island's oldest church. **Sant' Eufemia** ❽ (Mon–Sat 9am–noon; Sun Mass only) faces the great Gesuati church across the water on Dorsoduro *(see page 180)*. Sant' Eufemia, marred by remodelling, survives as a bizarre mix of Veneto-Byzantine capitals, rococo stuccowork and 18th-century paintings.

Since this is Giudecca, the church is overshadowed by a neighbouring mill, and by the decaying industrial wasteland behind. Next door, on the western edge of the island, lies **Mulino Stucky** ❾, a neo-Gothic

industrial relic. The novelist L.P. Hartley looked "almost with affection on the great bulk of Stucky's flour mill, battlemented, pinnacled, turreted, machicolated, a monument to the taste of 1870, that might have been built out of a child's box of bricks". Giovanni Stucky, the overbearing Swiss owner, was murdered by one of his workers in 1910. After decades of neglect, and arson in 2003, this fortress-like former grain silo, pasta factory and flour mill is being converted into a mix of affordable housing, hotel and convention centre. Giudecca residents hope that

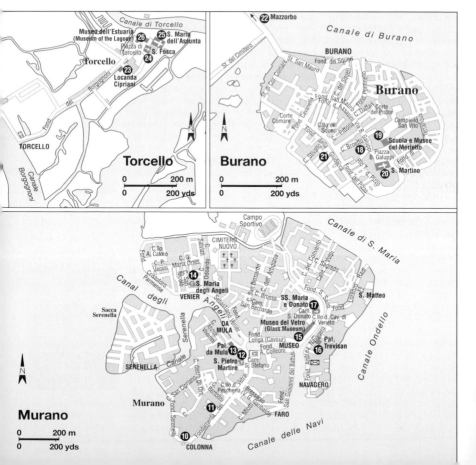

this grandiose monument to the Victorian age may yet come to symbolise an economic regeneration.

Murano

"The most curmudgeonly of the Venetian communities, where it always feels like early closing day", moaned the writer Jan Morris. Yet Murano is proud of its past as a highly celebrated glassmaking centre and a summer resort for the nobility. In the 18th century, the island was noted for its villas, gambling clubs and literary salons. However, the closure of many churches and the rapaciousness of the glass factories has somewhat blunted its appeal.

On a sunny day, Murano can pass for a smaller version of Venice, but it can be very bleak in winter, with scruffiness and commercialism outweighing picturesque charm. Nonetheless, Murano makes a pleasant enough stopping-off point on the way to austere Torcello. The majority of visitors are enticed by the glassmaking, although an impressive Byzantine church and a cluster of bars also add to Murano's appeal.

Murano glass is an acquired taste, which many lifelong Venice fans fail to acquire. While few visitors would turn down an antique Murano mirror or an 18th-century chandelier, modern Murano glass is another matter. It errs on the side of virtuosity and garishness rather than refinement and elegance. Still, the skill of the glassblowers makes an impressive display, while the crisis in the glass industry means that prices are competitive at the artistic end of the spectrum.

Resist the touts on Riva degli Schiavoni, offering free boat trips to Murano. Freedom is costly, with victims marooned in one glass factory and subjected to heavy selling techniques. Instead, travel independently and select the showrooms you wish to see at leisure.

Visitors who only want a brief visit to Murano should stay on board until **Museo**, the third stop, close to the glass museum. However, serious shoppers will choose **Colonna** ❿, the best stop for exploring the myriad glass factories.

The quayside opens onto **Fondamenta dei Vetrai** ⓫, the heart of the glassmaking district, with the 16th-century Palazzo Contarini on the left. The showrooms along the quayside offer a chance to admire the glassblowers' skills.

Barovier e Tosso (Fondamenta Vetrai 28) is noted for its collectors' items, but kitsch creations abound in Murano, from peacock-shaped glasses to gondola vases. Towards the end of the quayside, a bridge crosses the canal to the left bank and the church of **San Pietro Martire** ⓬ (9am–noon, 3–6pm). This Gothic church has a Renaissance portal and a newly restored altarpiece by Bellini (1488) depicting a "holy conversation" between Doge Barbarigo and the Virgin, the temporal and spiritual powers. This is a harmonious work: the drapery of the Madonna's blue cloak is deliberately blurred, with the rich colours creating a soft atmosphere.

Further down the quayside, just before Ponte Vivarini, stands the **Palazzo da Mula** ⓭, a glassworks set in a Gothic palace and Byzantine walled garden. From here, there is a picturesque view looking west along Canale degli Angeli to the abandoned church of **Santa Maria degli Angeli** ⓮.

From Palazzo da Mula, cross the main bridge over Canale Grande and turn to the right, following the quaysides of Fondamenta Cavour to the **Museo del Vetro** ⓯ (10am–5pm; closed Wed), the Glass Museum. This occupies the Gothic Palazzo Giustinian, originally the seat of the bishop of Torcello, which was transferred here after the earlier settlement was abandoned.

Given the Far Eastern fakes flooding the Venetian market, buy "Murano" glass only where you see the trademark *Vetro Artistico Murano*. (For details see www.muranoglass.com or call Hello Venezia, tel: 041-2424.)

The refinement of Venetian glass developed on the island of Murano made it a byword for superb chalices, chandeliers, mirrors and goblets. Most of the island's furnaces welcome spectators.

Although the palace retains a few original frescos, it is essentially a showcase for Murano glass, from platters and beakers to crystal chalices and the finest chandeliers. Non-Venetian pieces include a Roman mosaic bowl, matched by mosaics from the local church of Santi Maria e Donato. As well as Renaissance enamelled glassware, there are satirical scenes mocking the Austrian rulers, art-nouveau objets d'art, and the glittering blue Coppa Barovier, a Gothic wedding chalice, adorned with allegorical love scenes.

Murano's finest church

On the right bank, facing the museum, lies the classical **Palazzo Trevisan** , with its interior frescoed by Veronese. On the left bank, just north of the glass museum is a beguiling church reflected in the water. **Santi Maria e Donato** ⑰ (8.30am–noon, 3.30–7pm) is the finest church on Murano, despite a misguided 19th-century restoration. This 7th-century church, remodelled in Veneto-Byzantine style, boasts 12th-century apses, decorated with blind arches and loggias leaning over the canal. As in Santa Fosca on Torcello, the brick and terracotta apses are studded with zigzag friezes and dog-tooth mouldings.

The charm of the interior has survived much tampering, with its Gothic ship's-keel ceiling, Greek marble columns and Veneto-Byzantine capitals. The apse is dominated by a luminous Byzantine-style mosaic of the Madonna and Child, rivalled by a beautiful altarpiece by Paolo Veneziano (*c*.1310).

However, the highlight is the patterned mosaic floor, depicting interlaced foliage and allegorical animals. The pattern includes fragments of ancient glass mosaics, recalling the finest Murano craftsmanship. When leaving Murano from the Museo boat stop, look out for the jaunty lighthouse *(faro)* located on the east of the island.

Burano

This most vibrant of Venetian islands makes a cheery stop en route to Torcello, its polar opposite. Hemingway mocked the islanders for having nothing better to do than make boats and babies. However, Burano is better known as the home of fishermen and lace-sellers. Weary visitors may be relieved to find that there are few cultural sights but atmosphere aplenty. Burano is one of the friendliest islands, partly the product of its self-sufficiency: a history of modest prosperity has made it less dependent on tourism than many other islands. To help preserve its character, the community regularly rejects applications for hotels.

Burano feels like an authentic old fishing village, with nets hung out to dry and boxes of crabs blocking the doorways. Burano romantics even portray lacemaking as an aesthetic extension of the net-mending tradition. After several glasses of wine, visitors can easily imagine them-

Navigational channels are marked by bricole, *sturdy poles roped together, while* paline *are individual poles, often striped, for tethering private craft.*

BELOW: basilica of Santi Maria e Donato.

selves transported to a Greek island, aided by visions of bobbing boats in the dappled sunlight.

From the ferry stop, follow the flow to **Via Galuppi** , the main street, lined with fishermen's cottages. Tradition has it that the houses were painted different colours to enable fishermen to recognise their homes from out at sea.

When not ruining their eyesight poring over lace, the fishermen's wives painted the family homes in bold colours, often adding geometrical motifs over the doorways. By the same token, when ashore, the fishermen spent their time mending nets or boat-building. Burano remains the best place for boat-building, with craftsmen building by eye, not by design. The street is lined with lace shops and traditional trattorias, the place for the best crab and squid dishes. After a visit to the lace school, visitors learn to distinguish between Taiwanese products and genuine Burano lace, as light as tulle.

Piazza Galuppi, the colourful town square, is home to the **Scuola e Museo del Merletto** (10am–4pm; closed Tues), the lace school and museum, housed in a Gothic palace. Given the difficulties of preserving lace, most samples on display tend to be from the 19th century, including a fine wedding train. Lace has been made in Venetian convents since medieval times, but the *punto in aria* method, using a needle and thread, only emerged in the 16th century. The art fell into decline with the Industrial Revolution, but was saved from extinction on Burano by the creation of a lacemaking school in 1872. By the turn of the century, the local industry sustained 5,000 people, but factory-made lace also fell out of fashion. Ironically, the islanders now import Taiwanese lace to boost their scant sales of hand-made lace.

Genuine hand-made Burano-point lace is ridiculously expensive: but then, it takes 10 women up to three years to make a single tablecloth.

From here, the leaning tower of **San Martino** (8am–noon, 3– 6pm) looms into view. The 16th-century church is best-known for its paintings, especially a Tiepolo *Crucifixion*. A short walk leads to **Fon-**

Map on page 196

TIP

Da Romano on Burano's Piazza Galuppi (tel: 041-730030) is one of those canny seafood restaurants where previous owners accepted paintings as payment for meals.

BELOW: Burano, the home of fishermen and lacemakers.

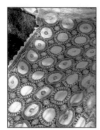

Burano lace – beware of imitations.

damenta della Giudecca N, and a stretch of colourful quaysides. The more adventurous should consider a boat trip to an atmospheric Franciscan retreat: Burano is the only sensible embarkation point for the lush island of **San Francesco del Deserto** (tel: 041-528 6863).

From the quays close to the church there is an idiosyncratic, family-run shuttle service in a *sandolo*, a traditional rowing boat. Alternatively, on the way back to the ferry, cross the footbridge to **Mazzorbo** N, a former island for exiles. The verdant island is unremarkable, but there are evocative views towards Venice. The salt marshes and mudflats around Burano are being reinstated to restore the lagoon's ecological balance and act as a sea defence against high tides and storms.

Torcello

The long boat trip to Torcello helps one appreciate the remoteness of this evocative island, the earliest centre of Venetian civilisation. It is strange to think that Venice arose from these solemn marshes, a 7th-century settlement uprooted from its mainland home of Altinum. As an autonomous island and trading post, Torcello flourished, with 10,000 inhabitants in the 10th century. Decline set in with the rise of Venice, hastened by the silting up of this corner of the lagoon, which turned Torcello into a malarial swamp after the 14th century. Now only about 50 people live here permanently.

The novelist George Sand captured the pastoral mood of her visit in the 1830s: "Torcello is a reclaimed wilderness. Through copses of water willow and hibiscus bushes run saltwater streams where petrel and teal delight to stalk." But where Sand celebrated life, other commentators have seen the haunting spirit of a ghost town. Ruskin mused on the poignant scene, "this waste of wild sea moor, of a lurid ashen grey… the melancholy clearness of space in the warm sunset, oppressive, reaching to the horizon of its level gloom".

From the jetty, a canal towpath leads through the lush countryside to the Byzantine complex. **Locanda Cipriani** N, a deceptively modest rural inn, lies just beyond the bridge. Film stars and royals have feasted on the self-consciously simple seafood dishes. Hemingway, who stayed here while working on his Venetian novel, has one of his characters give a simplified view of the creation of Venice: "Torcello boys were all great boatmen. So they took the stones off all their houses on barges… and they built Venice." Certainly, as the city declined, building materials were often recycled, first on Murano and Burano, and then in Venice itself.

At the end of the path stands the austerely lovely basilica of **Santa Fosca** N (10.30am–6pm). Built by Greeks, it was designed as a *martyrium*, housing the relics of a martyr. The church is a coherent masterpiece, a harmonious structure

Nature Trips

It is often easy to be overwhelmed by this city of stone, and forget that La Serenissima is only a tiny portion of a vast lagoon that comprises hundreds of islands, archaeological sites, monasteries, farms, fortresses and wetlands, home to hundreds of species of birds. The *vaporetti* operate a reasonable service through the lagoon, concentrating on tourist classics like the glass-blowers' island, Murano, and the brightly painted fishermen's houses on Burano and Torcello, where the earliest settlers arrived. Fortunately, you can now explore some of the lagoon on the public-ferry system. Moreover, thanks to enterprising ecologists, you can visit previously unchartered waters with the experts *(see page 228)*. Trips use public transport or a chartered boat to visit previously inaccessible islands, churches, excavation sites and the beautiful market-garden island of Sant' Erasmo. One trip uses a wooden *bragozzo*, a flat-bottomed boat capable of navigating the shallow channels of the shifting wetlands. Here, you have the chance to see daily life out on the lagoon, from the giant nets belonging to squid fishermen to sightings of men in waders plunging their hands into the squelchy mud in search of lagoon fish.

combining Romanesque with Byzantine elements. The basilica was built in the 11th century, at the same time as Santi Maria e Donato in Murano, and boasts the same blind arcading and geometrical motifs. The outer walls are girded by an octagonal portico resting on stilted arches, with sculpted columns. The portico balances the thrust of the dome and vaults, and also heightens the sense of interior space. The central plan, a Greek cross inscribed within an octagon, is emblematic of Byzantine architecture, with the pentagonal apses echoing oriental forms. The Byzantine interior is barrel-vaulted, but the planned dome was never built.

Santa Fosca is linked by a portico to **Santa Maria dell'Assunta** ❷❺ (10.30am 6pm, 4.30pm in winter), a model of an early Christian church. To Ruskin, the stark exterior was reminiscent of a storm refuge. The cathedral is the oldest monument in the lagoon, founded in AD 639 as an episcopal seat. The basilica was modelled on those in Ravenna, but modified in the 9th and early 11th centuries to create a superb Veneto-Byzantine building. The church was first restored in 1008, with the raising of the floor and creation of a crypt: the lovely mosaic floor dates from this period.

The dignified interior is punctuated by slender Greek marble columns, bearing Byzantine capitals. Among the treasures included here are the original 7th-century altar, the pulpit, the ceremonial throne, and a Roman sarcophagus containing the relics of St Heliodorus, the first bishop of Altinum. The iconostasis is painted with Byzantine panels and supported by marble peacocks drinking from the fountain of life.

The solemnity of the architecture is counterpointed by the richness of the **Mosaics**. These date from the 7th century, with some in the apse from the 9th century. A masterpiece of

Byzantine design adorns the central apse: a slender, mysterious Madonna bathed in a cloth of gold. The frieze of the Twelve Apostles close by dates from the 12th century. Henry James admired these "grimly mystical mosaics", with the Apostles "ranged against their dead gold backgrounds as stiffly as grenadiers presenting arms". The 13th-century *Last Judgement* counterbalances the apse mosaics and is the most compelling narrative sequence. One should read it from top to bottom, with the *Crucifixion* leading to the *Descent into Limbo*, the *Day of Judgement* and, at the bottom, the *Weighing of Souls*.

Although sections of the work have been over-restored, it is still engrossing, with angels, devils and disembodied corpses competing for attention.

After climbing the newly restored belltower, glance at the vestiges of the 7th-century **baptistry**, built on a circular plan like the Roman baths. Also on the piazza is **Attila's Throne**, a Roman potentate's marble seat. Nearby stands the Torcello museum, the **Museo dell' Estuario** ❷❻

Map on page 196

Torcello, the oldest Venetian settlement, has a sarcophagus adorned with a winged lion; a lovely iconostasis is also supported by sculpted lions and peacocks drinking from the fountain of life, symbolising, perhaps, the eternal spirit of Venice.

BELOW: Torcello's Santa Maria dell' Assunta and museum.

TIP

Ferries for the main islands: For San Giorgio take line 82; for the Lido, take lines 1, 51, 52, 61, 62, 82; for Murano (52, 41, 42, also Alilaguna services); for Burano and Torcello (12,14); for Giudecca (41, 42, 82). For current information call 041-2424 or 041-730761.

(Tues–Sun 10.30am–5pm). While not outstanding, the museum is a quiet complement to the site, spread over two buildings, the former town hall and city archives. Exhibits include mosaics from Ravenna and fragments from Torcello's *Last Judgement*, lost during a clumsy restoration in 1853. Compared with the largely intact and original buildings, these are the broken shards of a lost civilisation.

Like Ruskin, most writers strike an elegiac note when faced with the collapse of this early Venetian settlement: "The lament of many human voices mixed with the fretting of the waves on the ridges of the sand." However, if you are fortunate, and the crowds are in abeyance, you may share George Sand's enchantment with Torcello: "The air was balmy and only the song of cicadas disturbed the religious hush of the morning."

If the ferry fails to come, or if you are overcome by the exquisite aromas from the Locanda Cipriani, retire to lunch at its gentrified rustic rival, the **Osteria Ponte del Diavolo**.

The Lido

This long strip of land, sandwiched between the city of Venice and the Adriatic, belongs neither to Venice nor the mainland. This reflects the Lido's prime function, to protect Venice from the engulfing tides. In spirit, it is a place apart, not quite a traditional summer resort nor a residential suburb. After the time warp of historic Venice, the sight of cars, large villas and department stores can be disconcerting. Yet the island cannot be dismissed as soulless. There is a touch of unreality about the Lido, as there is about Venice itself, hence its role as a superior film-set. In this faded fantasy, neo-Gothic piles vie with art-nouveau villas and a mock-Moorish castle.

In the Romantic era, Byron and Shelley raced on horseback along the empty sands, but the advent of sea-bathing in the 1840s brought the fashionable élite and the world in its wake. The English and Germans were the chief culprits, but by the 1880s the Venetians had also succumbed to the spell of sun, sand and sea. The island became the world's

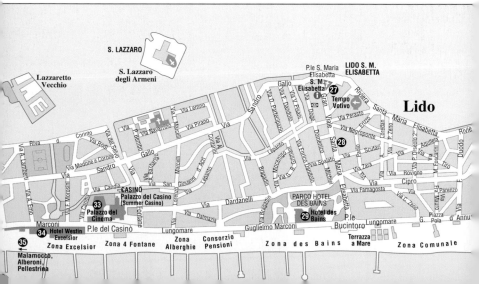

first lido, spawning a rash of brash or glitzy imitators across the globe. Ruskin railed against the crowds of uncouth smokers who filled "his" steamers: the populace "smokes and spits up and down the piazzetta all day, and gets itself dragged by a screaming kettle to the Lido next morning to sea-bathe itself into capacity for more tobacco". The once windswept dunes gave way to mass tourism in the 1920s, with D.H. Lawrence decrying the beach as "a strand with an endless heap of seals come up for mating".

However, the Lido is also Thomas Mann's Venice, a place of decadence and spiritual dislocation. Curiously, this does not dispel its staid reputation as a bourgeois retreat. The Lido has long been a bulwark of conservatism, residential rather than industrial, conventional yet cosmopolitan.

Since the Lido cannot compete with the historical riches of the rest of Venice, it remains the preserve of residents and visitors staying on the island. Although most day-trippers stray no further than the beaches and smart hotels, the Lido offers more

subtle pleasures, from *belle époque* architecture to a gentle cycle ride along the sea walls to Malamocco.

The ferries from San Marco deposit visitors among the traffic at the edge of the shopping district. Close to the jetties stands the 16th-century church of **Santa Maria Elisabetta ㉗**, with the main shopping street beyond. **Gran Viale Santa Maria Elisabetta ㉘** cuts across the island from the lagoon shore to the Adriatic. An air of gracious living still permeates the broad promenade, leading to the **Lungomare**, the seafront promenade and the focus of the summer evening *passeggiata* (promenade). Beyond are the best Adriatic beaches, private pockets of sand bedecked with colourful cabins.

The Lido is home to several of the city's most elegant hotels, including the **Hôtel des Bains ㉙** (Via Lungomare Marconi 17). Thomas Mann's stay in this eclectic Edwardian palace helped inspire *Death in Venice*. Even Mann's beach spelt foreboding: "Evening too was rarely lovely, balsamic with the breath of flowers and shrubs from the nearby park."

The Art Deco Hôtel des Bains, where Visconti shot Death in Venice (1971), *based on the evocative novella by Thomas Mann (1875–1955) who stayed here.*

BELOW: the lagoon.

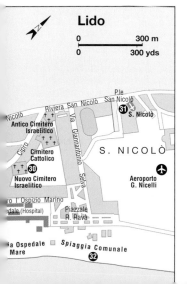

Venice Film Festival

Venice, the world's oldest film festival, now rivals Cannes in prestige and outshines the Côte d'Azur in terms of glamour. Founded as a showcase for Fascist Italy, the festival's success belies its unpromising origins. The 10-day jamboree provides a more romantic visual backdrop than Cannes, conducive to "secret" celebrity assignations in Harry's Bar and stirring speedboat chases across the lagoon, designed to outwit or ensnare any lurking paparazzi. Recently, the festival has gone all out for Hollywood glitz, even if worthy arthouse winners, such as Mike Leigh's *Vera Drake*, tend to triumph in the end.

In the 2004 festival, most plaudits went to Al Pacino's Shylock in *The Merchant of Venice*, a choice that delighted the partisan home crowd. Not that the festival failed to recognise talent at the very outset. Spencer Tracy was nominated for his role in *Dr Jekyll and Mr Hyde* in the first edition, and Venice has celebrated such vintage performances as Greta Garbo in *Anna Karenina* (1935) and Laurence Olivier's *Hamlet* (1948). Although early directors of the calibre of John Ford and Auguste Renoir brought glamour to the Lido, the festival has a checkered past, frequently beset by bureaucracy and political wrangling. The glory days coincided with New Wave cinema in the 1960s, a fame sealed by movies from Godard, Pasolini, Tarkovsky and Visconti. Since the 1980s, there have been constant charges of jury bias, and controversial directors have not always fared well in Venice. Nonetheless, there has been a revival in the festival's fortunes, both in terms of audience appreciation and in film quality. The Golden Lion (Leon d'Oro) award may now mean more, particularly since the presentation ceremony is once again back in the Fenice opera house, resplendent after its restoration.

During the September festival, the Lido recovers a little of its turn-of-the-century lustre. Stars can be spotted sipping bellinis on the terrace of the top hotels or parading along the seafront. The resort's *belle époque* Hôtel des Bains has both starred in *Death in Venice* and stood in for Cairo in *The English Patient*, while the Fascistic Palazzo del Cinema is still the heart of the festival.

In the 2004 festival, Tom Cruise, Meryl Streep, Denzel Washington and Steven Spielberg were all on the red carpet, with Spike Lee and Scarlett Johanssen on the jury. The Venetian audiences enjoy basking in the presence of the stars, and then bringing them down to earth. Thwarted in his bid to pilot his plane onto the Lido beach, John Travolta had to settle for staying in Missoni's yacht, moored by St Mark's. Classic festival chaos meant that several stars were left standing at their own premieres, while delays led to Johnny Depp's and Kate Winslet's premiere finishing at 4am. But for gossip-mongers, the highlight was Lauren Bacall's sour put-down of her Antipodean co-star, Nicole Kidman, as "no film legend".

Whatever the failings of the films, the city always shines. The Lido is awash with sleek movie stars scurrying from screenings to someone's private yacht. The 2004 film festival coincided with Disney's remake of *Casanova*, transforming the city into a surreal film-set, with the libertine's stagecoach and plumed horses thundering across St Mark's, towards the newly erected gallows. Since shooting coincided with unseasonal flooding, the 500 extras in period costume all started slipping in the waterlogged square. Yet the film festival closed in style when the same piazza was turned into an open-air cinema for the premiere of Spielberg's *Shark Tale*, projected onto the world's largest inflatable screen. As the producer said: "More than anything, we are in show-business – this is the show part." ❏

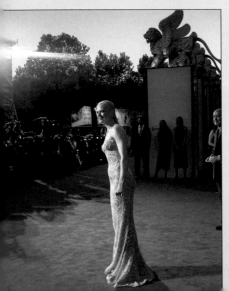

LEFT: Oscar-winning actress Nicole Kidman performs for the paparazzi.

Beaches

Following the seafront north leads to the public beach and airstrip. **Nuovo Cimitero Israelitico ㉚**, the Jewish cemetery, lies on Via Cipro, the street cutting across the island. The cemetery dates back to 1386 and reflects the special status of Jews in Venice *(see page 172)*. Via Cipro leads to the lagoon shore and **San Nicolò ㉛**, a church and Benedictine monastery. where the doge prayed after the Marriage of the Sea ceremony on Ascension Day. From here, there is a clear view of the **Fortezza di Sant'Andrea** on the island of Le Vignole, the impressive bastion that defended the lagoon *(see page 209)*.

If beaches appeal, bear in mind that most are private and charge a fee, unlike the **Spiaggia Comunale ㉜**, the scruffy public beach in the east of the island. Reports of pollution in the Adriatic do not deter the crowds. At the grander end of the seafront stands the **Palazzo del Cinema ㉝**, typical of the functionalist buildings of the Fascist era, and the focus of the Venice Film Festival. On Lungomare Marconi, along the seafront, stands the **Hotel Westin Excelsior ㉞**, inspired by exotic Moorish models and Veneto-Byzantine traditions.

A cycle ride or leisurely walk lead south past the grand hotels and manicured beaches, following the sea walls into oblivion. The route passes **Malamocco ㉟**, the site of the first capital of the lagoon before it was engulfed by a tidal wave. Although there are no traces of the 8th-century capital, this fishing village has several seafood restaurants and a bell-tower recalling the campanile of San Marco. The spit eventually peters out in the sand dunes of **Alberoni**, with the windswept views beloved by Goethe now only visible across golf courses.

Beyond is the island of **Pellestrina**, a narrow strip of land bounded by the *murazzi*, the great sea walls that protect the lagoon city. For the first time since the city's creation, the sea defences are being radically re-thought and a mobile dam is being built nearby: whether to save Venice from the sea, or as an act of political folly, only time will tell. ❑

Map on page 202

TIP

Book lagoon visits with the nature and archaeology specialists, Natura Venezia (www.natura-venezia.it; tel: 041-932003); trips may include a rustic lunch of sardines, sea-bass, sole and lagoon fish.

BELOW:
Lido di Venezia.

THE MINOR ISLANDS

The smaller islands of the lagoon show a different face of Venice: among the delightful backwaters are a famous cemetery, isolated monasteries and a rural way of life

A drift between the industrial and the rural world, the lesser-known islands of the Venetian lagoon are abandoned to birdsong, howling dogs and the prayers of monks. Apart from the religious communities who cherish their isolation, the minor islands are searching for a new identity. In the past, they served specific functions, with the city

defences bolstered by the islands close to the Lido, the monastic islands clustered around San Marco, and outlying islands used as hospitals or munitions stores. Remoteness rendered the islands suitable for such esoteric uses as quarantine centres and lunatic asylums, hermitages and monastic retreats – even cemeteries, leper colonies and dog sanctuaries. Many of these survive, although some have been transformed into market gardens and vineyards.

Nonetheless, about 20 of the 34 lagoon islands are virtually abandoned, although reclusive millionaires, cultural associations and hotel chains are waiting in the wings. At intervals, the Italian State, daunted by the future upkeep of the islands, auctions or leases certain minor treasures, usually on the understanding that any forts and monasteries are restored.

Although the fate of such islands as Lazzaretto Vecchio and Poveglia still hangs in the balance, success stories abound, from the university on San Servolo to the luxury resort on San Clemente and the opening up of the former quarantine island of Lazzaretto Nuovo.

Yet thanks to the shifting tides and the shallowness of the lagoon, the islands preserve a pastoral way of life, one that is rarely visible to visitors who stay close to the shore. At low

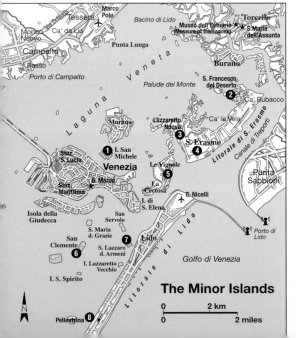

The Minor Islands

0   2 km
0   2 miles

tide, the shrimp fishermen leave their boats and seem to walk across water; families picnicking on remote sandbanks appear from nowhere and then disappear again with the tide. With the blur of mainland pollution merging into a heat haze, you may catch sight of the vivid plumage of a migratory bird or two, or spot a solitary reed-cutter tramping over the mudflats. In the *valli* fisheries, locks are checked and the fish directed into different ponds while, to the east of Torcello, the salt pans continue to be worked. Children play happily in the vineyards of Le Vignole while their uncles tend to their market gardens on neighbouring Sant'Erasmo, and the sun-worshippers simply stretch out on the sandbars of Pellestrina.

The autumn **Galuppi Festival** is a successful way of opening up unusual sites, with concerts staged in Franciscan churches, forts and former leper colonies on the islands of San Francesco del Deserto, Sant'Erasmo and San Lazzaretto Nuovo. Even if many islands are served by ferry, island-hopping is not always easy, so bargaining with fishermen is recommended for a rewarding view of Venice beyond the confines of St Mark's. The holy grail is a plate of risotto steeped in black cuttlefish sauce – ideally cooked by a lapsed monk in an isolated tavern deep in the lagoon.

San Michele

San Michele ❶, site of the city cemetery (7.30am–4pm), is known as "the island of the dead". From afar, its silhouette is swathed in mist, floating as ethereally as a city in the afterlife. As the island closest to Venice, it is served by ferries from the Fondamente Nuove. The quayside and adjoining alleys serve the business of death: monumental masons vie with funeral florists, both doing their briskest business in winter. From the shore, one's eye is drawn to the contrast between the solemn cypress trees, black against the sky, and the high, rose-coloured brick walls.

Just by the landing-stage lies **San Michele in Isola**, a cool, austere Renaissance church by Coducci. As the first church faced in white Istrian stone, San Michele set a building

Map on page 206

Coducci's innovative Renaissance church.

BELOW: San Michele, "island of the dead".

Although the writer Jan Morris is enchanted by the cemetery's "seductive desolation", Venetian nurse Livio Nardo has a sunnier relationship with San Michele, and says of it: "It's the most cheerful cemetery in the world, as cemeteries go. You've got good company there – Stravinsky and Ezra Pound. We get tourists committing suicide in Venice just so they can be buried there."

BELOW: church of San Michele cloisters.

trend throughout the Veneto. Beside the church is a domed Gothic chapel and cloisters leading to the cemetery.

This was where Napoleon decreed the dead should be despatched, away from the crowded city graves. The Austrians used the former monastery as a political prison, but the island is now tended by Franciscans. Although there are sections for foreigners here, the Jews bury their dead in a separate cemetery on the Lido. Famous foreigners are allowed to rest in peace, but more modest souls tend to be evicted after 10 years. The rambling cemetery is lined with gardens stacked with simple memorials or domed family mausoleums awaiting further members. Here lie the tombs of several dogal families, obscure diplomats, and the victims of malaria or the plague. The grounds are studded with grotesque statuary, encompassing the monumental and the municipal, the cute and the kitsch.

In the eastern corner is the Protestant *(Evangelisti)* section, containing the grave of American poet Ezra Pound (1885–1972). Untended and overgrown, this is also the last resting place of obscure Swiss, German and British seamen. In the *Greci* or Orthodox section lie the tombs of the composer Igor Stravinsky (1882–1971) and the ballet impresario Diaghilev (1872–1929), along with the tombs of long-forgotten Russian and Greek aristocrats. The British architect David Copperfield has recently been entrusted with creating an extension to the cemetery, including gardens, funerary chapels, footbridges and even a crematorium.

San Francesco del Deserto

Another fascinating island is **San Francesco del Deserto ❷** (9–11am, 3–5pm; closed Monday), a Franciscan retreat. Since there are no ferry services, visitors will need to hire a *sandolo*, a Venetian rowing boat, from **Burano**, the closest inhabited island *(see page 200)*. Legend has it that St Francis visited on his return from the Holy Land, symbolised by a tree that supposedly sprouted from the saint's staff. This early Franciscan community has been abandoned only twice, after an outbreak of malaria and military occupation, yet remains the only monastery to be spared desecration by Napoleonic troops.

Although donations are appreciated, the monastery exudes an air of self-sufficiency, from the serene friars to the cloisters, church and well-tended vegetable gardens. A contemplative mood is induced by the lofty cypresses and emblematic Franciscan paintings. Up to ten friars live here, along with visiting novices and laymen on retreats.

Lazzaretto Nuovo and Sant'Erasmo

These diverse neighbouring islands can all be reached on line 13 from Fondamente Nuove, beginning with **Lazzaretto Nuovo ❸**, a former monastery, quarantine island and military garrison (weekends 9am–11.30am or by arrangement; tel 041-

520 6713 or 041-244 4011). This austere, newly opened island was a
Benedictine monastery until 1468,
when it became a quarantine centre
for Venetian ships suspected of har-
bouring contagion. Designed to combat the spread of diseases transported
via oriental ports, the island became
a model for quarantine centres all
over the Mediterranean, from Malta
to Marseilles. It was dubbed "new"
(nuovo) to distinguish it from **Lazzaretto Vecchio**, off the Lido, the
"old" quarantine island for plague
victims. In Austrian times, the island
was converted into a military garrison, with a gunpowder-and-munitions factory.

The most impressive building is
the **Teson Grande**, a barn-like 16th-
century structure, complete with historical graffiti. The imposing bastions
also make an atmospheric nature trail,
with misty views over the lagoon.

Facing Lazzaretto is **Sant'
Erasmo ❹**, the large market garden
in the heart of the lagoon. This aloof
island may be home to just 800 people, most of them subsistence farm-
ers, but the community now benefits
from rural tourism. Venice's vegetable garden is famed for its production of radicchio, asparagus and
artichokes, delivered to the Rialto
market by boat. Yet Sant'Erasmo
also attracts walkers, cyclists and
canoeists in summer, when the small
beach becomes a magnet for Venetian families and teenage boat-boys.

There are several ferry stops on
the island, but **Fermata Capannone**
is the closest to Venice and is convenient for the beach, sole trattoria, fort
and canoeing club. **Torre Massim-
iliana**, the Austrian fort once used as
a barracks and munitions dump, has
been well renovated but awaits conversion into a lagoon museum.

Le Vignole and its fortress

Le Vignole ❺ lies just south of
Sant' Erasmo but can also be viewed
from the northern end of the **Lido**.
Its sole claim to fame is that it
served as the main plank in the
Venetian defensive system. The
Sant'Andrea fort, designed by Sanmicheli in 1543, guarded the lagoon,
with chains stretching right across
the water from here to a matching
fortress on the Lido. The lagoon entrance was thus completely sealed
off and reinforced by lines of cannons resting on rafts.

Although dilapidated, the fort is
still visible, forming an arched bastion with apertures at water level to
accommodate more cannon. The
island remains popular with Venetians, thanks to its patchwork of vineyards and smallholdings. In summer,
the adults congregate in a makeshift
café, while children dive off their parents' boats.

Plans are afoot to turn the neighbouring monastic island of **La Certosa** into a conservation area, with a
bridge linking it to Le Vignole. As
the largest abandoned island in the
lagoon, La Certosa has the space
and the history to provide archaeological and nature trails.

When shopping for
fruit and vegetables in
Venice itself, request
produce that is
nostrano ("our own"),
meaning grown on
Sant'Erasmo.

BELOW:
one of the smaller
of the lagoon's 34
islands, with channel
and tide markers.

Cruising the Brenta Canal

The Brenta Canal is a placid showcase for Venice's rural treasures, sumptuous villas which are regularly open to visitors. This limpid area linking Venice and Padua is known as the Riviera del Brenta, reflecting its role as a summer retreat for the Venetian nobility. In echoes of the Grand Tour, visitors can take a canal-boat *(burchiello)*, which crawls along the Brenta to Padua, passing over 50 sumptuous villas. The route involves nine swing-bridges and five locks, a reminder that there is a 10-metre difference in water level between Venice and Padua.

The Veneto possesses the blueprint for the patrician villa, a harmonious rural retreat framed by waterside formal gardens and a working farm estate. Characterised by a classical portico, and modelled on a Graeco-Roman temple, these Palladian gems have influenced architectural styles the world over. From Renaissance times, the Venetian nobility commissioned these residences as retreats from the summer heat. The villa also represented the glorification of the dynasty and a practical investment of profits earned from maritime trade. In summer, the villa became a society haunt, originally a focus for humanist

gatherings, but later a setting for lavish festivities, notably gambling, a Venetian vice. To this end, most villas have a *barchessa*, a colonnaded wing used as a summer house, banqueting hall or gambling pavilion.

From Venice, the first masterpiece is **Villa Foscari**, better known as La Malcontenta because of its troubled romantic past. This distinctive villa was designed for the Foscari family, and is still owned by their descendants. Raised on an elevated pedestal to protect it from floods, it has a temple-like facade mirrored in the Brenta and a vaulted *piano nobile* modelled on the interiors of Roman baths.

Further along, set on a scenic bend in the canal, is the late-baroque **Villa Widmann**, decorated in fanciful French rococo style. The galleried ballroom is adorned with Arcadian scenes. The grounds are lined with cypresses, horse-chestnut and limes, and dotted with neoclassical statuary, centred on an ornamental lake. Barchessa Valmarana, which faces Villa Widmann across the water, is all that remains of a villa destroyed in the early 20th century to avoid death duties. Although reduced to its colonnaded guest wings, this glorious relic has been restored and contains frescos rivalling its more famous neighbours.

Closer to Padua is **Villa Pisani**, a palatial masterpiece which owes much to French classicism. A ballroom frescoed by Tiepolo is matched by grandiose grounds dotted with follies, an appropriate setting for Mussolini and Hitler's first meeting in 1934. At Stra, just beyond Villa Pisani, looms **Villa Foscarini Rossi**, a testament to the ambitions of the Foscarini dynasty, including Doge Foscarini, a past owner. The Palladian-inspired villa contains baroque *trompe l'œil* frescos depicting allegories of war and peace, science and the arts. The heroic adventurer, Lord Byron, a previous resident, must have felt at home.

Booked through Venetian travel agencies, the Brenta barge cruise and villa visits make a lovely day trip from Venice. Cruises run from April to October and include entrance fees to selected villas. Although the barges stop by the grandest villas, these can also be reached independently, but more mundanely, by car, train and bus (www.riviera-brenta.it). ❏

LEFT: cruising past Villa Pisani.

The southern lagoon

Known as **"The Hospital Islands"**, these former asylums and leper colonies are treated with disdain by Venetians, despite their newer incarnations as resorts or cultural centres. **San Clemente ❻**, just south of Giudecca, began as a monastery, but, in the 19th century, became a lunatic asylum for women, later mutating into a psychiatric hospital until 1992. Since 2003, the island has been an austerely luxurious resort, playing up its past as a monastery rather than a madhouse. Despite insane prices, the island retreat is a lovely spot, with low-key restaurants and bars, open to visitors and guests *(see page 213)*.

Between Giudecca and the Lido lies **San Servolo** island, which rose to prominence as a Benedictine monastery, but then became a nunnery until 1615. After welcoming refugee nuns from Crete, a former Venetian colony, San Servolo started operating as a hospital. In 1725, it became an asylum for Venetian "maniacs of noble family", of whom there were many. The asylum was built within the monastic shell, with the church remodelled and new wards created. Byron often passed the island on his marathon swims from the Lido to the Grand Canal. His friend Shelley referred to the asylum as "a windowless, deformed and dreary pile... which calls the maniacs, each one from his cell, to vespers". The French poet Théophile Gautier, who visited in 1850, also found it deeply dispiriting: "It had been no great task to adapt their use from monks to madmen."

However, in recent years the restored complex has been given a new lease of life as a prestigious craft centre and as Venice International University, with English the medium of instruction. San Servolo has managed to preserve its 18th-century pharmacy and library as well as the cloisters and its lush grounds.

Santa Maria delle Grazie, immediately south of Giudecca and currently abandoned, began as a medieval crusaders' staging post, but swiftly became a monastic site, military base, munitions dump and hospital for infectious diseases.

San Lazzaro

San Lazzaro degli Armeni ❼ (3.25–5.25pm), an island off the Lido, is one of the most intriguing monasteries in the lagoon, distinguished by its onion-shaped cupola. (This Armenian enclave is served by line 20 from San Zaccaria, with the 3.10 ferry the only practicable option).

The Armenians, along with the Greeks and Jews, form the oldest foreign community in Venice, having settled in the city from the 13th century onwards and remained on good terms with the Republic. The island was a leper colony until 1717, when the Armenians were granted asylum from Turkish persecution. The leader, Mechitar the Consoler, had been driven from the monastery he had established in the Peloponnese. Today, the island is a scholarly centre for

Map on page 206

Many sections of the lagoon are unnavigable because of the mudflats and sandbanks – but skilled boatmen can weave through the shifting channels and sandbars, guided by the bricole, the distinctive navigational markers.

BELOW: the Hotel San Clemente, a romantic retreat set on its own private island.

Map
on page
206

TIP

For information on ferries call 041-2424 or 041-730 761 as these can be infrequent. For San Lazzaro degli Armeni take line 10 or 20 (best at 3.10pm from San Zaccaria); for San Servolo line 20; for San Francesco del Deserto lines 12 or 14 to Burano then water taxi; for San Michele, known as Cimitero, lines 41 or 42; for Lazzaretto Nuovo line 13; for Sant'Erasmo line 13 is best; also 42 and 52.

BELOW: San Lazzaro degli Armeni.

Armenian culture, supported by the 8-million strong Armenian diaspora. The setting is idyllic, with the church and cloisters surrounded by orchards, gardens and strolling peacocks. The remodelled Romanesque church is decorated with starry mosaics, the air laden with incense. The 18th-century refectory is where the courteous, trilingual monks and seminarians eat in silence while the Scriptures are intoned in classical Armenian.

The picture gallery contains fine Venetian and Armenian paintings, while the museum displays bizarre exhibits, from Phoenician artefacts to an Egyptian mummy. The library's priceless books and manuscripts are rivalled by the typesetting hall, which has an ancient printing press capable of reproducing 36 languages.

Although the printing centre closed in 1993, the Armenian press is still run from this nerve centre. One room is dedicated to Byron, because of his enthusiasm for Armenian culture and his contribution to an Armenian–English dictionary in 1816. Browning, Longfellow and Proust were equally impressed by this serene monastery.

Changing fortunes

The southern part of the lagoon, from the Lido to Pellestrina and Chioggia, now forms part of the controversial mobile-dam project known as MOSE, intended to save the city from flooding (see page 39). New lagoon gates are being built at the three entrances to Venice Lagoon: at the Lido, Malamocco and Chioggia inlets. The new lock-gate will operate at the Malamocco inlet and be backed up by breakwaters, which are also being built just beyond each lagoon inlet.

Lazzaretto Vecchio, an island for stray dogs, has been a pilgrims' hostel, hospital and military site, but is mooted to become a sports complex. The first plague outbreak in the 14th century led to the creation of an isolation centre, which became Europe's first permanent quarantine hospital for plague victims.

Poveglia, a distinctive humpback island, hugs the southern shore of the Lido. It was once a powerful centre, but decline set in after the devastation of the Genoese war in 1380. Poveglia's chequered past includes a spell as a noble summer residence, a barracks and munitions depot and, until the 1960s, a hospice and retirement home. Despite its virtual abandonment, the island is coveted as a potential secluded holiday resort or marina.

Pellestrina ❽, the sandy gash which protects Venice from the open sea, makes a relaxing summer excursion. (It is best reached from the Lido, with bus 11 to Alberoni connecting with the ferry for a five-minute boat ride to Pellestrina.) This ribbon of land forms a natural barrier strengthened by the *murazzi*, the great sea walls. The island is a haunt of sunbathing Venetians or solitary walkers, with a quaint fishing village, gossipy bars and jaunty cottages. As part of the newly reinforced dyke which helps preserve Venice for generations to come, Pellestrina makes a fitting end to an exploration of the lagoon.❑

RESTAURANTS & BARS

Restaurants

BURANO

Al Pescatori
Piazza Galuppi. Tel: 041-730 650. Closed Wed. €€
This welcoming restaurant serves fish and game. Try the seafood risotto or tagliolini with cuttlefish (seppie).

Da Romano
Piazza Galuppi. Tel: 041-730 030. Closed Sun D and Tues. €€
This old-established restaurant is the best on Burano. Set in the former lace school, the pretty interior is lit by glass lamps and adorned with paintings donated by visiting artists. You can dine on the terrace.

GIUDECCA

Altanella
Calle delle Erbe. Tel: 041-522 7780. No credit cards. €€–€€€
Friendly trattoria favoured by Elton John, who has a home around the corner. Only fish dishes on offer.

I Do Mori
Fondamenta Sant'Eufemia. Tel: 041-522 5452. Closed Sun. €€
Formed by a breakaway group from Harry's Bar, this is the place for those who can't afford the elevated prices of the originals. The food is sound Venetian home cooking, with a preponderance of fish dishes (try the scampi risotto) as well as pasta and pizzas.

Harry's Dolci
Fondamenta San Biagio. Tel: 041-522 4844. Closed Tues and Nov–Feb. €€€
Pop over to Harry's Dolci for a waterside American brunch – it's "Harry's without the hype", but with better views and prices. Try the Venetian risotto, curried chicken or baccalà mantecato, and sip a signature Bellini in the bar. Tasty pastries served outside mealtimes. Vaporetto: Sant' Eufemia.

Hotel Cipriani
Fondamenta San Giovanni. Tel: 041-520 7744. Closed Nov–March. €€€€
Set in the city's most luxurious hotel, Cipriani is an elegant spot spilling onto a glorious terrace. The setting is exquisite, the service divine and the prices deadly. Or try the more informal Cip's Club (D only; €€€). Both offer rare views across to St Mark's. Free launch service from St Mark's pier. Book.

THE LIDO

Liberty Restaurant
Hôtel des Bains, 17 Via Lungomare Marconi. Tel: 041-526 5921. €€€
This art-deco restaurant is perfectly pleasant, but the opulent setting is more impressive than the food. There is an additional beach restaurant as well as buffets and snacks around the pool.

Taverna Summertime
Hotel Westin Excelsior, 41 Lungomare Marconi. Tel: 041-526 0201.€€€€
This summery restaurant spreads out under an attractive terrace overlooking the beach. Good buffet and delicious grilled fish. Book.

MURANO

Trattoria Busa alla Torre
3 Campo Santo Stefano. Tel: 041-739 662. L only. €€
Classic Venetian fish and seafood restaurant which has been an inn since 1420 and a wine-store since the 12th century. Clams, fish grills and lagoon vegetables.

SAN CLEMENTE

San Clemente Palace
Tel: 041-244 5001. €€–€€€€
This former monastery is now a luxury hotel with four restaurants. Ca' dei Frati is the most enchanting, with views across to San Marco, while La Laguna is a casual poolside affair. Free private launch from St Mark's.

TORCELLO

Locanda Cipriani
29 Piazza Santa Fosca. Tel: 041-730 150. Closed Tues, and Jan. €€€€
This remote but lovely inn run by the nephew of Arrigo Cipriani, the owner of Harry's Bar, is a local institution. Try the grilled fish, fillet steak or risotto alla torcellana. Book.

Bars & Cafés

The Lido has a wide range of atmospheric bars: the **Bar Maleti Lido** by the jetty is the place for ice cream, cocktails or snacks; **Cafe del Lido** (Via Michiel) wine-and-cocktail bar is a tribute to art-deco opulence; **Pachuka** is a popular beach bar, restaurant and disco-bar with live music and DJ-led events staged on San Nicolò beach. Giudecca has **Bar Zitelle**, a simple but appealing waterfront bar next door to the more pretentious **Cip's Club** (Zitelle waterbus stop). **San Clemente** has some smart resort bars, including one resembling an English gentlemen's club. **Sant' Erasmo** has one bar-restaurant, situated by the beach and ferry stop. On most of the minor islands, visitors would be better off bringing a picnic.

PRICE CATEGORIES

Prices for three-course dinner per person with a half-bottle of house wine:
€ = under €30
€€ = €30–€50
€€€ = €50–€70
€€€€ = more than €70

TRANSPORT

GETTING THERE AND GETTING AROUND

GETTING THERE

Visitors from abroad are most likely to arrive by air. Although other modes of travel offer benefits, all require extra time.

By Air

The main airport for Venice is **Marco Polo** on the edge of the lagoon, 13 km (8 miles) from the city centre. However, Ryanair and other airlines confusingly also refer to **Treviso** as "Venice airport". This is, in fact, 30 km (19 miles) to the north of Venice and far less convenient. You may wish to choose a flight-plus-hotel package to Venice, which can often be cheaper and easier than travelling independently. There are direct flights to Marco Polo from the major European capitals, as well as low-cost flights operated by Easyjet (to Marco Polo) and Ryanair (to Treviso). From North America, flights to Venice are usually via London, Rome, Milan, Frankfurt or Amsterdam. From Australia and New Zealand, flights are generally via Rome or Milan. Contact the airport switchboard on 041-260 6111; flight information on 041-260 9260. The lost-property office is on 041-260 9222.

By Car

Travelling to Venice by car from abroad is not cheap. Costs include petrol, motorway tolls, hotels en route and the car-park fees in Venice. You will require a current driving licence (with an Italian translation unless it is the standard EU licence) and valid insurance (green card). Arriving by car is generally best avoided, since it will have to be left in a car park outside Venice.

By Train

For those arriving in Venice from abroad, there are international and Eurostar services from London (changing in Paris), Moscow, Munich, Nice, Paris, Vienna, St Petersburg and Zurich – but train fares are often more expensive than flights. Within Italy, there are direct services to Venice from Bologna, Padua, Genoa, Ferrara, Milan, Turin and Verona.

Once at Venice's Santa Lucia station, call in at the tourist office in the entrance hall and buy your *vaporetto* (ferry) ticket from the kiosk just outside the station, by the waterfront. For travel within Italy or abroad, buy train tickets from Italian travel agents, which saves queuing for ages at the station. For train information, call 8488-88088;

www.trenitalia.it; for lost property call: 041-785 238, and for left luggage call: 041-523 1107.

GETTING AROUND

The best way to get around far-flung parts of the city is by boat – once you have mastered a few key ferry routes, water transport is quite straightforward, although most of the time you will probably be walking, which is often more practicable in the city centre.

Car Parks

Visitors arriving in Venice by car will need to leave their vehicle at the entrance to the city. The multi-storey car park at Piazzale Roma is close to the centre and has good ferry services but is pricey (www.asmvenezia.it). The island of Tronchetto forms the largest car park in Europe (tel: 041-520 7555; www.veniceparking.it). Although cheaper, it is further away and less accessible by ferry. You may have to wait over half an hour for a ferry, so weigh up cost against convenience. Prices vary, depending on the car and the season, but €20 per day is a minimum and queues can be extremely long in summer. Ferry line 82 links Tronchetto with central Venice.

The Airports

A large number of charters (and Ryanair flights) arrive at Venice-Treviso airport, 30 km (19 miles) from Venice, and may include a bus link to the city centre. If this is not provided, take the No. 6 bus from outside the terminal.

Both scheduled and charter flights arrive in Venice-Marco Polo Airport (tel: 041-260 6111), on the edge of the lagoon. You can buy your bus or water travel pass from the special office in the arrivals hall, en route to the terminal exit. From here to the city centre, you have a choice of routes. Splashing out on a water taxi (from around €80; beware of extras) is a magical way to see Venice for the first time. Or pre-book a water taxi at €25 per person (minimum 2 passengers) with Bucintoro Viaggi; tel: +39-041-521 0632; www.bucintoroviaggi.com). Alternatively, there are car taxis (from around €30) to Piazzale Roma, close to Venice bus terminal (tel: 041-523 7774/041-936 137) and the city waterfront.

In addition, there are ATVO bus services (tel: 041-520 5530; www.atvo.it) to Piazzale Roma, with tickets (€3) on sale in the airport lounge. The journey takes 30 minutes, ending close to the waterside, where you can catch a ferry (vaporetto). You can also buy a travel pass from the transport office there. Alternatively, if you are staying on the Lido (for land taxis on the island, tel: 041-526 0059) or in central Venice, close to San Marco, then a water bus is an appealing yet inexpensive way to reach the city from the airport. A free shuttle bus takes you to the airport waterfront, where water taxis and the fast Alilaguna lagoon shuttle boat await. These services (just over an hour; €10) connect with Murano, the Lido, the Arsenale area, San Zaccaria and San Marco (tel: 041-523 5775; www.alilaguna.com). Check times with the booking office in the airport.

City Ferries

Ferries or water buses are known as vaporetti (for timetable information tel: 041-2424). It is worth buying a one-day, three-day or weekly travel pass, which will allow you to travel on any city ferries during this period, including the islands (with a supplement for boats to the airport). The travel passes are expensive (much more than the Venetians pay), but are cheaper and less fuss than buying individual trips, and also help subsidise city transport for Venetians, acting as an indirect tourism tax. The passes are bought in the form of a Venice Card (with the blue version covering transport and the orange version including museum access too, and virtually half-price passes for "juniors", those 29 and under). A 24-hour blue "senior" pass costs €14 (€28 for orange); a three-day senior pass costs €29 (€47 for orange); and a weekly pass costs €51 (€68 for orange). If you are found without a ticket, a fine is payable on the spot. The passes can be bought online (www.venicecard.com), in the tourist office, or at Piazzale Roma, among other places. The times displayed are generally reliable, but double-check with a boatman. The most confusing landing-stages are at San Zaccaria (Riva degli Schiavoni), San Marco and Fondamente Nuove because they are spread out along the quaysides, with different services running from different jetties. The traghetto is a useful gondola ferry that crosses the Grand Canal at certain strategic points (40 cents), thus saving extra walking.

Pick up an up-to-date transport map (€1) from the tourist offices and check gondola prices.

Main ferry routes

Line 1 is the most romantic and runs the length of the Grand Canal, stopping everywhere. Line 82 is the quickest way from the station to central Venice, the Lido and Giudecca, and makes fewer stops than line 1.

Ferries for main islands

For San Giorgio take line 82; for the Lido, take lines 1, 51, 52, 61, 62, 82; for Murano, 52, 41, 42, also Alilaguna services; for Burano and Torcello, 12 or 14; for Giudecca, 41, 42, 82.

Ferries for minor islands

Double-check return times before setting out, as ferries can be infrequent. For San Lazzaro degli Armeni take line 10 or 20 (at 3.10pm from San Zaccaria); for San Francesco del Deserto, 12 or 14 to Burano then water taxi; for San Michele, known as Cimitero, 41 or 42; for Lazzaretto Nuovo, 13; for San Servolo, 20; for Sant'Erasmo, 13 from Fondamente Nuove is best; also 42, 52 from Piazzale Roma. For current information on ferries, call 041-2424 or 041-730 761.

Gondolas

Everyone expects to try this once. Prices are fixed, with extra paid for music or evening trips (€73 for 50 minutes or €91 after 8pm). Agree a route with the gondolier, but, for romance, stick to the back canals rather than the Grand Canal.

Water Taxis

Even if many islands are served by ferry, island-hopping is not always easy, so bargaining with fishermen is recommended for a rewarding view of Venice beyond the confines of St Mark's. To travel in style, pick up a pricey water taxi on the taxi stand on Riva degli Schiavoni, near San Marco (or call: 041-522 2303 or 041-723 112).

Boat Holidays

For a houseboat holiday around the Venetian lagoon (in an eight-berth cruiser), contact Connoisseur Boats in the UK (tel: 0870-774 9933). Venetian tide information service tel: 041-241 1996.

ACCOMMODATION

SOME THINGS TO CONSIDER BEFORE YOU BOOK THE ROOM

Hotels

In theory, the closer you are to San Marco, the higher the price, but there are exceptions, with several pricey hotels on the Lido, Giudecca and San Clemente. Given its closeness to St Mark's and the spread of upmarket hotels and newly converted boutique hotels, the Castello district is an obvious choice, with lagoon views available from the hotels on Riva degli Schiavoni. Delightful, central and convenient though the San Marco area is, it feels resolutely touristy, so Venice fans or second-time visitors would do well to broaden their horizons. This can mean choosing an inn or a boutique hotel in Castello, or an island resort such as San Clemente, or even an individualistic boutique hotel in the up-and-coming Cannaregio area. Although no longer a bargain, the tranquil, romantic Dorsoduro district is charming, with small but sought-after mid-market hotels. For families with young children, the Lido makes a good choice, with its sandy beaches and bike rides, but remains the least Venetian area of Venice. The budget alternative is the station area, which is convenient rather than attractive. If forced to stay outside the city, avoid soulless Mestre and opt for atmospheric Padua or Treviso, a 30-minute train ride from Venice.

Timing and booking

Since there is almost no off-season in Venice, hotels can easily be fully booked all year round, though the recent opening or refurbishment of so many luxury hotels means there is a wide choice at the top end of the market. In any case, make reservations well ahead of peak seasons such as Christmas, New Year, Carnival (February), Easter, May–June and September. When booking a hotel, ask which is the nearest square/church and ferry stop. **Official booking service: Venezia Si** represents over 90 per cent of Venetian hoteliers and offers a free booking service, even at the last minute (from abroad, call: +39-041-522 2264; in Italy, call freephone 800-843 006; www.veneziasi.it). However, if in a search for a bargain, first try all the usual accommodation-only websites.

Cost and quality

Venice is the most costly city in Italy and its hotels are notoriously expensive. A simple, central hotel is often the same price as a mid-market hotel elsewhere in Italy. The basic rules in Venice are: book early, and check where your room faces, and what the price differential is between poky rooms and palatial rooms. A typical hotel can offer a choice between an expensive large room overlooking the Grand Canal, and a poky back room overlooking a bleak courtyard. Even so, a room with a view can cost half as much again as one without a view.

A Place of Your Own

Apartments represent charm and excellent value, particularly since one can eat at home, on fresh produce selected from the Rialto markets. Occupying a glorious Gothic *palazzo* a stone's throw from an old-fashioned wine shop, cheese shop or fish market, is a delightful way to experience the intimacy of neighbourhood Venice, and feels light years away from the tourist bustle, even if apartments are central. Most owners are linked to foreign agents or tour operators. The London-based **Venetian Apartments** (tel: (44) 0208-8878 1130; www.venice-rentals.com) specialises in stylish, unusual city apartments. Apartments range from a bijou residence under the eaves to a Gothic palace with fabulous views over the Grand Canal. The apartments, which must be booked for at least a week, range from about £600 to £2,000 weekly. However, the company takes great pride in matching the right apartment to the right client. Apartments can be booked by guests from anywhere in the world.

SAN MARCO

Luxury

Gritti Palace
Campo Santa Maria del Giglio
Tel: 041-794 611
Fax: 041-520 0942
www.luxurycollection.com
Hemingway, Winston Churchill and Greta Garbo all stayed in this 15th-century palace. As the most patrician hotel in Venice, it is renowned for its formal luxury, Grand Canal setting and discreet service. Doge Andrea Gritti lived here, and the hotel still has the air of a private *palazzo*, with Murano chandeliers and 16th-century damask furnishings. The charm appeals to Europeans in particular; the Hemingway suite is the loveliest.

Luna Baglioni
Calle Vallaresso/Calle de l'Ascension
Tel: 041-528 9840
Fax: 041-528 7260
www.baglionihotels.com
The Luna's claim to fame is that it is the oldest hotel in Venice, a former Knights Templar lodge (1118) for pilgrims en route to Jerusalem. Set just off San Marco, the hotel boasts noble Venetian decor and an 18th-century ballroom with original frescos; impressive restaurant, and the grandest breakfast room in Venice.

Monaco e Grand
Calle Vallaresso
Tel: 041-520 0211
Fax: 041-520 0501
E-mail: mailbox@hotelmonaco.it
Since being bought by Benetton, this luxury hotel has been revamped, creating a mix of slick contemporary and classic Venetian style. Chic bar and waterfront breakfast room; Il Ridotto, the former Venice casino, is on the first floor. While the hotel is more luxurious and has great views, the new Palazzo Salvadego annexe is more Venetian and less pricey.

The mood of this distinctive hotel is vaguely medieval in inspiration, which, depending on taste, can be romantic or rather austere. Bedrooms are both intimate and comfortable.

Moderate

Santo Stefano
Campo Santo Stefano
Tel: 041-520 0166
Fax: 041-522 4460
www.hotelsantostefano.com
Set in a medieval watchtower overlooking one of the city's most stylish squares, the hotel has a friendly, unjaded attitude, a change from Venetian indifference; spa baths throughout; courtyard; breakfast served on the square.

Expensive

Westin Europa & Regina
Corte Barozzi, Via XXII Marzo
Tel: 041-240 0001
www.westin.com/europaregina
Lovely waterfront position facing the church of La Salute, this 18th-century palace has been renovated, and the stucco-work and damask tapestries shown off to greater effect. Spacious bedrooms decorated in Venetian style; Grand Canal rooms are in great demand.

Saturnia & International
Via XXII Marzo
Tel: 041-520 8377
Fax: 041-520 5858
www.hotelsaturnia.it

PRICE CATEGORIES

All prices for a double room; bear in mind that the same hotel may well have rooms in two price brackets or more; in the off-season, it's worth bargaining in pricier hotels.
Luxury: over €500
Expensive: €280–500
Moderate: €150–280
Inexpensive: under €150

BELOW: Monaco e Grand's palatial dining room.

Flora
Calle della Pergola, off Larga
XXII Marzo
Tel: 041-520 5884
www.hotelflora.it
A sought-after family-run
hotel set in a quiet alley
near St Mark's. Bed-
rooms can be palatial or
poky, with the best
being numbers 45, 46
and 47, graced with *fin
de siècle* furnishings.

Breakfast in the
secluded courtyard
garden, with well-head.
**La Fenice et des
Artistes**
Tel: 041-523 2333
www.fenicehotels.it
Set within a stone's
throw of the Fenice
opera house, this hotel
is popular with singers
and musicians; there's
a new and an old sec-

tion, both furnished in
traditional style.
Locanda Novecento
Calle del Dose
Tel: 041-241 3765
www.locandanovecento.it
An exotic touch of
Marrakesh in Venice,
with funky Moroccan
lamps, Turkish rugs,
Thai beds; beamed ceil-
ings; cosy bedrooms;
sleek bathrooms;

honesty bar; courtyard
for breakfasts.

Inexpensive

Locanda Art Deco
Calle delle Botteghe
Tel: 041-277 0558
A quiet, good-value inn in
a 17th-century *palazzo*
enlivened by art-deco
touches. Just off Campo
Santo Stefano.

CASTELLO

Luxury

Danieli
Riva degli Schiavoni
Tel: 041-522 6480
Fax: 041-520 0208
www.luxurycollection.com/danieli
Set on the bustling
waterfront, this world-
famous hotel boasts a
splendid covered Gothic
foyer, built around a
courtyard, and plush
rooms with parquet
floors and gilded bed-
steads; splendid rooftop
restaurant; supercilious
service. (Avoid staying in
the hotel's charmless
modern extension).
Londra Palace
Riva degli Schiavoni
Tel: 041-520 0533
Fax: 041-522 5032
www.hotelondra.it
This elegant yet
restrained hotel has
been restored to its old
splendour, creating a
fresh yet timeless feel.
Tchaikovsky composed
his Fourth Symphony
here in 1877. Lagoon
views; romantic bar and
Do Leoni, an excellent
restaurant; the staff are
far more welcoming than
in other top hotels.
Metropole
Riva degli Schiavoni
Tel: 041-520 5044

Fax: 041-522 3679
www.hotelmetropole.com
This patrician family-
owned boutique hotel
decorated in grand 19th-
century style has been
romantically renovated
and dotted with eclectic
antiques and objets
d'art; trendy bar; lovely
garden courtyard; views
over the lagoon or canal;
attentive service; bed-
rooms can be cosy (try
number 350) or amus-
ingly kitsch (try 251).

Expensive

Colombina
Calle del Remedio
Tel: 041-277 0525
www.colombinahotel.com
Boutique hotel close to
St Mark's with bedrooms
designed with a muted,
modern take on Venetian
style; slick marble bath-
rooms; balconies with
view of the Bridge of
Sighs. New annexe also
furnished in tasteful tra-
ditional style; visitors can
arrive by water.
Gabrielli Sandwirth
Riva degli Schiavoni
Tel: 041-523 1580
Fax: 041-520 9455
E-mail: hotel.gabrielli@libero.it
Old-world family-run
waterfront hotel mired in

a delightful 18th-century
time warp; charming
inner courtyard for breakfast; reliable restaurant;
panoramic roof terrace;
by Arsenale ferry stop.
Liassidi Palace
Ponte dei Greci
Tel: 041-520 5658
Fax: 041-522 1820
www.liassidipalacehotel.com
This new boutique hotel
occupies a Gothic palace
on a side canal behind
Riva degli Schiavoni; it
boasts a muted yet sleek
interior with exposed
beams; bar but no
restaurant; stuffy ser-

vice; the individualistic
bedrooms range from
art deco to Bauhaus.
Locanda Vivaldi
Riva degli Schiavoni
Tel: 041-277 0477
Fax: 041-277 0489
www.locandavivaldi.it
Lagoon-front location

BELOW: Danieli, a landmark hotel.

enjoyed by most bedrooms (many with jacuzzi); breakfast on roof terrace; Vivaldi's music piped into the public rooms, a reminder that the composer lived here and worked in the church next door.

Moderate

Palazzo Schiavoni
Fondamenta dei Furlani
Tel: 041-241 1275
www.palazzoschiavoni.com
A mix of rooms and apartments in a tasteful

new conversion beside the Scuola di San Giorgio, complete with the odd frescoed ceiling; good choice for families.

Santa Marina
Campo Santa Marina
Tel: 041-523 9202
Fax 041-520 0907
www.santamarina.it
Set between the Rialto and Campo Santi Giovanni e Paolo, this is a pleasant if slightly lacklustre hotel redeemed by friendly, helpful staff; breakfast on the terrace.

Inexpensive

Bucintoro
Riva degli Schiavoni
Tel: 041-522 3240
This popular family-run hotel prides itself on the stunning views from all bedrooms, especially from the top floors. Bedrooms are all basic, but front rooms look out over San Giorgio, while side rooms enjoy a sweeping vista over the Riva degli Schiavoni.

Casa Querini
Campo San Giovanni Novo
Tel: 041-241 1294/4231

Small inn by Campo Santa Maria Formosa; low-key decor; spacious, unexceptional rooms and pleasant staff; *vaporetto* stop: San Zaccaria.

Locanda La Corte
Calle Bressana
Tel: 041-241 1300
www.locandalacorte.it
Small Gothic palace off Campo Santi Giovanni e Paolo; decorated in a muted version of traditional Venetian style; charming inner courtyard for breakfast; bedrooms overlook the canal or the courtyard.

DORSODURO

Moderate

Accademia Villa Marevege
Fondamenta Bollani
Tel: 041-521 0188
www.pensioneaccademia.it
Gracious, highly sought-after wisteria-clad villa; situated at the Grand Canal end of Rio San Trovaso; atmospheric bedrooms; delightful canalside gardens.

Ca' Pisani
Rio Terra Foscarini
Tel: 041-277 1478
www.capisanihotel.it
Set in a historic *palazzo*, this designer hotel has shaken up the staid world of Venetian hotels by offering a sharp art-deco design in a Gothic palace near the Accademia; satellite TV and e-mail facilities, a novelty for mid-range Venetian hotels; trendy bar (with original Futurist artwork) and bistro.

DD.724
Dorsoduro 724
Tel: 041-277 0262
Fax: 041-296 0633

A reaction to all the gilt and brocade on offer elsewhere, this is a new, stylish yet welcoming designer hotel close to the Guggenheim; contemporary art complements the warm minimalism of the setting, making it popular with artists and curators; flatscreen TVs, great breakfast and willing staff. (The hotel name is also the address).

La Calcina
Fondamenta Zattere ai Gesuati
Tel: 041-520 6466
www.lacalcina.com
Romantic inn on the Zattere overlooking the Giudecca canal, where art critic and aesthete John Ruskin lodged in 1876.Charming roof terrace; uncluttered bedrooms (try number 127); waterside La Piscina dining room and terrace; also other suites and apartments to let near by.

Inexpensive

Ca' della Corte
Corte Surian
Tel: 041-715 877
Fax: 041-722 345
www.cadellacorte.com
Inn with apartments housing from 2–8 people in a modernised period *palazzo* close to the station; tea- and coffee-making facilities; oriental rugs and Venetian masks; daily cleaning service included; number 175 is the biggest and best.

Locanda San Barnaba
Calle del Traghetto
Tel: 041-241 1233
www.locanda-sanbarnaba.com
Small inn close to Ca' Rezzonico; 16th-century frescoed palace run by the ancestral owner; traditional Venetian style; pleasant bedrooms (ask for frescoed bedroom); inner canalside courtyard for breakfast.

Locanda San Trovaso
Fondamenta delle Eremite
Tel: 041-277 1146
www.locandasantrovaso.com

Unpretentious inn on a quiet canal in Dorsoduro. Terracotta floors and damask wallpaper; reasonable bathrooms; no television or telephone; roof terrace; choose room 2 or 4.

PRICE CATEGORIES

Prices for a double room; bear in mind that the same hotel may well have rooms in two price brackets or more; in the off-season, it's worth bargaining in pricier hotels.
Luxury: over €500
Expensive: €280–500
Moderate: €150–280
Inexpensive: under €150

CANNAREGIO, SANTA CROCE AND SAN POLO

Luxury

Grand Hotel Dei Dogi
Fondamenta Madonna
dell'Orto
Tel: 041-220 8111
Fax: 041-722 278
www.deidogi.boscolohotels.com
Daring new luxury hotel
on the edge of the
lagoon in a quiet part of
town; a former
monastery that is still
an oasis of calm; quiet,
tasteful decor; the
largest and loveliest
hotel garden in Venice;
offers a free shuttle
boat to St Mark's;
loveliest rooms in the
lagoon villa.

Expensive

Ai Mori d'Oriente
Fondamenta della Sensa
Tel: 041-711 000
Fax: 041-714 209
www.hotelaimoridoriente.it
Quirky boutique hotel
with lots of character
and eclectic or exotic
touches; welcoming
staff; *vaporetto:*
Madonna dell'Orto or
San Marcuola).

Bellini
Lista di Spagna
Tel: 041-524 2428
Fax: 041-715 193
www.boscolohotels.it
An upmarket Boscolo-
managed hotel en route
to the train station. Set
in a refurbished palace
overlooking the Grand
Canal, with Murano
chandeliers in evidence;
good buffet.

Moderate

Abbazia
Tel: 041-717 333
Fax: 041-717 949
www.abbaziahotel.com
Set close to the station
but a haven of calm,
this former Carmelite
foundation has been
sensitively restored;
beamed ceilings in

tasteful bedrooms;
abbey courtyard
and garden.

Ca' d'Oro
Tel: 041-241 1212
Fax: 041-241 4385
www.hotelcadoro.it
Set in a historic *palazzo*
near the Ca d'Oro ferry
stop, this quiet, cosy
hotel offers a range of
rooms from slightly
poky to the palatial
(with coffered ceilings).

Giorgione
Santi Apostoli
Tel: 041-522 5810
Fax: 041-523 9092
www.hotelgiorgione.com
Set near the Ca' d'Oro,
this historic family-run
hotel dates back to the
14th century, but decor
is in traditional Venetian
style, with chandeliers
and Murano glass. The
breakfast room opens
onto a brick courtyard;
free afternoon coffee
and cakes.

**Locanda Ai Santi
Apostoli**
Strada Nuova
Tel: 041-521 2612
www.locandasantiapostoli.com
A discreet family-run inn
in a *palazzo* overlooking
the Grand Canal (room
11 has the most charm
and best view); inter-
connecting family
rooms; sitting room.

San Cassiano
Calle della Rosa, Santa Croce
Tel: 041-524 1768
Fax: 041-721 033
www.sancassiano.it
This Grand Canal hotel
has as much faded
charm as any Gothic
palazzo. About half the
rooms have canalside
views looking across to
the Ca' d'Oro but vary
dramatically in size,
quality and price. The

stairs are steep and
there is no lift, but a
gondola jetty.

Inexpensive

Ca' Gottardi
Strada Nuova
Tel: 041-275 9333
Set opposite Ca'
Pesaro, this small inn is
run by a fourth-genera-
tion family of gondo-
liers.

Ca' Pozzo
Sottoportego Ca' Pozzo
Ghetto Vecchio 1279
Tel: 041-524 0504
Fax: 041-524 4099
Small, simple hotel in
the Ghetto Vecchio area
designed in a modern,
minimalist style; pastel
hues, exposed beams
and modern art.

Locanda Antico Doge
Campo Santi Apostoli
Tel: 041-241 1570
www.anticodoge.com
Set on a busy but
pleasant square;
grand breakfast room;
damask-draped bed-
rooms in a *palazzo*
that once belonged to
the Doge Marin Falier.

Locanda Leon Bianco
Corte Leon Bianco
Tel: 041-523 3572
www.leonbianco.it
Simple but romantic
budget hotel overlook-
ing the Grand Canal;
tucked away in an inner
courtyard; tiled doors
and mahogany beds.

BELOW: San Clemente Palace, a romantic hideaway.

THE ISLANDS

Luxury

Cipriani
Isola della Giudecca 10
Tel: 041-520 7744
Fax: 041-520 3930
www.orient-expresshotels.com
Set on the tip of Giudecca, the Cipriani is the most glamorous of Venetian hotels. Among its comforts are lavish bedrooms furnished with Fortuny fabrics, a swimming pool, gardens and tennis courts, a yacht harbour, piano bar and, of course, the water-launch service which whisks guests to San Marco. **Palazzo Vendramin**, a glorious patrician palace, benefits from the full Cipriani service, as does **Palazzetto Nani Barbaro**.
San Clemente Palace
Isola di San Clemente
Tel: 041-244 5001
Fax: 041-244 5800
www.sanclemente.thi.it
Luxury, romantic hideaway resort in converted monastery; three restaurants and bars; pool; spa and lovely grounds, a rar-

ity for Venice. 10 minutes by private shuttle from St Mark's.
Westin Excelsior
Lungo Marconi, Il Lido
Tel: 041-526 0201
Fax: 041-526 7276
www.westin.com
Luxury beach hotel with a facade reminiscent of a Moorish castle. Sports facilities, private beach and a free launch service to Venice. Better for business or families rather than romance.

Expensive

Grand Hotel des Bains
Lungo Marconi, Il Lido
Tel: 041-526 5921
Fax: 041-526 0113
www.starwood.com/italy
Atmospheric and luxurious *belle époque* hotel that starred in *Death In Venice*; still popular with the stars during the Film Festival; faces its private beach on the Lido.
Hungaria Palace
Gran Viale 28, Il Lido
Tel: 041-242 0060
A dignified period hotel on the Lido with some

charm; classical concerts in winter; attentive service; book early for the Film Festival.

Moderate

Locanda Cipriani
Isola di Torcello
Tel: 041-730 150
www.locandacipriani.com
Small, rustic inn set in a seemingly remote spot with an excellent homely restaurant; run by a branch of the famous Cipriani family; objets d'art; garden dining.
Quattro Fontane
Via Quattro Fontane, Il Lido
Tel: 041-526 0227
www.quattrofontane.com
Peaceful, quirky, much-loved mock-Tyrolean hotel; comfortable rather than luxurious.

Inexpensive

Lato Azzurro
Via Forti, Isola di Sant'Erasmo
Tel: 041-244 900
www.latoazzurro.it
Simple but sporty hotel on Sant'Erasmo, Venice's market garden;

only local produce served in the restaurant; bicycles, kayaks and beach nearby; family-friendly; gay-friendly; ferries to central Venice.

PRICE CATEGORIES

Prices for a double room; bear in mind that the same hotel may well have rooms in two price brackets or more; in the off-season, it's worth bargaining in pricier hotels.
Luxury: over €500
Expensive: €280–500
Moderate: €150–280
Inexpensive: under €150

BUDGET

Bed & Breakfasts

Request the "Where to Stay – Non-Hotel Accommodation" from the tourist office. It lists bed and breakfasts, which are mostly under €150 per room. There are almost 100 official B&Bs in Venice, but the lack of details and websites makes the choice a minefield. One top B&B is **Casa de Uscoli**

(Campo Pisani, San Marco 2818; tel: 041-241 0669), which is near Campo Santo Stefano and the Accademia bridge. The four bedrooms and lovely sitting room are decorated with ethnic pieces. Another of the better central B&Bs is **Palazzo Duodo** (Calle dei Fabbri; tel 041-522 5832; www.palazzoduodo.com). On Giudecca, try **B&B**

De Zorzi (Fondamenta San Giacomo, Giudecca 197; tel: 041-528 6380), which has views over St Mark's Basin. A good upmarket B&B in the Castello district is **Ponte Chiodo** (3749 Ponte Chiodo; tel: 041-241 3935; www.pontechiodo.it), which has six rooms and a small garden for breakfast, reading or relaxing in fine weather.

Youth Hostels

There are five youth hostels in Venice, with three on Giudecca, the best location. Particularly recommended: **Ex Junghans** (Giudecca 394; tel: 041-521 0801) and **Ostello Venezia** (Fondamenta delle Zitelle, Giudecca 86; tel: 041-523 8211; www.ostellionline.org).

ACTIVITIES

THE ARTS, NIGHTLIFE, FESTIVALS, SHOPPING AND SIGHTSEEING

THE ARTS

For most visitors, evening entertainment takes the form of concerts, Venice's strongest suit, or even opera, especially now that the Fenice opera house has been restored. To find out what's on, the best sources of information are *Leo*, the tourist office's free listings magazine, and the invaluable free booklet, *A Guest in Venice*, available from any of the grand hotels. As for theatre, plays are exclusively in Italian, with Teatro Goldoni the loveliest theatre. Since foreign films are virtually always dubbed into Italian, your best bet for seeing films in English is during the Venice Film Festival in September, when entertainment tends to be more cosmopolitan.

Concerts and Opera

Venice is deeply musical, and many of the sounds of the city are free: visitors wandering the canals will often hear music students laboriously practising their Chopin or Schubert. Vivaldi, Monteverdi and Wagner lived in Venice, and Vivaldi's concerts are commonplace. Autumn spells the start of the Venice opera season at the newly reopened

La Fenice (tel: 041-786 511; www.teatrolafenice.it) and the start of the classical music season *(see page 225)*. Music can usually be listened to in lovely settings, especially in churches, oratories and the *scuole*, the charitable confraternity seats *(see page 158)*.

Confraternity concerts

The **Scuola Grande di San Teodoro** (tel: 041-521 8294) stages concerts in the confraternity house; the singers and orchestra are dressed in 18th-century costume. Concerts are also held in the splendidly decorated confraternity houses of **Scuola Grande di San Rocco**, **Scuola Grande dei Carmini**, **Scuola Grande di San Giovanni**

Evangelista and the **Ospedaletto**. Many of the best concerts are conducted by the Accademia di San Rocco, a musical ensemble which stages baroque recitals in traditional Venetian settings.

Church concerts

One of the most popular concert churches is **La Pietà** (Riva degli Schiavoni), the lovely rococo church linked to Vivaldi, both a magnificent setting for the Venetian composer's work and for concerts of baroque music. Classical concerts are also held in the vast Gothic church of **I Frari**, in Tintoretto's church of **Madonna dell'Orto**, and in the basilica of **La Salute**. The Renaissance church of **Santa Maria dei**

BOOKING AND DISCOUNT CARDS

Hello Venezia (tel: 041-2424; www.hellovenezia.it; open 7.30am–8pm) is the place to book opera, concerts, ballet and events. You can also book the useful Venice Card here, a discounted combined ticket allowing access to all the museums on San Marco, including the Museo Correr, with similar schemes for Ca' Rezzonico and Palazzo Mocenigo. In the case of churches, two passes cover

many of the best churches: **Chorus**, the pass for the main churches (tel: 041-275 0462), and its rival, **Associazione Sant' Apollonia**, for others (tel: 041-270 2464). **Venezia Si** is an organisation representing over 90 per cent of Venetian hoteliers, but it also accepts bookings for major exhibitions and concerts (from abroad call: +39-041-522 2264; in Italy call freephone 800-843 006; www.veneziasi.it).

Miracoli, the Rialto market church of **San Giacometto** and the neighbourhood **Santa Maria Formosa** are also evocative settings for concerts. On St Mark's Square, the **Ateneo di San Basso** (tel: 041-521 0294) is the setting for concerts of Vivaldi and Mozart's works.

Palaces and theatres

Concerts are also staged in the city's greatest palaces, from **Ca' Vendramin-Calergi** (usually Wagner) to **Ca' Rezzonico** (18th-century music). The **Querini-Stampalia** (tel: 041-271 1411) is a small gallery providing an intimate yet sumptuous setting for evening and lunchtime recitals. **Teatro Malibran** (tel: 041-786 601) is a gem of an opera house that has recently reopened in the heart of the city (by Corte del Milion).

Outdoor concerts

In summer, key squares in the Dorsoduro district are turned into open-air concert venues, including Campo Pisani, just off Campo Santo Stefano.

Cinema and Theatre

Teatro Goldoni (tel: 041-240 2011; www.teatrostabilveneto.it) stages plays by the Venetian dramatist Goldoni, and is also a music venue.

As far as films are concerned, the usual American and international releases are shown, but are usually dubbed into Italian. Key cinemas include: **Accademia** (in Dorsoduro) and the **Rossini** (close to San Luca). **Giorgione Movie d'Essai**, in the Cannaregio district, usually shows foreign films in their original language. (Take *vaporetto* line No. 1 to the Ca' d'Oro stop.)

An exception to the rule of showing works in Italian only is the glitzy Venice Film Festival, held in late August and early September, when films are shown in their original versions. Venice is the oldest film festival in the

world, and second in prestige only to Cannes. Today the festival concentrates on art-house

FESTIVALS AND EVENTS

Venice is busy all year round, with the Lenten Carnival and the September Film Festival flagged as the most popular events. While there are almost 100 regattas on the lagoon, the key one is in September. This also happens to be the most culturally aware month since, apart from the Historical Regatta, there is the Film Festival and either the Art Biennale or Architecture Biennale, depending on the year. Most city water festivals are child-friendly and often accompanied by fireworks, while Carnival is the time for dressing up and parading around. For more on the main festivities, see Carnival *(page 66–9)* and Water Festivals *(pages 70–1)*. In November, the opera season restarts at the newly restored La Fenice and the Festival Musica Internazionale opens in various locations, focusing on chamber music, baroque works, ballroom dancing, piano recitals, jazz, big-band music and even Spanish guitar. Major art exhibitions take place throughout the year. For current events, pick up a copy of the free *Leo* listings magazine from the tourist office. For upcoming events, call the tourist office (041-529 8711) or check the official Venice websites (www.turismovenezia.it; and www.culturaspettacolovenezia.it)

February: Carnevale (Carnival) is considered the colourful opening to the city's festive season. (Since accommodation is then scarce, book in good time.)

So e Zo i Ponti (fourth Sunday of Lent) is a non-competitive

marathon crossing bridges and canals.

25 April: Festa di San Marco is the celebration of the city saint, with a ceremonial Mass in the Basilica and the romantic presentation of a *bocolo* (rosebud) to women.

May: Festa della Sensa (Sunday after Ascension Day) is a re-enactment of the Marriage of Venice with the Sea, followed by a gondola regatta off the Lido. **La Vogalonga**, the "long row", a marathon rowing race, takes place in early May. **Il Palio Delle Quattro Antiche Repubbliche Marinare** is a major regatta in honour of the four ancient maritime republics, which take turns to host it. Venice next has the honour in 2007.

June: Venezia Suona, the summer music festival, is held in the streets and squares of the city. The **Sagra di San Pietro** on 29 June is dedicated to St Peter and centred on the church of the same name, with concerts in the city's first cathedral. The **Regata del Cento Vele** (Hundred Sails Regatta) is held sometime in June.

June–November: Art Biennale (odd years only). Contemporary art show La Biennale (tel: 041-521 8898; www.labiennale.org) is staged in the Giardini gardens, in Teatro Piccolo Arsenale, and in other locations around the city. **Architecture Biennale (even years only)** is the contemporary architecture show; tel: 041-523 0428; www.iuov.it/ citiesonwater).

Early July: Murano Regatta is held off the island of Murano and is accompanied by feasts and music. **San Pellegrino Regatta** celebrates racing and cooking.

July (third weekend): Festa del Redentore (Festival of the Redeemer). This bridge of boats across the Giudecca canal is a

TRANSPORT

ACCOMMODATION

ACTIVITIES

A – Z

LANGUAGE

celebration in thanksgiving for the city's survival from an outbreak of plague; an exceptional fireworks display takes place on the water.

July–September: Summer in the Villas. Concerts, feasts and festivals in the Riviera del Brenta villas, reached on a boat trip from Venice (tel: 041-560 0690, and also 041-529 8711; www.turismovenezia.it).

August: Casino concerts. The Casino in Palazzo Vendramin-Calergi is the setting for occasional summer rock concerts, with tickets including entrance and some chips. **Ferragosto** (15 August, the Assumption) is celebrated with fireworks and concerts including on Torcello.

Early September (ten days): Venice Film Festival. Films are shown in their original versions and, while art-house movies rather than blockbusters tend to win the awards, the festival attracts a glitzy Hollywood crowd. Nightlife is more cosmopolitan during the festival and centred on the Lido by day and San Marco by night *(see page 204)*.

September (first Sunday): Regatta Storica (Historic Regatta) is the finest regatta in Venice. It includes a procession up the Grand Canal led by craft and costumed Venetians, and is followed by gondola races. **Sagra del Pesce**, the Burano fish festival and regatta, also includes a music festival held on the island of Burano.

September: Festival Galuppi, named after a Burano composer, is a successful way of opening up curious sites, with concerts staged in Franciscan churches, forts and former leper colonies on the islands of San Francesco del Deserto, Sant'Erasmo, and San Lazzaretto Nuovo; also concerts and organ recitals in Ca' Rezzonico, La Pietà and in La

Salute in central Venice (book on 041-522 1120).

October: Festival del Mosto (Grape Harvest) takes place on the island of Sant'Erasmo; the small quantity of grapes is an excuse for a feast and party.

November: Festa della Madonna della Salute, on the 21st, is a procession across the Grand Canal on floating pontoons to La Salute basilica; the festival is in thanksgiving for the city's survival from the plague. November also marks the start of the **Venice Opera Season** at the newly re-opened La Fenice (tel: 041-786 511). The **Festival Musica Internazionale**, the city's classical-music season, begins at the same time and runs until the end of December. Locations include the luxury hotels on the Lido (especially the Hungaria Palace; tel: 041-242 0060). November is also the start of the **Chamber-music season at Teatro Malibran** (contact Società Veneziana di Concerti on 041-786 764).

November–December: Winter concert season: organ concerts and choral singing in Venetian churches (concerts in La Pietà, the Gesuati, San Zulian, San Trovaso and also the Ospedaletto music room); 18th-century chamber music in Ca' Rezzonico (the Museum of the 18th century) and in the ballroom of Museo Correr. **Piano competition at La Fenice. San Sevolo Jazz festival** is on the island of San Servolo (tel: 041-276 5001).

December–January: Christmas concerts in Saint Mark's Basilica, La Fenice and La Pietà. Display of Murano glass cribs *(presepi)* in various churches. **New Year's Eve:** a celebrity pop and rock concert in one venue, and a classical concert in La Fenice. **Regata della Befana:** The Epiphany Regatta on 6 January is the first race of the New Year.

NIGHTLIFE

Venetian nightlife may be distinctly tame, yet it is far from dead, and much improved in recent years. It is no longer a case of a cosy meal out followed by a gondola ride echoing to the strains of Céline Dion's greatest hits. Not that the simple watery Venetian pleasures should be mocked. Nothing beats the furtive feeling of slipping down the Grand Canal at night on a No. 1 *vaporetto* and watching persons unknown mingling inside a glittering *palazzo*, or even the innocent pleasure of eating an ice cream while sauntering down the breezy Zattere, looking at illuminated water-craft going full tilt.

The traditional take on the city is that entertainment tends to be low-key, focused on piano bars, the historic cafés around San Marco and chic hotel bars. Given that the average age of Venetians is 45, most people opt for cosy drinks in a bar, followed by a meal out. It is also true that conservative Venetians of all ages favour the traditional bars known as *bacari*. (The best *bacari* are covered in the **Restaurants and Bars** listings in the Places section.) Since a number of these bars close early, the recommendations below are for late-night *bacari*, as well as the full range of nightspots, from jazz clubs and lounge bars to Irish pubs, cocktail bars and designer wine bars.

Venetians have clearly become more adventurous of late. By diversifying the bar scene, revamping the top hotel bars, opening stylish designer bars, and bringing the *bacaro* concept up to date, Venice has surreptitiously acquired a burgeoning new nightlife scene.

While the core clientele of middle-aged Venetians are not about to be shaken from their slumbers by hard-core clubbing, the local nightlife scene is buzzing. Age distinctions are now blurred, with cost and personal style the determining factors, rather than age. By the same token, the best places, excluding the grand hotel bars, are as popular with Venetians as with visitors. If romance and glamour are the goals, then the waterfront-hotel piano bars possess it in abundance. If elegant designer bars, jazz or lounge-music clubs appeal, then most are within walking distance of St Mark's. If you want to sample some of the reinvented *bacari*, new spins on the traditional Venetian bars, then slip off to quiet *campi* and *calli* in Castello, San Polo or Dorsoduro. Instead, if you feel more at home among the rustic copper pots of the traditional *bacari*, or in a semblance of an Irish pub, then set off to Cannaregio or, if it's still early evening, catch the cramped but authentic wine bars clustered around the Rialto market.

Given the ageing Venetian population, the historic centre of Venice has no recommended dance venues – only a few staid and distinctly old-fashioned nightclubs and one "disco club". For brasher and younger nightlife, especially nightclubs, many young Venetians dance the night away with tourists in the clubs on the Lido di Jesolo on the Adriatic coast. (You will need to go there by car, taking a road with a high accident rate.)

Alternatively, in the summer, the nightlife scene switches to the Lido in summer and focuses on the seafront and the grand hotels. As for winter fun, during **Carnival** Venetian nightlife comes into its own, with open-air balls, people-watching, and strolling from café to café *(see page 66)*. Also in the winter, visitors should try to visit the gorgeous **Casino** in **Palazzo Vendramin-Calergi** on the Grand Canal (tel: 041-529 7111; see: www.casinovenezia.it; open Oct–March; *vaporetto:* San Marcuola, lines 1 or 82). Smart clothes are required, with jacket and tie for men. The casino focuses on "classic" table games rather than on "American" slot machines.

The following nightlife options are presented by area. Fortunately, if you don't feel like straying far from San Marco, the most romantic spots tend to be near by, with the top hotel bars overlooking the waterfront on Riva degli Schiavoni or the Grand Canal. However, the Dorsoduro area covers some of the most charming spots, ranging from classic cocktail bars to tastefully gentrified wine bars, while Cannaregio favours more idiosyncratic nightlife, from the best of traditional wine bars *(bacari)* to eclectic music clubs and ethnic haunts which are satisfyingly diverse for such a conservative city. Even so, bear in mind that the hottest spots are often tucked away down labyrinthine alleys.

San Marco

Centrale (Piscina Frezzeria, off Frezzeria; open 6.30pm–2am, closed Sun) is an inviting new haunt for metropolitan night owls of all ages. Set in a converted cinema, itself carved out of an ancient *palazzo*, this stylish lounge bar is moody and modern, a great place for chilling out with cocktails or dinner, all smoothed along by host Alfredo's engaging personality *(see page 104)*. In terms of class and style, its only rivals are the top hotel bars and **Harry's**, though, on a good night, **Bacaro Lounge** puts on the style *(see page 105)*. **Martini Scala** (Campo San Fantin) offers a slightly lacklustre piano bar and supper club handily open from 10pm until 3am. **Bacaretto** (Calle delle Botteghe) is a bar and inn popular with ordinary Venetians (closed weekends). **Café Torino** (Campo San Luca) is a youthful late-night drinking den. **Malvasia Vecchia** (Corte Malatina, 11pm–4am) is a youth-oriented club with eclectic sounds and reasonably priced drinks that moves to the Lido in summer.

Castello

Most upmarket nightlife revolves around the international hotels on the Riva degli Schiavoni, including **Londra Palace** with its piano bar, dinner jazz and waterside terrace, and the **Danieli**, with its great bar and terrace. By contrast, the **Metropole** (tel: 041-524 0034) boasts an exotic oriental Zodiac Bar and holds DJ-led lounge and classic chill evenings every Thursday, accompanied by food- and wine-tastings. Nightlife is more Venetian as one retreats to the authentic wine bars behind San Zaccaria. One such is **Enoteca Mascareta**, a low-key temple to wine and the long lost art of conversation *(see page 141)*. **Inishshark** (Calle del Mondo Novo; Tel: 041-523 5300; closed Mon; *vaporetto:* Rialto) is the place for Guinness, bar snacks, Celtic music and live sport on television.

Dorsoduro

Campo Santa Margherita is the centre of Venice's nightlife, and is awash with buzzing, youth-oriented bars. The red-tinged **Caffè Rosso** competes with the futuristic **Orange** lounge bar (with garden) and the friendly but fake **Green Pub**, leaving the more low-key **Margaret Duchamp** bar to cater to a sophisticated crowd. A cool clientele, with the occasional fashion victim, is drawn to the equally cool atmosphere. Despite its appeal, prices are reasonable and service friendly. **Imagina** (Rio Terra canal) is an arty, designer bar that comes into its own at night, with eclectic music and late-night snacks. Cocktails tend to draw a bohemian crowd of painters and writers, while it becomes more relentlessly youth-orientated as the night wears on. **La Rivista**, near by, is also recommended *(see page 187)*. **Linea d'Ombra** (Ponte dell'Umilta, Zattere) is a chic late-night port of call behind La Salute, especially good in

HOTEL BARS

In terms of glamour, class and romance, only **Harry's Bar** and **Centrale** can compete with the top hotel bars. Most hotel bars have been revamped recently, and aim for a slightly differing clientele. Mired in a comforting time warp, the stuffy, unduly formal international bars still predominate, but tend to be softened by fabulous rooftop views or waterside terraces. Certain classic hotels have tweaked the formula to make their bars more distinctive, even moving into the contemporary music scene, as is the case with the **Metropole**. All the best bars make an atmospheric choice for cocktails or a post-prandial brandy or grappa, with the mood enhanced by piano music and

starlit views. The **Monaco e Grand Hotel** has been overzealously revamped by Benetton, but the waterside bar remains an appealing spot, with better views than Harry's Bar. For elegance, atmosphere and more life than most top hotel bars, visitors can opt for the **B-Bar** at the **Bauer**, or the revamped bars at the Metropole and neighbouring **Londra Palace**. In terms of history, atmosphere and class, the bars at the **Gritti Palace** and the **Danieli** are timeless, as is the rooftop view from **Gabrielli & Sandwirth**. For a more remote, waterside setting, the bars at the **Cipriani** (including **Cips**), **San Clemente Palace** and **Dei Dogi** are recommended. *(See Hotel listings for details).*

cometto) is an idiosyncratic yet deservedly popular meeting place, especially for pre-dinner or late-night drinks *(see page 125).* **Bacaro Jazz**, on the San Marco side of the Rialto bridge (facing Fondaco dei Tedeschi), is a cocktail bar with jazz videos and occasional live artists. **Osteria Ruga Rialto** (Ruga Rialto; tel. 041-521 1243) offers live jazz, blues and reggae as well as dinner and drinks in a rustic setting. **Easybar** (Campo Santa Maria Mater Domini, closed Thur) is a cool mix of traditional Venice and contemporary Milan, offering a lounge ambience and a chance to enjoy a classic *spritz al bitter*. **Novecento** (Campiello Sansoni) doubles as a jazz club and pizzeria.

summer when the floating water terrace comes into its own. **Senso Unico** (Calle della Chiesa, close to the Guggenheim) styles itself as an English pub but does an equally good line in wine and bar snacks. **Suzie Café** (Campo San Basilio) stages live music in summer, from rock to reggae and blues. **Vinus** (corner of Crosera San Pantalon and San Rocco) is a friendly wine bar serving plates of ham and cheese and occasional live music. For a late-night ice cream, coffee or liqueur at one of Venice's best *gelaterie*, head to **Paolin** (Campo Santo Stefano), one of the few open very late (until midnight in summer). Try the pistachio or lemon ice cream, or confine yourself to cocktails.

Cannaregio

Fondamenta della Misericordia is the nightlife hub in this northern part of town. Here, lining the once abandoned quaysides, are a cluster of nightspots with atmosphere and fairly decent food: **Cantina Iguana**, a Mexican cantina, **Paradiso Perduto** and

Sahara *(see page 175).* Bustling Paradiso Perduto is the liveliest nightspot (tel: 041-720 581; open until 2am from Thursday to Sunday) with live jazz, folk and ethnic music. Near by, on Fondamenta degli Ormesini is the boisterous **Pub Da Aldo**, with a well-stocked bar, or try **Fiddler's Elbow** (Corte dei Palli) for much of the same. For traditional Venetian haunts, the alleys off Strada Nuova (especially the Campo Santi Apostoli end) conceal excellent *bacari*, such as **La Vedova** *(see page 175),* but avoid the charmless tourist traps on Strada Nuova itself. The side streets close to the Ca' d'Oro gallery (off Strada Nuova) also conceal plenty of traditional bars, as do some of the seemingly bleak quaysides.

San Polo and Santa Croce (Rialto Area)

Antica Birraria (Campo San Polo) is a beer-hall and jazz-and-blues venue set in an atmospheric barn of a building, a former naval boat shed. The Rialto's romantic **Bancogiro** (Campo San Gia-

SHOPPING

To enjoy the excitement of finding something truly Venetian, you need curiosity, conviction and a comfortable income. Shopaholics would do well to focus on arts and crafts, especially luxury fabrics, glassware, marbled paper and genuine masks. The full range of Italian designer goods are on sale in Venice, but prices tend to be higher than on the mainland. The most elegant designer boutiques are on **Calle Vallaresso**, **Salizzada San Moisè**, the **Frezzeria** and **Calle Larga XXII Marzo**, west of San Marco. The classic fabric and haberdashery quarter is the **Mercerie**, a maze of alleys sandwiched between San Marco and the Rialto. More everyday shops lie between Campo San Salvador and Santo Stefano and in the Castello district, while the **Rialto fish and vegetable market** is the most intoxicating place for foodstuffs. The Rialto shopping alleys are also lively in the early evening, with **Ruga Vecchia di San Giovanni** home to good food shops. If you hanker after ersatz designer bags and belts, fake Louis Vuitton or Gucci, the

African traders will catch your attention around Calle Larga XXII Marzo or on bustling Riva degli Schiavoni.

What and Where to Buy

Art

Contini (Calle dello Spezier, off Campo Santo Stefano) is the grandest art gallery in Venice.

Books

Mondadori (Salizzada San Moise) is a cool, central late-night bookshop, gallery and multimedia centre with Bacaro, an equally cool bar, attached. **Libreria Sansovino** (San Marco 84) specialises in books on Venice.

Carnival costumes

Flavia hires or sells carnival costumes (Campo San Lio, tel: 041-528 7429). Before buying a mask, always check what it is made of and ask the seller to tell you how it fits into the Venetian tradition: it may be a character from the *commedia dell'arte*. For women, the *civetta* is a flirtatious, catlike mask while the *colombina* is more ladylike (see page 68 for details). Some of the most genuine and appealing mask shops lie in the Castello district, in the quiet canals behind San Zaccaria. One such shop is **Ca' del Sol** (Fondamenta del Osmarin; tel: 041-528 5549) and, virtually next door, **Atelier Marega**. **Mondonovo** is one of the most creative mask-makers (Rio Terra Canal, off Campo Santa Margherita, tel: 041-528 7344).

Department store

Coin (Salizzada San Giovanni Crisostomo) is one of very few department stores in Venice.

Luxury fabrics and lace

Venice is well known for its Fortuny fabrics – silks and velvets, plain or gloriously patterned. **Venetia Studium** (Calle Larga XXII Marzo, tel: 041-522 9281) produces exclusive fabrics, including Fortuny designs, from scarves to cushion covers to lamps, and delicately patterned fabrics and soft furnishings. **Jesurum** (Merceria del Capitello, tel: 041-520 6177) has been selling princely household linen, including embroidered sheets, since 1870. **Frette** (Calle Larga XXII Marzo, tel: 041-522 4914) sells fine linens, exquisite sheets, cushions and bathrobes. Frette recently contributed to the restoration of Ca' Foscari, Venice University, acting in the long tradition of Venetian patronage.

Marbled paper

Between San Marco and the Rialto are shops selling marbled paper. Called *legatoria* or "bookbinding", this ancient craft gives paper a decorative marbled veneer and is today used for photo albums, writing cases, greeting cards, diaries and notebooks. Try **Paoli Olbi** (Calle della Mandola) or **Legatoria Piazzesi** (Santa Maria del Giglio, tel: 041-522 1202).

Murano glass

Refrain from buying glass until you have visited the Murano Glass Museum and watched the glass being made at a factory. Only buy glass guaranteed by the **Vetro Artistico Murano** trademark (www.muranoglass.com). Also, resist the hard sell before you know what you like. One of the most prestigious contemporary glassmakers is **Venini** (shop on Piazzetta Leoncini, San Marco, with factory and showrooms on Fondamenta Vetrai 50, Murano, tel: 041-273 7211). **Barovier e Toso** (Fondamenta Vetrai 28, tel: 041-527 4385) is equally respected and in simpler taste than many others. **Murano Collezioni**, 1cd Fondamenta Manin, Murano, tel: 041-736 272 is a showroom for several of the best brands. **Archimede Seguso** is a prestigious firm, with a shop close to St Mark's (Frezzeria, tel: 041-739 234).

Prints

La Stamperia del Ghetto (Calle del Ghetto Vecchio) includes general and Jewish themes.

OTHER ACTIVITIES

Guided Tours

Most of the big agencies around St Mark's Square and off Calle Vallaresso offer pleasant but predictable city tours and visits to the islands. The latter can consist of a hard sell in a glass factory in Murano, so check the itinerary carefully (and read the Murano section; pages 197–8). The best cultural walking tour is of the Jewish Ghetto (conducted in English or French only), which can be booked through the tourist office or the Jewish Museum (tel: 041-715 359). For murk and mystery, try the Secret Itinerary (tel: 041-522 4951 and 041-520 9070) around the Doge's Palace (tours in English, French, Italian booked in advance; see page 97). For a free guided tour of Basilica San Marco, book on 041-270 2420. Other curious walking tours include Casanova's Venice and Wagner's Venice (tel: 041-523 2544). There's also a Romantic Venice walking tour (tel: 041-630 761). For church visits and tours, contact Chorus (tel: 041-275 0462) and Associazione Sant' Apollonia (tel: 041-270 2464), which both deal with different churches. Venice Walks (tel: 041-520 8616) run a ghost tour and a Dorsoduro walk, while Venice Events do tours on art and architecture as well as on merchants and courtesans (tel: 041-523 9979; www.veniceevents.com). For a current list of all city walks, the best source is *Leo*, the free listings magazine, available from the tourist office.

SIGHTS AND ATTRACTIONS

The locations and opening times of most sights are featured within the Places chapters. These include museums, churches, belltowers, palaces, galleries and historic monuments. Bear in mind that there will always be unexpectedly closed sections of galleries and churches in Venice: ongoing restoration is a feature of the city. Changes in opening times and sights are listed in the *Leo* magazine, free from the tourist office. For details on the civic museums, see www.musei civicivenezia.it. Tickets for most events can be booked through Hello Venezia (041-2424) or through tourist agencies around San Marco.

the church and Paolin ice-cream parlour). As for art, the Scuola Grande di San Giorgio degli Schiavoni is a lovely choice, even for young children: Carpaccio's engrossing scenes are like fairy tales peopled by dragons, knights, princesses and lions. The Secret Itinerary around the Doge's Palace is also good fun as it covers prisons, secret passages and torture chambers. Older children may enjoy the Naval Musem, with its boats and guns.

Nature Excursions

For a different side of Venice, try a nature ramble on the lesser-known lagoon islands. These tours, which visit market gardens, fishing ponds, sandbars, salt pans and mudflats, are aimed at increasing the ecological awareness of visitors and Venetians alike. On a visit to a fish farm in the lagoon, you might see bream, sea bass and eels (which feed in the lagoon in spring). Other tours visit wildlife, including mute swans, kingfishers, cormorants, coots, grey herons and egrets. The Lido tourist office (Gran Viale 6/a, Lido) is the best-informed about such tours, including the exploration of Torcello, Burano and Sant'Erasmo's market gardens. For nature and archaeological visits around the minor islands, the specialists are Limosa, who run Natura Venezia (tel: 041-932 003). Since their stance is broadly ecological and against the mobile dam, to understand the interventionists' case, first call into the Punto Laguna interactive display for an overview of Venice lagoon (tel: 041-529 3582, Campo Santo Stefano). The Archeoclub d'Italia also organises trips to ancient fortifications on the lagoon. To enjoy this area on an individual basis, catch a ferry (line 13) to Sant'Erasmo, Venice's market garden.

Children's Activities

Everyday activities can be entertaining, from jumping on and off boats to chasing pigeons or watching glassmaking displays on Murano. Crossing the Grand Canal on the *traghetto* (gondola-ferry) is inexpensive and fun, especially if children stand up, as the natives do. Climbing towers is another engaging activity: the best are probably San Giorgio (on the island of the same name) and the Campanile on St Mark's Square. In fine weather, take a boat to the islands, with Burano probably the most fun for children. As for sport, tennis, riding and sailing are all available, as well as cycling on the Lido and Sant'Erasmo. The Lido beaches are an option, but are private and expensive, so choose a hotel with a private beach. In Venice, only Hotel Cipriani and San Clemente Palace have pools. For invigorating walks, try the Zattere quaysides in Dorsoduro. Apart from waterside views, there are numerous cafés and *gelaterie* where you can eat pasta or ices while sitting on jetties over the water. Venetian children occasionally play in the Giardini Pubblici, the city's main park in Eastern Castello, but most prefer pigeon-chasing, ball games and clambering on well-heads in their local parish squares, especially Campo San Giacomo dell'Orio, Campo San Polo and Campo Santa Margherita. Campo Santo Stefano is also child-friendly, with free toys set up for young children (beside

Sports

Venice is not a destination for spectator sports, with the exception of regattas, which are part sporting events, part festivities. For a list of current water festivals and the odd football match on the island of Sant'Elena, pick up a free copy of *Leo*, the listings magazine issued by the city tourist office. Despite the water, Venice is not a great place for swimmers. Holidaymakers regularly swim in the Adriatic, but the more fastidious may prefer to stick to the hotel pool. While many hotels on the Lido have pools, only two in central Venice (the Cipriani and San Clemente Palace) have this luxury. Cycling, riding, sailing, tennis and golf are also possible on the Lido. To book a bicycle on the Lido, call 041-526 8019 (Gran Viale SM Elisabetta 21b). In Dorsoduro district, the Bucintoro rowing club (tel: 041-522 2055; www.bucintoro.org) is the place to learn Venetian-style rowing or even try sailing in traditional lagoon vessels.

TRANSPORT

ACCOMMODATION

AN ALPHABETICAL SUMMARY OF PRACTICAL INFORMATION

ACTIVITIES

B udgeting for Your Trip

Bear in mind that, given its unique location, Venice is the most expensive city in Italy, so make use of any travel passes and discounts on offer and use water taxis sparingly. Boat transport is expensive as it acts as an indirect city subsidy and tourism tax. But you will not need to use ferries every day, so plan island trips to run on the same or consecutive days and buy the right transport pass accordingly (for instance, plan to see Murano, Burano and Torcello on the same day). The Museum Card is a worthwhile combined ticket for the museums around St Mark's. The Venice Card is a useful museum-and-transport discount card which can be pre-booked from abroad (www.venicecard.com) or in

Venice, either from the tourist office or from Hello Venezia (tel: 041-2424; www.hellovenezia.it). As for meals, avoid bland "tourist menus"; instead choose a simple but atmospheric Venetian tapas bar (bacaro) as a budget option (see Restaurants and Bars listings at the end of each chapter). In most places, there is a premium imposed on sitting down; even so, it is often worth it to appreciate the atmosphere of a grand San Marco café, for instance.

Business Hours

Shops are usually open from 9am–12.30pm or 1pm and again from 3pm or 3.30pm–7.30pm. Most of them, apart from those aimed mainly at tourists, are closed on Sunday. Office hours are normally 7.30am–12.30pm and

3.30pm–6.30pm. Government offices are usually only open to the public in the mornings. Churches tend to be open from 7.30am–noon, and then from 3.30pm or 4pm–6.30pm or 7pm. However, the following 14 churches have now formed an association that charges for entry. In return, they offer longer opening hours, usually from 10am–5pm, Monday–Saturday and 1–5pm Sunday. Called **Chorus**, this important group offers individual tickets or a good-value pass covering the following churches: Santa Maria del Giglio; Santo Stefano; Santa Maria Formosa; Santa Maria dei Miracoli; the Frari; San Polo; San Giacomo dell'Orio; San Stae; Madonna dell'Orto; San Pietro di Castello; San Sebastiano; Il Redentore; Sant'Alvise and the Gesuati (tel: 041-275 0462 for

A – Z

LANGUAGE

details). Museums tend to close on Monday (opening times are given in the colour section of the book).

C limate

The Venetian climate is notoriously capricious, with a spectrum of weather possible in one day. January can be bitterly cold, wet and windy and then illuminated by warm sunshine. Humidity affects the hottest and coldest days. Venice in the height of summer can be oppressively muggy, but there is always the Lido to escape to. The weather is hottest in August, with an average temperature of 24°C (75°F). Most rain falls in March to April and November to December, but acqua alta, which occurs between the autumn and spring, is the condition Venetians loathe: exceptionally high tides often flood the low-lying areas of the city, including San Marco. Although it rarely snows in Venice, the city is exposed to fog and two harsh winds: the bora blows from the Steppes in winter and is linked with low atmospheric pressure, while the sirocco brings hot weather from the Middle East. That said, Venice experiences sunny days and limpid lagoon light in all seasons. The loveliest months of the year are probably May, June and September, but even the dark depths of winter, swathed in romantic mists, have their appeal. In spring, the city can be highly dramatic, viewed from the top of San Giorgio, with the wind buffeting the tower and the bobbing boats on the lagoon. Average temperatures are: January 3.8°C (38.8°F), April 12.6°C (54.6°F), July 23.6°C (74.4°F) and October 15.1°C (59.1°F).

Clothing

Clothes for the capricious Venetian climate can be tricky. If visiting between October and April, consider a raincoat, scarf, umbrella and warm outdoor clothes for the chilly evenings, windy ferry trips and frequent fogs. The secret to an enjoyable stay is to dress in layers of clothing and to bring comfortable walking shoes. If you are unlucky enough to experience acqua alta, the seasonal flooding, you can avoid most of it by walking on duckboards and, if necessary, by buying cheap but ingenious pull-on "plastic-bag boots" from kiosks. Although wet, it is, in fact, a strange and exciting experience. Take some beachwear if visiting Venice in summer. Shorts are acceptable for visiting the Lido beaches or smaller islands, but less so for the city itself. To avoid offence, dress decently in churches – women should cover up their arms and shoulders, and both sexes should avoid wearing shorts. Smart casual wear is accepted in all but the grandest hotels and restaurants, but most Venetians dress smartly when dining out.

Consulates

Venice has almost 40 consulates, but many foreign nationals will need to contact their embassies in Rome or consulates elsewhere. The British consulate is now in Mestre, mainland Venice; tel: 041-505 5990; The nearest United States consulate is in Milan (Largo Donegani 1; tel: 02-290 351). The nearest Canadian Consulate is in Padua; tel: 049-878 1147. Australian and Irish citizens will need to contact their embassies in Rome. (For a full list of consulates in Venice, see: www.corpoconsolarevenezia.com.

Crime and Safety

Venice is an exceptionally safe city, no matter what thriller-writers would have one believe. Stringent security measures in St Mark's basilica mean that all bags have to be left in the Ateneo San Basso on Piazzetta dei Leoncini, a free left-luggage service. The key numbers in the event of an emergency are listed in the yellow box above.

EMERGENCY NUMBERS

For certain difficulties, including lost passports, see Consulates. For illness, see Health and Medical Care. In general, these are the most useful emergency telephone numbers:
112/113: Police
118: Ambulance.
115: Fire brigade
116: Road assistance.
041-274 7070: Venice City police.
041-785 620: Venice railway police.
041-5294111: Venice Hospital switchboard: Ospedale Civile Venezia (by the Zanipolo church, Santi Giovanni e Paolo).
041-533 54111: Harbour authorities.

D ay Trips

If you are staying in Venice for a while and the waterscape is making you restless, then consider a day trip to one of the mainland cities in the Veneto: either workaday Chioggia, for a good fish lunch, or, for culture, to the historic university city of Padua (about 40 minutes by train from Venice). The other delightful trip is to visit the Palladian villas along the Brenta Canal (see page 210) on a boat trip offered by the tourist board and a number of operators around the St Mark's and Calle Vallaresso area. Alternatively, consider visiting romantic Verona (approximately 90 minutes away by train), engaging and vibrant Bologna (two hours by train) or even art-studded Florence (three hours by train). Ring the following number for train timetables throughout Italy: tel: 8488-88088.

Directions

In Venice, official addresses can be meaningless, with numbers in the thousands merely linked to the sestiere or district but giving no indication of the street name. In theory, street names are not given in official addresses to avoid confusion, since those same names may exist elsewhere; in practice, this merely complicates the issue. When searching for a new place, check which is the nearest *campo*, church or monument.

Disabled Travellers

Venice presents considerable challenges, so careful pre-planning is required, especially for those with limited mobility: wheelchair access, steps, queues, and getting on and off ferries and gondolas all present hazards; few museums and relatively few hotels have adequate access and facilities. For service and guidance for the disabled in Venice, call 041-274 6144. Ca' Rezzonico and the Doge's Palace are fully accessible, apart from the prisons and the Secret Itinerary; the Museo Correr is partially accessible. In the UK, contact Holiday Care (0845-124 9971; www.holidaycare.org.uk) for lists of accessible accommodation in Italy. In the US, contact Access-Able (www.access-able.com).

E conomy

There is a gaping gulf between mainland and historic Venice. While the mainland communities of Mestre and the port of Marghera are essentially industrial, dealing with shipping, petrochemicals, metalworking and food processing, the economy of historic Venice depends on tourism. This embraces independent, package and conference tourism as well as the cruise sector, and

ELECTRICITY

220 volts. You will need an adaptor to operate British three-pin appliances and a transformer to use 100- to 120-volt appliances.

such crafts as glassmaking, lacemaking and mask making, in addition to restoration and antique-dealing. The city is trying to foster a crafts revival to stem the tide of families moving to the mainland. Tourism and the craft industry are supplemented by the declining sectors of fishing, boat-building and market-gardening.

Entry Regulations

For visits up to three months, visas are not required by visitors from EU countries, the US, Canada, Australia or New Zealand. A valid passport (or in the case of those from EU member countries, a valid identification card) is sufficient. Nationals of most other countries require a visa, which must be obtained in advance from an Italian embassy.

G overnment

Venice is the capital of the Veneto, the wealthy region in north-eastern Italy which has one of the highest per capita incomes in Italy. Venice and the mainland communities come under the same local government. Despite a referendum in which the city decided to retain its links with the mainland communities, the relationship makes for uneasy bedfellows: historic Venice and modern Mestre have very different needs. As in the US, the city mayor wields considerable power. Over the last 10 years the control of the municipality has swung between the left and right, but with very little practical difference being made to the daily life of the Venetians. The present administration may be left of centre, but in reality, factional infighting between the two communities of mainland Venice and historic Venice means that the city is likely to experience continuing turmoil. The issue that divides the city most is the construction of the new mobile dam, with the right broadly in favour but the left (and most environmentalists) either sceptical or opposed to the project.

H ealth and Medical Care

Before travelling, ensure you have a valid health and personal insurance policy. An Italian pharmacist is qualified to advise on minor health complaints. Night pharmacists *(farmacie)* operate on a rota system, so consult your hotel or check the sign posted on any pharmacist. If you are seriously ill, telephone 118 or go to the Pronto Soccorso (casualty department) of the nearest hospital. In central Venice, this is the Ospedale Civile, Campo Santi Giovanni e Paolo (San Zanipolo), tel: 041-529 4516 (casualty) beside the church of Santi Giovanni e Paolo and also accessible by water taxi. On the Lido, call the medical centre on 041-526 1750. Tap-water is generally safe to drink, but Venetians prefer to drink mineral water. Take mosquito repellent in the summer, especially for lagoon trips.

M edia and Internet

International publications can be found in Venice. The main Italian papers *(Il Corriere della Sera, La Repubblica)* publish northern editions, but the most useful local daily is *Il Gazzettino*, which carries information on transport, entertainment and on duty chemists. This is presented clearly, so anyone with a smattering of Italian should understand it. To find out what's on, pick up a copy of the *Leo* listings magazine from the tourist office (in English and Italian) as well as the free booklet, *Un Ospite a Venezia/A Guest in Venice* from one of the grand hotels. Venice has a cluster of internet cafés, including The Telecom Centre (Campo San Salvador) and Network Café (San Polo).

Money

The unit of currency in Italy is the Euro. There are 5, 10, 20, 50, 100, 200 and 500 Euro notes, and 1, 2, 5, 10, 20 and 50 cent coins. Banks are open Monday–Friday from 8.30am–1.30pm and

TRANSPORT
ACCOMMODATION
ACTIVITIES
A – Z
LANGUAGE

sometimes from 2.30–3.30pm or from 3.30–4.30pm. You will need your passport when changing money. ATMs have instructions in foreign languages. Most hotels do not accept travellers' cheques. Major credit cards are accepted by most large stores and restaurants, but are less common than in North America or Northern Europe. Always check to avoid embarrassment. Foreign-exchange offices give a less favourable rate of exchange than banks but are plentiful around the San Marco and Rialto areas.

P opulation and Size

The city is built on 118 islands, 4 km (2 miles) off the mainland. The Venetian lagoon covers an area of over 500 sq. km (193 sq. miles), which is roughly divided – biologically speaking – between the "dead" and the "living" lagoons. Venice itself comprises 45 km (28 miles) of canals and 400 bridges. Of the 320,000 inhabitants of Venice (including the mainland communities), 60,000 live in historic Venice, about

PUBLIC HOLIDAYS

Banks and most shops are closed on the following public holidays:
New Year's Day *(Capodanno)* 1 January
Epiphany *(Befania)* 6 January
Easter Monday *(Lunedì di Pasqua)* varies
Liberation Day *(Anniversario della Liberazione)* 25 April
May Day *(Festa del Lavoro)* 1 May
August holiday *(Ferragosto)* 15 August
All Saints *(Ognissanti)* 1 November
Immaculate Conception *(Immacolata Concezione)* 8 December
Christmas Day *(Natale)* 25 December
Boxing Day *(Santo Stefano)* 26 December

45,000 have homes on the islands and the remainder inhabit the mainland. The numbers in historic Venice have fallen by more than 50 percent since 1945. This is because the cost of accommodation and the demands of living in Venice are provoking an exodus to the mainland. This has also resulted in the population of central Venice, which has an average age of 45 years, considerably older than the European average.

Postal Services

Post offices are generally open Monday–Friday 8.30am–1.30pm. In Venice, the main post office is at Fondachi dei Tedeschi on the St Mark's side of the Rialto (8am–7pm), where you can also pay direct and pay afterwards. Stamps *(francobolli)* are available from tobacconists *(tabacchi)* and card shops. The postal service is not renowned for its speed, so if you need to send an urgent letter, ask for "posta prioritaria". In a real emergency, send a telegram, either from a post office, or from Telecom Italia.

Public Toilets

Although the situation is improving, these are still in short supply, so most visitors will need to resort to bars and museums. The best-kept (paying) ones are by the tourist office on St Mark's waterfront, by the Giardini Ex-Reali.

R adio and Television

In general, Italian television ranges from bad to appalling. It is worth watching, however, just so that you appreciate the quality at home – wherever you live. Better hotels are fitted with satellite television, with channels in English, French, German and possibly Japanese.

Religious Services

Visitors to St Mark's Basilica are channelled along set routes, so Catholics might consider visiting

from 7–9.45 am, when only worshippers are welcome. For a full list of church services, pick up the free *A Guest in Venice* from any of the grand hotels.

S tudent Travellers

Students with a valid card often get discounts on tours, civic museums and other services. (The Rolling Venice Card is worth getting to ensure further discounts). Members of the EU who can prove they are under 18 are entitled to free entry to State museums.

T elephones

Italy has the highest mobile-phone ownership in Europe but public telephones abound, though most only accept phone cards *(schede telefoniche)*, which are sold at news-stands and *tabacchi* for €2.50 and €5. The main Telecom Italia office is in Piazzale Roma (8am–9.30pm), where you can make phone calls; the call is metered and paid upon completion. If calling from a hotel, expect a steep mark-up. You can also call using a British BT chargecard or one of the cards issued by Sprint, mci, AT&T and other North American long-distance telephone companies (calls are charged to your home address). To call Venice from abroad, dial +39-041 plus the number you require. If calling Venice from within Italy, including from within Venice itself, dial 041, plus the number.

Tipping

In Italy, it is customary to tip for certain services, so it is worth carrying loose change (which also comes in handy for using to ensure decent light in front of key treasures in city churches). Most restaurants impose a cover charge *(pane e coperto)* of approximately €7. In addition, there is often a 10 percent service charge *(servizio)* added to the bill. If the menu says that service is included, then a small additional tip is discre-

TOURS, TICKETS AND SERVICES

Hello Venezia, tel: 041-2424 (7.30am–8pm); transport timetables; street directions; also for booking opera, concerts, ballet, events. **Venice Card** (museum and transport discount card), tel: 041-2424 (booked through Hello Venezin). Doge's Palace (information service; tel: 041-271 5911). **Doge's Palace Secret Itinerary** (booking required; tel: 041-520 9070). **San Marco** for a free guided visit (tel: 041-270 2420). **Chorus** (pass for the main Venetian churches) tel: 041-275 0462. **Associazione Sant'Apollonia** (the rival church association), tel: 041-270 2464. For the **Jewish Museum**, ghetto and cemetery tours, tel: 041-715 359.

For **Wagner's apartments** and the **Casino tour**, tel: 041-523 2544. **Romantic Venice** walking tours, tel: 041-630 761. **Natura Venezia**, tel: 041-932 003; www.limosa.it (nature visits round the lagoon). **Punto Laguna**, tel: 041-529 3582; www.salve.it (Campo Santo Stefano, information about Venice lagoon and the mobile dam). **La Biennale**, tel: 041-521 8898 (the major city art festival). **Venetian Hoteliers Association** (for hotels and events), tel: 041-522 8004 (freephone in Italy: 8008-43006). **Tourism complaints**, tel: 041-529 8710; e-mail: complaint.apt@ turismovenezia.it

tionary. If service is not included, then leave between 12 and 15 percent of the bill. Gondoliers need not be tipped but water taxi drivers may expect a small tip. Tips to local guides depend on their ability and the length of the trip: €2.50 to €5 per person. In certain churches, there is often a custodian (or elderly "helper") near by who will be pleased to open the door. A tip of around €1.50 per person is appropriate.

Tourist Offices

Italian ENIT (State tourist) offices abroad:
ENIT Australia: Level 26, 44 Market Street, Sydney. Tel: 02-9262 1666.
Canada: 175 Bloor Street East, Suite, 907-South Tower, Toronto M4W 3R8. Tel: 416-925 4882.
ENIT UK: 1 Princes Street, London W1R 8AY. Tel: 020-7408 1254.
ENIT USA. New York: 630 5th Avenue, Suite 1565, New York, NY 10111. Tel: 212-245 4822.
Chicago: 500 N Michigan Avenue, Suite 2240, Chicago, IL 60611. Tel: 312-644 0996.
California: 12400 Wilshire Bld, Suite 550, Los Angeles CA 90025. Tel: 310-820 0098.

Tourist offices in Venice

The main St Mark's tourist office is on the western corner of Piazza San Marco and offers both general information and booking for some tours and events: APT Venezia, San Marco 71/f, Calle dell'Ascensione/Procuratie Nuove (tel: 041-529 8711; fax: 041-523 0399; 9am–3.30pm Mon–Sat). The equally convenient but less busy office is on the St Mark's waterfront, in a pavilion beside the public gardens. It also has a good Venice-themed bookshop: APT Venezia, Ex-Giardini-Reali (tel: as above; 10am–6pm Mon–Sat). The tourist office at the railway station is also handy: APT Venezia, Ferrovia Santa Lucia (8am–6.30pm), as is the one at the airport: APT Marco Polo (9.30am–7.30pm). This mostly deals with accommodation and transport tickets. To contact the central tourist office by e-mail: info@turismovenezia.it; website: www.turismovenezia.it (events, itineraries, excursions, hotels, and advice).

Websites

Websites on Venice:
www.turismovenezia.it – tourist office/APT

www.comune.venezia.it – official website of the Comune di Venezia (city council): background; events; cultural sites (incomplete listings only); guide to city services, including transport
www.hellovenezia.it – public transport timetables, booking events; Venice Card
www.actv.it – Venetian public water transport
www.atvo.it – shuttle bus from airport to Venice
www.alilaguna.com – Alilaguna Lines – airport-city water shuttle
www.venicecard.it – city discount card for transport and museums
www.museiciviciveneziani.it – Venice city museums – Italian only
www.chorusvenezia.org – information and pass for main Venetian churches
www.provincia.venezia.it/assap – information about the other main churches
www.teatrolafenice.it – opera and concerts at La Fenice
www.labiennale.org – information on the Biennale art festival
www.palazzograssi.it – major exhibitions at Palazzo Grassi
www.guggenheim-venice.it – the Guggenheim collections
www.galleriaccademia.org – the Accademia collections
www.regione.veneto.it/cultura/musei – museums in the Veneto
www.museoebraico.it – the Jewish Museum
www.jewishvenice.com – Jewish Venice and tours
www.ilburchiello.it – booking boat trip on the Brenta Canal between Venice and Padua
www.veneziasi.it – Venetian Hoteliers Association, for booking
www.corpoconsolarevenezia.com – list of consulates in Venice
www.limosa.it – nature tours around the lagoon islands
www.salve.it – the ecology and protection of Venice
www.veniceinperil.org – Venice in Peril is the prestigious British-led organisation that funds restoration projects to save the city
www.savevenice.com – Save Venice is the parallel American-led organisation

TRANSPORT

ACCOMMODATION

ACTIVITIES

A – Z

LANGUAGE

L ANGUAGE

UNDERSTANDING THE LANGUAGE

It is well worth buying a good phrase book or dictionary, but the following will help you get started. Since this glossary is aimed at non-linguists, we have opted for the simplest options rather than the most elegant Italian.

Communication

Yes *Sì*
No *No*
Thank you *Grazie*
Many thanks *Mille grazie/Tante grazie/Molte grazie*
You're welcome *Prego*
All right/That's fine *Va bene*
Please *Per favore* or *per cortesia*
Excuse me (to get attention) *Scusi* (singular), *Scusate* (plural)

Excuse me (in a crowd) *Permesso*
Excuse me (sorry) *Mi scusi*
Could you help me? (formal) *Potrebbe aiutarmi?*
Certainly *Ma, certo/Certamente*
Can I help you? (formal) *Posso aiutarla?*
Can you show me...? *Può indicarmi...?*
Can you help me? *Può aiutarmi, per cortesia?*
I need... *Ho bisogno di...*
I'm lost *Mi sono perso*
I'm sorry *Mi dispiace*
I don't know *Non lo so*
I don't understand *Non capisco*
Do you speak English/French? *Parla inglese/francese?*
Could you speak more slowly?

Può parlare piu lentamente, per favore?
Could you repeat that please? *Può ripetere, per piacere?*
here/there *qui/là*
yesterday/today/tomorrow *ieri/oggi/domani*
what *quale/come?*
when/why/where *quando/perchè/dove?*
Where is the lavatory? *Dov'è il bagno?*

Greetings

Hello (Good day) *Buon giorno*
Good afternoon/evening *Buona sera*
Good night *Buona notte*
Goodbye *Arrivederci*
Hello/Hi/'bye (familiar) *Ciao*

PRONUNCIATION TIPS

Italians claim that pronunciation is straightforward: you pronounce it as it is written. This is approximately true, but there are a couple of important rules for English speakers to bear in mind: **c** before **e** or **i** is pronounced ch, eg. *ciao, mi dispiace, la coincidenza*. **Ch** before **i** or **e** is pronounced as **k**, eg. *la chiesa*. Likewise, **sci** or **sce** are pronounced as in sheep or shed respectively. **Gn** in Italian is rather like the sound in onion, while **gl** is

softened to resemble the sound in bullion.

Nouns are either masculine (**il**, plural **i**) or feminine (**la**, plural **le**). Plurals of nouns are most often formed by changing an **o** to an **i** and an **a** to an **e**, eg. *il panino*: *i panini*; *la chiesa*: *le chiese*. As a general rule, words are always stressed on the penultimate syllable unless an accent indicates that you should do otherwise.

Like many languages, Italian has formal and informal words

for "you". In the singular, **Tu** is informal while **Lei** is more polite. In general **Voi** is reserved for you plural, though in some places it is also used as a singular polite form. For visitors, it is simplest – and probably safest to avoid offending anyone – to use the formal form unless invited to do otherwise. There is, of course, rather more to the language than that, but you can get a surprisingly long way in making friends by mastering a few basic phrases.

Mr/Mrs/Miss *Signor/Signora/ Signorina*
Pleased to meet you (formal) *Piacere di conoscerla*
I am English/American *Sono inglese/americano*
Irish/Scottish *irlandese/scozzese*
Canadian/Australian *canadese/australiano*
How are you (formal/informal)? *Come stà (Come stai)?*
Fine, thanks *Bene, grazie*
See you later *A più tardi*
See you soon *A presto*
It's wonderful (a phrase that can equally be applied to food, beaches, the view) *È meravigliosa/favolosa*

Telephone calls

The area code *il prefisso telefonico*
May I use your telephone, please? *Posso usare il suo telefono?*
Hello (on the telephone) *Pronto*
My name is *Mi chiamo/Sono*
Could I speak to...? *Posso parlare con...?*
Sorry, he/she isn't in *Mi dispiace, è fuori*
Can he call you back? *Può richiamarla?*
Can I leave a message? *Posso lasciare un messagio?*
Please tell him I called *Gli dica, per favore, che ho telefonato*
Hold on *Un attimo, per favore*
A local call *una telefonata locale*

Do you have any vacant rooms? *Avete camere libere?*
I have a reservation *Ho una prenotazione*
I'd like... *Vorrei*
a single/double room (with a double bed) *una camera singola/doppia (con letto matrimoniale)*
a room with twin beds *una camera a due letti*
a room with a bath/shower *una camera con bagno/doccia*
for one night *per una notte*
for two nights *per due notti*
How much is it? *Quanto costa?*

Is breakfast included? *È compresa la prima colazione?*
half/full board *mezza pensione/ pensione completa*
Do you have a room with a balcony/view of the sea? *Avete una camera con balcone/ con vista mare?*
With a bath/shower *con doccia/ con bagno*
Is it a quiet room? *È una stanza tranquilla?*
The room is too hot/cold/ noisy/small *La camera è troppo calda/fredda/rumorosa/piccola*
Can I see the room? *Posso vedere la camera?*
Could you show me another room please? *Potrebbe mostrarmi un'altra camera?*
What time does the hotel close? *A che ora chiude l'albergo?*
I'll take it *La prendo*
big/small *grande/piccola*
What time is breakfast? *A che ora è la prima colazione?*
Please give me a call at... *Mi può chiamare alle...*
Come in? *Avanti!*
Can I have the bill, please? *Posso avere il conto, per favore.*
Can you call me a taxi please? *Può chiamarmi un taxi, per favore?*
dining room *la sala da pranzo*
key *la chiave*
pull/push *tirare/spingere*

I'd like... *Vorrei...*
coffee *un caffè*
small, strong and black *un espresso*
with hot, frothy milk *un cappuccino*
with warm milk *un caffelatte*
weak *un caffè lungo*
tea *un tè*
lemon tea *un tè al limone*
herbal tea *una tisana*
hot chocolate *una cioccolata calda*
(bottled) orange/lemon juice *un succo d'arancia/di limone*
orange squash *l'aranciata*
fresh orange/lemon juice *una spremuta di arancia/di limone*
a glass/bottle of *un bicchiere/una bottiglia di*

Prezzo in terrazza/al tavolo **Terrace/table price (often double what you pay standing at the bar)**
Si paga alla cassa **Pay at the cash desk**
Si prende lo scontrino alla cassa **Take the receipt** *(lo scontrino)* **to the bar to be served; this is common procedure**
Signori/Uomini **Gentlemen (lavatories)**
Signore/Donne **Ladies (lavatories)**

fizzy/still mineral water *acqua minerale gasata/naturale*
with/without ice *con/senza ghiaccio*
red/white wine *vino rosso/ bianco*
beer *una birra*
a gin and tonic *un gin tonic*
an aperitif (vermouth, cinzano, etc.) *un aperitivo*
milk *latte*
(half) a litre *un (mezzo) litro*
ice cream *un gelato*
pastry/brioche *una pasta*
sandwich *un tramezzino*
roll *un panino*
Anything else? *Desidera qualcos'altro?*
Cheers *Salute*

I'd like to book a table *Vorrei riservare un tavolo*
Have you got a table for... *Avete un tavolo per...*
I have a reservation *Ho fatto una prenotazione*
lunch/supper *il pranzo/la cena*
I'm a vegetarian *Sono vegetariano/a*
Is there a vegetarian dish? *C'è un piatto vegetariano?*
May we have the menu? *Ci dia la carta?*
wine list *la lista dei vini*
What would you like? *Che cosa prende?*
What would you recommend? *Che cosa ci raccomanda?*

PASTA

cannelloni stuffed tubes of pasta
farfalle bow- or butterfly-shaped pasta
penne pasta quills, smaller than *rigatoni*
ravioli and **tortellini** different types of stuffed pasta
tagliatelle long strips of pasta

Typical pasta sauces include:
aglio e olio garlic and olive oil
arrabbiata spicy tomato
burro e salvia butter and sage
matriciana ham and tomato
panna cream
pesto with basil and pine nuts
ragù meat sauce

What would you like to drink?
Che cosa desidera da bere?
a carafe of red/white wine *una caraffa di vino rosso/bianco*
the dish of the day *il piatto del giorno*
home-made *fatto in casa*
cover charge *il coperto/pane e coperto*
The bill, please *Il conto, per favore*
Is service included? *Il servizio è incluso?*
Keep the change *Va bene così*
I've enjoyed the meal *Mi è piaciuto molto*

Menu Decoder

Antipasti – starters
antipasto misto **mixed hors d'œuvres; cold cuts of meat, cheeses, roast vegetables (ask for details)**
caponata **aubergine, olives, tomatoes**
insalata caprese **tomato, basil and mozzarella salad**
insalata di mare **seafood salad**
insalata mista/verde **mixed/green salad**
melanzane alla parmigiana **fried or baked aubergine with parmesan and tomato**
mortadella/salame **similar to salami**

peperonata **grilled peppers drenched in olive oil**

Primi – first courses
Typical first courses include soup, risotto, gnocchi or myriad pastas in a wide range of sauces.
gli asparagi **asparagus**
il brodetto **fish soup**
il brodo **broth**
crespolini **savoury pancakes**
gnocchi **potato-and-dough dumplings**
la minestra **soup**
il minestrone **thick vegetable soup**
pasta e fagioli **pasta and bean soup**
il prosciutto (cotto/crudo) **(cooked/cured) ham**
i suppli **rice croquettes**
i tartufi **truffles**
la zuppa **soup**

Secondi – main courses
Typical main courses are fish, seafood or meat-based, with accompaniments *(contorni)*, including vegetables, that vary greatly from region to region.

La carne – meat
arrosto **roast meat**
al ferri **grilled without oil**
al forno **baked**
alla griglia **grilled**
involtini **skewered veal, ham, etc.**
stagionato **hung, well-aged**
ben cotto **well-done (steak, etc.)**
al puntino **medium (steak, etc.)**
al sangue **rare (steak, etc.)**
l'agnello **lamb**
la bresaola **dried salted beef**
la bistecca **steak**
il capriolo/cervo **venison**
il carpaccio **wafer-thin raw beef**
il cinghiale **wild boar**
il controfiletto **sirloin steak**
le cotolette **cutlets**
il maiale **pork**
il fagiano **pheasant**
il fegato **liver**
il filetto **fillet**
il manzo **beef**
l'ossobuco **shin of veal**
la porchetta **roast suckling pig**
il pollo **chicken**

polpette **meatballs**
la salsiccia **sausage**
saltimbocca (alla Romana) **fried veal escalopes with ham**
le scaloppine **escalopes**
lo stufato **braised, stewed**
il sugo **sauce**
il vitello **veal**

Frutti di mare – seafood
Beware the word *surgelati*, meaning frozen rather than fresh.
affumicato **smoked**
alle brace **charcoal grilled**
ai ferri **grilled without oil**
alla griglia **grilled**
fritto **fried**
ripieno **stuffed**
al vapore **steamed**
acciughe **anchovies**
l'anguilla **eel**
l'aragosta **lobster**
il baccalà **dried salt cod**
i bianchetti **whitebait**
il branzino **sea bass**
i calamari **squid**
i crostacei **shellfish**
le cozze **mussels**
il fritto misto **mixed fried fish**
i gamberi **prawns**
il granchio **crab**
il merluzzo **cod**
le molecche **soft-shelled crabs**
le ostriche **oysters**
il pesce **fish**
il pesce spada **swordfish**
il risotto di mare **seafood risotto**
le sarde **sardines**
la sogliola **sole**
le seppie **cuttlefish**
la triglia **red mullet**
la trota **trout**
il tonno **tuna**
le vongole **clams**

I legumi/la verdura – vegetables
a scelta **of your choice**
gli asparagi **asparagus**
la bietola **(similar to spinach)**
il carciofo **artichoke**
le carote **carrots**
il cavolo **cabbage**
la cicoria **chicory**
la cipolla **onion**
i contorni **side dishes (vegetables)**
i funghi **mushrooms**
i fagioli **beans**

i fagiolini **French beans**
le fave **broad beans**
il finocchio **fennel**
l'insalata mista **mixed salad**
l'insalata verde **green salad**
la melanzana **aubergine**
le patate **potatoes**
le patatine fritte **French fries**
i peperoni **peppers**
i piselli **peas**
i pomodori **tomatoes**
il radicchio **red endive (red, slightly bitter lettuce)**
rucola **rocket**
spinaci **spinach**
la verdura **vegetables**
la zucca **pumpkin/squash**

La frutta – fruit

le arance **oranges**
le banane **bananas**
il cocomero **watermelon**
le ciliege **cherries**
i fichi **figs**
le fragole **strawberries**
i frutti di bosco **fruits of the forest**
i lamponi **raspberries**
la mela **apple**
la pesca **peach**
la pera **pear**
l'uva **grapes**

I dolci – desserts

la cassata **Sicilian ice cream with candied peel**
il dolce **dessert/sweet**
le frittelle **doughnuts (for carnival)**
un gelato **ice cream**
una granita **water ice**
una macedonia di frutta **fruit salad**

un semifreddo **semi-frozen dessert (many varieties)**
il tartufo (nero) **(chocolate) ice-cream dessert**
il tiramisù **cold, creamy rum-and-coffee dessert**
la torta **cake/tart**
zabaglione **sweet dessert made with eggs and Marsala**
la zuppa inglese **trifle**

Basic foods

l'aceto **vinegar**
l'aglio **garlic**
il burro **butter**
il formaggio **cheese**
la frittata **omelette**
il grana **parmesan cheese**
i grissini **bread sticks**
l'olio **oil**
la marmellata **jam**
il pane **bread**
il parmigiano **parmesan cheese**
il pepe **pepper**
il riso **rice**
il sale **salt**
la senape **mustard**
le uova **eggs**
il yoghurt **yoghurt**
lo zucchero **sugar**

Sightseeing

l'abbazia (la badia) **abbey**
la basilica **church**
il belvedere **viewpoint**
la biblioteca **library**
il castello **castle**
il centro storico **old town/historic centre**
la chiesa **church**
il duomo/la cattedrale **cathedral**

il fiume **river**
il giardino **garden**
il lago **lake**
il mercato **market**
il monastero **monastery**
i monumenti **monuments**
il museo **museum**
il parco **park**
la pinacoteca **art gallery**
il ponte **bridge**
i ruderi **ruins**
gli scavi **archaeological site**
la spiaggia **beach**
il tempio **temple**
la torre **tower**
l'ufficio turistico **tourist office**
il custode **custodian**
Suonare il campanello **Ring the bell**
aperto/a **open**
chiuso/a **closed**
Chiuso per la festa **Closed for the festival**
Chiuso per ferie **Closed for the holidays**
Chiuso per restauro **Closed for restoration**

At the Shops

What time do you open/close?
A che ora apre/chiude?
Closed for the holidays (typical sign) Chiuso per ferie
Can I help you? (formal) Posso aiutarla?
I'm just looking Stò soltanto guardando
How much does it cost?
Quant'è, per favore?
Do you take credit cards
Accettate carte di credito?
I'd like... Vorrei...

NUMBERS

1	Uno	13	Tredici	70	Settanta
2	Due	14	Quattordici	80	Ottanta
3	Tre	15	Quindici	90	Novanta
4	Quattro	16	Sedici	100	Cento
5	Cinque	17	Diciassette	200	Duecento
6	Sei	18	Diciotto	500	Cinquecento
7	Sette	19	Diciannove	1,000	Mille
8	Otto	20	Venti	2,000	Duemila
9	Nove	30	Trenta	5,000	Cinquemila
10	Dieci	40	Quaranta	50,000	Cinquantamila
11	Undici	50	Cinquanta	1 million	Un Milione
12	Dodici	60	Sessanta		

this one/that one *questo/quello*
Have you got...? *Avete...?*
Can I try it on? *Posso provare?*
the size (for clothes) *la taglia*
the size (for shoes) *il numero*
It's too expensive/cheap
È troppo caro/economico
It's too small/big *È troppo
piccolo/grande*
brown/blue/black *marrone/
blu/nero*
green/red/white/yellow
verde/rosso/bianco/giallo
pink/grey/gold/silver
rosa/grigio/oro/argento
I'll take it/I'll leave it *Lo
prendo/lo lascio*
This is faulty. Can I have a
replacement/refund? *C'è un
difetto. Me lo potrebbe
cambiare/rimborsare?*
Anything else? *Altro?*
Give me some of those *Mi dia
alcuni di quelli lì*
(half) a kilo *un (mezzo) kilo*
100 grams *un'etto*
200 grams *due etti*
More/less *Più/meno*
A little *Un pochino*
That's enough *Basta così*

Types of shops

bakery/cake shop *la panetteria/
pasticceria*
bank *la banca*
bookshop *la libreria*
boutique/clothes shop *il negozio
di moda*
butcher's *la macelleria*
chemist's *la farmacia*
delicatessen *la salumeria*
department store *il grande
magazzino*
fishmonger *la pescheria*
florist *il fioraio*
grocer *alimentari*
greengrocer *l'ortolano/
il fruttivendolo*
ice-cream parlour *la gelateria*
jeweller *il gioielliere*
market *il mercato*
news-stand *l'edicola*
post office *l'ufficio postale*
shoe shop *il negozio di scarpe*
stationer's *la cartoleria*
supermarket *il supermercato*
tobacconist *il tabaccaio* (also
sells travel tickets, stamps,
phone cards)

Travelling

Transport

airport *l'aeroporto*
aeroplane *l'aereo*
arrivals/departures *arrivi/
partenze*
boarding card *una carta
d'imbarco*
boat *la barca*
bus *l'autobus/il pullman*
bus station *l'autostazione*
coach *il pullman*
connection *la coincidenza*
ferry *il traghetto*
ferry terminal *la stazione
marittima*
first/second class *la prima/
seconda classe*
flight *il volo*
hydrofoil *l'aliscafo*
left luggage *il deposito bagagli*
platform *il binario*
port *il porto*
porter *il facchino*
railway station *Ferrovia (la
stazione ferroviaria)*
return ticket *un biglietto di
andata e ritorno*
single ticket *un biglietto di sola
andata*
smokers/non-smokers *fumatori/
non-fumatori*
station *la stazione*
stop *la fermata*
taxi *il taxi*
ticket office *la biglietteria*
train *il treno*
WC *il gabinetto*

At the station

(trains, buses and ferries)
Can you help me please? *Mi può
aiutare, per favore?*
Where can I buy tickets? *Dove
posso fare i biglietti?*
What time does the train leave?
A che ora parte il treno?
What time does the train arrive?
A che ora arriva (il treno)?
Can I book a seat? *Posso
prenotare un posto?*
Is this seat free/taken? *È
libero/occupato questo posto?*
You'll have to pay a supplement
Deve pagare un supplemento
Do I have to change? *Devo
cambiare?*

Where does it stop? *Dove si
ferma?*
You need to change in Rome
Bisogna cambiare a Roma.
Which platform does the train
leave from? *Da quale binario
parte il treno?*
The train leaves from platform
one *Il treno parte dal binario uno*
When is the next train/bus/
ferry for Rome? *Quando parte
il prossimo treno/pullman/
traghetto per Roma?*
How long does the crossing
take? *Quanto dura la traversata?*
How long will it take to get
there? *Quanto tempo ci vuole
per arrivare?*
Is this the right stop? *È la
fermata giusta?*
Can you tell me where to get
off? *Mi può dire dove devo
scendere?*

Directions

right/left *a destra/a sinistra*
first left/second right *la prima a
sinistra/la seconda a destra*
Turn to the right/left *Gira a
destra/sinistra*
Go straight on *Va sempre diritto*
Is it far away/nearby? *È
lontano/vicino?*
It's 5 minutes' walk *Cinque
minuti a piedi*
opposite/next to *di fronte/
accanto a*
up/down *su/giù*
traffic lights *il semaforo*
junction *l'incrocio, il bivio*
building *il palazzo (it can just as
easily be a modern block of flats
as a Gothic palace)*
Where is ....? *Dov'è ....?*
Where are ....? *Dove sono ....?*
Where is the nearest bank/
petrol station/bus stop/hotel/
garage? *Dov'è la banca/il
benzinaio/la fermata di autobus/
l'albergo/l'officina più vicino?*
How do I get there? *Come si
può andare? (or: Come faccio per
arrivare a...?)*
How long does it take to get
to...? *Quanto tempo ci vuole per
andare a...?*
Can you show me where I am on
the map? *Può indicarmi sulla
cartina dove mi trovo?*

FURTHER READING

Literature and Biography

Lord Byron, *Childe Harold's Pilgrimage*, classic poetic epic.
Giacomo Casanova, *Memoirs*.
Michael Dibdin, *Dead Lagoon*, a subtle detective story.
Ernest Hemingway, *Across the River and into the Trees* (1952), not his best, but evocative, nonetheless.
Henry James, *The Wings of the Dove* (1902) and *The Aspern Papers* (1888), evocative accounts from one of the greatest observers of Venice.
Donna Leon, *Friends in High Places*, one of a gritty detective series set in Venice.
Thomas Mann, *Death in Venice* (1912), haunting tale.
Ian McEwan, *The Comfort of Strangers* (1981), an eerie novel that stays on the mind.
Marcel Proust, *Albertine Disparue* (1925), translated as *The Fugitive* or *The Sweet Cheat Gone*.
Andrea di Robilant, *A Venetian Affair* (2003), an appealing historical romance by an aristocratic Venetian.
Muriel Spark, *Territorial Rights* (1979), an engaging read.
Sally Vickers. *Miss Garnet's Angel*, whimsical, spinsterish tale of an art trail in Venice.
Jeanette Winterson, *The Passion* (1987), bizarre work set in Napoleonic Venice.

History, Art and Architecture

Roberta Curiel, *The Ghetto of Venice*, a history of the city's Jewish community.
Umberto Franzoi, *Palaces and Churches along the Grand Canal*, well-illustrated palace-by-palace guide.
J.R. Hale (Ed.), *Renaissance Venice* (1973).
Christopher Hibbert, *Venice, Biography of a City* (1988).
Deborah Howard, *Architectural History of Venice* (2003).
Emily Lane (Ed.), *Venetian 17th-Century Painting* (1979).
Frederick C. Lane, *Venice, a Maritime Republic*, a core (if dry) historical account.
Michael Levey, *Painting in 18th-Century Venice* (1959), a sound introduction.
Francesco da Mosto, *Francesco's Venice* (2004), lavish romp through Venetian culture by an aristocratic Venetian architect.
John Julius Norwich, *A History of Venice* (1988), *The Rise to Empire* (1980), *The Greatness and Fall* (1981), engaged and engaging historian of Venice.
Marco Polo, *The Travels of Marco Polo* (1958).
John Ruskin, *The Stones of Venice* (1851–3), influential book on Venetian art history.
John Steer, *A Concise History of Venetian Painting* (1970).
Sabina Vienello, *The Churches of Venice* (1993).

Travel Memoirs

Toby Cole (Ed.), *Venice, a Portable Reader* (revised 1995), literary extracts by celebrated visitors.
Charles Dickens, *Pictures from Italy* (1846).
J.W. von Goethe, *Italian Journeys* (1786–8).
William Dean Howells, *Venetian Life* (1866) and *Italian Journeys* (1867), by the American consul in Venice.
Henry James, *Italian Hours*, includes a portrait of Venice in the 1860s and 1870s.
Jonathan Keates, *Italian Journeys* (1991), sharp yet persuasive travel memoir.
J.G. Links, *Venice for Pleasure* (1966), a quirky classic.
Ian Littlewood, *Venice: a Literary Companion* (1991), informed, literary presentation of lesser-known Venice.
Mary McCarthy, *Venice Observed* (1961, revised 1982), acerbic look at Venice from an intelligent observer.
Jan Morris, *Venice* (revised 1993), purple prose meets anecdotal account.
Mrs Oliphant, *The Makers of Venice* (1898), quirky personal account of Venetian doges, travellers and painters.
John Pemble, *Venice Rediscovered* (1995), thoughtful and critical account of Venice as a cultural icon.
Mark Twain, *A Tramp Abroad* (1880).

Other Insight Guides

Insight Guides: in-depth coverage and lavish photos. Italian titles include: *Northern Italy, Southern Italy, Rome, Florence, Tuscany, Sicily* and *Sardinia*.
Insight Pocket Guides feature a pull-out map and tailor-made itineraries; ideal for short breaks. Italian titles: *Venice, Rome, Milan, Florence, Sicily, Naples, Umbria* and *Tuscany*.
Insight Compact Guides are mini-encyclopaedias. Titles include *Florence, Milan, Rome, Tuscany, Venice, The Italian Riviera* and *The Italian Lakes*.
Insight Fleximaps detailed laminated maps that are durable and weatherproof. Italian maps include *Florence, The Italian Lakes, Milan, Rome, Sicily, Tuscany* and *Venice*.

ART & PHOTO CREDITS

AKG-images London 2/3, 4B, 16, 20, 25, 27, 63R, 64, 78/79, 134, 143T, 146
Alinari 115
The Art Archive 22, 32
Bridgeman Art Library 3B
Corbis 31, 212
Mary Evans Picture Library 21, 69
Frederico Fritz 51
Glyn Genin/Apa 7BR, 14, 33, 40, 42, 87, 89, 91, 98, 99, 100T, 101, 105, 120, 140, 153, 159, 161T, 172, 183, 191, 199, 201, 203T, 203, 205, 208
Getty Images 65, 148
Tore Gill/ACE 67
Heathledge.net/HL Net Team 94T
John Heseltine 5, 9BR,, 23L/R, 24, 46, 47, 48, 66, 112
Isola San Clemente 211, 220
Benjamin W.G. Legde 17, 18, 19, 39, 144
Londra Palace Hotel 130
Ross Miller/Apa 1, 4T, 35, 37, 49, 98T, 102T, 114T, 116, 118T, 132T, 133T, 135, 140T, 147T, 154T, 168T, 173T, 181T, 193T, 195T/B, 200, 207T
Anna Mockford & Nick Bonetti/Apa 6TR, 6BR, 7TR, 7CL, 7CR, 8TR, 8CR, 8BL, 9CR, 12/13, 41, 44L/R, 45, 52, 68, 72, 73, 75, 76, 80/81, 82, 90, 92, 93, 94, 96T, 96, 97, 102,

103, 104, 109, 117, 119, 121, 122T, 123, 125, 127, 129, 131T, 131, 133, 136T, 136, 137, 138, 142, 145T, 145, 147, 149, 150, 151, 154, 155, 156, 157T, 157, 159T, 160T, 162, 165, 167, 168, 169, 170, 171T, 171, 173, 174, 177, 180, 182T, 182, 184, 185, 186, 187, 192, 193, 196T, 197, 198, 207, 217, 218
James Morris/Axiom 113T, 181
Museo Teatrale Alla Scala 63L
National Portrait Gallery 110B
Vladimir Pcholkin/ACE 86
Gerd Pfeiffer 38
Popperfoto 36
Sarah Quill/Venice Picture Library/Bridgeman 95
Alessandra Santarelli/Apa 239
Science Photo Library 34
Sipa Press/Rex Features 204
R. Solomon Guggenheim Foundation 114
Villa Pisani 210
Bill Wassman 10/11, 53, 74, 77, 100, 108, 110T, 113, 118, 124, 126, 164, 176, 190, 209

PICTURE SPREADS

Pages 60/61: Top row, left to right: AKG- images London, Bridgeman Art Library, Glyn Genin/Apa

Centre row: Anna Mockford & Nick Bonetti/Apa,
Bottom row: Bridgeman Art Library
Pages 70/71 Top row, left to right: Ros Miller/Apa, Getty Images, Getty Images
Centre row: Corbis, AKG-images London
Bottom row: Bridgeman Art Library
Pages 106/107 Top row left to right: Scala/Firenze, Glyn Genin/Apa; Centre row: John Heseltine, Glyn Genin/Apa
Bottom row: both by John Heseltine
Pages 188/189 Top row, left to right: Anna Mockford& Nick Bonetti/Apa, Scala/Firenze
Centre row: AKG-images London
Bottom row: AKG-images London, Bridgeman Art Library

Production:
Linton Donaldson, Sylvia George

Map Production James Macdonald, Maria Randell, Laura Morris and Stephen Ramsay
© 2005 Apa Publications GmbH & Co Verlag KG (Singapore Branch)

VENICE STREET ATLAS

The key map shows the area of Venice covered by the atlas
section. An index of street names and places of interest
shown on the maps can be found on the following pages.
For each entry there is a page number and grid reference.

Map Legend

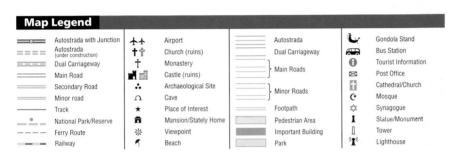

	Autostrada with Junction	✈✈	Airport		Autostrada	⛵	Gondola Stand
	Autostrada (under construction)	†✝	Church (ruins)		Dual Carriageway	🚌	Bus Station
	Dual Carriageway	†	Monastery		Main Roads	❶	Tourist Information
	Main Road	🏰🏛	Castle (ruins)			✉	Post Office
	Secondary Road	∴	Archaeological Site		Minor Roads	✝	Cathedral/Church
	Minor road	∩	Cave		Footpath	☾	Mosque
	Track	★	Place of Interest		Pedestrian Area	✡	Synagogue
	National Park/Reserve	🏠	Mansion/Stately Home		Important Building	⚲	Statue/Monument
	Ferry Route	❄	Viewpoint		Park	�🍺	Tower
	Railway	🏖	Beach			🗼	Lighthouse

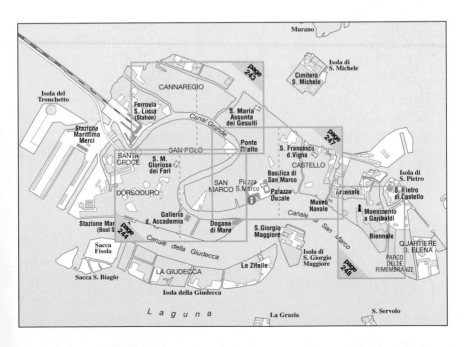

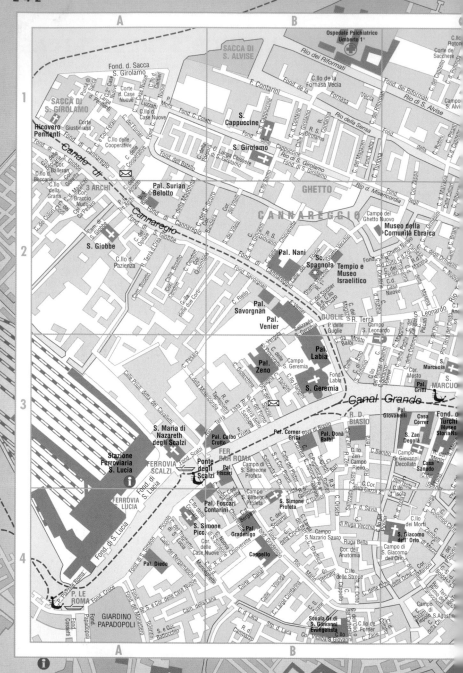

A   B

GIARDINO
PAPADOPOLI

Autorimessa
Air Terminal

S.
Andrea

Autorimessa

Cam. di S. Andrea

Piazzale
Roma

P.LE ROMA
R. NUOVO

S. CROCE

R. Cossetti

Rio Terra di S. Andrea

R. di S. Andrea

Nuovo di S. Andrea

Fond. di S. Andrea

Rio Terra dei Tabacchi

R. Bernardo

Fond. d.
Fabbrica
delle

Campazzo Tre Ponti
d. Tabacchi Ponti

Burchielle

Fond. delle Burchielle

Cam. di S. Maria Maggiore

Fond. dei Pensieri

Fond. d.
Tre Ponti

Bernardo

Fond. d. Rio Nuovo

R. Nuovo

Cor.
Correra

Rio Terra dei Pensieri

delle

Fond. Rizzi

Chiesa
S. M. Maggiore

Fond. di S. Maria

Sestiere di
S. Croce

Procuratie

C. Larga Fond.

C. Bergami

Fond. Procuratie

Fond. di S. Maria
Maggiore

Fond. Minotto

Fond. del Magazen

Pal.
Condulmer

Campo d.
Tolentini

C. d. Lavadori

C. del Cristo

Fond. del Gaffaro

S. Nicolò
dei Tolentini

R. Cimesin

R. d. Chioverette

C. dietro l'Archivio

Campazzo

Scuola Gr. di
S. Giovanni
Evangelista

S. Giovanni
Evangelista

Archivio di Stato

San
Rocco

Chiesa S. M.
Gloriosa
dei Frari

Scuola
Grande di
S. Rocco

Campo di
Casteforte
S. Rocco

C. del Malcanton

Cor.
del Gallo

C. de Basego

R. Nuovo
Fond. del Rio Nuovo

C.llo
delle
Mosche

Campo
S. Pantalon

S. Pantalon

C. Larga Foscari

Ca'
Fosc

C.llo dei
Squellini

Rezzon
Museo Settec
Venezi

S. Barnaba

Campo
S. Barnaba

C. del Traghe

DORSODURO

S. del Cristo
Teresa

Fond. Teresa

C. Camerini

C. dell'Olio

Cor. Nuova

C. Stretta

C. della Madonna

Cor.
Bonazzo

Cor.
S. Marco

Cor. Contarini

Fond. Rossa

Pal.
Foscarini

Scuola Gr.
di S. Maria
d. Carmini

S. Margherita

Campo di
S. Margherita

Rio Terra dei Carmini

Pal.
Cigogna

Calle dei Guardiani

Pal.
Zenobio

Ist. Sup.
d'Arte
Applicate

S. Maria dei
Carmini

Cor. del
Forno

Fond. dello Squero

Fond. Gerardini

Rio Terra Canal

C. Bernardo

C. Lunga S. Barnaba

S. Angelo
Raffaele

Campo dell'
Angelo Raffaele

Bevilacqua Nave

San
Sebastiano

Campazzo
S. Sebastiano

Cam. di
S. Basegio

Cam.
dietro il
Cimitero

C. Avogaria

C.llo
Avogaria

C.llo
Balastro

C. Balastro

C. della Ch.

Cor.
dei Morti

Ospedale
Ognissanti

Chiesa Ognissanti

Cam.
Ognissanti

Pal.
Brandolin

S. Trovaso

Campo S.
Trovaso

Stazione
Marittima

Banchina di S. Basegio

S. BASILIO

Fondaco

Zattere P.

Lungo

ZATTERE

Fond. Zat

Canale della Giudecca

0   200 m

0   200 yards

Fond. S. Biagio

A   B

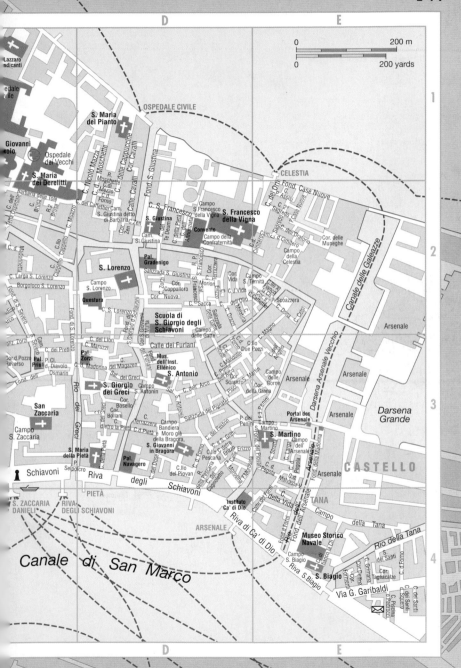

Lazzaro
ndicanti

edale
vile

OSPEDALE CIVILE

CELESTIA

S. Maria
del Pianto

Giovanni
iolo

Ospedale
dei Vecchi

S. Maria
dei Derelitti

Fond. Case Nuove

Cor. delle
Muneghe

S. Francesco
della Vigna

Campo
S.Francesco
della Vigna

Campo della
Confraternità

Convento

S. Giustina

S. Giustina detto
di Barbariac Zen

C. S. Francesco

Campo
della
Celestia

Canale delle Galeazze

S. Lorenzo

Pal.
Gradenigo

Campo
S.Ternità

Campo
S. Lorenzo

Cor.
Coppallora

Campo
della
Vida

Questura

Cor.
Nuova

Arsenale

Scuola di
S. Giorgio degli
Schiavoni

Campo
delle Gatte

Calle del Furlani

Dàrsena Arsenale Vecchio

Mus.
dell'Inst.
Ellénico

Pal.
Zorzi

C. del Lion

C. Maruzzi

C. del Preti

Pal.
Priuli

P. Cl.
d. Diavolo

Arsenale

Arsenale

Osmarin

S. Antonio

Campo
delle
Gorne

Darsena
Grande

S. Giorgio
dei Greci

Campo
S. Antonin

Arsenale

San
Zaccaria

Cor.
Bosello

Cor.
Bollani

Portal des
Arsenale

Arsenale

Campo
S. Zaccaria

Campo
Bandiera
e Moro gia
della Bragora,

S. Martino

Campo
dell'
Arsenale

S. Maria
della Pietà

S. Giovanni
in Bragora

CASTELLO

Pal.
Navagero

Schiavoni

Selpolcro

Riva

degli

Schiavoni

Instituto
Ca' di Dio

TANA

Campo

della

Tana

S. ZACCARIA
DANIELI

RIVA
DEGLI SCHIAVONI

PIETA

ARSENALE

Riva di Ca' di Dio

Rio della Tana

Museo Storico
Navale

Canale di San Marco

Campo
S. Biagio

S. Biagio

Via G. Garibaldi

D

E

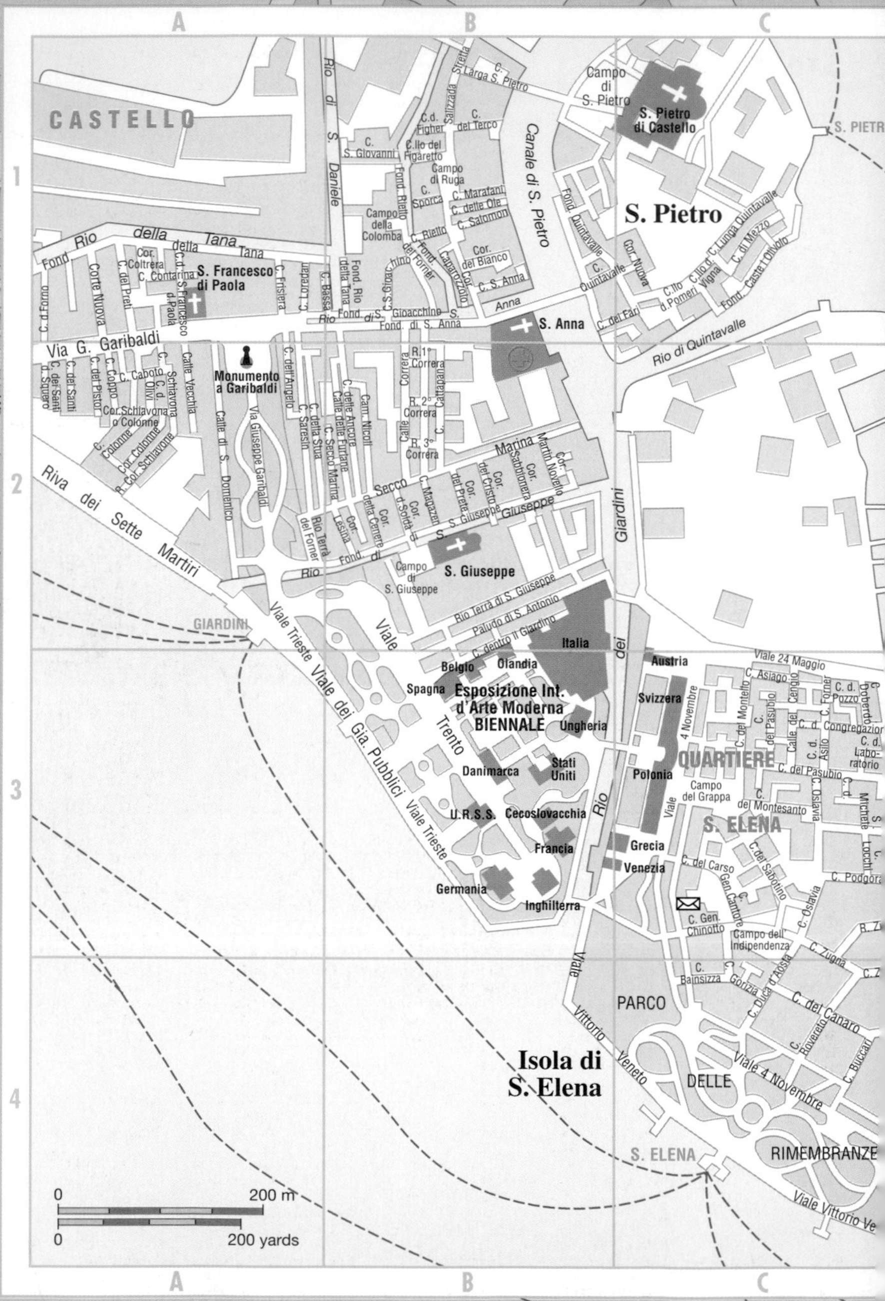

CASTELLO

Campo di S. Pietro
S. Pietro di Castello
S. PIETRO
S. Pietro

Rio di Quintavalle

Rio della Tana
Fond Rio della Tana
Corte Nuova
C. Coltrera
C. Contarina
C. del Pozzi
S. Francesco di Paola

Campo della Colomba
Campo di Ruga
C. Figher
C. del Terro
C. Marafanti
C. delle Ole
C. Salomon
Cor. del Bianco
C. S. Anna

S. Anna

Via G. Garibaldi
Monumento a Garibaldi

Via Giuseppe Garibaldi
Calle di S. Domenico

Riva dei Sette Martiri

GIARDINI

Viale Trieste Via Gia Pubblici Viale Trieste

Campo di S. Giuseppe
S. Giuseppe

Rio Terra di S. Giuseppe
Paludo di S. Antonio
C. dietro i Giardini

Italia
Belgio
Olanda
Spagna
Esposizione Int. d'Arte Moderna
BIENNALE
Ungheria
Trento
Danimarca
Stati Uniti
U.R.S.S. Cecoslovacchia
Francia
Germania
Inghilterra

Austria
Svizzera
Polonia
Grecia
Venezia

QUARTIERE
S. ELENA
Campo del Grappa
Campo del Montesanto

Viale 24 Maggio
C. Asiago
4 Novembre
Viale

Campo della Indipendenza
C. Gen Chinotto

PARCO
Vittorio Veneto
Isola di S. Elena

DELLE
Viale 4 Novembre
S. ELENA
RIMEMBRANZE
Viale Vittorio Ve

0   200 m
0   200 yards

STREET INDEX

General Index